# FUNDAMENTALS
# OF ECOSYSTEM SCIENCE

# FUNDAMENTALS OF ECOSYSTEM SCIENCE

KATHLEEN C. WEATHERS, DAVID L. STRAYER, AND GENE E. LIKENS

AMSTERDAM • BOSTON • HEIDELBERG • LONDON
NEW YORK • OXFORD • PARIS • SAN DIEGO
SAN FRANCISCO • SINGAPORE • SYDNEY • TOKYO
Academic Press is an imprint of Elsevier

Academic Press is an imprint of Elsevier

225 Wyman Street, Waltham, MA 02451, USA
525 B Street, Suite 1800, San Diego, CA 92101-4495, USA
84 Theobald's Road, London WC1X 8RR, UK

**Notices**
Knowledge and best practice in this field are constantly changing. As new research and experience broaden our understanding, changes in research methods, professional practices, or medical treatment may become necessary.

Practitioners and researchers must always rely on their own experience and knowledge in evaluating and using any information, methods, compounds, or experiments described herein. In using such information or methods they should be mindful of their own safety and the safety of others, including parties for whom they have a professional responsibility.

To the fullest extent of the law, neither the Publisher nor the authors, contributors, or editors assume any liability for any injury and/or damage to persons or property as a matter of products liability, negligence or otherwise, or from any use or operation of any methods, products, instructions, or ideas contained in the material herein.

**Library of Congress Cataloging-in-Publication Data**
A catalog record for this book is available from the Library of Congress

**British Library Cataloguing-in-Publication Data**
A catalogue record for this book is available from the British Library.

ISBN: 978-0-12-088774-3

For information on all Academic Press publications
visit our website at http://store.elssevier.com

Printed in the United States of America
13 14 15 16   9 8 7 6 5 4 3 2 1

# Contents

## 6. The Carbon Cycle   109
### JONATHAN J. COLE

## 7. The Nitrogen Cycle   137
### PETER M. GROFFMAN AND EMMA J. ROSI-MARSHALL

## 8. The Phosphorus Cycle   159
### ELENA M. BENNETT AND MEAGAN E. SCHIPANSKI

# IV
# SYNTHESIS

## 9. Revisiting the Ecosystem Concept: Important Features That Promote Generality and Understanding   181
### MICHAEL L. PACE

## 10. Ecosystems in a Heterogeneous World   191
### STEWARD T.A. PICKETT AND MARY L. CADENASSO

## 11. Controls on Ecosystem Structure and Function   215
### KATHLEEN C. WEATHERS, HOLLY A. EWING, CLIVE G. JONES, AND DAVID L. STRAYER

# Preface

This book provides an introduction to the content, ideas, and major findings of contemporary ecosystem science. We wrote the book primarily for beginning graduate students and advanced undergraduates but it should also be useful to a broad range of academic scientists and resource managers, and even to dedicated amateurs who seek an introduction to the field. Ecosystem science is a rigorous, quantitative science; we assume that readers of the book will have had an introductory class in ecology and basic understanding of chemistry and math. The book deliberately covers multiple approaches to understanding ecosystems (e.g., the use of experiments, theory, cross-system comparisons), in multiple environments (terrestrial, freshwater, and marine; managed, built, and natural ecosystems), across all parts of the world (although many examples come from the authors' experience in North America).

The origins of this book stem from an intensive two-week Fundamentals of Ecosystem Ecology class (the FEE class) that we have taught to graduate students from around the world every year or two at the Cary Institute of Ecosystem Studies since 1989. We, and many of the chapter authors, have played central roles in the development, evolution, and running of the FEE class since its origin.

We decided upon an edited book for several reasons, not the least of which was its genesis in this team-taught course. While we shepherded and integrated the chapters and their contents, we also deliberately allowed—and even encouraged—multiple approaches, and as a result, multiple "voices" will be evident throughout the book. We believe that this diversity reflects some of the myriad perspectives and approaches that are fruitfully brought to bear on the field of ecosystem science.

The book contains six major sections. The opening chapter introduces the concept of the ecosystem, explores some of the consequences of this concept, describes the intellectual tools of the science, and briefly reviews the history of this young science. Chapters 2 through 8 lay the foundation for the study of ecosystems, and cover the two major branches of ecosystem science: energetics (Chapters 2–4) and biogeochemistry (Chapters 5–8). These chapters present the core content of ecosystem science—the movement and fate of energy and materials in ecosystems—in some detail. In the synthetic Chapters 9–11, we revisit major themes that cut across multiple areas of study in ecosystem science. Authors of these chapters review the power and utility of the ecosystem concept, the roles of heterogeneity in space and time, and the importance of various types of controls in ecosystems. Chapters 12–16 take ecosystem science into the real world by illustrating, through five case studies, the value of ecosystem science in identifying and solving a range of environmental problems. The book closes with Chapter 17, co-authored by several current Cary Institute postdoctoral associates, which lays out some challenges and needs for the future. Today's ecosystem science is evolving rapidly, with major new discoveries and ideas emerging every year. The ultimate shape and contributions of this science remain to be discovered.

This book benefited from the persistent and hard work of the Academic Press team, especially Jill Cetel, Candice Janco, and multiple graphic artists. We were also fortunate to have received helpful and critical reviews of chapters from colleagues, including Clifford Ochs and several anonymous reviewers who teach ecosystem science; their comments substantially improved the book. We thank the authors of various chapters for their scholarship, patience, goodwill, and commitment to bringing this project to fruition. The Cary Institute's assistant, Matt Gillespie, was an enormous help as well. Finally, generations of FEE students were and continue to be an impetus and inspiration to us and the field of ecosystem science.

# INTRODUCTION

# 1

# Introduction to Ecosystem Science

*Kathleen C. Weathers, David L. Strayer, and Gene E. Likens*

**Cary Institute of Ecosystem Studies, Millbrook, NY**

Humans have devised many intellectual systems to understand and manage the complicated world in which we live, from physics to philosophy to economics. In this book, we present one such intellectual system, ecosystem science, that tries to make sense of the complex natural world and help us better manage it. As you will see, ecosystems can be highly varied in size and character, from a little pool of water in a tree cavity, to a redwood forest, to a neighborhood in a city, to a frigid river, to the entire globe (Figure 1.1). Nevertheless, a common set of tools and ideas can be used to analyze and understand these varied and complicated systems. The results of these analyses are both intellectually satisfying and useful in managing our planet for the benefit of humankind and nature. Indeed, because of the growing demands placed on the living and nonliving resources by humans, it could be argued that ecosystem science is one of the essential core disciplines needed to understand and manage the modern planet Earth.

This book defines the ecosystem, describes the chief characteristics of ecosystems and the major tools that scientists use to analyze them, and presents major discoveries that scientists have made about ecosystems. It also lays out some of the important questions for the future. This book is not specifically about ecosystem management, but throughout the book some of the management implications of ecosystem science are described.

## WHAT IS AN ECOSYSTEM?

*An ecosystem is the interacting system made up of all the living and nonliving objects in a specified volume of space.*

This deceptively simple definition both says much and leaves out much. First, as with other systems (Box 1.1), ecosystems contain more than one object, and those objects interact. More surprisingly, living and nonliving objects are given equal status in ecosystem science. A particle of clay and the plant drawing its nutrition from that clay are both parts of

**FIGURE 1.1**   Some examples of ecosystems: (a) the frigid Salmon River, Idaho; (b) a residential neighborhood in Baltimore, Maryland; (c) a biofilm on a rock in a stream; (d) a section of the southern ocean containing a phytoplankton bloom; (e) a redwood forest in the fog in California; (f) a tree cavity; (g) the Earth (Photocredits: 1a - John Davis; 1b - Baltimore Ecosystem Study LTER; 1c - Colden Baxter; 1d - US government, public domain; 1e -Samuel M. Simkin; 1f -Ian Walker; 1g - NASA, http://visibleearth.nasa.gov/).

an ecosystem, and therefore equally valid objects of study. This viewpoint contrasts with physiology and population ecology, for example, in which the organism is the object of study, and the nonliving environment is conceived of as an external influence on the object of study. Finally, the definition implies that ecosystems have definite boundaries, but does not tell us how we might go about setting or finding the boundaries to an ecosystem.

There are some unexpectedly powerful advantages to this simple definition. First, by including all living and nonliving objects in a specified space, it is possible to use the tool of mass balance to follow the movement and fate of materials (Box 1.2). Material that comes into an ecosystem must either stay in the ecosystem or leave—there is simply no

## BOX 1.1

### SOME NONECOLOGICAL SYSTEMS

Thinking about some of the many familiar examples of nonecological systems may help you understand how ecosystems are described and compared. A system is just a collection of more than one interacting object. A few familiar systems include the group of planets rotating around the sun as a system (the solar system); the group of electrons, protons, and neutrons forming an atom; and the system of banks that controls the money supply of the United States (the Federal Reserve System). Just as with ecosystems, we can describe these systems by their structures, their functions, and the factors that control them.

A description of system structure often begins with the number and kinds of objects in the system. Thus, we might note that our solar system contains eight or nine planets; or that the copper atom has 29 electrons, 29 protons, and 35 neutrons; or that the Federal Reserve System contains a seven-member Board of Governors, 12 banks, and 26 branch banks. Systems have functional properties as well—the copper atom exchanges electrons with other atoms in chemical reactions, and the Federal Reserve System exchanges money with

other banks. Systems may be described according to their controls as well. Gravity and rotational dynamics control the motions of the planets, and the copper atom is controlled by strong and weak atomic forces, whereas the Federal Reserve System is controlled by the decisions of its Board of Governors (who, in turn are chosen by a president who is elected by the voters of the United States). All of these descriptions allow us to understand how each system works. Perhaps more importantly, they let us compare one system to another—our solar system with those of other stars; the copper atom with the cadmium atom; our current banking system in the United States with that of France, or with that of the United States in the nineteenth century. Ecosystem scientists likewise describe ecosystems in various ways to understand them better, and to allow comparisons across ecosystems.

Systems science, the general field of understanding all kinds of systems, is well developed. Many of the conceptual frameworks for ecosystem science are those of system science (e.g., Hogan and Weathers 2003).

other place for the material to go. Mass balance offers a convenient quantitative tool for measuring the integrated activity of entire, complicated systems without having to measure the properties and interactions of each of its parts. It also allows ecosystem scientists to estimate the size of a single unknown flux by difference. Consequently, it will become evident throughout the book that ecosystem scientists often use the powerful tool of mass balance.

Second, defining an ecosystem as we have done makes it possible to measure the total activity of an ecosystem without having to measure all the parts and exchanges within the ecosystem. This is sometimes referred to as a "black-box" approach, because we can

## BOX 1.2

## MASS BALANCE

To see just how useful the tool of mass balance can be, suppose we are trying to evaluate whether a lake ecosystem is taking up or releasing phosphorus. We could try to measure all the exchanges between parts of the ecosystem (e.g., the uptake of phosphorus by phytoplankton and rooted plants; the consumption and excretion of phosphorus by the animals that eat phytoplankton and plants; the release of phosphorus during the decay of phytoplankton, plants, and animals; and dozens of other exchanges), then simply sum up all of these measurements. It would take an enormous amount of work to measure all the exchanges, and our final answer would be fraught with large uncertainties. Alternatively, we could define a lake ecosystem

that was bounded by the lakeshore, the overlying air, and the bedrock deep beneath the lake sediments. Using mass balance, we note that the amount of phosphorus being retained by the lake ecosystem is simply the amount of phosphorus going into the lake minus the amount that is leaving the lake. Now we just have to measure the exchanges across the ecosystem boundary (stream water and ground water going into and out of the lake; rain, snow, and particles falling on the lake; and any animals entering and leaving the lake; hard enough!) to calculate whether the lake is taking up or releasing phosphorus. In the case of Mirror Lake, New Hampshire (Figure 1.2), almost 40% of incoming phosphorus is retained by the lake.

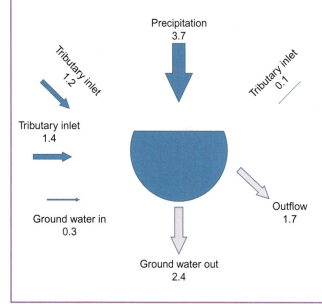

**FIGURE 1.2** Average phosphorus inputs and outputs in kilograms/year to Mirror Lake, NH. Total average inputs = 6.7 kilograms/year; total average outputs = 4.1 kilograms/year. Inputs − outputs = 2.7 kilograms/year or 39.7% retention of phosphorus in the lake. *(Data from Winter and Likens 2009.)*

Precipitation
3.7

Tributary inlet
1.2

Tributary inlet
0.1

Tributary inlet
1.4

Outflow
1.7

Ground water in
0.3

Ground water out
2.4

measure the function (input and output) of a box (the ecosystem) without having to know what is in the box (Figure 1.3). Sometimes ecologists debate whether it is philosophically possible to predict the properties of a complex system by studying its parts (reductionism) or whether it is necessary to study intact systems (holism). It is not necessary to accept the philosophical claims of holism, though, to recognize that studies of whole systems may be a much more efficient way than reductionism to understand ecosystems. Such a holistic approach to ecosystems is a powerful tool of ecosystem science, and is often combined with reductionist approaches to develop insights into the functioning and controls of ecosystems.

Third, the definition gives the investigator complete flexibility in choosing where to set the boundaries of the ecosystem in time and space. The size, location, and timescale at which ecosystems are defined can therefore precisely match the question that the scientist is trying to answer. Boundaries often are drawn at places where fluxes are easy to measure (e.g., a single point on a stream as it leaves a forested-watershed ecosystem) or so that fluxes across the boundary are small compared to cycling inside the ecosystem (e.g., a lake shore). Nevertheless, boundaries are required to make quantitative measures of these fluxes. It is true that ecosystems frequently are defined to be large (e.g., lakes and water-sheds hectares to square kilometers in size) and are studied on the scale of days to a few years, but there is nothing in the definition of ecosystem that *requires* ecosystems to be defined at this scale. Indeed, as you will see, an ecosystem may be as small as a single rock or as large as the entire Earth, and can be studied for time periods as long as hundreds of millions of years.

Fourth, defining an ecosystem to contain both living and nonliving objects recognizes the importance of both living and nonliving parts of ecosystems in controlling the functions and responses of these systems. There are examples throughout the book in which living organisms, nonliving objects, or both acting together determine what ecosystems look like (structure) and how they work (function). Furthermore, the close ties and strong interactions between the living and nonliving parts of ecosystems are so varied and so strong that it would be very inconvenient to study one without the other. Thus, the

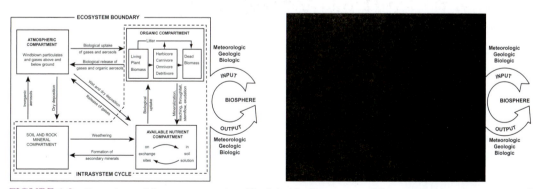

FIGURE 1.3 Two views of the same ecosystem. The left side shows some of the parts inside an ecosystem and how they are connected, as well as the exchanges between the ecosystem and its surroundings, whereas the right side shows a black-box approach in which the functions of an ecosystem (i.e., its inputs and outputs) can be studied without knowing what is inside the box. (*Modified from Likens 1992.*)

inclusion of living and nonliving objects in ecosystems has practical as well as intellectual advantages.

Finally, we note one further property of ecosystems—they are open to the flow of energy and materials. It might be theoretically possible to define particular examples of ecosystems that are closed systems, not exchanging energy or materials with their surroundings, but nearly all ecosystems as actually defined have important exchanges of energy and materials with their surroundings. Indeed, such exchanges are one of the central subjects of ecosystem science. We note in particular that most ecosystems depend on energy inputs from external sources, either as energy from the sun or as organic matter brought in from neighboring ecosystems.

Now consider briefly what is missing from the definition. We have already noted that the definition does not specify the time or space scales over which an ecosystem is defined, or where exactly the boundaries are placed. Ecosystems are not required to be self-regulating, permanent, stable, or sustainable. They are not required to have any particular functional properties. For example, they need not be in balance or efficient in the way that they process materials. Our definition does not require ecosystems to have a purpose. Although ecosystems change over time, the basic definition does not suggest anything about the nature or direction of that change. It might seem like a shame not to include such interesting attributes in a definition of ecosystem (O'Neill 2001), and indeed some ecologists have included such attributes in their definitions, but we think it is neither necessary nor helpful to include them in a basic definition. They may, however, be useful hypotheses and the subject of fruitful research projects. For instance, we might hypothesize that as forest ecosystems recover from disturbances like fire or clear-cutting, they retain a higher proportion of nutrient inputs. This viewpoint is quite different than saying that ecosystems *are* systems that tend to maximize efficiency of use of limiting nutrients.

## WHAT ARE THE PROPERTIES OF ECOSYSTEMS?

All systems have characteristic properties that allow us to describe them and compare them with other similar systems (Box 1.1). How might we describe the properties of ecosystems?

### What Is in an Ecosystem?

We might begin simply by listing the contents of an ecosystem. Plants and animals occur in most ecosystems. As we will see later in the book, the number and kinds of plants and animals can have a strong influence on ecosystem function. Many ecosystems also contain people. Historically, many ecologists treated humans as being outside of the ecosystem, or deliberately studied ecosystems without people, but it has become increasingly common to treat people and our institutions as parts of ecosystems (e.g., Pickett et al. 2001, 2011; see Chapter 17). Certainly the structure and function of many modern ecosystems cannot be understood without considering human activities.

Almost all ecosystems contain microbes (bacteria and fungi); although not as conspicuous as plants and animals, their activities are vital to ecosystem functioning. Viruses occur in most ecosystems, and may play important roles as regulators of plant, animal, and microbial populations. Ecosystems also contain water and air, which are themselves resources for many organisms and also serve as media in which organisms and nonliving materials can be transported. Finally, ecosystems contain an enormous variety of nonliving materials, organic and inorganic, solid and dissolved. These nonliving materials, including such disparate items as dead wood, clay particles, bedrock, oxygen, and dissolved nutrients, interact with the living biota and exercise strong influences on the character and functioning of ecosystems. Thus, the total inventory of an ecosystem can be very long; it might contain thousands or millions of kinds of items, living and nonliving.

## Ecosystems Have Structure

This complexity allows for an essentially infinite number of possible descriptions of ecosystem structure. Nevertheless, only a few descriptions of ecosystem structure are commonly used by the scientists who study ecosystems. Often ecosystems are described by the numbers and kinds of objects that they contain, focusing on key materials or organisms. Thus, we may describe an ecosystem as having a plant biomass of $300 \text{ g/m}^2$, or a deer population of $5/\text{km}^2$, or a nitrogen content of $200 \text{ kg/ha}$. Sometimes ecosystem scientists describe ecosystems by the ratios of key elements such as the nitrogen : phosphorus ratio of a lake ecosystem. If we were interested in the role of biological communities in regulating ecosystem function, we would refer to the biodiversity (especially the species richness) of the organisms in the ecosystem. We may be interested in the spatial variation, as well as the mean value, of any such key variables (see Chapter 10). Thus, we may describe ecosystems as being highly patchy as opposed to relatively homogeneous in nitrogen content or biodiversity. Finally, scientists often describe ecosystems by their size or location (e.g., latitude, altitude, biogeographic realm, or distance from the coast).

## Ecosystems Perform Functions

In the broadest sense, ecosystems consume energy and transform materials. As with all systems subject to the second law of thermodynamics, some of the useful energy that comes into ecosystems in forms such as solar radiation, chemical energy (e.g., organic matter), or mechanical energy (e.g., wind) is degraded to heat and becomes unable to perform further work. In particular, living organisms need a continual source of energy to maintain biochemical and physiological integrity, as well as to perform activities such as swimming, running, and flying. Curiously, although these biological energy transformations are only a part of the energy transformations that occur in an ecosystem, most studies of energy flow through ecosystems treat only forms of energy that can be captured and used by living organisms (i.e., solar radiation and chemical energy), and ignore such purely abiotic processes as the conversion of kinetic energy to heat by flowing water. Organisms can capture solar energy or chemical energy from inorganic compounds (photosynthesis and chemosynthesis, respectively), store energy, obtain energy from other organisms (e.g., predation), or convert energy into heat (respiration). Patterns of energy flow through ecosystems can be of direct interest to humans who harvest wild populations, and can tell ecosystem scientists a good deal about how different ecosystems function.

Ecosystems also transform materials in various ways. Materials that come into the ecosystem may be taken up by some part of the ecosystem and accumulate. In some cases, this accumulation may be temporary so that the ecosystem acts as a sort of capacitor, releasing the material at a later time. The lag time between atmospheric deposition of sulfate onto a terrestrial ecosystem and its export in stream water from that system is an example. Ecosystems may also be a source of material, releasing their internal stores to neighboring systems. Weathering of soils and bedrock is a prime example. Finally, and perhaps most interesting, ecosystems transform materials by changing their chemical and physical states (see Chapter 5). Nitric acid contained in rainwater falling on a forest soil may react with the soil and form calcium nitrate in soil water. The nitrate in the solution may then be taken up by a plant and incorporated into protein in a leaf. At the end of the growing season, the leaf may fall into a stream where it is eaten by an insect and chopped into small leafy bits, which then wash out of the ecosystem. The description of chemical and biological transformations by ecosystems forms the field of biogeochemistry (Schlesinger 1997; see Chapter 5), a major part of modern ecosystem sciences (and this book). Many biogeochemical functions are important to humans (e.g., the removal of nitrate by riparian forests in the Mississippi River basin), as well as essential to understanding how different ecosystems work.

Ecosystems often are described by their functions as well as their structures. One of the most common functional descriptions of ecosystems is whether the system is a source or a sink of a given material; that is, whether the inputs of that material to the ecosystem are less or more, respectively, than the outputs of that material from the ecosystem. In the special case of energy flow through ecosystems, the degree to which an ecosystem is a source or a sink is described by the P/R (gross photosynthesis to respiration) ratio for the system. At a steady state, ecosystems with a P/R ratio less than 1 must import chemical energy (usually organic matter) from neighboring ecosystems and are called heterotrophic; those with a P/R ratio greater than 1 export chemical energy to neighboring ecosystems and are called autotrophic. Another useful functional description is the residence time of a given material in an ecosystem; that is, the average amount of time that a material spends in an ecosystem. Residence time is calculated by dividing the standing stock of the material in the ecosystem by its input rate.

Recently, people have begun to formally recognize that ecosystem structures and functions may have economic value. For instance, ecosystems provide lumber, they purify water and air, they regulate the prevalence of human diseases, and they provide pollination for crop plants. These and many other goods and services provided by ecosystems are now commonly called "ecosystem services"—the benefits that people derive from ecosystem structures and functions (e.g., Millennium Ecosystem Assessment 2005; Kareiva et al. 2011). Developing ways to estimate quantitatively the value of ecosystem services is an important and developing field at the intersection of ecology and economics.

## Ecosystem Structure and Function Are Controlled by Many Factors

Unlike systems like the solar system, the dynamics of which are controlled by just a few factors, ecosystem structure and function depend on many factors. Ecosystem scientists have learned much about how ecosystems are controlled, and much of the remainder of this book will be concerned with this subject (see Chapter 11). Ecosystem structure and function often are affected by organisms (including humans), either through trophic activities such as herbivory, predation, and decomposition, or through engineering activities (Jones et al. 1994) such as burrowing, shelter construction (beaver dams), and the like (see Box 11.1 in Chapter 11). Likewise, the nonliving parts of ecosystems often control ecosystems by determining supplies and movement of air, water, key nutrients, and other materials. Temperature is another abiotic factor that has strong effects on ecosystems. Finally, because most ecosystems are open and exchange energy and materials with the ecosystems that surround them or that preceded them, the structure and function of an ecosystem can be strongly affected by its spatial and temporal context (see Chapter 10).

## Ecosystems Change Through Time

Ecosystems change through time (see Chapters 10 and 11). These changes may be gradual and subtle (the millennial losses of minerals from a weathering soil) or fast and dramatic (a fire sweeping through a forest). Both external forces (changes in climate or nutrient inputs) and internal dynamics (aging of a tree population, accumulation or depletion of materials in a soil or a lake) are important in driving temporal changes in ecosystems. In some cases, changes are directional and predictable (e.g., soil weathering, the filling of a lake basin), while in other cases changes may be idiosyncratic and difficult to predict (e.g., the arrival of an invasive species, disturbance by a hurricane). Understanding and predicting how ecosystems change through time is of great theoretical and practical interest, and is a major part of contemporary ecosystem science.

## How Do We Classify or Compare Ecosystems?

Thus, ecosystem scientists use structure, function, control, and temporal dynamics to classify and compare ecosystems. For instance, it is common to see ecosystems described as rich in nitrogen (structure), sinks for carbon (function), fire-dominated (control), or recently disturbed (dynamics). All of these attributes of ecosystems can provide useful frameworks to classify ecosystems, and ultimately to organize and interpret the vast amount of information that scientists have collected about ecosystems. Similar descriptions and classifications are evident throughout the book.

# WHY DO SCIENTISTS STUDY ECOSYSTEMS?

Scientists have been motivated to study ecosystems for several reasons. To begin with, if ecosystems truly are the "basic units of nature" on Earth, any attempt to understand our planet and the products of evolution on it must include ecosystem science as a central theme. Indeed much of ecosystem science has been motivated by simple curiosity about how our world and how systems—whether ecological, social, or socio-ecological—work. Many salable products such as timber and fish are taken directly from "wild" ecosystems, so many early ecosystem studies were done to try to better understand the processes that supported these products and ultimately increase their yields. Especially in the past 20 years, we have come to realize that the valuable products of nature include far more than obviously salable products like timber and fish. Wild ecosystems also provide us with clean air and water, opportunities for recreation and spiritual fulfillment, protection from diseases, and many more "ecosystem services" (e.g., Millennium Ecosystem Assessment 2005; Kareiva et al. 2011). Human economies and well-being are wholly embedded in and dependent on wild ecosystems. Thus, many contemporary ecosystem studies are concerned with how ecosystems provide this broad array of services, how human activities reduce or restore the ability of ecosystems to provide these services, and ultimately trying to reconcile the growing demands of human populations with the needs of both nature and ourselves for functioning ecosystems.

# HOW DO ECOSYSTEM SCIENTISTS LEARN ABOUT ECOSYSTEMS?

Depending on the problem that they are studying, ecosystem scientists use a wide variety of approaches and an array of simple to sophisticated tools to measure different aspects of ecosystem structure and function. We offer a few examples here; however, new approaches and tools emerge every year, and with them come more ways to open black boxes in ecosystem science (see Chapter 17).

## Approaches for Learning about Ecosystems

There are multiple approaches by which scientists can understand ecosystem structure, function, and development, both qualitatively and quantitatively. Five approaches are especially important in ecosystem science, including (1) natural history or observation, (2) theory and conceptual models, (3) long-term study, (4) cross-ecosystem comparison, and (5) experiments (modified from the lists of Likens 1992; Carpenter 1998). These approaches are complementary to one another (Table 1.1), and are best used in combination. Almost every scientific question of any size or importance requires the use of two or more of these approaches to get a satisfactory answer.

### *Natural History*

A good deal can be learned about ecosystems simply from watching them and documenting what is observed in some fashion. Do fallen leaves decay in place, wash away into a stream, or burn in episodic fires? Is the soil deep and rich, or shallow and rocky? Does it freeze in the winter? As a result, our understanding of an ecosystem often is based on simple observations of its natural history. Indeed, without such careful observations, even the most sophisticated studies can go astray by formulating nonsensical questions or omitting key observations or measurements. Not surprisingly, careful natural history studies (such as Forbes' "The Lake as a Microcosm," discussed later) were important precursors to modern ecosystem science. Although these forerunners of ecosystem science often included speculation about ecosystem processes, they did not have the technical means to easily measure such functions as net ecosystem productivity or nutrient cycling, or to quantify trophic transfers.

## Long-Term Studies

Long-term studies (i.e., those lasting for more than 3 to 5 years—the length of most grants or the time it takes to earn a PhD!) are relatively rare in ecology as a whole. However, long-term studies are especially good at providing insight into slow processes (e.g., changes associated with forest succession), subtle changes (e.g., changing chemistry of precipitation), rare events (e.g., effects of hurricanes or insect outbreaks), or processes controlled by multiple interacting factors (e.g., fish recruitment; Likens 1989; Lindenmayer and Likens 2010; and see the Long-Term Ecological Research Program (LTER) of the National Science Foundation, http://www.lternet.edu). Sometimes long-term understanding can be obtained by short-term analyses of materials that record history, such as soil or sediment cores, otoliths (fish ear-stones), or written historical records. For example, analysis of pollen, diatoms, pigments, geochemistry, and minerals in lake sediment can reveal the history of terrestrial vegetation, phytoplankton, soils, and lake level—in short, the history of the development of the linkages between terrestrial and aquatic ecosystems. It is from long-term studies or their surrogates that scientists have documented climatic, atmospheric, geochemical, and organismal changes over decades to billions of years.

## Cross-Ecosystem Comparison

Comparative studies have served two important roles in ecosystem science. Most simply, scientists often have measured some variable associated with ecosystem structure or function across a series of ecosystems to identify typical values of that variable, show how it varies among types of ecosystems, and generate hypotheses about what factors might

**TABLE 1.1** Strengths and limitations of approaches to understanding ecosystems. Natural history observations and understanding underpin all of these approaches.

| Approach | Some Strengths | Some Limitations |
|---|---|---|
| Theory | Flexibility of scale; integration; deduction of testable ideas | Cannot develop without linkage to observation, experiment |
| Long-term observation | Temporal context; detection of trends and surprises; test hypotheses about temporal variation | Potentially site specific, difficult to determine cause |
| Comparison | Spatial or inter-ecosystem context; detection of spatial pattern; test hypotheses about spatial variation | Difficult to predict temporal change or response to perturbation |
| Ecosystem experiment | Measure ecosystem response to perturbation; test hypothesis about controls and management of ecosystem processes | Potentially site specific; potentially difficult to rule out some explanations; hard to do |

*After Carpenter (1998).*

control that variable. An example of such an analysis is shown in Table 2.1 in Chapter 2. Alternatively, scientists often test whether some factor controls an ecosystem by comparing ecosystems that differ in that factor and not (to the extent possible) in any other relevant characteristic (Cole et al. 1991). For instance, if we wanted to test whether phosphorus inputs control primary production in lakes, we might try to measure primary production in a series of 10 lakes of similar size, depth, and terrain that differ in their phosphorus inputs. In practice, it often is difficult to find such a perfect series of well-matched study sites.

### Experiments

Experiments, whether conducted in the laboratory or in the field, are powerful ways to reveal controls on ecosystem structure and function (Likens 1985; Carpenter et al. 1995). There are no rules about the size of experimental units: manipulations have been made across hundreds of square kilometers (e.g., iron fertilization experiments conducted in the ocean) and within square centimeters. Often, the goal of experiments is to measure an ecosystem's response to a change in a single variable while holding all others as constant as possible. For example, to understand whether phytoplankton in lakes were controlled by phosphorus or by other nutrients such as nitrogen and carbon, scientists in the Experimental Lakes area of Canada added phosphorus, nitrogen, and carbon to one-half of a lake (cut in two by a massive curtain) and just nitrogen and carbon to the other half. They then compared responses—such as the amount of primary production—in each half of the lake to see what effects the treatments had (see Chapter 8). This whole-lake experiment helped to demonstrated that phosphorus was a major factor controlling algal productivity in lakes.

### Theory and Conceptual Models

As in other sciences, ecosystem scientists routinely use theory and conceptual models. Such theories and models are highly varied in structure and purpose (Canham et al. 2003; Pickett et al. 2007). Models may be as simple as a statistical regression (see Chapter 11) or a box-and-arrow diagram drawn on a napkin, or as complex as a detailed simulation model (Figure 1.4). Models are highly flexible, can cover scales of time and space that are difficult to study using other approaches, and often can provide quick answers at low cost. They also are very useful as a way to organize facts and ideas; to generate, sharpen, or narrow hypotheses; and to guide research activities. Scientists often make rapid progress by tightly coupling theory and models to other approaches.

## What Do Ecosystem Scientists Measure?

Ecosystem scientists are inherently interested in the connections between structure and function of ecosystems and how they develop over time. Thus, many of the examples of measurements or values in this book are related to structure and function, such as biomass of a species, or rates of carbon cycling. They are what is often found on the $x$ or $y$ axes of graphs, or are used as treatments or are measured as responses in experiments. Ecosystem structure is sometimes measured by variables such as leaf area index or the number of trophic levels in a lake (see Chapter 11). Productivity (Chapters 2 and 3), rates of decomposition (Chapter 4), or mineralization (Chapter 7) over time or space, or the accumulation of some element of interest can be indicators of ecosystem function. Ecosystem development is often described by changes in structure, function, and their relationship over time (e.g., linked changes in soil and vegetation over millennia; Ewing 2002).

Many, if not most, of our measurements of ecosystem function are indirect. Sometimes we can measure function directly, such as measurement of gas exchange, but these measurements are almost inevitably made on a tiny fraction of the ecosystem (e.g., individual leaves within a grassland or bottle of water from a lake). To estimate a flux over a larger area of a grassland, for example, an ecosystem scientist might deploy eddy covariance instruments that measure carbon dioxide, water, temperature, and wind speed and direction continuously at a place within the grassland. From these measures, a model can be used to infer carbon dioxide flux into or out of the ecosystem.

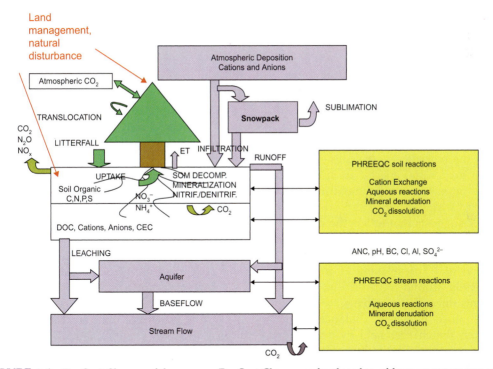

FIGURE 1.4 DayCent-Chem model processes. DayCent-Chem was developed to address ecosystem responses to combined atmospheric nitrogen and sulfur deposition. DayCent-Chem operates on a daily time step and computes atmospheric deposition, soil water fluxes, snowpack and stream dynamics, plant production and uptake, soil organic matter decomposition, mineralization, nitrification, and denitrification (left side of figure) while utilizing PHREEQC's (an aqueous geochemical equilibrium model) low-temperature aqueous geochemical equilibrium calculations, including $CO_2$ dissolution, mineral denudation, and cation exchange, to compute soil water and stream chemistry (right side of figure). ET = evapotranspiration; DOC = dissolved organic carbon; CEC = cation exchange capacity; ANC = acid neutralizing capacity; BC = base cations (Ca, Mg, K, Na). The model requires considerable site-specific environmental data to run. *(From Hartman et al. 2009, Figure 1.3.)*

Scientists often choose indirect measures because they are easier to make across larger parts of a system or across more systems. As another example, the measurement of chlorophyll-a is often used as an indicator of primary productivity in aquatic ecosystems. However, chlorophyll-a is not a direct measure of productivity, rather it is a measure of the presence of a pigment used in photosynthesis, and the photosynthetic process is the source of building biomass. Likewise, the carbon : nitrogen (C:N) ratio in soil is often used as an indicator of litter or soil quality, and is often used to predict decomposition rates, or rates of nitrogen cycling (see Chapters 4 and 5). To make these indirect measures useful, empirical relationships between direct and surrogate measures must be established– quantifying these relationships is an active area of research (see Chapter 17).

## Some Tools in the Ecosystem Scientist's Toolbox

Ecosystem scientists try to answer a diverse range of questions about a wide array of characteristics of the most varied kinds of ecosystems, using any of several scientific approaches. It will therefore come as no surprise that ecosystem scientists use an enormous number of specific scientific techniques in their investigations, some simple, some sophisticated, some developed within the discipline, and some borrowed and adapted from other disciplines. These techniques are far too numerous to list and discuss in an introductory textbook. Nonetheless, several tools are worth introducing here because they are characteristic of ecosystem science and will appear repeatedly in the coming chapters.

### *Balances: Mass and Charge*

*Mass balance* (Box 1.2) is a major tool in ecosystem science, especially for ecosystems of which the boundaries are defined by their watersheds. The laws of thermodynamics tell us that matter and energy are not created or destroyed. When both inputs and outputs of energy or matter can be measured relatively completely and accurately it is possible to construct a mass balance and infer processes. For example, an unbalanced watershed mass balance suggests that either the element of interest is being retained in (inputs > outputs) or leaking from (outputs > inputs) the ecosystem (see Chapters 5 and 9). The watershed mass balance approach was pioneered in the 1960s by scientists at the Hubbard Brook Experimental Forest, New Hampshire (Bormann and Likens 1967), and has been used powerfully around the world to understand the abiotic and biotic movement of a suite of elements through ecosystems.

The other powerful "balance" tool that ecosystem scientists use is *charge balance*. In water, the charges held by positive ions (cations) and negative ions (anions) must balance each other. That is, for every anion (such as chloride) in an aqueous solution, there must be a corresponding cation (such as sodium). Why is this tool so useful? Charge balance tells us, for example, that when an anion moves through a forest soil from ground water into a stream, it must be accompanied by a corresponding cation (see Chapter 5). The sum of all the negative charges brought by anions must be balanced by the same number of positive charges. Charge balance also makes it possible to check whether the major ions in a water sample have been measured correctly; a charge imbalance tells us that a measurement error has been made or that we have not quantified all the cations or anions that are important in a sample.

### Tracers

As useful as balances are as tools, they tell us about the bulk (or net) movements of materials through ecosystems, and rarely allow us to distinguish among different pathways of material movement within ecosystems. All nitrogen atoms look alike to a mass balance. Tracers are tools that allow ecosystem scientists to distinguish among particular pathways of material movement by labeling just some of the atoms or molecules of interest. Ecosystem scientists have used several tracer methods, which have been enormously powerful in understanding how ecosystems work.

Radioisotopes (Box 1.3) were some of the first tracers used in ecosystem science. Radioisotopes can be detected and quantified at very low concentrations, so they make excellent tracers, and have had many applications in ecosystem science. In the mid-twentieth century, ecosystem scientists added small amounts of radioisotopes to ecosystems to trace the movement of water and the uptake and movement of carbon and limiting nutrients through ecosystems. Radioisotopes are no longer added to ecosystems as tracers because of associated health risks, but they continue to be used widely in laboratory studies and measurements (e.g., to measure microbial production; see Chapter 3). They also are used in "natural abundance" studies where ecosystem scientists use the very low natural abundance of

---

### BOX 1.3

## ECOLOGICAL TRACERS: ISOTOPES

Most elements exist in several forms that contain different numbers of neutrons (but the same number of protons and electrons, and basically the same chemical properties). For example, about 99% of the carbon on Earth is $^{12}C$, which contains six protons, six electrons, and six neutrons, but about 1% of the carbon is $^{13}C$, which contains seven neutrons. A tiny amount ($\sim 0.0000000001\%$) of the carbon is $^{14}C$, which has eight neutrons. Some isotopes are stable, while others are radioactive (i.e., they spontaneously decay into other elements or isotopes). In the case of carbon, $^{12}C$ and $^{13}C$ are stable isotopes, whereas $^{14}C$ is a radioisotope that decays into nitrogen ($^{14}N$) with a half-life of 5730 years. Some isotopes that commonly make an appearance in ecosystem science include the radioisotopes $^{3}H$ (tritium), $^{14}C$, $^{32}P$, and $^{35}S$, and the stable isotopes $^{2}H$ (deuterium), $^{13}C$, $^{15}N$, $^{18}O$, and $^{34}S$, although many other isotopes have been used in specialized studies (see Figure 1.4).

The concentration of stable isotopes is usually expressed in a "del" ($\delta$) notation that compares the abundance of the heavier isotope to that of the lighter isotope.

Thus, the abundance of $^{13}C$ in a sample is expressed as:

$$\delta^{13}C(\%_o) = \left( \frac{\left( \frac{^{13}C}{^{12}C} \right)_{sample}}{\left( \frac{^{13}C}{^{12}C} \right)_{standard}} - 1 \right) \times 1000$$

The standard in this case is Vienna Pee Dee Belemnite (a particular kind of fossil). Negative $\delta$ values indicate that the heavier isotope is less abundant in the sample than in the standard, while positive $\delta$ values indicate that the heavier isotope is more abundant in the sample than in the standard.

---

radioisotopes to trace the movement of materials through ecosystems, rather than adding radioisotopes to ecosystems. For example, Caraco and her colleagues (2010) observed that the concentration of $^{14}$C in organic matter washed into the Hudson River from the soils of its watershed was very different from that of organic matter produced by photosynthesis within the river. They could therefore use $^{14}$C to trace movement of terrestrial organic matter through the Hudson River food web, and show that modern zooplankton were being supported in part by carbon that was captured by primary production thousands of years ago (Figure 1.5).

Stable isotopes have largely taken the place of radioisotopes as tracers outside the laboratory (Box 1.3). Although much more difficult to measure and often expensive to use, stable isotopes do not present a health risk to humans and wildlife. Stable isotopes are available for many elements of ecological interest, including hydrogen, nitrogen, carbon, oxygen, sulfur, and others. Stable isotopes often are added to ecosystems (or to laboratory experiments) and followed as they move through the system. For example, Templer and her colleagues (2005) added a stable isotope of nitrogen, $^{15}$N, to forest plots in the Catskill

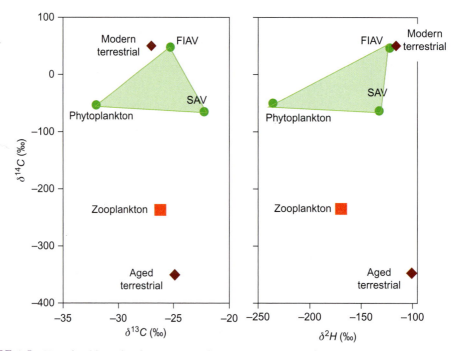

FIGURE 1.5  Use of stable and radioisotopes to determine the source of organic matter supporting zooplankton in the Hudson River (Caraco et al. 2010). Isotope bi-plots show $^{14}$C vs. $^{13}$C (left side) and $^{14}$C vs. $^{2}$H (right side). Sources of carbon from modern primary production are shown near the tops of the graphs (FlAV = floating-leaved aquatic vegetation; SAV = submersed aquatic vegetation). If zooplankton were composed of carbon and hydrogen from these sources, then the data for isotopic composition of zooplankton should fall in the same region of the graph as the sources. Instead, zooplankton fall far outside this region of the graph, showing that they must be composed of organic matter from both modern and "aged" sources (i.e., organic matter thousands of years old from the soils of the Hudson River's watershed). *(From Caraco et al. 2010.)*

Mountains, NY, and then followed it into soil, microbial biomass, understory plants, tree roots, wood, and leaves, and found that most of the nitrogen stayed in the soil. Alternatively, ecosystem scientists often use natural abundance studies of stable isotopes to follow the movement of materials through ecosystems.

Substances other than isotopes can be used as tracers as well. For instance, certain fatty acids cannot be synthesized by animals and are made only by particular kinds of algae. By analyzing the fatty acid content of zooplankton and fish, we can trace the contribution of different kinds of algae throughout the food web. Caffeine, which is not readily degraded in conventional sewage treatment plants, is sometimes used as a tracer for sewage. The kinds of substances that can be used as tracers are highly varied, limited only by the ingenuity and analytical capabilities of the investigator.

### Spatial Data

Where are the regions of high and low productivity around the globe? How do they change over the seasons? These are questions that can now be answered largely as a result of the availability of remote sensing tools and spatially explicit data. The ability to collect, represent, and analyze spatially explicit data has risen exponentially over the past decade. Remote sensing and the georeferencing of basic data on landscape characteristics such as elevation, water bodies, land cover, and geological materials have opened the door to a description of ecosystem structure over large areas. Geographic information systems (GISs) allow analysis of the relationships between these structures and fluxes in or out of these systems. For example, the variation in atmospheric deposition across the mountainous terrain of Acadia National Park or Great Smoky Mountain National Park can be described by a GIS model that links empirical measurements to landscape features that are described in the GIS (Figure 1.6). Such spatially explicit models greatly enhance our ability to identify places on the landscape and times that may be subject to particularly high levels of atmospheric deposition (Weathers et al. 2006). GIS and other technologies are being used creatively and hold tremendous potential for understanding ecosystem processes across heterogeneous landscapes. Other newly emerging tools and techniques are described in Chapter 17.

## FROM THERE TO HERE: A SHORT HISTORY OF THE ECOSYSTEM CONCEPT IN THEORY AND PRACTICE

Ecosystem science is a relatively young discipline, largely developed since the mid-twentieth century (Hagen 1992; Golley 1993; indeed, the term *ecology* was coined only in 1866). The concept of an ecosystem was first formally proposed by the English botanist Arthur Tansley in 1935, although related ideas were in circulation for at least a century before this. For instance, the idea of a biosphere (a region near the Earth's surface in which living organisms are a dominant geochemical force) was outlined by the French scientist Jean-Baptiste Lamarck in 1802; the term *biosphere* was coined in 1875 by an Austrian geologist, Eduard Suess, in describing the genesis of the Alps; and the concept of a biosphere was fully elaborated by the Russian mineralogist Vladimir Vernadsky in 1926. Other

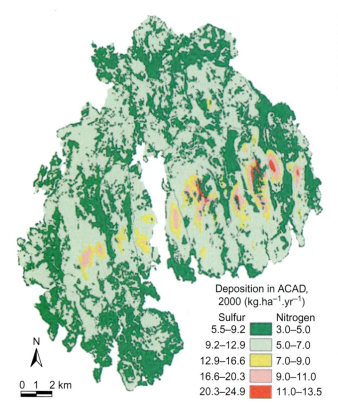

FIGURE 1.6 Atmospheric deposition of nitrogen and sulfur for the year 2000 to Mount Desert Island study area of Acadia National Park, Maine (ACAD). Deposition estimates are based on a GIS-based empirical model. *(From Weathers et al. 2006.)*

Deposition in ACAD, 2000 (kg.ha$^{-1}$.yr$^{-1}$)

| Sulfur | Nitrogen |
|---|---|
| 5.5–9.2 | 3.0–5.0 |
| 9.2–12.9 | 5.0–7.0 |
| 12.9–16.6 | 7.0–9.0 |
| 16.6–20.3 | 9.0–11.0 |
| 20.3–24.9 | 11.0–13.5 |

N

0  1  2 km

important precursors to the modern idea of the ecosystem included Karl Möbius' (1877) use of the term *biocoenosis* to refer to the biotic community associated with oyster beds; Stephen Forbes' (1887) essay on "The Lake as a Microcosm," which explored the myriad of ecological interactions that existed within a bounded area (a lake) to produce a single system; and K. Friedericks' (1930) use of the idea of holocoens (Jax 1998). Although Vernadsky's ideas perhaps were closest to modern ideas of the ecosystem, they were not widely influential outside of the former USSR, and none of the other early concepts really captured the idea that organisms and their abiotic environment could be integrated into a single system.

In 1935, Tansley brought all of these ideas together by writing, "The fundamental concept appropriate to the biome [i.e., all living organisms] considered together with all the effective inorganic factors of its environment is the *ecosystem*." He further stated: "It is the systems so formed which, from the point of view of the ecologist, are the basic units of nature on the face of the earth." Tansley's definition finally explicitly recognized the close interactivity (indeed the inseparability) of living and nonliving entities sharing the same physical space, and is remarkably similar to the definition of ecosystem that many ecologists use 75 years later. Just a few years after Tansley's paper appeared (1942), Raymond Lindeman, a young American ecologist, published a paper laying out a conceptual framework that defined trophic levels and allowed the analysis of energy flow through ecosystems. Because modern ideas about material cycles had been around since the mid-nineteenth century (Gorham 1991), much of the essential conceptual foundation for ecosystem science and its two major branches, material cycling and energy flow, was thus in place by 1942. However, it would take a few more decades before ecosystem studies formed a large part of ecology.

What remained was for the concept of ecosystems to be publicized and widely accepted by ecologists, and for scientists to find suitable tools for studying these newly defined "ecosystems." Of course, many scientists and techniques made important contributions to advance and shape what is now ecosystem science, but a few key contributions are worth special mention. Readers who are interested in more information about the development of the ecosystem concept and its use may want to read the detailed histories published by Hagen (1992), Golley (1993), and Kingsland (2005).

A key advance in the adoption of the ecosystem concept and approach by working ecologists was the appearance of a popular textbook by Eugene Odum (1953 and subsequent editions through 2004). Odum's textbook was organized around the ecosystem concept, and was enormously influential in introducing ecosystem science to generations of ecologists. This text showed with enthusiasm and clarity the possibility and value of quantitative, large-scale studies, how the ecosystem approach could be applied to both aquatic and terrestrial habitats, and the application of this approach for understanding complicated interactions and linkages at large scales (Likens 1992, 2001). Odum and his brother Howard T. Odum also conducted pioneering field studies showing how the ecosystem concept could be insightfully applied in nature (e.g., Odum and Odum 1955; Odum 1957). Odum's textbook was closely followed by a high-profile article in *Science* by Francis Evans (1956) that recommended the ecosystem as "the basic unit in ecology."

The first Big Science initiative in ecology, the International Biological Program of 1964−1974, was organized around systems ecology and exposed hundreds of ecologists around the world to measurements of productivity, nutrient cycling, and decomposition, and the development of ecosystem models, despite controversy and criticism about the program (Committee to Evaluate the IBP 1975; Mitchell et al. 1976; Aronova et al. 2010). Thus, by the late 1960s, the basic ideas of ecosystem science were familiar to most ecologists.

Among all the tools that developed with the science, we highlight two important advances here. First, radioisotopes were widely used in the 1940s through 1960s to trace movement of materials within and between ecosystems (see the earlier section "Tracers"). In the wake of the development of atomic weapons, agencies such as the United States Atomic Energy Commission (AEC) and equivalent agencies in other countries were looking for peaceful uses of radioactive materials. The timing of their interest coincided with the rise of ecosystem science, and led the AEC and similar agencies to provide radioisotopes and funding for many of the early studies on the movement of materials through ecosystems (Golley 1993).

Second, and more significantly, ecosystem scientists began to conduct large-scale experiments on entire ecosystems. As the essentially reductionist approach of the IBP showed, it is very difficult to understand or predict the behavior of entire complex ecosystems from the bottom up by measuring all of their many pieces and trying to model how the whole system will behave. Instead, a direct experimental approach can be used to cut through the Gordian knot of ecosystem complexity, and reliably show how the system actually reacts to some perturbation. It took a few decades for such whole-ecosystem experiments to become a common and accepted tool. Perhaps because of the pervasive influence of "The Lake as a Microcosm" and the clear boundaries to lakes, many of the earliest whole-ecosystem experiments were performed on lakes (Likens 1985; Carpenter et al. 1995). For instance, models and small-scale experiments were unable to resolve a bitter controversy in the 1960s about whether excessive phosphorus caused lakes to become offensively eutrophic, but a whole-lake experiment was conclusive (see Figure 8.1 in Chapter 8). Likewise, by adapting the small-watershed technique from hydrology in the 1960s, ecosystem scientists could quantify inputs and outputs of materials to and from terrestrial ecosystems and treat entire watersheds as experimental subjects (Bormann and Likens 1967; Likens et al. 1970). Perhaps more than any other tool, whole-ecosystem experiments made Tansley's concept a practical subject of scientific study. Ecosystem experiments are now an important tool for scientists to study subjects as varied as the effects of toxins, food-web structures, disturbances, and limiting nutrients in all types of ecosystems (Table 1.1).

As a result of these advances, during the period from approximately 1935 to 1975, ecosystem science moved from being just an interesting concept to a central position in contemporary ecology. Ecosystem scientists, from the roots of the discipline to the present, have worked to unravel the complexity of entire ecosystems of all sizes and forms, from a water-filled cavity in a tree, to a small vernal pool, to a large lake, to a forested watershed, to an entire city, to the total biosphere. The ecosystem concept provides a comprehensive framework for study of the interactions among individuals, populations, and communities and their abiotic environments, and for study of the change in these relationships both temporally and spatially (adapted from Likens 1992).

# References

Aronova, E., Baker, K.S., Oreskes, N., 2010. Big science and big data in biology: From the International Geophysical Year through the International Biological Program to the Long-Term Ecological Research (LTER) network, 1957–present. Hist. Stud. Nat. Sci. 40, 183–224.

Bormann, F.H., Likens, G.E., 1967. Nutrient cycling. Science 155, 424–429.

Canham, C.D., Cole, J.J., Lauenroth, W.K. (Eds.), 2003. Models in ecosystem science. Princeton University Press, Princeton, NJ.

Caraco, N., Bauer, J.E., Cole, J.J., Petsch, S., Raymond, P., 2010. Millennial-aged organic carbon subsidies to a modern food web. Ecology 91, 2385–2393.

Carpenter, S.R., 1998. The need for large-scale experiments to assess and predict the response of ecosystems to perturbations. In: Pace, M.L., Groffman, P.M. (Eds.), Successes, limitations, and frontiers in ecosystem science. Springer-Verlag, New York, NY, pp. 287–312.

Carpenter, S.R., Chisholm, S.W., Krebs, C.J., Schindler, D.W., Wright, R.F., 1995. Ecosystem experiments. Science 269, 324–327.

Cole, J., Lovett, G., Findlay, S. (Eds.), 1991. Comparative analyses of ecosystems: Patterns, mechanisms, and theories. Springer-Verlag, New York.

Committee to Evaluate the IBP, 1975. An evaluation of the International Biological Program. National Academy of Sciences.

Evans, F.C., 1956. Ecosystem as the basic unit in ecology. Science 123, 1127–1128.

Ewing, H.A., 2002. The influence of substrate on vegetation history and ecosystem development. Ecology 83, 2766–2781.

Golley, F.B., 1993. A history of the ecosystem concept in ecology: More than the sum of its parts. Yale University Press, New Haven, CT.

Gorham, E., 1991. Biogeochemistry: Its origins and development. Biogeochemistry 13, 199–239.

Hagen, J.B., 1992. An entangled bank: The origins of ecosystem ecology. Rutgers University Press, New Brunswick, NJ.

Hartman, M.D., J.S. Baron, D.W. Clow, I.F. Creed, C.T. Driscoll, H.A. Ewing, et al., 2009. DayCent-Chem simulations of ecological and biogeochemical processes in eight mountain ecosystems in the United States. United States Geological Survey Scientific Investigations Report 2009-5150.

Hogan, K., Weathers, K.C., 2003. Psychological and ecological perspectives on the development of systems thinking. In: Berkowitz, A.R., Nilon, C.H., Hollweg, K.S. (Eds.), Understanding urban ecosystems: A new frontier for science and education. Springer-Verlag, New York, pp. 233–260.

Jax, K., 1998. Holocoen and ecosystem—On the origin and historical consequences of two concepts. J. Hist. Biol. 31, 113–142.

Jones, C.G., Lawton, J.H., Shachak, M., 1994. Organisms as ecosystem engineers. Oikos 69, 373–386.

Kareiva, P., Tallis, H., Ricketts, T.H., Daily, G.C., Polasky, S. (Eds.), 2011. Natural capital: Theory and practice of mapping ecosystem services. Oxford University Press, New York, NY.

Kingsland, S.E., 2005. The evolution of American ecology, 1890–2000. Johns Hopkins University Press, Baltimore, MD.

Likens, G.E., 1985. An experimental approach to the study of ecosystems. J. Ecol. 73, 381–396.

Likens, G.E. (Ed.), 1989. Long-term studies in ecology: Approaches and alternatives. Springer-Verlag, New York.

Likens, G.E., 1992. The ecosystem approach: Its use and abuse, excellence in ecology, vol. 3. Ecology Institute.

Likens, G.E., 2001. Ecosystems: Energetics and biogeochemistry. In: Kress, W.J., Barrett, G. (Eds.), A new century of biology. Smithsonian Institution Press, Washington and London.

Likens, G.E., Bormann, F.H., Johnson, N.M., Fisher, D.W., Pierce., R.S., 1970. Effects of forest cutting and herbicide treatment on nutrient budgets in the Hubbard Brook watershed ecosystem. Ecol. Monogr. 40, 23–47.

Lindeman, R.L., 1942. The trophic-dynamic aspect of ecology. Ecology 23, 399–418.

Lindenmayer, D.B., Likens., G.E., 2010. Effective ecological monitoring. CSIRO Publishing and Earthscan, London, UK.

Millennium Ecosystem Assessment, 2005. Ecosystems and human well-being: Synthesis. Island Press, Washington, DC (also available at http://www.maweb.org/documents/document.356.aspx.pdf).

Mitchell, R., Mayer, R.A., Downhower, J., 1976. An evaluation of three biome programs. Science 192, 859–865.

Odum, E.P., 1953. Fundamentals of ecology. W.B. Saunders, Philadelphia, PA.

Odum, H.T., 1957. Trophic structure and productivity of Silver Springs, Florida. Ecol. Monogr. 27, 55–112.

Odum, H.T., Odum, E.P., 1955. Trophic structure and productivity of a windward coral reef community on Eniwetok atoll. Ecol. Monogr. 25, 291–320.

O'Neill, R.V., 2001. Is it time to bury the ecosystem concept? (With full military honors, of course.) Ecology 82, 3275–3284.

Pickett, S.T.A., Cadenasso, M.L., Grove, J.M., Nilon, C.H., Pouyat, R.V., Zipperer, W.C., et al., 2001. Urban ecological systems: Linking terrestrial ecological, physical, and socioeconomic components of metropolitan areas. Annu. Rev. Ecol. Syst. 32, 127–157.

Pickett, S.T.A., Kolasa, J., Jones, C.G., 2007. Ecological understanding: The nature of theory and the theory of nature. Academic Press, Burlington, MA.

Pickett, S.T.A., Cadenasso, M.L., Grove, J.M., Boone, C.G., Groffman, P.M., Irwin, E., et al., 2011. Urban ecological systems: Foundations and a decade of progress. J. Environ. Manage. 92, 331–362.

Schlesinger, W.H., 1997. Biogeochemistry: An analysis of global change, second ed. Academic Press, San Diego, CA.

Tansley, A.G., 1935. The use and abuse of vegetational concepts and terms. Ecology 16, 284–307.

Templer, P.H., Lovett, G.M., Weathers, K.C., Findlay, S.E.G., Dawson, T.E., 2005. Influence of tree species on $^{15}$N sinks and forest N retention in the Catskill Mountains, New York, USA. Ecosystems 8, 1–16.

Weathers, K.C., Simkin, S.M., Lovett, G.M., Lindberg, S.E., 2006. Empirical modeling of atmospheric deposition in mountainous landscapes. Ecol. Appl. 16, 1590–1607.

Winter, T.C., Likens, G.E., 2009. Mirror Lake: Interactions among air, land, and water. University of California Press, Berkeley.

# ECOLOGICAL ENERGETICS

## INTRODUCTION

All organisms need materials such as carbon, nitrogen, and phosphorus to build molecules, cells, and other structures, and energy to build and maintain those structures against the relentless forces of entropy. Not surprisingly, the two main branches of ecosystem science deal with the movement and fate of materials and energy (*biogeochemistry* and *ecosystem energetics*, respectively). This section of the book (Chapters 2–4) introduces ecosystem energetics (primary production, secondary production and consumer energetics, and decomposition), and Section III deals with biogeochemistry (Chapters 5–8).

Studies of energy flow through individuals, populations, communities, and ecosystems form a large part of past and present-day ecosystem science. Historically, ecosystem scientists studied energy flow for several reasons. Many of the earliest studies (i.e., before 1950) were motivated by the idea that the allowable harvest from a wild population (e.g., a fishery) would be related to the amount of energy flowing into that population, so that studies of energy flow would help to estimate sustainable yield. Although historically important, this is no longer a primary motivation for ecological energetics (but see Libralato et al. 2008 for a modern example). More generally, ecologists recognize that energy is essential for *all* life; thus, studies of energy flow track the movement of a key resource. Because all organisms require energy, it provides a common currency that allows ecologists to make comparisons across all organisms and habitats. That is, it allows ecologists to compare the activities of such disparate organisms as plants, mice, moose, and microbes using the same single currency that is required by all of them.

Some ecologists have gone further to regard energy as *the* key resource, making the case that energy can be substitutable with other resources (e.g., water, nutrients) so that deficiencies in any resource can be ameliorated if enough energy is available. In this world view, which was held by a minority of ecologists, energy is the ultimate limiting resource, so pathways of energy flow might reveal pathways of control in ecosystems. Finally, energy flow often is roughly proportional to other key activities (e.g., grazing, flows of elements), so it could be argued that energy flow is the most appropriate single measure of the importance of a population (if we *must* reduce a population to a single number), because it roughly summarizes the multiple activities that the population performs.

# UNITS USED IN STUDIES OF
# ECOLOGICAL ENERGETICS

If you've taken a physics class recently, you know that the proper units of energy content and flow are joules ($kg\text{-}m^2/s^2$) and watts (joules/s), respectively. It may seem confusing, then, that ecologists studying energy flow almost never express their results in terms of joules or watts. Rather, most ecologists implicitly equate energy with biomass, because biomass is the carrier of energy in organisms, and is easier to measure than energy content. Biomass thus implies energy content, and the production or destruction of biomass implies energy flow. Consequently, ecologists usually express energy in units of biomass (i.e., grams of live mass, dry mass, ash-free dry mass, or organic carbon). Other units sometimes used in ecological energetics are the mass of oxygen produced or consumed by photosynthesis or respiration, or calories (an obsolete unit of energy content). Table 1 shows conversions between units commonly used in ecological energetics.

**TABLE 1** Approximate conversion factors between energetic units used in ecological studies. Except for the conversion between joules and calories (which is exact), the conversion factors are approximate and can vary substantially among organisms and among tissues in an individual organism. Both the photosynthetic quotient and the respiratory quotient are assumed to equal 1.

| Units Converted From | Units Converted To | | | | | | |
|---|---|---|---|---|---|---|---|
| | Joules | Calories | Carbon (g) | Oxygen (g) | Dry Mass | Wet Mass | Ash-Free Dry Mass |
| Joules | 1 | 0.239 | $2 \times 10^{-5}$ | $6 \times 10^{-5}$ | $5 \times 10^{-5}$ | $2.5 \times 10^{-4}$ | $4.3 \times 10^{-5}$ |
| Calories | 4.18 | 1 | $9 \times 10^{-5}$ | $2.5 \times 10^{-4}$ | $2 \times 10^{-4}$ | $1 \times 10^{-3}$ | $1.8 \times 10^{-4}$ |
| Carbon (g) | $4.5 \times 10^4$ | $1 \times 10^4$ | 1 | 2.7 | 2.2 | 11 | 1.9 |
| Oxygen (g) | $1.7 \times 10^4$ | $4 \times 10^3$ | 0.375 | 1 | 0.8 | 4 | 0.7 |
| Dry mass | $2 \times 10^4$ | $5 \times 10^3$ | 0.45 | 1.2 | 1 | 5 | 0.9 |
| Wet mass | $4 \times 10^3$ | $1 \times 10^3$ | 0.09 | 0.24 | 0.2 | 1 | 0.17 |
| Ash-free dry mass | $2.3 \times 10^4$ | $6 \times 10^3$ | 0.5 | 1.4 | 1.2 | 6 | 1 |

*Modified from Cummins and Wuycheck (1971), Peters (1983), Benke (1993), Cattaneo and Mousseau (1995), and other sources.*

# References

Benke, A.C., 1993. Concepts and patterns of invertebrate production in running waters. Verh. Int. Ver. Theor. Angew. Limnol. 25, 15–38.

Cattaneo, A., Mousseau, B., 1995. Empirical analysis of the removal rate of periphyton by grazers. Oecologia 103, 249–254.

Cummins, K.W., Wuycheck, J.C., 1971. Caloric equivalents for investigations in ecological energetics. Mitt. Int. Ver. Theor. Angew. Limnol. 18, 1–158.

Libralato, S., Coll, M., Tudela, S., Palomera, I., Pranovi, F., 2008. Novel index for quantification of ecosystem effects of fishing as removal of secondary production. Mar. Ecol. Prog. Ser. 355, 107–129.

Peters, R.H., 1983. The ecological implications of body size. Cambridge University Press, New York.

# Primary Production: The Foundation of Ecosystems

*Michael L. Pace*[1] *and Gary M. Lovett*[2]

[1]University of Virginia, Charlottesville
[2]Cary Institute of Ecosystem Studies, Millbrook, NY

## INTRODUCTION

Primary production is the storage of energy through the formation of organic matter from inorganic carbon compounds. Primary production is carried out by autotrophic organisms. The term *autotrophic* is derived from the Greek words *autos*, meaning self, and *trophikos*, meaning pertaining to food. Autotrophs are "self-feeders." Higher plants as well as some microbes (e.g., algae) are autotrophs. Plants and algae conduct the most familiar form of primary production—photosynthesis—where carbon dioxide is incorporated into organic matter using energy from sunlight. In most ecosystems primary production is carried out by a variety of species and the diversity of autotrophs influences primary production (e.g., Tilman et al. 2006). The accrual of organic matter by primary producers represents the first step in the capture, storage, and transfer of energy in most ecosystems.

There are several reasons why ecologists consider primary production a fundamental ecosystem process. The ecosystem carbon cycle begins with the fixation of carbon (i.e., incorporation of $CO_2$ into organic matter). Herbivores consume this organic carbon produced by autotrophs to support their growth and metabolism. Other components of the food web such as detritivores and predators also depend directly or indirectly on primary production for their energy supply. Primary producers require nutrients such as nitrogen and phosphorus to build biomolecules such as proteins and nucleic acids. The uptake and cycling of nitrogen, phosphorus, and other elements accompanies primary production, and the ratio of elements that ultimately comprises primary producers influences many ecological processes (Sterner and Elser 2002). The formation of organic matter by primary producers is also a key process of the global carbon cycle. Primary production and the short- and long-term fate of this fixed carbon influences atmospheric carbon dioxide concentration. The study of primary production in terms of rates, controls, trophic interactions, biogeochemical cycles, and storage of the end-products of primary production is, therefore, central to ecosystem science.

The results of primary production are often quite evident as, for example, the rapid growth of lawn grass during spring. In terrestrial ecosystems the accumulation of biomass by primary producers provides important structure. For example, in forests, tree growth leads to branch and root formation and the accumulation of wood. These structural elements are critical components affecting many physical, chemical, and biological processes in a forest (Box 11.1). Analogous growth of marine kelp forests in the sea creates structure and habitat that support many types of organisms.

Primary production may also be cryptic. Measurement of phytoplankton biomass day to day in the sea or in a lake would usually reveal little variation. It would seem that no biomass is being produced because there is no accumulation, but in this case, loss processes such as grazing by herbivores are as rapid as the increase in phytoplankton. Production might be high even though biomass of the phytoplankton does not change. In contrast, when growth rates are consistently in excess of loss rates, so-called "blooms" of phytoplankton result and can lead to massive, sometimes noxious, accumulations of algal scums. Rather than being cryptic, these scums caused by excess primary production are conspicuous and represent a serious environmental problem in many water bodies.

## COMPONENTS OF PRIMARY PRODUCTION

Primary production is by definition a rate with units of mass per area (or volume, if measured in water) per time. For example, primary production data are often presented as grams carbon per square meter per day ($g \, C \, m^{-2} \, d^{-1}$). The absolute amount of plant material produced in an ecosystem is sometimes referred to as production or yield (mass per unit area or volume) as, for example, the total mass of corn plants generated in a field. Time, however, is generally implicit in this use of production and yield. For example, the production of a corn field typically refers to a mass per unit area for a growing season. In this chapter the terms *production* and *primary production* will always refer explicitly to rates with the time attribute of the rate specified.

Biomass is distinct from primary production. The biomass of primary producers is mass per area or volume independent of time. Biomass is often approximately correlated with primary production. However, it is possible as noted earlier to have low biomass but relatively high rates of primary production as often observed in the ocean. Alternatively, slow-growing plants may represent a substantial biomass but have relatively low rates of primary production.

Primary production encompasses a number of processes that require definition and that pose problems for measurement. The components of primary production are clarified by following the flow and fates of carbon through a generalized ecosystem (Figure 2.1). Primary production begins with the fixation of $CO_2$ into organic matter. Gross primary production (GPP) represents this first step accounting for all the carbon dioxide fixed into

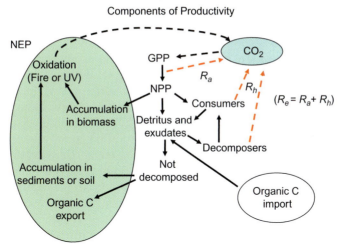

FIGURE 2.1    Components of productivity; see text for definitions. *(Figure modified from Lovett et al. 2006.)*

organic matter irrespective of any respiratory losses (Figure 2.1). Net primary production (NPP) is the difference between GPP and autotrophic respiration ($R_a$):

$$NPP = GPP - R_a \tag{2.1}$$

Conceptually, NPP is the rate at which organic matter is made available for other uses beyond simply supporting energy costs (i.e., respiration) of the primary producers. Net primary production is consumed, converted to detritus, or accumulated in biomass. The portion of the NPP that is consumed and respired by heterotrophic organisms ($R_h$) is cycled back to the atmosphere as $CO_2$. Ecosystem respiration ($R_e$) is the sum of $R_a$ and $R_h$ (Figure 2.1).

Ecosystem respiration typically does not consume all the organic carbon that is either produced within or imported to the ecosystem (Figure 2.1). Some organic carbon accumulates in biomass (e.g., wood in trees) and detritus (e.g., organic matter in soils and sediments). Some organic matter is exported (e.g., organic carbon exiting a river ecosystem and entering the ocean). Together these rates of accumulation and export represent net ecosystem production (NEP). The balance of carbon flows requires that NEP is equivalent to the difference between GPP and $R_e$:

$$NEP = GPP - R_e \tag{2.2}$$

Because $R_e$ is the sum of $R_a$ and $R_h$ and NPP is the difference between GPP and $R_a$, NEP can also be expressed as:

$$NEP = GPP - R_a - R_h = NPP - R_h \tag{2.3}$$

In other words, *NEP is the portion of gross primary production that is not respired by autotrophs or heterotrophs.* This residual production either accumulates as carbon in biomass or detritus, is exported from an ecosystem, or is lost through fire or photo-oxidation.

Interestingly, NEP can be either positive or negative. How is this possible? One way this can occur is if the primary production of an ecosystem is stopped or severely reduced (the GPP in Eq. 2.2 $\sim$ 0), but the respiration of stored organic matter continues. For instance, consider a forest that has just been clear-cut so that there is little or no primary production but decomposers are still consuming (and respiring) the organic matter in the forest floor. Another way that negative NEP can occur is if an ecosystem imports organic carbon, and these imports are respired by heterotrophs along with the carbon produced within an ecosystem. In both cases the total respiration of the ecosystem exceeds gross primary production ($R_e > GPP$), thus NEP is negative. Ecosystems with negative NEP are referred to as heterotrophic ecosystems—these systems respire more carbon than they produce and the excess respiration either depletes carbon stored in the system or is subsidized by imports of carbon from outside the ecosystem. In contrast, ecosystems with positive NEP are autotrophic ecosystems. Ecosystems with negative NEP are quite common and include many lakes, streams, rivers, and estuaries (Caraco and Cole 2004). These distinctions about relative NEP are important in considering carbon sequestration by ecosystems (Box 2.1; Chapter 6).

We can also consider NEP in the context of organic carbon accumulation ($dC_{org}$) in an ecosystem by considering a mass balance of inputs and losses:

$$dC_{org} = GPP + I - R_e - Ex - Ox_{nb} \tag{2.4}$$

where the new terms are:

$$I = \text{imported organic carbon}$$
$$Ex = \text{exported organic carbon}$$
$$Ox_{nb} = \text{nonbiological oxidation of organic carbon (e.g., fire or photo-oxidation)}$$

Since NEP is equal to GPP $- R_e$, Eq. (2.4) can be written as:

$$dC_{org} = NEP + I - Ex - Ox_{nb} \tag{2.5}$$

Organic carbon accumulation ($dC_{org}$) in ecosystems sequestered over long time periods (centuries to millennia) provides a sink for atmospheric $CO_2$ and is very important to those studying global carbon budgets (Box 2.1; Chapter 6).

Not all primary production results from aerobic photosynthesis where water is split and oxygen is produced in the fixation of carbon. Under anoxic conditions, some microorganisms can fix carbon, for example, using hydrogen sulfide ($H_2S$) instead of water and producing sulfur instead of oxygen. Further, some microorganisms, primarily archaea and bacteria, have chemosynthetic abilities and are also primary producers. There are many types of chemosynthetic reactions but all oxidize inorganic molecules to produce energy, which is used to fix $CO_2$ as organic matter (Box 2.2). For example, nitrifying bacteria convert ammonia to nitrite or nitrite to nitrate, and in the process derive energy sufficient to convert $CO_2$ to organic matter.

---

BOX 2.1

## NET ECOSYSTEM PRODUCTION AND CARBON SEQUESTRATION

The fate and especially long-term storage of primary production in the biosphere can influence carbon dioxide in the atmosphere. For example, the current burning of fossil fuels by humans that is causing atmospheric $CO_2$ to increase represents the mining of ancient primary production long stored in the earth. Is it possible to partially reverse the current course of $CO_2$ increase by storing increased amounts of contemporary primary production in long-term reservoirs? This type of question drives research on the carbon cycle and carbon sequestration in ecosystems. Consideration of carbon sequestration, however, requires clarity in terminology and specification about timescales over which sequestration occurs. In some systems NEP is equated to carbon sequestration; however, this is not necessarily correct. For instance, a portion of NEP may be exported as organic carbon rather than sequestered in the ecosystem. In addition, today's sequestered carbon might become tomorrow's atmospheric $CO_2$. Consider a regenerating forest that grows for 50 years accumulating carbon in wood (90%) and soil organic matter (10%) at a rate of 100 g C m$^{-2}$ y$^{-1}$ so that 5000 g C m$^{-2}$ is stored after 50 years. If the forest burns in year 51 and all the wood is consumed in the fire, the sequestered carbon is only the 10% stored in the soil (assuming it did not burn). Consideration of the timescale of carbon storage is important given discussions to develop carbon markets and global sinks for $CO_2$.

These general issues can be clarified by revisiting the definition of NEP in the context of an ecosystem budget for organic carbon (Lovett et al. 2006). Remember Eq. (2.5) that $dC_{org} = NEP + I - Ex - Ox_{nb}$.

Clearly, NEP is not simply equivalent to carbon sequestration ($dC_{org}$). It is possible that in some ecosystems $I$, $Ex$, and $Ox_{nb}$ are low, but most ecosystems lose some carbon ($Ex$) as dissolved organic carbon and receive organic inputs ($I$) from the atmosphere and/or adjacent ecosystems. Further, if an area burns, $Ox_{nb}$ is high and $dC_{org}$ is strongly affected but NEP is not. Schemes for carbon sequestration must consider NEP and the fluxes $I$, $Ex$, and $Ox_{nb}$ in the context of the particular ecosystems where carbon will be stored. Because some measurement systems provide an instantaneous estimate of NEP, the imports, exports, and nonbiological oxidation must be accounted for before organic carbon accumulation can be calculated. Moreover, the timescale of probable carbon sequestration should be explicit so that periodic events like fires and floods can be incorporated into calculations.

---

In most ecosystems that receive significant light energy, chemosynthesis is only a small proportion of primary production. For example, in three Swedish lakes chemosynthetic primary production by methane-oxidizing bacteria (which transform methane to acquire energy, Box 2.2) was only 0.3% to 7% of total primary production (Bastviken et al. 2003). However, in unlighted ecosystems such as the deep realms of soils, sediments, and caves where suitable reduced compounds are present (e.g., ammonium, sulfides, methane, and hydrogen),

# BOX 2.2

## CHEMOSYNTHESIS

Chemosynthesis exploits chemical energy to convert inorganic carbon compounds into organic matter, in contrast with photosynthesis, which exploits the energy of light to produce organic matter. Chemosynthetic reactions are carried out by prokaryotic microorganisms, principally bacteria and archaea (referred to as "bacteria" in the following). Energy is produced in chemosynthetic reactions from oxidizing reduced compounds. There are a variety of chemosynthetic bacteria that carry out these reactions including nitrifying bacteria (oxidizing $NH_4$ or $NO_2$), sulfur bacteria (oxidizing $H_2S$, S, and other sulfur compounds), hydrogen bacteria (oxidizing $H_2$), methane bacteria (oxidizing $CH_4$), iron and manganese bacteria (oxidizing reduced iron and manganese compounds), and carbon monoxide bacteria (oxidizing CO). This is not an exhaustive list and new modes of chemosynthesis as well as new chemosynthetic bacteria are still being discovered.

Chemosynthetic reactions often occur at the interface of aerobic and anaerobic environments where the end-products of anaerobic decomposition as well as oxygen are available. Thus, these reactions are most often apparent in soils and sediments where oxygen is depleted. For example, methane is produced by anaerobic bacteria that convert fermentative end-products like acetate to methane. Methane builds up in anaerobic zones of soils, sediments, and stratified water columns. Methane-oxidizing bacteria grow at the interface of the aerobic–anaerobic zone exploiting methane that moves out of the anaerobic area. The chemosynthetic reaction of methane oxidation is:

$$CH_4 + O_2 \rightarrow CO_2 + 4\,H^+ \text{ and } 2\,e^-$$

The energy generated by this reaction is represented by the reducing power of the hydrogen ions and electrons produced. These are coupled to biochemical reactions used to fix inorganic carbon. For methane-oxidizing bacteria the initial organic compound produced in the coupled oxidation-reduction reaction is formaldehyde (HCHO), which is a precursor for further organic synthesis.

Understanding of chemosynthetic processes is still advancing with new findings that reveal reactions in environments where they were not previously believed to occur. For example, methane oxidation can occur in anaerobic environments where microbes use sulfate or nitrate to oxidize methane. Raghoebarsing et al. (2006) studied a freshwater canal polluted with high concentrations of agricultural runoff and documented anaerobic methane oxidation conforming to the following reaction:

$$5\,CH_4 + 8\,NO_3^- + 8\,H^+ \rightarrow \begin{array}{l} 5\,CO_2 + 4\,N_2 \\ + 14\,H_2O \end{array}$$

The microbial community found in the canal was able to use methane and nitrate as a sole energy source and did not require oxygen to convert methane to carbon dioxide. The energy gained from this reaction is used to fuel growth (via the fixed $CO_2$). Further research is likely to bring to light novel mechanisms by which microbes use chemicals in their environment as energy sources to fix carbon.

chemosynthetic organisms can be the main primary producers (e.g., Sarbu et al. 1996). Indeed, in the thermal vent regions of the deep sea entire ecosystems run on energy derived from chemosynthetic microorganisms. Sulfides and other reduced compounds that emerge with geothermal fluids from these vents are converted by microorganisms to energy through chemosynthetic reactions. In these settings chemosynthetic primary production supports a variety of consumers with high local biomass (Lutz and Kennish 1993; Van Dover et al. 2002). Regardless of whether gross primary production is powered by chemosynthesis or photosynthesis, the carbon flow pathways in Figure 2.1 still apply and the definitions of GPP, NPP, R, and NEP are equivalent.

## MEASURING PRIMARY PRODUCTION

Methods to measure primary production vary as a function of the types of autotrophs in an ecosystem—an algal assemblage in a lake or stream requires a different approach compared to trees in a forest. Primary production methods also vary in terms of the processes that are included or excluded. For example, some methods measure GPP while other methods include autotrophic respiration and therefore measure NPP. The timescale of the measurement may determine which of the processes in Figure 2.1 are included. For example, measurement of grassland primary production is often accomplished by clipping and weighing plant material produced over a given time interval (e.g., a growing season). This measurement represents NPP not GPP because $R_a$ has occurred during the course of the measurement. Furthermore, any losses to herbivores that were not excluded and that occur in this period are not measured in the biomass accumulation and must either be considered negligible or estimated to provide a correction.

In aquatic ecosystems, "bottle methods" are often used wherein a sample is collected and incubated for a few hours to measure the uptake of radioactive inorganic carbon ($^{14}$C) or a change of dissolved oxygen. Other techniques include continuously monitoring chemical constituents such as oxygen or pH to assess overall ecosystem respiration and primary production. For aquatic and wetland vascular plants various harvest and morphometric methods are used.

In terrestrial ecosystems, including fields and forests, both harvest and incremental growth observations are used to measure production. More recently, continuous monitoring of $CO_2$ exchange over terrestrial ecosystems has been employed to estimate production over large areas. The actual area measured by these latter approaches varies substantially from system to system as a function of plant cover, terrain complexity, wind, and weather conditions.

This text does not emphasize methods but we turn now to a brief discussion of some aquatic and terrestrial methods for measuring primary production. Our purpose is to compare and contrast the methods in terms of the components of primary production (Figure 2.1) that are included in or excluded by the technique. By considering the methods we hope to deepen understanding of the process of primary production and to increase the reader's appreciation of some of the complexities inherent in this measurement.

## Aquatic Methods

One of the most common primary production methods used in aquatic ecosystems dominated by fast-growing phytoplankton and benthic algae is measurement of the incorporation of $^{14}$C. The technique is extremely sensitive so even very low rates of primary production can be measured. To measure phytoplankton production, water samples are collected, a trace amount of $^{14}$C-labeled bicarbonate ($H^{14}CO_3$) is added, and the sample is incubated in situ or in the laboratory under specified light conditions. At the end of the incubation, the water is filtered. The $^{14}$C captured on the filter after any residual bicarbonate is removed by acidification represents primary production. The length of incubation determines whether significant respiration of $^{14}$C by phytoplankton occurs ($R_a$) and the method typically measures a quantity that falls somewhere between GPP and NPP. Other complexities need to be considered including the loss of radioactive dissolved organic compounds, death of phytoplankton during the incubation, temporal variations of light (e.g., daily light cycle), and possible artifacts from enclosing phytoplankton in bottles. The incubation time, and hence measurement period, is usually a few hours, and rates are typically extrapolated to represent daily production.

## Terrestrial Methods

The phytoplankton $^{14}$C method contrasts with approaches to forest production. One standard approach to measuring forest primary production is through a combination of leaf fall (foliar production) and wood production estimates. The estimate of wood production takes advantage of the strong correlation of woody biomass with tree diameter. Allometric equations that quantify the relationship between diameter and mass are available in the literature for many tree species. These equations are generated by harvesting trees and measuring both morphometric characteristics and the biomass of selective components. With these relationships, repeated measurements (usually over several years) of tree diameters in a stand of trees can be used to calculate the accumulation of woody biomass. This approach estimates NPP rather than GPP because $R_a$ is occurring during the measurement period. Foliar and wood production constitute most of the NPP in forests, but it is important to note that this method ignores many other parts of the total NPP, each of which can be important in some places and times. For instance, understory plants can contribute significantly to NPP in some ecosystems. Losses to herbivory are usually small but can sometimes be very important, as for example, during insect outbreaks or in grasslands. Seed production can be important but is sometimes episodic (e.g., masting) and therefore difficult to measure accurately. Root production is also part of the primary production but is also very difficult to measure, thus most terrestrial primary production data are presented as ANPP, above-ground net primary production. Root production can be equal to or greater than ANPP in some ecosystems, but measurement of this process has vexed ecologists for decades. One current method is to use a video camera to repeatedly measure the growth of individual roots along the face of a clear sampling tube inserted into the ground. Although this method is promising, all root production estimates involve great uncertainties.

The aquatic and terrestrial methods outlined earlier have been used extensively but are being supplemented or replaced by methods that rely on in situ measurement of gas exchange to estimate primary production. These new techniques provide much greater temporal resolution and increase the spatial scale of the estimates of primary production (because the gas measurements are typically representative of larger spatial areas). To illustrate these approaches, consider measurements of oxygen concentration made continuously in a water body with an in situ oxygen electrode (Figure 2.2). Oxygen increases during the day as a consequence of oxygen production by photosynthesis (GPP) and decreases at night as a consequence of oxygen consumption by respiration ($R_e$). In addition, oxygen exchanges ($D$) with the atmosphere as a consequence of the relative concentrations of oxygen in the water and atmosphere. $D$ can be positive or negative depending on whether oxygen in the water is undersaturated or oversaturated relative to the atmosphere. Thus, the daily change in oxygen is described as:

$$\Delta O_2 = GPP - R_e + D \tag{2.6}$$

where $R_e = R_a + R_h$ (Figure 2.1). The loss of oxygen at night plus or minus atmospheric exchange is equal to respiration ($R_{night}$):

$$\Delta O_{2night} = R_{night} + D \tag{2.7}$$

Assuming respiration at night equals respiration during the day ($R_{day}$), the gain of oxygen during the day is equal to GPP plus respiration ($R_{day} = R_{night}$) plus atmospheric exchange ($D$). Hence, GPP can be readily calculated as:

$$GPP = \Delta O_{2day} + (R_{night}) + D \tag{2.8}$$

The advantages of this method are numerous. Instruments to measure oxygen allow continuous observations so that production can be estimated repeatedly rather than just a

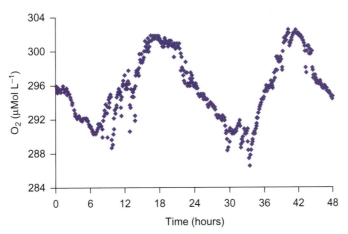

**FIGURE 2.2**   Oxygen dynamics in Peter Lake, a small lake in Michigan, over 48 hours beginning at midnight. Oxygen declines at night are due to respiration and increases during the day are due to photosynthesis. These daily changes in oxygen provide a basis for estimating primary production. *(From data from the authors.)*

few times. Potential artifacts related to sample enclosure as required in the $^{14}C$ method are eliminated. The technique is less subject to problems of extrapolation of primary production for an ecosystem, because the method inherently provides estimates across broad scales (e.g., an entire lake each day). This method, as for any technique, also has important uncertainties such as the assumptions about the equivalence of day and night respiration as well as questions of scale (e.g., what portion of an aquatic ecosystem is represented by the oxygen measurements). Nevertheless, this type of method is greatly improving the resolution and the accuracy of primary production measurements of ecosystems (e.g., Roberts et al. 2007).

An analogous gas-exchange approach in terrestrial ecosystems is called *eddy covariance* (sometimes called eddy flux or eddy correlation). In this method a fast-response $CO_2$ sensor is paired with a multidirectional wind speed sensor on a tower extending above a vegetation canopy. The sensors measure the $CO_2$ concentrations associated with updrafts and downdrafts as the turbulent air mixes into the canopy. The flux of $CO_2$ into and out of the canopy on these air currents is calculated using algorithms programmed into a computer, and the difference (efflux − influx), integrated over time, is termed the *net ecosystem exchange*, or NEE. (By convention, NEE is negative if the net flux of $CO_2$ is into the canopy and positive if the net flux is out of the canopy.) Because the release of $CO_2$ from the ecosystem includes both autotrophic and heterotrophic respiration, NEE is essentially an instantaneous measurement of NEP. In some cases, nighttime measurement of NEE ($CO_2$ efflux at night) is used to estimate ecosystem respiration ($R_e$, including both $R_a$ and $R_h$), and GPP is calculated as the sum of NEE and $R_e$. NPP cannot be readily calculated because it is very difficult to separate the autotrophic and heterotrophic components of $R_e$.

This method has some major advantages—its fast response allows for observation of short-term physiological and meteorological controls on production, and it naturally integrates over a substantial area (typically on the order of hectares) upwind of the tower. It also allows direct measurement of NEP, which, if organic carbon losses from the system are negligible, is a good estimate of the organic carbon accumulation rate in the ecosystem. On the other hand, it is difficult to apply in areas where the terrain or the vegetation canopy is uneven, and it does not measure NPP, which is very important in terrestrial ecological studies.

# REGULATION OF PRIMARY PRODUCTION

Primary production by photosynthesis obviously requires light, which attenuates rapidly with depth in water and from the top of the canopy to the ground on land. This limits maximum light to upper waters of aquatic ecosystems and to terrestrial plant canopies. Primary producers found in deeper waters and on the ground beneath canopies are shaded and exhibit adaptations that enhance carbon fixation at low light intensities. Primary production tends to increase with increasing light concentration up to a maximum (Figure 2.3) and can often be described by a saturating function (Jassby and Platt 1976). This relationship is useful for modeling primary production. The relationship can be quantified by measuring primary production per unit biomass at different light intensities and fitting a two-parameter model that includes the initial slope of the

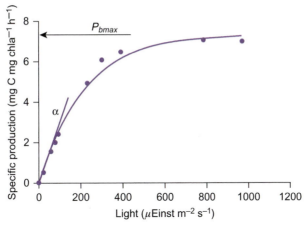

FIGURE 2.3    Relationship of net primary production to light for the Hudson River phytoplankton. Parameters are defined in the text. *(Redrawn from Cole and Caraco 2006 using additional data from the authors.)*

increase ($\alpha$) and the maximum rate of photosynthesis ($P_{bmax}$). A light-production relationship combined with detailed data on light intensity for an ecosystem provides a means to estimate net primary production over time and space. Thus, light is a key variable used to model primary production within and among ecosystems. However, total light input to an ecosystem is not the only factor determining primary production. Other factors are important in limiting primary production, particularly temperature, nutrients, and water.

Primary production is nutrient-limited in most ecosystems. In 1840 Justus Leibig, a German agronomist and chemist, first proposed the idea that a single factor limits production. In terrestrial ecosystems water and/or specific nutrients such as potassium, calcium, nitrogen, or phosphorus are often in shortest supply. In aquatic ecosystems, the nutrients nitrogen and phosphorus frequently are most limiting. Single-factor limitation is a useful but simplistic view for two reasons. First, organisms can use one resource to obtain another. For instance, a tree with sufficient light but insufficient nitrogen can grow more roots to obtain more nitrogen, so in effect both light and nitrogen limit the growth of a tree. Second, within an ecosystem, there may be variation across space, time, or species in which the factor is limiting production. For example, in aquatic ecosystems diatoms are often limited by silica while other phytoplankton are limited by other elements such as phosphorus, nitrogen, or iron. Diatoms flourish in many ecosystems until silica is exhausted and then are replaced by other forms. Similarly, the NPP of a grassland may be limited by nitrogen in wetter areas and by water in drier areas, so the NPP of the entire ecosystem could be increased by either fertilization or irrigation. Thus, in a mechanistic sense, single-resource limitation does not completely account for the processes that regulate primary production of ecosystems. Nevertheless, the limiting resource concept is very useful for describing regulation of primary production, interpreting relative availability among nutrients (stoichiometry), and developing models about how ecosystems respond to changes in inputs.

Autotrophs synthesize organic matter de novo by definition but require a variety of inorganic elements to do so. These elements are described as either macronutrients, which constitute greater than 0.1% of organism wet weight, or micronutrients, which constitute less than 0.1%. The macronutrients of organic matter are C, N, H, O, P, S, K, Mg, Na, and Ca (plus Si, for diatoms and some land plants). Micronutrients include Fe, Mn, Zn, Cu, B, Mo, Cl, V, and Co, which are used mainly as enzyme cofactors. Some autotrophs have more specialized requirements including various trace metals and vitamins (e.g., vitamin $B_{12}$). Relative uptake and loss of macro- and micronutrients influence the stoichiometric composition of autotrophs. For example, limitation of primary production by nitrogen and phosphorus often results in autotrophs with high carbon-to-nitrogen and carbon-to-phosphorus ratios, and such ratios can constrain other ecosystem processes like herbivory and decomposition (Sterner and Elser 2002; Figure 3.7).

The ratio of the key elements carbon, nitrogen, and phosphorus can be quite variable in autotrophs. Terrestrial plant leaves have an enormous range of C:N and C:P ratios that reflect investment in structural carbon as documented by Sterner and Elser (2002), who summarized a large compilation of data from a variety of sources and sites. Mean foliar C:N and C:P ratios (expressed in moles) were 36 and 970, respectively (Sterner and Elser 2002). These high ratios contrast with marine seston (particulate matter collected on filters) from the ocean, which is dominated by phytoplankton cells with lower mean C:N and C:P ratios of 7.7 and 143, respectively. Freshwater seston ratios were intermediate with mean C:N and C:P of 30 and 307, respectively, probably reflecting the mixture of terrestrial detritus and phytoplankton cells suspended in the water as well as the chemical composition of phytoplankton, which is often depleted in P. Importantly, the ranges in ratios observed in marine seston are relatively small, larger in freshwater, and huge for terrestrial leaves (Figure 2.4; note the log scale). Animals maintain a more rigid C:N:P composition and must compensate when feeding on nitrogen- or phosphorus-poor autotrophic organic matter (Sterner and Elser 2002).

To illustrate nutrient limitation of primary production consider the results of several experimental additions of nutrients to ecosystems (Figure 2.5). An example of a single nutrient addition comes from the Southern Ocean, which is the oceanic region bordering the Antarctic continent. Iron was added to a 1000 km² area that was also marked with an inert tracer so that the labeled patch could be identified and followed as it diluted with the surrounding waters (Boyd et al. 2000). In the iron-addition patch NPP (measured with ${}^{14}C$) increased approximately five-fold relative to NPP measured outside the patch (Figure 2.5a). Similar results were obtained in another addition experiment when nitrogen and phosphorus were added to a lake (Carpenter et al. 2005). Primary production measured as GPP using continuous oxygen measurements increased two-fold (Figure 2.5b). Terrestrial ecosystems also respond to nutrient enrichment. For example, nitrogen and phosphorus additions enhanced forest primary production as measured by tree increments (Figure 2.5c). This forest fertilization study was conducted on different islands in the Hawaiian chain that vary in age of the geological substrate (Vitousek 2004). Nutrient limitation of production changed from primarily nitrogen on younger substrate to primarily phosphorus on older substrate (Figure 2.5c).

The increase of production in the lake example (Figure 2.5b) illustrates a common response to nutrient additions in ecosystems. Phosphorus is often the primary limiting

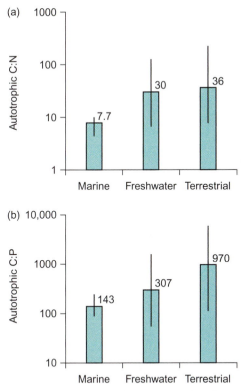

FIGURE 2.4   (a) Molar carbon to nitrogen (C:N) and (b) carbon to phosphorus (C:P) ratios of autotrophs from marine, freshwater, and terrestrial environments. Vertical line is the range of ratios for each environment. Number associated with each bar is the mean ratio. Note the log scale. Marine and freshwater ratios are based on samples of suspended particles filtered from water samples that represent a mixture of phytoplankton, other organisms, and detritus. Terrestrial ratios are based on leaves and may not represent an entire plant, especially those with woody structure. *(The means and ranges are values presented in Sterner and Elser 2002.)*

nutrient in lakes, but nitrogen is also needed in most cases to sustain increased primary production (Lewis and Wurtsbaugh 2008). The island forests (Figure 2.5c) also exhibited highest productivities in two of three cases with both nitrogen and phosphorus addition. Because of the coupled nature of nutritional requirements, relief from one form of nutrient limitation will often rapidly lead to limitation by a second nutrient. In addition, nutrients can facilitate the uptake of other limiting nutrients. Nutrient additions to enclosures in Lake Erie illustrate this colimitation and facilitated uptake (North et al. 2007). Iron additions alone had little effect on the accumulation of phytoplankton biomass (a surrogate for net primary production). Iron additions with other nutrients, however, were associated with increased biomass (Figure 2.5d). Independent measurements of nutrient status indicated the phytoplankton were strongly P-limited and moderately N-limited. Adding iron and phosphorus helped overcome the N-limitation by facilitating the uptake of nitrate, which requires Fe. Adding all three nutrients produced the greatest increase

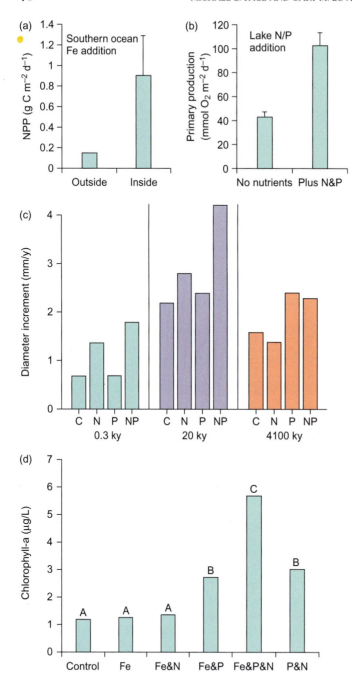

**FIGURE 2.5** Responses of primary productivity to (a) iron additions in the Southern Ocean (Boyd et al. 2000), (b) nitrogen and phosphorus additions in a lake (Peter Lake, MI; Carpenter et al. 2005), (c) nitrogen and phosphorus additions to Hawaiian forests growing on substrate (islands) of different ages (ky = thousands of years) (Vitousek 2004), and (d) additions of iron alone and combined with nitrogen and/or phosphorus for water isolated from Lake Erie (North et al. 2007), where letters (A, B, C) over bars indicate statistically different groups.

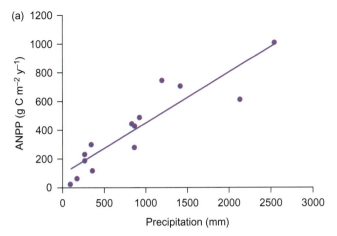

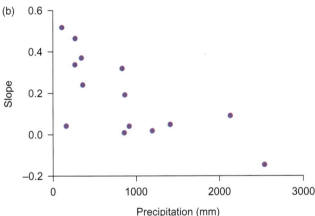

FIGURE 2.6 (a) Mean annual precipitation versus mean ANPP for a range of terrestrial ecosystems and (b) the slopes of the individual relationships of annual precipitation and ANPP for the same terrestrial ecosystems versus mean annual precipitation. *(Figure replotted from data in the supplement of Huxman et al. 2004.)*

in biomass (Figure 2.5d), leading to the conclusion that all three nutrients colimit production.

Terrestrial primary production is often correlated with precipitation in broad comparisons among ecosystems (Figure 2.6a) (Huxman et al. 2004). The values presented in Figure 2.6 are annual means of precipitation and ANPP for at least seven years from long-term study sites. Within a particular ecosystem represented by a point on the graph, the interannual relationship of precipitation and ANPP is variable. For example, low precipitation ecosystems like deserts and grasslands are generally quite sensitive to variation in precipitation and there is a positive relationship (positive regression slopes) between precipitation and ANPP in different years (Figure 2.6b). For ecosystems with precipitation greater than 1000 mm, slopes tend to be near zero; hence, these ecosystems are not sensitive to interannual variation in precipitation, and other factors are more limiting to primary production.

Herbivory can also regulate primary production. The most obvious direct effect of herbivores is to consume photosynthetic tissues and thereby reduce the biomass of primary producers. Herbivores also trample and damage primary producers during movement and feeding. These negative effects are partially compensated for by positive effects. Herbivore regeneration (via excretion or egestion) of limiting nutrients may stimulate photosynthesis (or partially compensate for lost photosynthesis due to the direct effects of grazing). In addition, herbivores disperse reproductive structures (seeds, cysts). Herbivores may also stimulate or reduce primary production indirectly by changing plant species composition through selective foraging because different plant species deplete and recycle nutrients with different efficiencies (de Mazancourt and Loreau 2000).

The amount of primary production directly consumed by herbivores is typically low in most ecosystems dominated by vascular plants, which are in many cases well defended against herbivores. For example, herbivores consume less than 10% of primary production in most terrestrial ecosystems (McNaughton et al. 1991). Herbivory in aquatic ecosystems is generally greater than in terrestrial ecosystems (Cyr and Pace 1993) especially for algal-based ecosystems where herbivores often consume more than 50% of primary production (Figure 2.7). Thus, the loss of primary production to herbivores differs considerably between an open-water setting where phytoplankton are heavily grazed, and a forest setting where, except during insect outbreaks, herbivory is typically light.

# RATES AND PATTERNS OF PRIMARY PRODUCTION

Primary production varies among ecosystems primarily as a function of light, nutrients, and moisture (the latter in terrestrial ecosystems). Local rates of primary production along with any imported material provide the energy that drives other ecosystem processes. Thus, relative rates or primary production help discriminate the capacity of different types of ecosystems. The most productive ecosystems include tropical forests, regions of oceanic upwelling, and shallow marine systems. These systems have productivities exceeding $700 \, \text{g C m}^{-2} \, \text{y}^{-1}$ (Table 2.1). The least productive aquatic ecosystems are lakes and streams with low nutrient inputs or in some cases low light conditions due to high turbidity from suspended sediments (e.g., the river in Table 2.1) or canopy shading in the case of small streams. Primary production in these ecosystems can be below $100 \, \text{g C m}^{-2} \, \text{y}^{-1}$ (Table 2.1). For terrestrial ecosystems the least productive ecosystems have low moisture, low nutrients, and/or short growing seasons—for example, deserts, arid shrublands, tundra, and boreal woodlands (Table 2.1). Primary production is less than $200 \, \text{g C m}^{-2} \, \text{y}^{-1}$ in these ecosystems. The most productive aquatic ecosystems are shallow-water marine ecosystems where light is ample and autotrophs are multicellular with complex structures or associations (e.g., corals and kelp). For ecosystems like coral reefs primary production is most often estimated as GPP (by measuring oxygen changes in water flowing across reef flats), and there are few estimates of NPP. Hence, the value in Table 2.1 of coral reef NPP greater than $1000 \, \text{g C m}^{-2} \, \text{y}^{-1}$ is approximate and based on the very high rates of GPP measured for reefs (Gattuso et al. 1998). Coral reefs and other shallow marine ecosystems sustain high rates of production even in the absence of high concentrations of

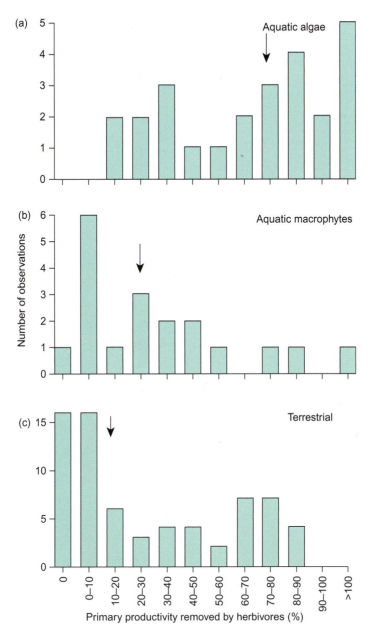

FIGURE 2.7   Relative distribution of herbivory as a percent of net primary production for ecosystems domi-nated by (a) algae, (b) aquatic macrophytes, and (c) terrestrial vegetation. Arrows indicate medians *(From Cyr and Pace 1993.)*

limiting nutrients, because nutrient recycling is very efficient. Tropical rainforests also maintain very high productivity even though tropical soils are often poor in nutrients. In these ecosystems plants form complex, diverse associations (e.g., canopy trees, vines,

**TABLE 2.1**  Net primary productivity of selected terrestrial and aquatic ecosystems. In most cases, data represent individual systems where an annual production estimate was made. Note differences among systems should not be interpreted finely (e.g., boreal forest has greater NPP than short grasslands) because the data do not represent the range of possible NPP values for given system types, which are often wide.

| Study Site | Ecosystem Type | NPP $(gCm^{-2}y^{-1})$ |
|---|---|---|
| | *Terrestrial* | |
| Toolik Lake, Alaska | Dry tundra | 65 |
| Curlew Valley, Utah | Shrubland | 110 |
| Toolik Lake, Alaska | Wet tundra | 120 |
| Schefferville, Quebec, Canada | Boreal woodland | 170 |
| Central Plains Experimental Range, Colorado | Short grassland | 200 |
| Bonanza Creek, Alaska | Boreal forest | 220 |
| Osage Prairie, Oklahoma | Tall grassland | 425 |
| Nylsvley Nature Reserve, South Africa | Tropical savanna | 435 |
| Cedar Creek, Minnesota | Temperate savanna | 450 |
| Andrews Experimental Forest, Oregon | Temperate coniferous forest | 535 |
| Guanica State Forest, Puerto Rico | Dry tropical forest | 550 |
| Harvard Forest, Massachusetts | Temperate deciduous forest | 650 |
| Harvard Forest, Massachusetts | Temperate mixed forest | 650 |
| Chakia, India | Tropical deciduous forest | 700 |
| Taita Experimental Station, New Zealand | Temperate evergreen forest | 725 |
| Ducke Forest, Manaus, Brazil | Tropical evergreen forest | 1050 |
| | *Aquatic* | |
| Hudson River, New York | River | 55 |
| Mirror Lake, New Hampshire | Oligotrophic lake | 65 |
| Walker Branch, Tennessee | Stream | 150 |
| Pacific Ocean, north of Hawaii | Oligotrophic ocean | 185 |
| Lake Mendota, Wisconsin | Eutrophic lake | 345 |
| Cap Blanc off Northwest Africa | Oceanic upwelling | 730 |
| Middle Atlantic Bight | Temperate continental shelf | 370 |
| Duplin River, Georgia | Salt marsh estuary | 760 |
| Off Southern California | Kelp forest | 730 |
| Various Sites | Coral reef | >1000 |

*Sources used for this Table are listed at the end of the Chapter.*

epiphytes), and along with abundant moisture and high light (in the canopy), tight nutrient recycling pathways promote high rates of primary production.

While local rates of primary production set the stage for many ecosystem processes, these rates collectively are also a major flux in the global carbon cycle, and hence global estimates of primary production are of interest, especially in the context of human impact on the carbon budget of Earth. The methods for scaling up productivity estimates are similar for aquatic and terrestrial ecosystems. Remote sensing, typically with multispectral scanners on satellites, provides an estimate of the "greenness" of areas on the surface of Earth. The greenness of an area is related to the light-capturing power of the ecosystem, which is then multiplied by estimates of the photosynthetically active radiation for that area and the efficiency of the ecosystem for capturing light energy in carbon fixation. In terrestrial ecosystems, this efficiency is estimated by models that include many factors regulating productivity, such as temperature, moisture, and nutrient supply. In marine ecosystems, the efficiency is generally estimated as a function of the sea surface temperature. In both cases, the models are verified against field measurements of productivity using methods like those described in the section "Measuring Primary Productivity."

Field et al. (1998) combined terrestrial and aquatic models to produce an analysis of primary production for the entire globe (Figure 2.8). Total global primary production based on this approach is approximately 105 Pg C y$^{-1}$ (1 Pg = $10^{15}$ g) with production split about equally between the terrestrial and marine realms (Table 2.2). Tropical rainforests, savannas, and cultivated areas dominate global terrestrial primary production, collectively accounting for 75% of the terrestrial total. Marine primary production areas are classified according to relative phytoplankton biomass (as measured by chlorophyll-a) as oligotrophic (<0.1 mg/m$^3$), mesotrophic (between 0.1 and 1 mg/m$^3$), and eutrophic (>1 mg/m$^3$). The mesotrophic areas contribute over half the marine total. Average NPP on land is 426 g C m$^{-2}$ y$^{-1}$ and in the ocean is 140 g C m$^{-2}$ y$^{-1}$. Field et al. (1998) argue that the lower

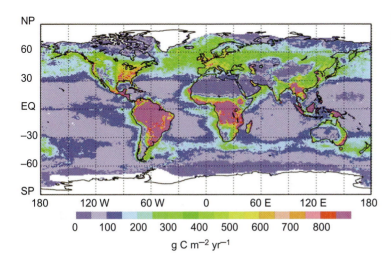

FIGURE 2.8 Global primary production. (*From Field et al. 1998.*)

TABLE 2.2　Global primary production estimated using remote sensing and terrestrial and marine models. Units are petagrams ($10^{15}$ grams) per year.

| Ocean | Pg/y |
| --- | --- |
| Oligotrophic | 11 |
| Mesotrophic | 27.4 |
| Eutrophic | 9.1 |
| Macrophytes | 1 |
| Total Marine | 48.5 |
| Land | |
| Tropical rainforests | 17.8 |
| Broadleaf deciduous forests | 1.5 |
| Broadleaf and needleleaf forests | 3.1 |
| Needleleaf evergreen forests | 3.1 |
| Needleleaf deciduous forests | 1.4 |
| Savannas | 16.8 |
| Perennial grasslands | 2.4 |
| Broadleaf shrubs | 1 |
| Tundra | 0.8 |
| Desert | 0.5 |
| Cultivation | 8 |
| Total terrestrial | 56.4 |
| Total global | 104.9 |

Source: (Data from Field et al. 1998)

areal average of the ocean is due to "competition for light between phytoplankton and their strongly absorbing medium." NPP in much of the ocean is also severely limited by very low nitrogen, phosphorus, and in some areas iron concentrations. Increasing these nutrients, as demonstrated in the iron fertilization experiment (see Figure 2.5), leads to substantial increases in phytoplankton biomass and primary production.

# FATES OF PRIMARY PRODUCTION

Primary production is consumed by herbivores, converted to detritus, stored in biomass, consumed by fire or photo-oxidation, or exported (Figure 2.1). Typically over a year, ecosystems accumulate little or no primary producer biomass with some notable

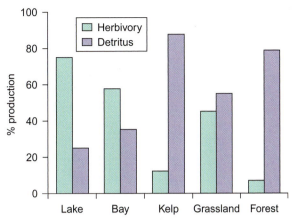

FIGURE 2.9 Relative fates of primary production to herbivory and detritus for phytoplankton in a freshwater lake ("Lake"), phytoplankton in a marine bay ("Bay"), kelp in a kelp dominated coastal system ("Kelp"), grasses in a grassland ("Grassland"), and trees in a forest ("Forest"). Note in some cases percentages do not add to 100 either because of errors in the estimates or other fates (not presented). *(From data provided in Cebrian 1999.)*

exceptions such as growing forests. In most ecosystems the two most immediate fates of NPP are consumption by herbivores and conversion to detritus. Ecosystems vary in the relative rates of these two processes with as much as 90% of primary production going to detritus as for the forest illustrated in Figure 2.9 (Cebrian 1999). However, in some terrestrial ecosystems grazers are abundant and herbivory is an important fate. For example, in the grass and shrub areas of Yellowstone National Park, elk and bison graze 45% of the annual primary production (Frank and McNaughton 1992). Similarly, in phytoplankton-based ecosystems much of the primary production is grazed (Figure 2.9). However, in other aquatic ecosystems, where the dominant primary producers are kelps (Figure 2.9), other types of seaweeds, and certain toxic or inedible algae, herbivory is low (<10 %), and the main fate of primary production is conversion to detritus.

Most NPP is ultimately respired by heterotrophs. These organisms close the ecosystem carbon cycle by converting carbon derived from primary producers back to $CO_2$. Heterotrophic respiration, particularly by bacteria, is a major carbon flux in all ecosystems.

Respiration of primary production is not 100% efficient and some residual organic matter accumulates over time in soils and sediments. This carbon is generally refractory (i.e., hard to decompose) or is sequestered in some way that minimizes degradation (e.g., complexing with minerals). The accumulation of unrespired organic carbon derived from primary production within an ecosystem accounts for a portion of net ecosystem production (Box 2.1). This carbon may have a long residence within an ecosystem (decades to centuries for carbon accumulated in woody plant biomass to millennia for some of the carbon buried in soils or sediments). Carbon exported from the system accounts for another portion of the NEP. For example, some of the organic matter accumulating in soils is soluble and referred to as dissolved organic carbon (DOC). DOC moves from terrestrial into aquatic ecosystems and export rates vary from roughly 0.1 to 10 g C m$^{-2}$ y$^{-1}$ (Aitkenhead and McDowell 2000) representing on the order of 0.1% to 10% of NPP in terrestrial ecosystems. Export can represent a much larger and even dominant fate of primary production in streams, rivers, and estuaries. In these flowing-water ecosystems short water residence time and periodic high discharge limit the development of phytoplankton and will often scour attached algae and aquatic plants transporting NPP downstream. Finally, some of the NEP can be oxidized back to $CO_2$ by abiotic processes such as by fire in terrestrial ecosystems or exposure to ultraviolet light in aquatic ecosystems. Overall, the nonrespiratory fates of primary production must be considered in an accounting of ecosystem carbon budgets, particularly when considering whether an ecosystem is a net exporter or sink for organic carbon as well as $CO_2$.

## A TALE OF SCALE

On a warm summer afternoon in a forest, scientists are busy studying primary production. A physiological ecologist, working from a tower in the canopy, has enclosed a leaf in a chamber and is measuring the leaf $CO_2$ exchange. On the same tower, but above the canopy, a micrometeorologist's eddy covariance system measures the $CO_2$ exchange of the entire forest. Meanwhile, on the ground, a plant ecologist checks baskets that collect litterfall and measures tree diameters to compare with measurements made in the same stand five years earlier. Nearby a geologist is surveying with specialized equipment looking for primary production from an ancient fern forest that is now sequestered in coal seams deep in the ground. The geologist suspects that storage of an era's worth of primary production now compressed and converted to coal will provide a significant energy resource for humans.

All of these measurements are attributes of primary production, but how are they related to each other? The physiological ecologist is measuring net photosynthesis of the leaf in her chamber, including the leaf's photosynthesis and respiration. To scale this up to the annual NPP of the whole forest, she would have to measure (or model) the net photosynthesis of all the leaves in the canopy for the entire year, subtract the respiratory losses for the nonphotosynthetic parts of the forest (e.g., stems, branches, and roots), and express the results per unit ground area rather than per unit leaf area. Needless to say there is a lot of uncertainty in such scaling.

The micrometeorologist is measuring NEE, which includes GPP and respiration of both autotrophs and heterotrophs ($R_e$). Integrated over a year, the NEE is equivalent to the annual NEP barring significant forms of exchange that are not measured. If the micrometeorologist estimates ecosystem respiration from his nighttime measurements, he may be able to calculate GPP, but not NPP. To compare his measurement with other GPP and NEP measurements, he would have to know the upwind area over which the flux tower integrates, and be certain that the other measurements are representative of the same area.

The plant ecologist is measuring accumulation of plant material in above-ground woody biomass and production of fine litterfall. To calculate above-ground NPP, he would also have to account for tree mortality, coarse litterfall (e.g., fallen branches), and losses due to herbivory and canopy leaching. To calculate total stand NPP, he would have to account for below-ground root biomass accumulation, root detritus production, and exudation of carbon from roots. To calculate NEP, he would need to combine his estimates of biomass carbon accumulation with measurements of soil carbon accumulation (which are very difficult to make in most forests), imports and exports of organic carbon (e.g., export by organic carbon leaching from the soil), and any losses of carbon due to fire during the measurement period.

The geologist is searching for the remains of past primary production. The coal that accumulated from an ancient forest is a component of the NEP of that forest. The geologist could calculate the NEP if she knew the time period over which the organic matter accumulated in the soil, and if she assumed (1) that the forest biomass was in steady state; (2) that there were no carbon imports, exports, or fires in the forest; and (3) that there were no losses of organic carbon from the stored coal during the millions of years that the organic matter was stored in the soil and transformed to coal in the rocks.

While all of these measurements pertain to primary production, each has a particular scale associated with it, and they are not comparable to one another without a significant effort at spatial and temporal scaling and a clear understanding of exactly which components of productivity are being measured. Nevertheless, each of these investigations provides insights of relevance to the others as our four researchers discuss later while having a beer together. The leaf measurements of the physiologist help explain the mechanisms that lead to the timing and rates of gas exchange by the forest. Knowing the types and amounts of plant matter accumulation provided by the plant ecologist allows the geologist to evaluate what forests and what conditions produced long-term preservation of organic matter. The studies of different scales and processes provide a richer view of primary production.

# SUMMARY

To summarize the main points of this chapter, primary production provides the organic carbon that ultimately supports the metabolism of autotrophs and heterotrophs in ecosystems. Understanding the pathways that organic carbon follows through an ecosystem leads to distinctions among GPP, NPP, and NEP. Measurement methods for primary production reflect the questions of interest, the types and life histories of primary producers considered, and scales over which rates are considered. Primary production is regulated by factors such as light, temperature, herbivory, and the supply of water and nutrients. Models of primary production in ecosystems cannot rely on a single limiting factor but instead must consider multiple potentially limiting processes. Net primary productivity varies widely among ecosystems as a function of temperature, light, nutrients, and precipitation (for terrestrial ecosystems) and covers a range from a few to more than a thousand grams of organic carbon produced per square meter each year. Global primary production is about half on land and half at sea and represents an important flux in the global carbon cycle. The most immediate fate of net primary production is either consumption by herbivores or conversion to detritus with the relative rates of these two processes varying widely among ecosystems. Ultimately the fate of most primary production is conversion back to $CO_2$ via respiration; however, some residual carbon accumulates in biomass and refractory organic matter. The storage and fate of this unrespired carbon is important in understanding ecosystems as carbon sources and sinks for atmospheric $CO_2$.

# References

Aitkenhead, J.A., McDowell, W.H., 2000. Soil C:N ratio as a predictor of annual riverine DOC flux at local and global scales. Global Biogeochem. Cycles 14, 127–138.

Bastviken, D., Ejlertsson, J, Sundh, I., Tranvik, L., 2003. Methane as a source of carbon and energy for pelagic food webs. Ecology 84, 969–981.

Boyd, P.W., Watson, A.J., Law, C.S., Abraham, E.R., Trull, T., Murdoch, R., et al., 2000. A mesoscale phytoplankton bloom in the polar Southern Ocean stimulated by iron fertilization. Nature 407, 695–702.

Caraco, N.F., Cole, J.J., 2004. When terrestrial organic matter is sent down the river: Importance of allochthonous C inputs to the metabolism in lakes and rivers. In: Polis, A., Power, M.E., Huxell, G. (Eds.), Food webs at the landscape level. University of Chicago Press, Chicago, pp. 301–316.

Carpenter, S.R., Cole, J.J., Pace, M.L., Van de Bogert, M., Bade, D.L., Bastviken, D., et al., 2005. Ecosystem subsidies: Terrestrial support of aquatic food webs from $^{13}C$ addition to contrasting lakes. Ecology 86, 2737–2750.

Cebrian, J., 1999. Patterns in the fate of production in plant communities. Am. Nat. 154, 449–468.

Cole, J.J., Caraco, N.F., 2006. Primary production and its regulation in the tidal-freshwater Hudson River. In: Levinton, J.S., Waldman, J.R. (Eds.), The Hudson River estuary. Cambridge University Press, New York, NY, pp. 107–120.

Cyr, H., Pace, M.L., 1993. Magnitude and patterns of herbivory in aquatic and terrestrial ecosystems. Nature 361, 148–150.

de Mazancourt, C., Loreau, M., 2000. Effects of herbivory and plant species replacement on primary production. Am. Nat. 155, 735–754.

Field, C.B., Behrenfeld, M.J., Randerson, J.T., Falkowski, P., 1998. Primary production of the biosphere: Integrating terrestrial and oceanic components. Science 281, 237–240.

Frank, D.A., McNaughton, S.J., 1992. The ecology of plants, large mammalian herbivores, and drought in Yellowstone National Park. Ecology 73, 2043–2058.

Gattuso, J.-P., Frankignoulle, M., Wollast, R., 1998. Carbon and carbonate metabolism in coastal aquatic ecosystems. Annual Review of Ecology and Systematics 29, 405–434.

Huxman, T.E., Smith, M.D., Fay, P.A., Knapp, A.K., Shaw, M.R., Loik, M.E., et al., 2004. Convergence across biomes to a common rain-use efficiency. Nature 429, 651–654.

Jassby, A.D., Platt, T., 1976. Mathematical formulation of the relationship between photosynthesis and light for phytoplankton. Limnol. Oceanogr. 21, 540–547.

Lewis Jr., W.M., Wurtsbaugh, W.A., 2008. Control of lacustrine phytoplankton by nutrients: Erosion of the phosphorus paradigm. International Review of Hydrobiology 93, 446–465.

Lovett, G.M., Cole, J.J., Pace, M.L., 2006. Is net ecosystem production equal to carbon storage? Ecosystems 9, 152–155.

Lutz, R.A., Kennish, M.J., 1993. Hydrothermal vent communities—A review. Rev. Geophys. 31, 211–242.

McNaughton, S.J., Oesterheld, M., Frank, D.A., Williams, K.J., 1991. Primary and secondary production in terrestrial ecosystems. In: Cole, J., Lovett, G., Findlay, S. (Eds.), Comparative analysis of ecosystems: Patterns, mechanisms, and theories. Springer-Verlag, New York, NY, pp. 120–139.

North, R.L., Guildford, S.J., Smith, R.E.H., Havens, S.M., Twiss, M.R., 2007. Evidence for phosphorus, nitrogen, and iron co-limitation of phytoplankton communities in Lake Erie. Limnol. Oceanogr. 52, 315–328.

Raghoebarsing, A.A., Pol, A., van de Pas-Schoonen, K.T., Smolders, A.J.P., Ettwig, K.F., Rijpstra, W.I.C., et al., 2006. A microbial consortia couples anaerobic methane oxidation to denitrification. Nature 440, 918–921.

Sarbu, S.M., Kane, T.C., Kinkle, B.K., 1996. A chemoautotrophically based cave ecosystem. Science 272, 1953–1955.

Sterner, R.W., Elser, J.J., 2002. Ecological stoichiometry: The biology of elements from molecules to biosphere. Princeton University Press, Princeton, NJ.

Tilman, D., Reich, D.B., Knops, J.M.H., 2006. Biodiversity and ecosystem stability in a decade-long grassland experiment. Nature 441, 629–632.

Van Dover, C.L., German, C.R., Speer, K.G., Parson, L.M., Vrijenhoek, R.C., 2002. Marine biology—Evolution and biogeography of deep-sea vent and seep invertebrates. Science 295, 1253–1257.

Vitousek, P.M., 2004. Nutrient cycling and limitation: Hawai'i as a model system. Princeton University Press, Princeton, NJ.

# References for Table 2.1

Brock, T.D., 1985. A eutrophic lake: Lake Mendota. Springer-Verlag, New York, NY, Wisconsin [Eutrophic Lake].

Cole, J.J., Caraco, N.F., 2006. Primary production and its regulation in the tidal-freshwater Hudson River. In: Levinton, J.S., Waldman, J.R. (Eds.), The Hudson River estuary. Cambridge University Press, Cambridge, UK, pp. 107–120 [River].

Dayton, P., 1985. Ecology of kelp communities. Annual Review of Ecology and Systematics 16, 216–245 [Kelp].

Fujieki, L.A., F. Santiago-Mandujano, P. Lethaby, C. Hannides, R. Lukas, and D. Karl. 2006. Hawaiian ocean time series data report 16: 2004. Available at http://hahana.soest.hawaii.edu/hot/reports/rep_y16.pdf.

Gattuso, J.-P., Frankignoulle, M., Wollast, R., 1998. Carbon and carbonate metabolism in coastal aquatic ecosystems. Annual Review of Ecology and Systematics 29, 405–434.

Kicklighter, D.W. 1999. NPP multi-biome: TEM calibration data, 1992. Data set. Available at http://www.daac.ornl.gov from Oak Ridge National Laboratory Distributed Active Archive Center, Oak Ridge, TN. [All terrestrial data].

Likens, G.E. (Ed.), 1985. An ecosystem approach to aquatic ecology: Mirror Lake and its environment. Springer-Verlag, New York, NY [Oligotrophic Lake].

Minas, H.J., Codispoti, L.A., Dugdale, R.C., 1982. Nutrients and primary productivity in the upwelling region off northwest Africa. Rapp. P.-v Reun. Cons. Int. Explor. Mer. 180, 148–183 [Upwelling].

Mouw, C.B., Yoder, J.A., 2005. Primary production calculations in the Mid-Atlantic Bight, including effects of phytoplankton community size structure. Limnology and Oceanography 50, 1232–1243 [Temperate Continental Shelf].

Pomeroy, L.R., Darley, W.M., Dunn, E.L., Gallagher, J.L., Haines, E.B., Whitney, D.M., 1981. Primary production. In: Pomeroy, L.R., Weigert, R.G. (Eds.), The Ecology of a Salt Marsh. Springer-Verlag, New York, NY, pp. 39–67. [Salt Marsh Estuary].

Roberts, B.J., Mulholland, P.J., Hill, W.R., 2007. Multiple scales of temporal variability in ecosystem metabolism rates: results from 2 years of continuous monitoring in a forested headwater stream. Ecosystems 10, 588–606.

# Secondary Production and Consumer Energetics

*David L. Strayer*

**Cary Institute of Ecosystem Studies, Millbrook, NY**

## INTRODUCTION

The energy captured by primary production supports animals, fungi, and heterotrophic bacteria and protozoans, which together constitute the community of consumers in ecosystems. These consumers include species that we harvest from the wild, species that we value for recreational or aesthetic reasons, and nuisance species. Consumers play two key roles in ecosystem energetics. Their respiration destroys the organic matter that serves as the medium of energy exchange in ecosystems, and thereby regenerates nutrients trapped in organic matter. This important role will be discussed in the next chapter on decomposition. However, not all the organic matter that a consumer eats is respired; some is captured and used for growth and reproduction of the consumer, which we call secondary production. This material is available to move up the food web. In this chapter, we will explore the basic energy budget of consumers and its ecological significance, and discuss the controls and prediction of secondary production, a particularly important and well studied part of consumer energetics. Finally, we will discuss briefly aspects of nutrient flow through consumer populations.

## CONSUMER ENERGETICS

### The Energy Budget of Consumers

Although there are many possible ways to budget energy flow through a consumer, a useful and widely used scheme is shown in Figure 3.1. Energy in food ingested ($I$) by a consumer may be either assimilated ($A$) or lost through egestion ($E$, sometimes called $F$,

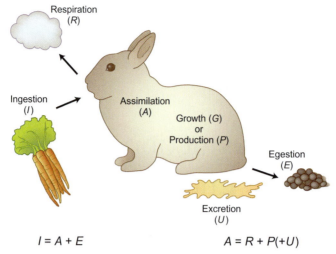

$$I = A + E \qquad\qquad A = R + P(+U)$$

FIGURE 3.1 Diagram of the consumer energy budget. $A$ = assimilation, $E$ = egestion, $I$ = ingestion, $P$ = production (growth), $R$ = respiration, $U$ = energy contained in nitrogenous compounds in urine.

for feces). Assimilated energy may be lost as respiration ($R$), excreted as the energy contained in nitrogenous wastes (usually called $U$, for urine), or used for growth ($G$). Growth often is called production ($P$), and may be further subdivided into somatic growth versus production of gametes and so forth, depending on the purposes of the study (i.e., production includes both growth and reproduction of the consumer). Bacteria and fungi don't "ingest" food, so the energy budget starts with assimilation. Terms like *consumption* or *demand*, although sometimes used in energy budgets, are undesirable because they could refer to more than one term in the energy budget.

Although I presented the energy budget as it applies to an individual organism, it is possible to write an analogous budget for a population of consumers, a group of populations, or even the entire community of consumers in an ecosystem. It is just more difficult to estimate the terms in the energy budget for a population or community than for an individual organism.

Two aspects of energy budgets are especially interesting to ecologists: the magnitude of the flows and the way energy is partitioned among the flows. The different terms of the energy budget each have special ecological significance. Ingestion describes the effect of the consumer on its food resource, egestion gives the input to the detritus pool, respiration is energy that is lost from the ecosystem, and production shows both the amount of energy that is available to the consumer to support growth and reproduction and the energy that is available to predators.

Several factors affect the magnitude of all of these terms in individual organisms (Figure 3.2). Mass-specific metabolic rates rise with increasing temperature. Specifically, resting respiration rates scale with the Boltzmann factor:

$$R \propto e^{-(E_i/kT)} \qquad\qquad (3.1)$$

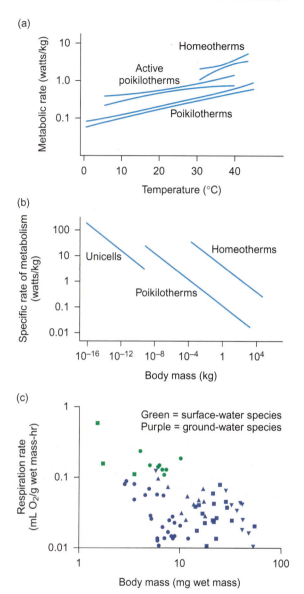

**FIGURE 3.2** Four primary determinants of metabolic rates of consumers. (a) Metabolic rates rise with rising temperature and are higher for homeotherms than poikilotherms. (b) Metabolic rates (per unit mass) fall with rising body size. *((a) and (b) redrawn from Peters 1983.)* (c) Metabolic rates may fall over evolutionary time in food-poor habitats. *(Data from Gourbault 1972.)*

where $e$ is the base of natural logarithms, $E_i$ is the activation energy of the average biochemical reaction, $k$ is Boltzmann's constant (a term from physics that relates the energy of a molecule to its temperature), and $T$ is the temperature (°K) (Gillooly et al. 2001). Temperature dependence is also commonly expressed using $Q_{10}$, the factor by which metabolic rates increase with a 10°C rise in temperature, although Gillooly et al. argued that the Boltzmann factor is mechanistically more reasonable and provides a better fit to data than $Q_{10}$. $Q_{10}$'s are often $\sim 2$, so metabolic rates often approximately double with a 10°C rise in temperature. Mass-specific metabolic rates are higher in small organisms than in large organisms, typically scaling as $M^{-0.25}$, where $M$ is individual body mass (Peters 1983). Respiration (and of necessity, A, I, and E) is much higher in homeotherms ("warm-blooded" species) than in poikilotherms ("cold-blooded" species; Peters 1983). Finally, metabolic rates are under evolutionary control, so they can respond to environmental and ecological pressures. For example, animals that live in ground waters, which are very poor in food, have lower metabolic rates than would be predicted from their body masses and temperatures.

The partitioning of energy among the parts of the energy budget can be described by a series of efficiencies. Many of these have been used by ecologists (Kozlovsky 1968), but three are of primary importance:

$$A/I = assimilation\ efficiency, \tag{3.2}$$

which describes how good a consumer is at extracting energy from its food

$$P/A = net\ growth\ efficiency, \tag{3.3}$$

which describes the partitioning between growth and respiration

$$P/I = gross\ growth\ efficiency, \tag{3.4}$$

a combination of the previous two efficiencies, which describes the overall efficiency with which food is converted to consumer tissue

Again, vague terms such as *ecological efficiency*, although widely used in the literature, should be avoided because they could refer to any of several efficiencies and lead to confusion. Typical values for these three efficiencies are given in Table 3.1. All three are highly variable, commonly depending on at least four variables: diet, temperature, metabolic type (homeothermy vs. poikilothermy), and physiological status (Figure 3.3). Among animals, assimilation efficiency depends strongly on the quality of the diet, so that

TABLE 3.1 Typical values (%) for the three most widely used ecological efficiencies.

| | Assimilation Efficiency (A/I) | Net Growth Efficiency (P/A) | Gross Growth Efficiency (P/I) |
|---|---|---|---|
| Plants | 1–2 | 30–75 | 0.5–1 |
| Bacteria | – | 5–60 | – |
| Poikilotherms | 10–90 | 10–60 | 5–30 |
| Homeotherms | 40–90 | 1–5 | 1–4 |

*From Kozlovsky (1968), Wiegert (1976), Humphreys (1979), May (1979), Schroeder (1981), Brafield and Llewellyn (1982), Valiela (1984), and del Giorgio and Cole (1998).*

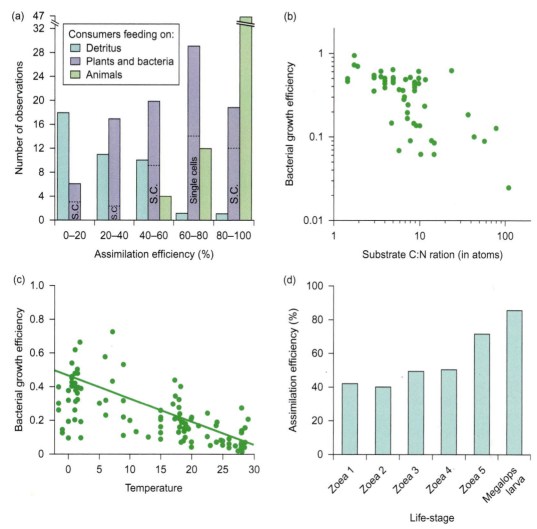

FIGURE 3.3   Factors that affect ecological efficiencies. (a, b) Diet: Both assimilation efficiency of marine animals (a) and net growth efficiency of aquatic bacteria (b) increase as diet quality increases. *(Redrawn from Valiela 1984 and del Giorgio and Cole 1998.)* (c) Temperature: Net growth efficiency of aquatic bacteria falls with rising temperature. *(Redrawn from Rivkin and Legendre (2001.)* (d) Physiological status: Assimilation efficiency varies across life stages in the crab *Menippe mercenaria. (Redrawn from Valiela (1984.)*

animals eating high-quality food (predators) have higher assimilation efficiencies than those eating low-quality food (herbivores and detritivores). Likewise, net growth efficiency of bacteria depends on the quality (e.g., nitrogen content) of the substrate. (These observations suggest that consumers are not always limited by the energy in their diets, contrary to a central assumption in classical ecological energetics, but often are limited by the availability of specific dietary components—protein, nitrogen, fatty acids, and so on. We will revisit this assumption later in the chapter.) Net growth efficiencies of bacteria (and perhaps protozoans) fall steeply with rising temperatures. Homeotherms have much lower net growth efficiencies than poikilotherms. In addition, ecological efficiencies may vary with the physiological state of the organism—for example, assimilation efficiency may vary with age.

Lindeman (1942) suggested that the low assimilation efficiency of herbivores (and detritivores) may be compensated for in part by a relatively high net growth efficiency. His argument was that herbivores have to spend less time than predators searching for and capturing food, and so might have lower respiratory costs than predators. Thus, gross growth efficiency would vary less across species than net growth efficiency. This hypothesis has not been tested in detail, although Welch (1968) found some evidence to support it.

## SECONDARY PRODUCTION

The remainder of this chapter focuses on secondary production, which has received more attention than the other terms in the ecological energy budget. Ecologists have focused on secondary production for two reasons. First, although we will see that secondary production often is difficult to estimate, it is at least much easier to estimate than other terms in the energy budgets of free-ranging organisms. Various methods have been developed to estimate assimilation or respiration of free-ranging organisms (dimethylsulfoxide reduction, activity of the electron transport system, tracer injections of radiocesium, or double-labeled water), but these are more or less experimental and have not been widely used by ecologists. Second, there is a strong and persistent idea among ecologists that the "purpose" of a food web is to transfer matter and energy into higher trophic levels, which may be useful to humans. (To see this bias, note that systems with high "efficiencies" are defined as those that transfer a lot of energy to higher trophic levels, not those that dissipate a lot of energy through respiration, even though the "purpose" of a food web could just as easily be said to be the destruction of organic matter as its transfer to higher trophic levels.) Production is the mechanism by which energy is transferred through a food web, so it naturally attracted ecologists who viewed a food web as a way to move energy up into useful higher trophic levels. Further, although this view is simplistic, secondary production seemed to early ecologists to be related to the yield of those higher trophic levels. Although I won't be discussing other energetic terms much, you will note that many of the conclusions that I reach about secondary production apply equally well to ingestion, assimilation, egestion, and respiration. Perhaps because humans harvest wild animals (i.e., higher trophic levels) more often from aquatic ecosystems than from terrestrial ecosystems, the vast majority (>90%) of work on secondary production has been done in aquatic ecosystems. Consequently, some generalizations about secondary production may actually be generalizations about aquatic ecosystems.

## DEFINITION OF SECONDARY PRODUCTION

*Secondary production is all heterotrophic production (=growth), regardless of its fate.* It includes the production of heterotrophic bacteria, fungi, protozoans, and animals. This definition of secondary production is commonly misinterpreted, in two ways. First, secondary production is sometimes confused with yield or biomass accumulation. To see the difference between production and biomass accumulation, consider an example. Suppose there are 10 rabbits in a field. Over the course of a year, 40 rabbits are born and grow to adult size, but 20 rabbits are run over by cars, 10 are eaten by foxes and owls, and 10 die of broken hearts (rabbits are very sensitive). After a year, there will again be 10 rabbits in the field, so there has been no accumulation of rabbit biomass. But secondary production (summed growth) of rabbit tissue was 40 rabbits. This tissue was grown by the rabbits and became available to consumers of rabbits. We might be tempted to argue that gross production was 40 rabbits, but net production (which might be what counts) was zero. There is no such thing as gross and net secondary production. The equivalent of gross secondary production (i.e., net secondary production plus consumer respiration) is assimilation by consumers. Further, note that accumulation of consumer biomass is inconveniently scale-dependent and tends to approach zero over large scales of space and time (otherwise we'd be up to our necks in rabbits), so is not often an interesting thing to study. As a result, ecologists rarely think about or measure biomass accumulation of consumers.

Less commonly, secondary production is defined as the production of primary consumers, with the production of their predators being referred to as tertiary production. This definition is based on an outdated view of food webs, in which microbes and omnivory were regarded as insignificant. If it is desirable to distinguish among the levels of the traditionally defined (nonmicrobial) food web, it may be helpful to refer to them as the second, third, and fourth trophic levels in the sense of Burns (1989).

# METHODS TO ESTIMATE SECONDARY PRODUCTION

Methods to estimate primary production (chiefly $CO_2$ uptake, $O_2$ production, and biomass accumulation) are well known, conceptually simple, and often easy to apply (see Chapter 2). In contrast, the highly varied methods used to estimate secondary production are relatively obscure, conceptually complicated, usually difficult to apply, and often encumbered with large uncertainties. Further, primary production is most often measured on the entire community of producers, whereas secondary production usually is estimated for individual populations or guilds of consumers, but almost never on the entire consumer community. Several approaches have been taken to estimate secondary production (Table 3.2): (1) relating the measurable uptake of a labeled substance to production; (2) combining estimates of the turnover rate of consumer tissue with estimates of consumer biomass; (3) combining demographic information with individual growth to calculate biomass accrued by a population; and (4) using empirical models.

Radioactive tracers are used to estimate bacterial or fungal production. Bacteria are incubated with trace amounts of tritiated thymidine or tritiated leucine. At these low concentrations, bacteria (and no other organisms) are assumed to take up and incorporate these labeled molecules into DNA or protein, respectively. After incubation, the amount of radioactive label taken up by bacteria is measured, and converted to units of carbon growth using a series of conversion factors. Fungi are similarly incubated with trace

TABLE 3.2   Overview of methods used to estimate secondary production (for details, see Downing and Rigler 1984; Benke 1984; Kemp et al. 1993; Servais 1995).

| Organism | Method | Data Requirements | Limitations |
| --- | --- | --- | --- |
| Bacteria | Tracers (radioactive nucleotides or amino acids) | Uptake of label | Subject to large errors because of (1) critical assumptions about fate and use of label and nonradioactive analogues, which may be hard to test; (2) uncertain conversion factors to get from uptake of label to carbon production |
| Fungi | Ergosterol synthesis (from radioactive acetate) | Uptake of label into ergosterol | Method still under development; potential problems similar to those for bacterial production |
| Animals with recognizable cohorts | Increment summation, mortality summation, Allen curve | Density and body size of animals at frequent intervals over the life of the cohort | Data intensive |
| Animals without recognizable cohorts | Growth increment summation, instantaneous growth | Density, body size, and growth rates of animals in various size classes throughout the year | Data intensive; growth rates often measured in the lab and extrapolated to the field |
| | Egg ratio | Density and development time of eggs, body mass of animals at death | Suitable only in the special case in which the body mass at death is known |
| | Size-frequency ("Hynes method") | Density and body size of animals in various size classes throughout the year | Data intensive |
| Any organism | Empirical models | Population biomass; perhaps body size, temperature, habitat type | Subject to large error; may be data intensive |

amounts of $^{14}C$-labeled acetate, which is incorporated into ergosterol, a chemical compound that occurs only in fungi. Organic carbon production is estimated from the amount of radiolabeled ergosterol measured after the incubation. To get annual production of microbes, incubations are run throughout the year in the various parts of the ecosystem under study. Although relatively simple in spirit, these radiotracer methods make important assumptions about the biochemical uptake, production, and destruction of labeled compounds, and factors for converting from uptake of radiolabel to production of organic carbon may be difficult to estimate. Thus, estimates of microbial production often have large (or uncertain) errors and must be interpreted cautiously.

Animal production is sometimes estimated as the product of standing biomass and the turnover rate of that biomass. Because turnover rates often change with animal size or age, the population usually is divided into size-classes. Thus,

$$P = \sum_i B_i g_i \tag{3.5}$$

where $B_i$ and $g_i$ are the standing biomass and instantaneous growth rates of the $i$th size-class, respectively. For exponential growth,

$$g_i = (1/D_i)\ln(m_{b+1}/m_b) \tag{3.6}$$

where $D_i$ is the development time (the length of time the animal spends in the $i$th size-class), and $m_{b+1}$ and $m_b$ are the body masses of the animals entering and leaving the $i$th size-class. Here, we need to know the biomass of each size-class in the field and the amount of time the animal takes to develop through each size-class. Both of these variables generally vary over the year. Thus, data requirements for estimating production are high. Care must be taken that the conditions under which the $D_i$ are measured mimic field conditions. Because field estimates of $B_i$ usually are burdened with large errors, estimates of production using this method typically have large errors.

For animals with distinct cohorts, production may be estimated by summing the product of mass gain and population size over the life of the cohort:

$$P = \sum_t ((m_{t+1} - m_t)(N_{t+1} + N_t)/2) \tag{3.7}$$

where $N_t$ is the mean population density at time $t$ and $m_t$ and $m_{t+1}$ are the mean body masses at two successive sampling times. This method requires good estimates of population size and body mass in the field over the life of the cohort, and is therefore data-intensive and subject to large errors. The size-frequency method uses an entirely different method to estimate production, but also requires data on body mass and abundance, so it also requires good estimates of population size and body mass in the field over the year.

Finally, production may be estimated by empirical models, usually of the form

$$P = (P/B)\overline{B} \tag{3.8}$$

where $\overline{B}$ is the mean annual biomass and $P/B$ is the annual turnover ratio. Estimates of $P/B$ are now readily available for many animals from empirical models based on body mass and temperature. These empirical models still require good estimates of $\overline{B}$, and are subject to large errors, but can be applied to a wide range of circumstances.

Further technical details on methods to estimate secondary production measurements are available in the works of Downing and Rigler (1984), Kemp et al. (1993), Benke (1984, 1993), Suberkropp and Weyers (1996), and Benke and Huryn (2006).

# CONTROLS AND PREDICTION OF SECONDARY PRODUCTION

Ecologists have devoted a lot of effort to understand what controls primary production (see Chapter 2), and most beginning ecology students know that primary production is controlled by and can be predicted from supply rates of a few key resources (e.g., nitrogen, phosphorus water, and light). In contrast, little has been written about the controls and prediction of secondary production. In part, this is because primary production has often been viewed as an aggregate measurement that encompasses all primary producers in an ecosystem (e.g., see Table 2.1 in Chapter 2), whereas secondary production has been viewed at the level of individual populations, or at most guilds of consumers. As we will see, secondary production is least predictable at the level of individual populations. Here, I will address the problems of predicting and understanding the controls on secondary production at three distinct levels: the production of an individual species of consumer, the production of a guild of consumers, and the production of the entire community of consumers. Perhaps surprisingly, predictions of secondary production become simpler and more precise as we move from individual populations to entire communities of consumers.

# PRODUCTION OF AN INDIVIDUAL SPECIES
## OF CONSUMER

Several papers (Plante and Downing 1989; Morin and Bourassa 1992; Benke 1993; Tumbiolo and Downing 1994; Cusson and Bourget 2005) have considered the problem of predicting the production of an individual species of consumer. All of these papers were based on empirical analyses of published data, were restricted to aquatic invertebrates, and reached similar conclusions (Figure 3.4):

- Secondary production is readily predictable, but with a confidence interval of about five-fold (in each direction around the mean, for a total width of 25-fold), from the average annual biomass of the population, the body size of the animal, and the temperature of the habitat.
- Biomass is by far the best single predictor of production; adding body size and temperature to the models adds little predictive power.
- Model coefficients suggest that production depends linearly on biomass (i.e., $B^{1.0}$), inversely on the fourth-root of body mass ($M^{-0.25}$), and on temperature with a $Q_{10}$ of 2 to 2.5. Production thus parallels the mass-dependence of many metabolic processes on $M^{-0.25}$ (Peters 1983).

Tumbiolo and Downing (1994) additionally found that production of marine invertebrates was correlated with water depth and habitat type (i.e., seagrass beds vs. unvegetated habitats). They interpreted these findings as evidence that production was affected by food quality, with higher production rates in places with high food quality. Tumbiolo and Downing's result is interesting because it suggests that $P/B$ (as opposed to $B$) is increased in shallow waters and seagrass beds, which implies an increase in mortality as well as growth in these food-rich environments. Thus, the whole pace of life may be increased by the high-quality food in plant beds, just as it apparently is reduced in food-poor ground waters (Figure 3.2).

Although these empirical models show that production of animal populations can readily be predicted (albeit with considerable error), all of them rely chiefly on an estimate of

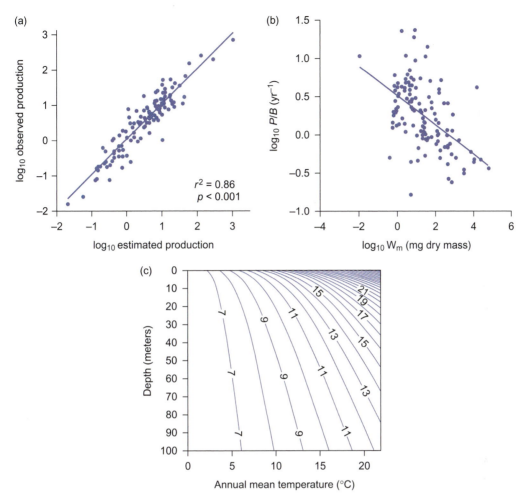

FIGURE 3.4 An example of an empirical model to predict secondary production of individual species of, in this case, marine benthic invertebrates. (a) Estimated versus measured production, showing precision and bias of model results ($\log_{10}P = 0.18 + 0.97\log_{10}B - 0.22\log_{10}W_m + 0.04T - 0.014T\log_{10}(z+1)$ ($P$ = production, $B$ = mean annual biomass, $W_m$ = individual body mass, $T$ = temperature, $z$ = water depth). (b) The effect of body size on annual turnover ($P/B$). (c) Effect of temperature and habitat location on turnover rates (annual $P/B$), for a species of average biomass (19 g/m$^2$) and large body size (1.2 g dry mass). *(Redrawn from Tumbiolo and Downing 1994.)*

mean annual biomass to do so. Benke (1993) argued that such models are not statistically valid because production is a mathematical function of biomass, so biomass-production plots are a case of self-correlation. In addition, mean annual biomass is not an ideal predictor because estimates of mean annual biomass often are costly and error-prone. In fact, in many cases, if the necessary data have been collected to estimate mean annual biomass satisfactorily, relatively little additional effort is required to gather the data to estimate production directly.

Models to predict production of consumer species without using mean annual biomass as an independent variable have not been developed, and probably would be difficult to build and be subject to huge errors. To see why, note that Eq. (3.8) can be expanded by replacing $B$ with $NM$. Thus,

$$P = (P/B)NM \tag{3.9}$$

where $M$ usually is easily measured, and existing models (Banse and Mosher 1980; Benke 1993) can be used to predict $P/B$ (with moderate to large error) from temperature and body mass. Consumer density ($N$), however, varies over many orders of magnitude and is at this point unpredictable. As a glance at any general ecology text will show, $N$ (the density or size of a population) is controlled by a wide range of ecological factors. The only general model to predict animal density (from body size; Peters 1983) is far too imprecise (the range in densities at a single body mass covers up to eight orders of magnitude!) to be used to predict density. As it seems unlikely that ecology will soon come up with a satisfactory general model to predict abundance of individual consumer species, I doubt that ecologists will be able to develop a useful model to predict production of consumer species that does not include mean biomass as a predictor variable.

## PRODUCTION OF A GUILD OF CONSUMERS

Studies of both animals and bacteria (Kajak et al. 1980; Cole et al. 1988; McNaughton et al. 1989, 1991; Wallace et al. 1999; cf. also Cyr and Pace 1993; Cebrian 1999) have shown that the production of a functional group of consumers is correlated with the supply rate of its food (Figure 3.5). This conclusion holds whether food levels are experimentally manipulated (Figure 3.6) or vary naturally across a series of ecosystems. These results suggest that production rates of guilds of consumers are often constrained by food supply. Nevertheless, the considerable scatter around the published regressions suggests that factors other than food supply also exert important control over production at the level of guilds of consumers. For example, there is increasing evidence (e.g., Sterner and Elser 2002) that bacterial and animal production may often be limited by nutrients (i.e., phosphorus, in lakes) rather than energy (Box 3.1), so that the quality as well as amount of primary production may set secondary production of consumer guilds (Figure 3.7). In any case, the scatter around regressions like those in Figure 3.5 is too great for food supply to be a practical predictor of production of consumer guilds.

In addition to the rate of food supply, whether the consumers are homeotherms or poikilotherms affects the production of the guild, with homeotherms having markedly lower rates of production (Figure 3.5; McNaughton et al. 1989, 1991), as expected.

Because of the scatter in the relationships between food supply and consumer guild production, it is difficult to estimate precisely the slopes of these relationships. Nevertheless, reduced major axis regression slopes of most of the published log-log regressions are between 1 and 1.5, suggesting that the production of a guild of consumers rises approximately linearly (or perhaps a little more steeply) with increasing food supply (Table 3.3). Thus, consumer production may be a constant or rising fraction of organic inputs as organic inputs to an ecosystem increase.

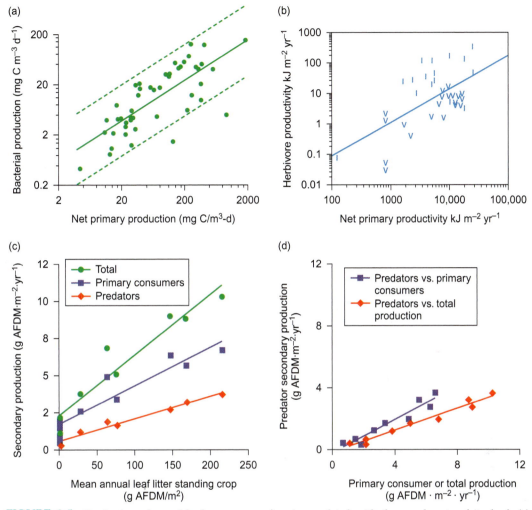

**FIGURE 3.5**  Production of a guild of consumers often is correlated with the supply rate of its food. (a) Bacterial production as a function of net primary production in various freshwater and marine pelagic ecosystems. *(Redrawn from Cole et al. 1988.)* (b) Herbivore production in terrestrial ecosystems as a function of net primary production. Dominant herbivores were vertebrates (V) or invertebrates (I). *(Redrawn from McNaughton et al. 1991.)* (c) Production of aquatic insects as a function of leaf litter standing crop in a small Appalachian stream from which litter was experimentally excluded. (d) Production of predatory insects as a function of production of prey insects in the same stream. *((c) and (d) redrawn from Wallace et al. 1999.)*

Guild-level analyses also show important energetic differences between aquatic and terrestrial ecosystems. Herbivore ingestion (as a percentage of primary production) is higher in aquatic than terrestrial ecosystems because primary producers tend to be more nutrient-rich in aquatic ecosystems than in terrestrial ecosystems (Figure 3.7). The higher nutrient content of aquatic primary producers should also lead to higher assimilation efficiencies in aquatic consumers than their terrestrial counterparts, and the relative rarity of homeothermy should lead to higher net growth efficiencies in aquatic ecosystems. Consequently,

**FIGURE 3.6** Setting up a whole-stream experiment to exclude inputs of leaf litter from a small stream at the Coweeta Hydrologic Laboratory, North Carolina (some results of this experiment are shown in Figure 3.5). (*Photograph by John Hutchens.*)

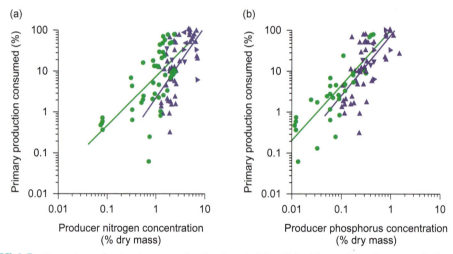

**FIGURE 3.7** Percentage of net primary production ingested by all herbivores in various aquatic (green symbols) and terrestrial (purple symbols) ecosystems, as a function of nitrogen (a) and phosphorus (b) content of the primary producers. This figure shows that food quality may influence metabolic activity by guilds of consumers. (*Redrawn from Cebrian and Lartigue 2004.*)

top-down control by herbivores may be most frequent in aquatic ecosystems (Cebrian and Lartigue 2004), and the ratio of herbivore production to primary production should tend to be very much higher in aquatic ecosystems than terrestrial ecosystems.

## PRODUCTION OF THE ENTIRE COMMUNITY OF CONSUMERS

In contrast to the previous cases, where only approximate, statistical estimates of production are available, production by the entire community of consumers in an ecosystem

TABLE 3.3    Relationships between resource supply and secondary production (or other measures of consumer activity) in ecosystems. The slope is the reduced major axis slope, not the ordinary least squares slope.

| Ecosystem Type | Measure of Consumer Activity | Slope of Relationship | Source |
|---|---|---|---|
| Lakes | Macrozoobenthos production | 0.8 | Kajak et al. (1980) |
| Aquatic ecosystems | Bacterial production | 1.1 | Cole et al. (1988) |
| Terrestrial ecosystems | Above-ground production | 1.8 | McNaughton et al. (1991) |
| Aquatic ecosystems | Ingestion by herbivores | 1.05 | Cebrian and Lartigue (2004) |
| Terrestrial ecosystems | Ingestion by herbivores | 1.8 | Cebrian and Lartigue (2004) |
| Various marine ecosystems | Ingestion by herbivores | 1 | Cebrian (2002) |

can be calculated exactly, at least in principle (Strayer 1988). Consider an ecosystem that receives an input of 100 g of organic matter, and is populated by a community of consumers, all of which (for simplicity) have net growth efficiencies of 30%. After all of these inputs have been assimilated by consumers, 70 g is lost by respiration, and 30 g remains in the system. Now this 30 g is assimilated in a second round of consumption, resulting in $0.3 \times 30$ g $= 9$ g of production and 21 g of respiration. This 9 g is then assimilated in a third round of consumption, giving 2.7 g of production and 6.3 g of respiration. By the time that the original 100 g of inputs is respired, a secondary production of 30 g $+ 9$ g $+ 2.7$ g $+ \ldots = 42.86$ g will have occurred.

More generally, all organic matter that enters an ecosystem at steady state and is not lost through nonrespiratory means (e.g., sedimentation, fire, photolysis) must be destroyed by respiration. (The assumption of steady state is not critical and may be relaxed simply by adding storage terms to the following equations.) Thus,

$$S = R + L \tag{3.10}$$

where $S$ is the net supply of organic matter to the ecosystem (i.e., net autochthonous primary production plus allochthonous inputs) to an ecosystem, $R$ is respiration of all consumers, and $L$ is nonrespiratory losses. By definition,

$$\varepsilon_g = P/(P + R) \tag{3.11}$$

where $\varepsilon_g$ is the net growth efficiency of consumers (the weighted mean; Strayer 1991) and $P$ is their production. Substituting and solving,

$$P = (S - L) \times \varepsilon_g/(1 - \varepsilon_g) \tag{3.12}$$

Similarly,

$$A = (S - L)/(1 - \varepsilon_g) \tag{3.13}$$

where $A$ is the summed assimilation of all consumers in the ecosystem, and

$$I = (S - L)/(\varepsilon_a \times (1 - \varepsilon_g)) \tag{3.14}$$

where $I$ is the summed ingestion by all consumers in the ecosystem, and $\varepsilon_a$ is the (weighted) mean assimilation efficiency of these consumers. Solutions for these equations for a range of conditions are shown in Figure 3.8. Because $\varepsilon_a$ varies over a wide range with diet of the consumer, estimates of $I$ from Eq. (3.14) are extremely approximate, and rarely will be useful. Often $S$ and $L$ are known with some precision, but $\varepsilon_g$ is variable, so estimates of total secondary production using this approach are likewise approximate. A reasonable guess for $\varepsilon_g$ for many ecosystems might be about 0.3, but it may vary from less than 0.1 to about 0.6 (Schroeder 1981; del Giorgio and Cole 1998; Rivkin and Legendre

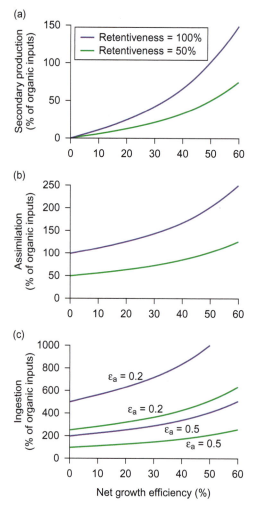

FIGURE 3.8   Calculated (a) production, (b) assimilation, and (c) ingestion by the entire community of consumers for a few combinations of net growth efficiency, assimilation efficiency, and ecosystem retentiveness. Production, assimilation, and ingestion are expressed as a percentage of net organic inputs to the ecosystem. Retentiveness is the fraction of organic inputs not subject to nonrespiratory losses (i.e., $(S-L)/S$). (*Modified from Strayer 1988.*)

2001). Furthermore, ecologists rarely measure secondary production by all consumers in an ecosystem, so there are few data to compare with these estimates (but see Table 3.4). Nevertheless, this analysis gives four interesting conclusions:

- Secondary production is large compared with primary production. If $\varepsilon_g = 0.3$, then secondary production is 43% of net organic inputs. It is even possible for secondary production to exceed primary production (if $\varepsilon_g > 0.5$). These numbers are much greater than the 10% figure often assumed by ecologists, based on a misapplication of Lindeman's old conclusions.
- Consequently, decomposers use a lot of consumer tissue; their diets are not necessarily dominated by plant tissue.
- Total secondary production may be smaller in systems dominated by homeotherms than those dominated by poikilotherms.
- The energy available for assimilation and ingestion by consumers is generally much greater than net organic inputs to an ecosystem.

# CONCLUSION

Let me close with three points about the controls and prediction of secondary production. First, perhaps counterintuitively, it is easier to predict the production of a guild of consumers than the production of a single population, and easier still to predict the production of the entire consumer community. If the biomass of a consumer population is unknown, then its production is essentially unpredictable. Even if consumer biomass is known, production

TABLE 3.4  Total secondary production (g C m$^{-2}$ yr$^{-1}$) in Mirror Lake, New Hampshire, estimated from direct measurements and by indirect means, using the equations in the text.

| Direct Estimate | |
| --- | --- |
| Pelagic bacteria | 6 |
| Benthic bacteria | 10.5 |
| Metazoan plankton | 2.5 |
| Metazoan benthos | 6 |
| Fish | 0.2 |
| **Total direct estimate** | **25.2** |
| **Indirect Estimate** | |
| Net organic inputs ($S$) | 60 |
| Nonrespiratory losses ($L$) | 24.9 |
| Assumed net growth efficiency ($\varepsilon_g$) | 0.4 |
| **Total indirect estimate ($P$)** | **23.4** |

*Modified from Strayer (1988), using data from Jordan et al. (1985).*

## BOX 3.1

# WE DON'T LIVE BY BREAD ALONE: CONSUMER BUDGETS FOR ELEMENTS OTHER THAN CARBON

Consumers process materials (i.e., nutrients) as well as energy (i.e., carbon). The conceptual framework for consumer energy budgets is easily modified to describe material processing by consumers, with one key difference: There are no respiratory losses for elements other than carbon and oxygen. For instance, following the notation presented in Figure 3.1 for energy, we can write the consumer nitrogen balance as:

$$I_n = A_n + E_n \qquad (3.B1)$$

$$A_n = P_n + U_n \qquad (3.B2)$$

where $I_n$, $A_n$, $P_n$, and $U_n$ are ingestion, assimilation, production (=growth), and excretion of nitrogen, respectively. Likewise, we can define a series of ecological efficiencies for nitrogen that are parallel to those defined for energy:

$A_n/I_n$ = assimilation efficiency of nitrogen, $\varepsilon_{an}$

(3.B3)

$P_n/A_n$ = net growth efficiency of nitrogen, $\varepsilon_{gn}$

(3.B4)

$P_n/I_n$ = gross growth efficiency of nitrogen

(3.B5)

Because there are no nonrespiratory losses of nitrogen (and most elements), net growth efficiencies of most elements will be much higher than net growth efficiencies for energy, especially for homeotherms. The mismatch between large respiratory losses of carbon and lesser losses of other elements should tend to progressively enrich organic matter in nutrients as it moves up the food chain.

A consumer may be limited by the energy content or the nutrient content of its diet, which can have important consequences for ecological interactions (e.g., nutrient cycling, foraging behavior) involving the consumer. Sterner and Elser (2002) explored this subject in detail; I will make only a few points here. First, when will a consumer be limited by nutrients, and when will it be limited by energy? To answer this question, we note that the elemental ratios (e.g., C:N, C:P) of most consumers do not vary much, and may be treated as constant within a species and life-stage (Sterner and Elser 2002). Put simply, a consumer will be nutrient-limited if its diet is so rich in energy (carbon) and so poor in nutrients that the carbon in its diet is more than enough to match the nutrients used for growth plus the demands of respiration. Putting this statement into mathematical terms:

$$I_c e_{ac} > (P_n/Q_g) + R \qquad (3.B6)$$

The left side of the equation shows the amount of carbon that is assimilated as the product of the rate at which carbon is ingested ($I_c$) and the assimilation efficiency for carbon ($e_{ac}$). The right side of the equation shows the amount of carbon needed for growth (which is the amount of nutrient used for growth, $P_n$, divided by the nutrient:carbon ratio of consumer tissue, $Q_g = P_n/P_c$) plus the amount of carbon needed to support respiration. After some algebra, we find that a consumer will be nutrient-limited if

$$c\varepsilon_{gc} > (Q_i/Q_g) \qquad (3.B7)$$

where $c$ is the ratio of the assimilation efficiencies for carbon and for the nutrient ($\varepsilon_{ac}/\varepsilon_{an}$), $\varepsilon_{gc}$ is the net growth efficiency for carbon, and $Q_i$ is the nutrient : carbon ratio of the diet. The consumer will be nutrient-limited if the left side of the equation is large and the right side is small. Thus, nutrient limitation will occur if the consumer is more efficient at extracting carbon than nutrients from its food, if it has a high net growth efficiency (for carbon), and if the consumer's body is much more nutrient-rich than its food. The opposite conditions will lead to energy limitation. This means that (1) homeotherms, with their very low growth efficiencies (Table 3.1), are more likely to be energy-limited than poikilotherms; (2) fast-growing consumers are more likely to be phosphorus-limited than slow-growing consumers, because fast-growing consumers have a high phosphorus : carbon content (because fast growth requires a lot of RNA, which is rich in phosphorus; Sterner and Elser 2002); and (3) consumers eating diets with high carbon : nutrient contents (e.g., terrestrial plants) are likely to be nutrient-limited (Sterner and Elser 2002). It is also worth noting that the energetic demands of respiration mean that the carbon : nutrient content of a consumer's ideal diet should always be much higher than the carbon:nutrient content of the consumer itself, and that cannibalism does not provide the ideal diet, from a stoichiometric point of view (to say nothing of its social shortcomings!).

We can squeeze a little more insight from Eq. (3.B7). When conditions are really poor, a consumer may spend all of its energy on respiration, and not grow at all. It may therefore be useful to consider respiration as consisting of two parts, a fixed maintenance respiration that occurs even when the consumer is not growing, and a variable respiration that depends on the production of the consumer. We can then write net growth efficiency as

$$\varepsilon_{gc} = \left( \frac{P_c}{(vP_c + R_{maint})} \right) \qquad (3.B8)$$

where the two terms in the denominator are the variable and fixed parts of respiration. Substituting this new definition of net growth efficiency into Eq. (3.B7), we find that

$$c\left( \frac{P_c}{(vP_c + R_{maint})} \right) > (Q_i/Q_g) \qquad (3.B9)$$

which allows us to make one final observation about when nutrient limitation of consumers is most likely to occur: When growth is slow, so that net growth efficiency approaches zero (del Giorgio and Cole 1998), consumers are less likely to experience nutrient limitation than when growth is fast.

There are several ways by which consumers can balance simultaneous demands for energy and multiple nutrients, or even specific biochemical compounds (Brett 1993; Sterner and Elser 2002). The consumer may adjust its diet to better meet its needs; microbial consumers may adjust the exoenzymes they produce to allow for easier assimilation of the compounds they need. Consumers may produce or draw on internal stores of critical compounds—the most familiar is energy storage as fat, but calcium may be deposited and withdrawn from bones. Finally, consumers may adjust the efficiency with which they extract and retain nutrients. Thus, assimilation, respiration, and recycling of elements may change as a consumer's diet and needs change.

can be predicted only approximately. The production of a guild of consumers often is constrained and predictable (at least loosely) by food supply. Finally, at the level of the entire consumer community, budgetary constraints tightly define the relationship among organic inputs, consumer activity, and nonrespiratory losses from the ecosystem, allowing for direct (if approximate) calculation of production of all consumers in the ecosystem. Thus, it is possible to predict the secondary production of all consumers on Earth more precisely than the production of an arbitrary individual population in a local ecosystem. This surprising result occurs because once we move up to the ecosystem level, we are able to apply powerful mass-balance constraints to the solution of the problem.

Second, expressing the total secondary production in an ecosystem by Eq. (3.12) highlights the linkages between consumer energetics and other aspects of ecosystem ecology. Obviously, consumer production depends on the supply of organic matter and nutrients to an ecosystem, including both autochthonous production and allochthonous inputs of organic matter and nutrients. Perhaps less obviously, consumer production also depends on processes that consume (e.g., fire), retain (e.g., debris dams), or export (e.g., floods) organic matter in an ecosystem. Likewise, the amount of organic matter that is buried, exported from an ecosystem, or is available to nonrespiratory fates (e.g., fire) depends on the number and physiological characteristics of consumers. Thus, consumers, exports, and nonrespiratory losses can be thought of as competitors for organic matter, and consumer activity is at the center of an interaction web that extends well beyond energetics. For instance, Rivkin and Legendre (2001) noted that bacterial respiration in the open ocean helps to determine how much organic matter sinks to the ocean depths and how much $CO_2$ is exported to the atmosphere.

Third, by comparison with primary production, there has been little explicit consideration of the controls and prediction of secondary production. To the extent that these topics have been considered, attention has been focused on the production of individual populations of animals or sometimes on guilds of consumers rather than on the entire community of producers. However, when secondary production is considered at the same level of aggregation as primary production (whole communities, not individual populations), it becomes more or less predictable. To a first approximation, secondary production at the community level appears to be controlled by the amount of organic matter supplied to the ecosystem, by the ability of the ecosystem to retain versus export organic matter, and by the importance of competing, nonrespiratory losses (e.g., fire). Further, it seems clear that resource quality and the availability of inorganic nutrients affect the secondary production of communities. Thus, at least roughly in parallel to primary production, rates of secondary production at the community level seem to be controlled by inputs of energy and a few key nutrients.

## References

Banse, K., Mosher, S., 1980. Adult body mass and annual production/biomass relationships of field populations. Ecol. Monogr. 50, 355–379.

Benke, A.C., 1984. Secondary production of aquatic insects. In: Resh, V.H., Rosenberg, D.M. (Eds.), Ecology of aquatic insects. Praeger Publishers, New York, pp. 289–322.

Benke, A.C., 1993. Concepts and patterns of invertebrate production in running waters. Verhandlungen der internationale Vereinigung für theoretische und angewandte Limnologie 25, 15–38.

Benke, A.C., Huryn, A.D., 2006. Secondary production of macroinvertebrates. In: Hauer, F.R., Lamberti, G.A. (Eds.), Methods in stream ecology, second ed. Academic Press, Amsterdam.

Brafield, A.E., Llewellyn, M.J., 1982. Animal energetics. Blackie and Son, London.

Brett, M.T., 1993. Comment on "Possibility of N or P limitation for planktonic cladocerans: an experimental test" (Urabe and Watanabe) and "Nutrient element limitation of zooplankton production" (Hessen). Limnol. Oceanogr. 38, 1333–1337.

Burns, T.P., 1989. Lindeman's contradiction and the trophic structure of ecosystems. Ecology 70, 1355–1362.

Cebrian, J., 1999. Patterns in the fate of production in plant communities. Am. Nat. 154, 449–468.

Cebrian, J., 2002. Variability and control of carbon consumption, export, and accumulation in marine communities. Limnol. Oceanogr. 47, 11–22.

Cebrian, J., Lartigue, J., 2004. Patterns of herbivory and decomposition in aquatic and terrestrial ecosystems. Ecol. Monogr. 74, 237–259.

Cole, J.J., Findlay, S., Pace, M.L., 1988. Bacterial production in fresh and saltwater ecosystems: A cross-system overview. Mar. Ecol. Progr. Series 43, 1–10.

Cusson, M., Bourget, E., 2005. Global patterns of macroinvertebrate production in marine benthic habitats. Mar. Ecol. Progr. Series 297, 1–14.

Cyr, H., Pace, M.L., 1993. Magnitude and patterns of herbivory in aquatic and terrestrial ecosystems. Nature 361, 148–150.

del Giorgio, P.A., Cole, J.J., 1998. Bacterioplankton growth efficiency in aquatic systems. Annu. Rev. Ecol. Systemat. 29, 503–541.

Downing, J.A., Rigler, F.H. (Eds.), 1984. A manual on methods for the assessment of secondary productivity in fresh waters, second ed. Blackwell Science Publishers, Oxford, UK.

Gillooly, J.F., Brown, J.H., West, G.B., Savage, V.M., Charnov, E.L., 2001. Effects of size and temperature on metabolic rate. Science 293, 2248–2251.

Gourbault, N., 1972. Recherches sur les Triclades paludicoles hypogés. Mémoires du Muséum National d'Histoire Naturelle 73, 1-249 + 3 plates.

Humphreys, W.F., 1979. Production and respiration in animal populations. J. Anim. Ecol. 48, 427–453.

Jordan, M.J., Likens, G.E., Peterson, B.J., 1985. Organic carbon budget. In: Likens, G.E. (Ed.), An ecosystem approach to aquatic ecology: Mirror Lake and its environment. Springer-Verlag, New York, pp. 292–301.

Kajak, Z., Bretschko, G., Schiemer, F., Leveque, C., 1980. Zoobenthos. In: Lecren, E.D., Lowe-McConnell, R.H. (Eds.), The functioning of freshwater ecosystems. Cambridge University Press, pp. 285–307.

Kemp, P.F., Sherr, B.F, Sherr, E.B., Cole, J.J. (Eds.), 1993. Handbook of methods in aquatic microbial ecology. Lewis Publishers, Ann Arbor, MI.

Kozlovsky, D.G., 1968. A critical evaluation of the trophic level concept. Part 1. Ecological efficiencies. Ecology 49, 48–60.

Lindeman, R.L., 1942. The trophic-dynamic aspect of ecology. Ecology 23, 399–418.

May, R.M., 1979. Production and respiration in animal communities. Nature 282, 443–444.

McNaughton, S.J., Oesterheld, M., Frank, D.A., Williams, K.J., 1989. Ecosystem-level patterns of primary productivity and herbivory in terrestrial habitats. Nature 341, 142–144.

McNaughton, S.J., Oesterheld, M., Frank, D.A., Williams, K.J., 1991. Relationships between primary and secondary production in terrestrial ecosystems. In: Cole, J.J., Lovett, G.M., Findlay, S. (Eds.), Comparative analyses of ecosystems: Patterns, mechanisms, and theories. Springer-Verlag, New York, pp. 120–139.

Morin, A., Bourassa, N., 1992. Modèles empiriques de la production annuelle et du rapport P/B d'invertébrés benthiques d'eau courante. Can. J. Fish. Aquat. Sci. 49, 532–539.

Peters, R.H., 1983. The ecological implications of body size. Cambridge University Press, UK.

Plante, C., Downing, J.A., 1989. Production of freshwater invertebrate populations in lakes. Can. J. Fish. Aquat. Sci. 46, 1489–1498.

Rivkin, R.B., Legendre, L., 2001. Biogenic carbon cycling in the upper ocean: Effects of microbial respiration. Science 291, 2398–2400.

Schroeder, L.A., 1981. Consumer growth efficiencies: Their limits and relationships to ecological energetics. J. Theor. Biol. 93, 805–828.

Servais, P., 1995. Measurement of the incorporation rates of four amino acids into proteins for estimating bacterial production. Microb. Ecol. 29, 115–128.

Sterner, R.W., Elser, J.J., 2002. Ecological stoichiometry: The biology of elements from molecules to the biosphere. Princeton University Press, Princeton, NJ.

Strayer, D., 1988. On the limits to secondary production. Limnol. Oceanogr. 33, 1217–1220.

Strayer, D.L., 1991. Notes on Lindeman's progressive efficiency. Ecology 72, 348–350.

Suberkropp, K., Weyers, H., 1996. Application of fungal and bacterial production methodologies to decomposing leaves in streams. Appl. Environ. Microbiol. 62, 1610–1615.

Tumbiolo, M.L., Downing, J.A., 1994. An empirical model for the prediction of secondary production in marine benthic invertebrate populations. Mar. Ecol. Progr. Series 114, 165–174.

Valiela, I., 1984. Marine ecological processes. Springer-Verlag, New York.

Wallace, J.B., Eggert, S.L., Meyer, J.L., Webster, J.R., 1999. Effects of resource limitation on a detrital-based ecosystem. Ecol. Monogr. 69, 409–442.

Welch, H.E., 1968. Relationships between assimilation efficiency and growth efficiency for aquatic consumers. Ecology 49, 755–759.

Wiegert, R.G. (Ed.), 1976. Ecological energetics. Dowden, Hutchinson, and Ross, Stroudsberg, PA.

# 4

# Organic Matter Decomposition

*Stuart E.G. Findlay*

**Cary Institute of Ecosystem Studies, Millbrook, New York**

## INTRODUCTION

*Decomposition* is used in two distinct senses in ecosystem science. At the macroscale, decomposition is the conversion of organic matter from large and recognizable physical forms to small particles, soluble compounds, and gases. At the molecular scale, elements are generally converted from complex organic molecules such as carbohydrates and proteins to simpler forms such as individual sugars, amino acids, and eventually to inorganic compounds such as ammonium and carbon dioxide. As these compounds are released, the chemical energy tied up in the organic bonds is available for energy demands of the organisms carrying out the decomposition.

It is important to distinguish the two scales of decomposition. In the macro view, materials "lost" from the recognizable parent material may well be useable as food resources by other organisms. Release of fine particles and soluble organic compounds and even reduced gases (methane) may represent significant resources for other portions of the ecosystem. Additionally, these compounds may be transported to other ecosystems where they may well represent a significant subsidy. For example, terrestrial inputs to lakes via leaf-fall, or organic matter carried by streams, may fuel the food web and appear as a major portion of the organic content of higher trophic levels (e.g., Pace et al. 2004). Simple sugars, nucleic acids, or amino acids released during macroscale decomposition can be easily incorporated by microbes and probably are removed quickly before there is much opportunity for transport. Ultimately, as bonds are cleaved, organic carbon (and its chemical potential energy) is released and may be oxidized to $CO_2$, a form with no further energetic value for consumers. In the simplest example, the release of $CO_2$ from organic matter is the reverse of carbon fixation (primary production) (Figure 4.1). Breaking of the bonds formed during carbon fixation provides that "fixed" energy to heterotrophs. Parallel with release of carbon is regeneration of other elements held in organic matter (e.g. nitrogen, phosphorus, sulfur) to simpler forms

STUART E.G. FINDLAY

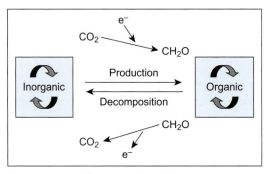

Ecosystem boundary

**FIGURE 4.1** Diagram illustrating conversion of oxidized carbon to the organic form (requires energy) and the back-reaction, which releases energy. Similar reactions occur for all the essential elements, which must be "fixed" into the organic form and may release energy upon breaking the organic bonds.

more available for assimilation by plants. Thus, decomposition completes the cycle begun with carbon fixation by releasing energy and elements to support other organisms.

In the absence of complete decomposition to $CO_2$ and inorganic nutrients, organic matter would accumulate and essentially sequester elements ultimately causing the ecosystem to wind down due to depletion of limiting elements. So decomposition is essential to maintain primary production, nutrient cycling, and other ecosystem processes. Other products of decomposition such as fine particles and dissolved organic matter allow for transport of organic carbon from locations of high productivity or large allochthonous loadings to downstream portions of flowing waters, deeper areas of lakes, or parts of estuarine and coastal systems connected by tidal exchange. Thus, decomposition in one location can subsidize energy flow in another. Organic matter sequestration in soils and sediments occurs to varying degrees in all ecosystems and has obviously occurred to a much greater degree in the geologic past resulting in large stockpiles of fossil fuels. Potential for future conversion of atmospheric $CO_2$ to longer-term storage is a critical factor in understanding how the global climate will change over the next decades (Chapters 6 and 17).

Most aquatic ecosystems are net heterotrophic (definition provided in Chapter 2; see, e.g., Teodoru et al. 2009), suggesting that they decompose large amounts of allochthonous material. Particulate plant litter is a major input to many ecosystems (leaves in headwater streams, plant litter in wetlands) and since local P/R is often less than 1 the portion of these inputs that is metabolized rather than stored or exported must be large relative to NPP. Understanding how decomposition proceeds (what are controls, which organisms are responsible) adds to knowledge of overall ecosystem function. Studies of particulate organic matter (POM) decay have logically been dominated by examination of plant litter since this is the main source of particulate detritus to most ecosystems. However, the degradation of animal and microbial biomass is a major term in subsequent carbon flow (see Chapter 3) and may represent an important pathway of nutrient transport (Bartz and Naiman 2005). For instance, the movement of anadromous salmon from the sea to small streams represents an important flux of nitrogen and the influence of this source can be seen in the terrestrial system surrounding the spawning stream (Naiman et al. 2002).

A wide array of macroinvertebrates (e.g., polychaetes and aquatic insects) rely on consumption of nonliving detritus in sediments or organic accumulations. Abundance or production of animals is often correlated with inputs of detritus (see Figure 3.6 in Chapter 3). By inference, this partially decomposed organic matter serves as a food resource although the exact pathways (microbial mediation or not) probably vary among organisms and among ecosystems. Microbial mediation occurs through at least two mechanisms: In some cases the microbial biomass associated with detritus is the predominant contributor to assimilable carbon (see Leal et al. 2011), or the action of microbial enzymes makes the nonliving detrital substrate more digestible by consumers. Whether microbes are involved directly, indirectly, or not at all, the transfer of detritus to higher trophic levels is an important path of energy flow in almost all ecosystems (see Chapter 3; Cebrian 1999).

The process of mineralizing the organic compounds in decaying organic matter returns many elements to a chemical form available for uptake by autotrophs or heterotrophic microbes and enhances transport to other ecosystems (see Chapter 7). For most ecosystems the pool of limiting nutrients (nitrogen and phosphorus) contained in organic matter is much greater than the pool of inorganic forms and so ecosystem productivity may be controlled by rates of decomposition. The fact that much of the particulate plant litter entering aquatic ecosystems has an overabundance of carbon relative to nitrogen, phosphorus, and such (with respect to the needs of consumers; (Box 3.1, Figure 4.8) implies that microbes metabolizing the organic carbon face a shortage of other elements unless external supplies are available. Most heterotrophic microorganisms have very efficient systems for acquiring external nutrients, and so as they grow there is a significant potential for immobilization of nutrients from the medium and incorporation in the detritus-microbe complex for some period of time.

This chapter will describe general processes of decomposition. Most of the basic concepts, processes, and even methodology are either similar or parallel for aquatic and terrestrial decomposition although certain aspects, metabolism of dissolved organic matter in particular, have received much more attention in aquatic ecosystems. The basic principles of organic matter decay do not differ greatly between aquatic and terrestrial ecosystems and, for instance, the importance of litter quality (lignin, nitrogen, etc.) has been demonstrated numerous times for both classes of ecosystems. There are, however, some substantial differences, the most obvious of which is the general importance of moisture availability in regulating organic matter decay and metabolic activity in many terrestrial systems (Sanderman and Amundson 2005).

Less obvious is the much greater opportunity for secondary reactions of decomposition products in soils than aquatic systems. The process of soil formation (humification) is key to many properties of terrestrial systems, and these processes can occur because removal of decomposition by-products is essentially zero for most soils. In many (but not all) aquatic systems, decomposition is balanced against physical transport (loss) and so there is often inadequate time for secondary recombination of decomposition by-products into new organic compounds. Additionally, incomplete decomposition within either flowing water or connected aquatic ecosystems allows for substantial cross-boundary fluxes of organic matter. The organic content of agricultural soils is a key control on their fertility and many agricultural practices such as plowing or adding manures are specifically intended to affect the balance between organic input and decomposition (Hendrix et al. 1986). Nutrient availability in agricultural soils is affected by rates of release from organic matter as well as immobilization of inorganic forms in microbial biomass growing on organic matter. The basic principles governing decomposition rates and processes apply across different ecosystems and I would argue there are more similarities than differences.

After describing a generalized model of decomposition, this chapter will discuss the organisms responsible for transforming the organic materials and then consider the factors that control decay rates. As organic matter decays, energy is made available for a wide array of heterotrophs via several pathways and inorganic nutrients may be either released or immobilized over several timescales. Lastly, gaps in our knowledge will be highlighted along with viable research approaches.

## DECOMPOSITION OF PLANT-DERIVED PARTICULATE MATTER

Studies of the disappearance of plant litter have been overwhelmingly dominated by measurements of mass loss from litter bags (Figure 4.2). Despite some concern about containment effects (Boulton and Boon 1991) this is a fairly standardized and straightforward way to quantify differences in decomposition among types of litter or ecosystems. In such studies, bags containing a known quantity of litter are placed in the environment and retrieved over a series of time points to determine how much mass remains. The general pattern to such data is a convex-up curve showing rapid mass loss early in the sequence with rates declining over time (Figure 4.3). There may or may not be some residual organic matter apparently resistant to decay during the study interval.

The shape of the curve is often represented by a negative exponential model (Figure 4.3) although there is no inherent reason that rate of mass loss from a complex mixture of organic compounds under varying environmental conditions should be described by such a model. The model is "first-order," meaning the rate of mass loss is proportional to the mass still

**FIGURE 4.2**  Photo of litter bag containing *Vallisneria americana* litter undergoing decomposition on the shore of the Hudson River. *(Photo Cornelia Harris.)*

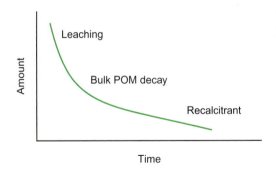

FIGURE 4.3 Hypothetical mass loss curve showing processes likely to be important during various phases.

present, so the actual quantity of mass disappearing over sequential time periods will get smaller as the amount of remaining material declines. The exponential constant (generally denoted as $k$ with units of $time^{-1}$) is a simple measure of differences in rates across types of litter, temperatures, presence/absence of certain organisms. and so on. In an extensive literature review, Enriquez et al. (1993) reported median $k$ values for various plant groups ranging across three orders of magnitude. Slowest were perennial leaves from broadleaf trees (0.001/day), intermediate were seagrasses and macroalgae (0.01/day), and fastest were microalgae (nearly 0.1/day). More complex models of mass loss are justified in some cases (Findlay et al. 1996), but the power of comparison to other observations argues for the simple and common model in most cases.

The measurement of disappearance of mass from a litter bag is a very coarse (or integrated) view of what is actually happening to the original organic matter. In fact, the actual pathway of disappearance has large implications for how that original organic matter might contribute to secondary production, be transported to other ecosystems, or interact with other element cycles. The predominance of any given pathway varies greatly among ecosystems and types of material but in general mass will be lost as soluble compounds are released (Figure 4.4), smaller particles are shed, and gases containing carbon, primarily $CO_2$, are released. Some of these products of mass loss (dissolved organic matter, DOM; fine particulate organic matter, FPOM) are fully capable of serving as a food resource for other organisms while the mineralization of organic carbon to $CO_2$ represents a dead end in terms of chemical potential energy. The partitioning between loss to other organic forms and $CO_2$ determines what organisms can derive energy from a unit input of POC (particulate organic matter). The relative magnitude of the various pathways depends on multiple factors, most of which have been fairly well studied.

Loss of particles depends on at least three things: fragility of the original material, physical stresses in the system, and perhaps most importantly the prevalence of animals capable of physically breaking litter into smaller pieces. Plant litters with a relatively low quantity of structural material are more susceptible to physical fragmentation, and for some fragile aquatic plants these losses can be rapid even without the activity of leaf-shredding invertebrates (Wallace and O'Hop 1985).

Loss of soluble organic compounds generally dominates the very early, rapid mass loss phase of decomposition soon after litter enters the water or is subject to precipitation/flooding in terrestrial systems. This part of mass loss appears as a very rapid decline over

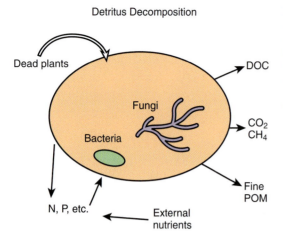

Detritus Decomposition

**FIGURE 4.4**  Illustration of the various pathways of organic matter decomposition and opportunities for immobilization of other nutrients (N, P) during microbial growth. Any of the components on the right side (DOC, nutrients) may be transported and used in other ecosystems. For many (but certainly not all) aquatic systems the input of detritus may be an export from another ecosystem.

the first few days followed by slower rates and a flattening of the curve. Quantities of release as well as constituents vary dramatically among litter types with mass loss in the first week or so ranging from negligible to more than 20%. These compounds are obviously available for subsequent metabolism by heterotrophic microbes and this can be a large, although short-term, subsidy.

Dissolved organic matter released from litter in aquatic systems or leached from soils can support food webs, interact with inorganic nutrient pools, alter light regimes, and can complex metals and toxic organic compounds in diverse ways (Findlay and Sinsabaugh 2003). Many of the principles and questions relevant to the study of POC decay apply equally to DOC although the likelihood of transport is much greater and protozoa and invertebrates play a much smaller role in DOC degradation.

The ultimate fate of POC is mineralization to $CO_2$, which, as mentioned earlier, is of no further energetic use to heterotrophs and often leaves the aquatic ecosystem. Generation of $CH_4$ (or other volatile organic compounds of low molecular weight) is susceptible to oxidation by the appropriate microbes (e.g., methane oxidizers) and so may contribute further to secondary production.

Measurement of mass loss from litter bags has been an informative, comparative, and integrative approach to studying decomposition (see Benfield 2006). However, the inability to identify which process is responsible for how much of the mass loss reduces the utility of litter bags in appreciating the subsequent uses of detrital organic matter and consequences for cycling of other elements. This technique also does not allow for study of longer-term decay processes since gases, small particles, and soluble compounds simply disappear from the litter bag. Decay of these components is often studied under artificial conditions of containment (such as bioassays of DOC consumption) or by integrative measures such as net $CO_2$ released from a fine sediment or soil. These latter approaches are nonspecific since $CO_2$ can derive from a range of OM present while the litter bag approach essentially follows a "cohort" of litter through early stages of decay. Measurements of specific processes such as $CO_2$ release or nitrogen immobilization during a litter bag study add greatly to understanding the macrodecomposition of POM.

# ORGANISMS RESPONSIBLE FOR DECOMPOSITION

It has been clear for over 40 years (see Kaushik and Hynes 1971) that microorganisms are responsible for the bulk of organic matter decay (i.e., conversion to $CO_2$), and recent improvements in microbial biomass and activity measurements have clarified their roles. The two classes of organisms most relevant for POM decay are bacteria and fungi. In general, their biomass is a few percent of the detrital carbon standing stock but their turnover can be rapid (1–10 d for bacteria, several days to weeks for fungi) and so they exert a considerable demand on organic carbon. Their relative biomass varies in a fairly consistent pattern with fungi having by far their greatest relative abundance on large particles of litter. For instance, they outweigh bacteria by more than 100-fold on standing dead wetland plant material. Bacterial biomass, relative to fungal biomass, increases as particle sizes decrease due to several mechanisms and it is often difficult to find fungi on particles smaller than a millimeter or so.

Most fungi in decaying litter have a filamentous morphology composed of hyphae used to penetrate plant cell walls and reproduction can't occur until enough hyphal mass has accumulated to support the reproductive structures. The effect of particle size is much stronger for fungi than bacteria such that even relatively small increases in abundance of large POM in a system will allow predominance of fungal over bacterial biomass (Findlay et al. 2002a). The difference in biomass across particles or ecosystems is relevant for food webs—for example, the food web in the surface litter of a pine forest is vastly different from the finer and more decayed humus layer (Berg and Bengtsson 2007; Figure 4.5). Moreover, fungi and bacteria differ in their catabolic and nutrient-acquisition capacities. For instance, fungi are more able to penetrate and degrade wood and other recalcitrant polymers such as chitin. On the other hand, bacteria typically have more efficient nutrient acquisition and so can draw down and assimilate nutrients at lower concentrations than most fungi.

During the decomposition process microbes convert nonliving organic carbon into microbial biomass with some concurrent loss of $CO_2$ to respiration. The net growth efficiency ($NGE = G/(G + R)$) where $G$ = growth and $R$ = respiration, describes the proportion of assimilated carbon ultimately available for consumption by other heterotrophs (see Chapter 3) as opposed to lost from the food web. Assimilation of this organic carbon into microbial biomass often requires some immobilization of inorganic nutrients from external sources (see Chapter 7). Therefore, low growth efficiencies suggest large net losses of organic carbon from the system and relatively little retention of inorganic nitrogen, phosphorus, and other elements in decomposer biomass. Given the importance of the NGE there has been considerable interest in determining its values during decomposition of diverse materials under natural conditions. Until measurement of microbial secondary production became routine (e.g., Gulis and Suberkropp 2006) most estimates were derived from lab estimates of growth on defined (often simple) compounds. These estimates tended toward the higher end of the range (as high as 75%), leading to overestimates of conversion of natural detrital carbon into microbial biomass. More recently, growth efficiencies have been determined for a range of aquatic ecosystems and values span 10% to 50% (del Giorgio and Cole 2000; Chapter 3) with most values below 30%. These NGEs mean that the vast majority of assimilated detrital carbon is lost as $CO_2$ and nutrient retention in microbial biomass will be smaller and more transient than previously believed.

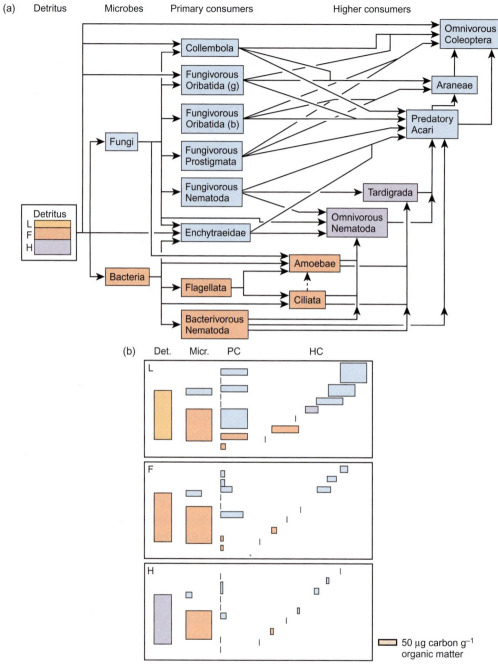

FIGURE 4.5    Example showing variability in soil food web structure derived from differences in the nature of detrital resource. The three boxes below the main figure show differences in consumer biomass for original litter (L), fragmented litter (F), and humus (H). Note large changes in the relative sizes of the consumer boxes depending on the basal carbon source. (*From Berg and Bengtsson 2007.*)

In many aquatic and terrestrial ecosystems there are invertebrates particularly adapted to ingesting large litter particles, thereby increasing overall mass loss. In streams, this functional group of invertebrates (mostly aquatic insects) has been described as "shredders" because of their important role in breaking apart leaf litter. Generation of small particles (or loss of large particles) is accelerated in the presence of these animals. When pesticides were used to reduce numbers of aquatic insects in a North Carolina stream, the quantity of fine particles exported decreased dramatically (Figure 4.6). Hieber and Gessner (2002) used litter bags with different mesh sizes to estimate that macroinvertebrates were roughly equal to microbes in accounting for loss of leaf mass. As discussed earlier, due to both inefficient feeding and a relatively low assimilation efficiency the fine particulate organic matter generated by shredder activity can be quantitatively significant and is suitable as food for a diversity of filtering and collecting organisms. In soils, earthworms, collembolans, and isopods play similar roles in large particle fragmentation.

In both terrestrial and aquatic ecosystems a significant fraction of macroconsumer secondary production is supported by consumption of detritus (e.g., Cummins and Klug 1979). There have been substantial shifts in our understanding of the trophic connections of detritivores (Findlay 2010). Early in the study of connections among detritus, microbes, and macroconsumers it was clear that the timing of increases in microbial abundance or

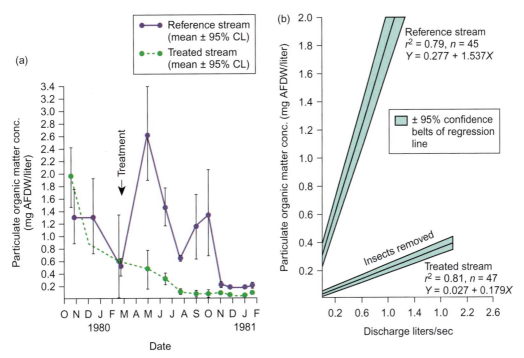

FIGURE 4.6 (a) Plot of FPOM export from an insecticide-treated stream vs. an untreated reference stream at the Coweeta Hydrologic Lab in North Carolina. Higher losses of FPOM from the reference stream relative to the insect-free stream at comparable water discharge rates (b) shows the positive effect of stream insects on release of FPOM from large particulate detritus. (*From Wallace et al. 1982.*)

activity were correlated with improved palatability of detritus to consumers (Arsuffi and Suberkropp 1984). These observations led to the proposal that the microbial biomass was the digestible portion of the detritus-microbe complex and much of the actual detrital organic matter was essentially unusable as a source of carbon or energy for the consumer (the "peanut butter and crackers" model; Cummins 1974). In this model the microbes are the digestible "peanut butter" and the plant material itself is analogous to the lower-quality crackers.

Once quantitative estimates of microbial biomass became common and it appeared that microbial carbon was insufficient to meet carbon demands of consumers (Findlay et al. 1986), other explanations for the observed correlations were proposed. Microbes inhabiting litter can alter the digestibility of the plant material itself by releasing extracellular enzymes capable of "predigesting" some of the macromolecules (Barlocher 1982) and there can be substantial production of extracellular polymers that can serve as a carbon source for consumers. Additionally, even relatively low assimilation efficiencies applied to the large quantities of ingested plant material would allow for the nonliving detritus to contribute significantly to overall consumer carbon demand. There is even a wider recognition that high microbial degradation can reduce detrital standing stocks, thus ultimately depleting the food resources for animals (Benstead et al. 2009). Microbes thus can both facilitate and compete with invertebrates for detritus.

The presence of microbial biomass somehow makes the pool of detrital organic matter more palatable and available to invertebrates. In contrast, there are also examples where microbial metabolism causes losses of organic carbon to $CO_2$, thereby reducing the pool of food for other consumers. As argued earlier, an appreciation of which pathways of mass loss are important at various times, places, and under what environmental conditions can greatly alter our conception of how allochthonous inputs contribute to secondary production. For instance, release of DOC can support bacterial growth but is generally unavailable for macroinvertebrates. Fine particles of organic matter can be used as a food resource by animals downstream or transported to other ecosystems, whereas conversion of detritus to $CO_2$ means that amount of carbon is of no further use to heterotrophs.

## CONTROLS ON DECOMPOSITION

For the sake of simplicity the various factors potentially controlling decay rates will be separated into *intrinsic* versus *extrinsic* factors although the two actually interact. For instance, an intrinsic factor such as plant nitrogen content will be affected by (and will eventually affect) environmental nutrient content. Similarly, low nutrient availability at a site or presence of herbivores (extrinsic factors) can alter plant biochemical composition (an intrinsic factor). Nonetheless, it is useful and informative to separate some inherent, species-specific controls on plant litter decay from regulation by environmental conditions.

Intrinsic controls are most often associated with either the bulk macromolecular composition of plant litter or the availability of some required nutrient that is present in low concentrations in the litter (together often referred to broadly as litter quality). Structural carbohydrates (e.g., cellulose, hemicellulose), often complexed with lignin, make up a major portion of plant biomass with obvious and well-known differences among plant taxa or functional types. In the broadest dichotomy, aquatic and terrestrial plants differ in decay rates due to the generally lower concentration of structural materials in aquatic plants (Enriquez et al 1993; Cebrian and Lartigue 2004). Also, nonvascular plants in general have less structural material and therefore decompose faster. In the realm of plant materials, lignin (a highly complex, uncharacterized macromolecule made up of diverse subunits containing phenolic rings; Figure 4.7) is one of the most recalcitrant plant materials and any plant with appreciable quantities of lignin will tend to decay slowly.

Schindler and Gessner (2009) found that leaf mass loss from coarse mesh bags was inversely related to the lignin content of the plant material across a range of litter types

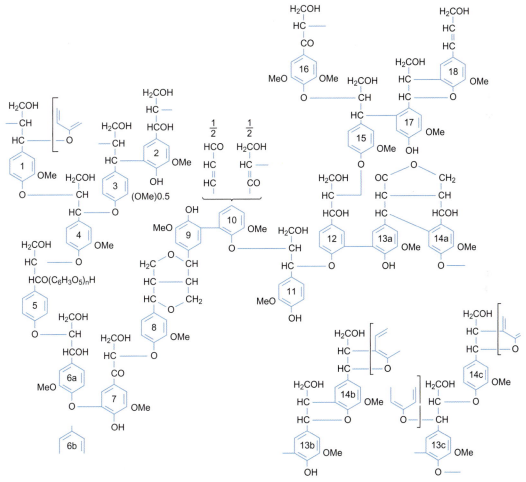

FIGURE 4.7 Representation of a portion of a lignin molecule showing the many types of compounds constituting this complex macromolecule. Enzymatic attack would require several different enzymes in contrast to a macromolecule made up of a consistent subunit where only a single type of enzyme would be necessary. Many of the compounds are ring structures indicating they are partially oxidized and therefore contain less energy than, for instance, more reduced forms of organic carbon such as methane.

TABLE 4.1   Example of range in lignin, nitrogen, and decay rates (k) for several common types of leaf litter.

| Species | Lignin (%) | SEM of Lignin | Mean N (%) | SEM of N | Mean $k$ (d$^{-1}$) | SEM of $k$ |
|---------|-----------|---------------|------------|----------|--------------------|-----------|
| Elm | 11.1 | 0.4 | 1.1 | 0.04 | $-0.026$ | 0.006 |
| Ash | 13.9 | 2.8 | 0.73 | 0.02 | $-0.017$ | 0.003 |
| Alder | 18.6 | 0.3 | 1.91 | 0.08 | $-0.01$ | 0.002 |
| Maple | 14.3 | 0.9 | 1.1 | 0.13 | $-0.01$ | 0.001 |
| Willow | 19.7 | 0.3 | 1.28 | 0.13 | $-0.01$ | 0.001 |
| Hazel | 23 | 3 | 1.15 | 0.06 | $-0.008$ | 0.0004 |
| Sycamore | 34.3 | 1.7 | 0.8 | 0.07 | $-0.008$ | 0.0006 |
| Oak | 23.9 | 0.5 | 0.45 | 0.03 | $-0.005$ | 0.0004 |
| Beech | 35.7 | 0.8 | 1 | 0.05 | $-0.003$ | 0.0002 |

*Values are from Schindler and Gessner (2009), who report a significant relationship between percent of lignin and the decay rate in coarse mesh litter bags. SEM = standard error of the mean.*

(Table 4.1). There are several reasons these macromolecules have significant effects on mass loss. Most obvious is simply their physical nature; compounds that play a role in supporting plant tissues must resist decay. These structural biomolecules can have complex physical structure (lignocellulose), making it difficult for enzymes to reach particular bonds. Second, the fact that they are polymeric and often heterogeneous means that microbes must release extracellular enzymes to break bonds (via hydrolysis or oxidation) to liberate the simpler subunits that they can break down. Moreover, some subunits (phenolic rings) are partially oxidized and so the energy yield is less than for a carbohydrate.

The other important class of materials affecting decay rates includes the nutrients (mainly but not exclusively nitrogen and phosphorus) that typically are underrepresented in plant litter relative to the needs of micro- or macroconsumers (Chapter 2, Box 3.1). To produce new biomass microbes require about 1 atom of nitrogen for about every 10 atoms of carbon. Accounting for the necessary loss of carbon to respiration means that organic detritus with less than 1 atom of nitrogen per 20 atoms of carbon will be poor in nitrogen relative to microbial demands (Figure 4.8). The relative paucity of nutrient can affect decay in two counteracting ways; slowing decomposition of low-nutrient litter due to the low biomass of decomposers, or increasing decomposition to compensate for low nutrient availability. In the first scenario the ultimate population size of decomposers and therefore rate of mass loss is limited by the quantity of nitrogen or phosphorus. In the alternative case, animals and/or microbes increase consumption to compensate for lower nutritive value and overall mass loss is greater. Both these cases assume the organic carbon compounds themselves do not limit decay.

Aside from the major structural components of plant material or the content of limiting nutrients (nitrogen, phosphorus), certain plant secondary compounds have been predicted to have strong effects on both decay rates and nitrogen cycling. Plant secondary compounds are not an essential part of plant metabolism but serve specific functions, often as

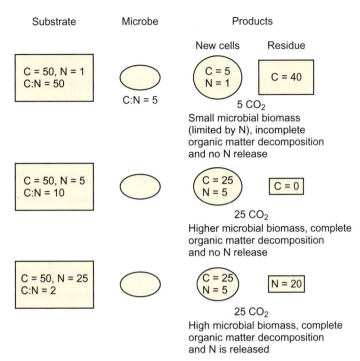

FIGURE 4.8 Effects of litter stoichiometry on potential nutrient immobilization. Assumptions are that the microbial decomposers have a biomass C:N of 5 and their growth efficiency is 50%. As microbes grow on a substrate they require 10 units of carbon (5 are lost to respiration) and 1 unit of nitrogen to make 1 new unit (5 carbon and 1 nitrogen) of microbial biomass. In the top case they become nitrogen-limited and cannot metabolize the residual carbon. The example assumes no external nitrogen supply but in the top case the residual carbon could be metabolized if a nitrogen source were available. In the second case the C:N ratio of the material is such that complete decomposition occurs, generating 25 units of new biomass and consuming all the detrital organic matter. In the last case there is excess nitrogen after microbial metabolism has consumed all carbon. Thus, in the first case detritus decomposition yields a "demand" for inorganic nitrogen, and in the last the system can release nitrogen to the environment.

defense against herbivores. Most attention has been given to a wide array of phenolic compounds since they should be inherently difficult to decompose and have the capability to bind proteins (Hattenschwiler and Vitousek 2000). Protein binding may inactivate enzymes important to the decay process and decrease the availability of this source of organic nitrogen. These secondary compounds vary among plant species and may be induced by herbivore attack on the living plants. Tannins, which affect protein metabolism by binding and possibly inactivating enzymes, are especially common secondary compounds. Effects of tannins on decomposition are demonstrable but not always strong. For instance, reindeer browsing on beech shifted tannin content but not uniformly across habitats or years (Stark et al. 2007). In a study of litter decay in a set of tropical streams Ardon et al. (2006) found little effect of variation in abundance of various classes of phenolic compounds. The effect of secondary compounds may be large in particular cases but is perhaps less general than consequences of variation in major macromolecules or macronutrient content.

A diverse array of extrinsic factors affects decay rates. In terrestrial ecosystems, the most important are temperature (Figure 4.9) and moisture. Many studies of decay have shown an increase in decay at warmer temperatures (e.g., Acuña et al. 2008) and recently it was demonstrated that diel variability in temperature could also affect mass loss (Dang et al. 2009). Despite the documented importance of temperature as a regulator of decomposition, some organisms carry out degradation even at fairly low temperatures. The best example may be the aquatic hyphomycete fungi, found in cold-water streams of which the temperature optimum is generally <10°C, allowing them to metabolize leaf litter in streams during winter.

Because most plant litters are poor in inorganic nutrients (nitrogen, phosphorus) relative to decomposer biomass, it is not surprising that environments with some external nutrient supply have more rapid decomposition. If the organic carbon in litter is available, then external nutrients allow for higher biomass of decomposers with resultant increases in carbon assimilation and hence mass loss (Suberkropp et al. 2010). Surface waters in particular can provide a nutrient subsidy that enhances detritus decay. Suberkropp and Chauvet (1995) showed a six-fold increase in mass loss of a common litter type across a range of ambient nitrogen concentrations in a series of streams. Similarly, Robinson and Gessner (2000) showed an increase in mass loss in leaf packs amended with slow-release phosphorus fertilizer. The stimulatory effects of external nutrients can be due to various processes. For instance, if inorganic nutrients are available in the medium, microbes will not necessarily elaborate extracellular enzymes to acquire nutrients from organic materials. This may allow reallocation to enzymes targeting organic carbon compounds and faster litter mass loss.

For aquatic ecosystems environmental pH is thought to constrain decomposer activity either through effects on microbes or by restricting abundances of leaf-shredding macroinvertebrates. Streams receiving acid mine drainage often show lower decay rates (see Niyogi et al. 2009). Acidic bogs can have pH as low as 2 or 3 (Mitsch and Gosselink 1993), which in combination with low oxygen availability leads to very slow decay. Often these bogs, which by definition get all their water from precipitation, also have low concentrations of inorganic nutrients and base cations so the direct pH effect may be hard to

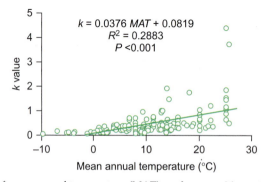

FIGURE 4.9   The effect of mean annual temperature (MAT) on decomposition rates (Zhang et al. 2008).

separate. Also, most extracellular enzymes have pH optima of 5 or higher and very low pH may affect the structure of these proteins. Low pH may also affect the diversity of macro- and microdecomposers inhabiting these systems, thereby removing potential synergistic effects of organisms on mass loss.

Microorganisms metabolizing organic carbon require an electron acceptor to acquire energy from carbon mineralization (Appendix). Oxygen is the most energetically favorable electron acceptor followed closely by $NO_3$, and so on. If these high-yield electron acceptors are absent, microbes use a wide diversity of inorganic and organic electron acceptors but the chemical energy yield is substantially lower. The lack of oxygen may depress decomposition by one or more mechanisms: First, lack of oxygen means less energetically efficient electron acceptors must be used and so there will be a smaller accumulation of microbial biomass. Lower biomass will generally be associated with lower rates of microbial respiration and therefore slower carbon loss. Second, the lower energy yield in the absence of oxygen means that a smaller proportion of the compounds in the detrital mixture will provide a positive energy gain. Therefore, some classes of compounds will no longer be degraded once oxygen has been depleted. Last, some organisms, notably macroinvertebrates, may be sensitive to low oxygen and therefore will not be present to consume or fragment detritus.

Physical conditions can play a large role in overall mass loss from large particles either due to temperature and moisture effects on biological decomposition or due to losses of particles to fragmentation (Langhans et al. 2008). Fragmentation and export can be significant with, for example, mass loss of seagrass due to export being roughly one-third as large as loss to respiration (Mateo and Romero 1997). In streams the direct physical effects of current velocity are more complex in part because higher flow can also allow different leaf-shredding organisms to attack the material (Reice 1977). Experiments in artificial streams designed to isolate the effects of physical stress have not uniformly revealed large effects on mass loss (cf. Canton and Martinson 1990; Ferreira et al. 2006). There is no direct analog to physical fragmentation in terrestrial ecosystems, but exposure to sunlight increases rates of decay for some types of plant litter through photodegradation (Austin and Vivanco 2006).

While these factors have been separated into intrinsic and extrinsic controls, they interact in many interesting and important ways. Several elegant experiments and analyses of literature data have tried to separate the effects of species shifts, nutrients, and temperature on differences in decomposition (e.g., Aerts and De Caluwe 1997; Dorrepaal et al. 2005). For example, transplant experiments where litter is moved from its native range to another location with different extrinsic attributes (warmer, more nutrients, etc.) can help reveal whether the intrinsic nature of the plant litter or the environmental conditions are more important in regulating decay. If decay is similar in both locations it suggests intrinsic control; if decay of the same material varies greatly across sites then extrinsic factors seem to exert greater control. Not surprisingly, both factors contribute significantly in most of these analyses and there are interesting feedbacks that are particularly relevant to issues of climate change and human alteration of nutrient regimes. For example, as atmospheric $CO_2$ increases we might expect higher C:N ratios in plant litter and therefore reduced decay rates and/or a greater demand for exogenous inorganic nitrogen to allow decomposition to proceed (Rier et al. 2002; Wetzel and Tuchman 2005).

Given the broad quantitative importance of decomposition processes and the ease of manipulation of many participating organisms there have been several attempts to investigate the effects of species diversity or richness of both plant litter and decomposer organisms on mass loss or respiration. Human activities frequently alter the richness of both the plants contributing litter to an ecosystem and the macro-organisms. For instance, planting monocultures, hybrids, or exotic tree species in riparian zones clearly alters the pool of POM and there are several examples of whole-ecosystem effects of such plantings (Leroy and Marks 2006; Swan and Palmer 2004). Additionally, human-caused climate change will likely lead to rapid change in species distribution. There will probably be some period of increasing richness during the period when both extant and new species are present, but ultimately species better suited to the new conditions will replace previously abundant species. Therefore, direct examination of effects of species richness of either the litter or detritivores has become a major research topic.

Recent studies have included invertebrates representing different taxa (Jonsson and Malmqvist 2000) or functional types (Heemsbergen et al. 2004). In general, these efforts have shown that decomposition is stimulated as species are added to the mixture; these effects usually are attributed to differences in functional capacity among test animals. Since microbes are responsible for the bulk of decomposition there have been several studies of bacterial taxonomic richness/diversity on decay of detritus. These studies typically show a leveling off of the effect of species richness above some number of species, suggesting there is some functional redundancy among taxa (Bell et al. 2005). Several studies have asked whether mixtures of litter decompose differently from what would be expected from their individual decay rates. The entire range of outcomes has been observed from faster than expected, slower than expected, and no effect (Swan and Palmer 2006; Lecerf et al. 2007; Srivastava et al. 2009). While individual results have been reconciled, there is yet to be a synthesis that accounts for the diversity of observations on consequences of mixing together different species of litter.

## INTERACTIONS WITH OTHER ELEMENT CYCLES

One of the key chemical characteristics of most (but certainly not all) plant litters is the relative shortage of some elements, most notably nitrogen and phosphorus. Plants undergoing normal senescence withdraw valuable nutrients from tissues destined for abscission or death at the end of the growing season. Therefore, microbes and other organisms using these detrital materials as a food resource are faced with a shortage of nutrients. Microbes can draw nutrients from the surrounding water or soil solution and so they often use the particulate organic matter as a carbon source while assimilating inorganic nutrients from their environment. This capability provides the mechanism whereby external nutrient supply can alter decomposition rates, but more importantly it allows ecosystems with large pools of detritus to have a substantial potential to remove and sequester nutrients. Tidal wetlands are well known for their capacity to act as a sink for inorganic nutrients, and while there are multiple mechanisms (plant uptake, denitrification, burial, etc.), immobilization in microbial biomass during litter decomposition is often dominant (Findlay et al. 2002b).

This interaction between carbon and other nutrients leads to some important implications of human-induced changes in element cycling. For example, as $CO_2$ increases in the atmosphere, plant tissues can become enriched in carbon, and if litter from these plants is available for decomposition it may require an external nitrogen or phosphorus source to balance the additional carbon. The converse effect is also plausible—as nitrogen and phosphorus concentrations increase there may be a stimulation of decay of previously nutrient-limited organic carbon pools. Therefore, $CO_2$ release may be enhanced as an indirect effect of human fertilization. Greater plant productivity may result from higher $CO_2$ availability, leading to increased litter production and accumulation (Lichter et al. 2008). In any case there are strong interactions between carbon compounds undergoing microbial attack and other elements necessary for biomass production and maintenance. Several components of these interacting processes are subject to alteration by human-accelerated supply of elements.

While many types of detrital organic matter are nutrient-poor, they all contain nitrogen, phosphorus, and other biologically relevant elements, and ultimately as the carbon is mineralized to $CO_2$, the organic forms of nitrogen, phosphorus, and the like are also released to the environment in simple forms available for uptake by plants and microbes. Unless the detrital material is permanently stored or recalcitrant, over reasonable timescales any elements in the original material or associated microbial biomass are eventually returned to active cycling. Therefore, rates of decay can be the limiting step in completing nutrient cycles in many ecosystems.

# SUMMARY

Processes of decomposition close the cycle begun by primary production by releasing energy for consumers and returning nutrients such as nitrogen and phosphorus to inorganic forms. Regulation of rates of decay and specific processes causing mass loss both affect where and when either energy or materials are available for consumption by organisms or assimilation by plants. The basic principles governing the rates and relative importance of processes are broadly similar across ecosystem types, and for instance the intrinsic composition of plant litter is almost always an important control on rates of decomposition. The biochemical composition also influences when (or whether) inorganic nutrients are released during the decay sequence versus being immobilized in the detritus-microbe complex during some phase of decay.

Particulate detritus and especially dissolved organic carbon move across ecosystem boundaries and can represent important subsidies to food webs in connected ecosystems. A wide array of microbes and animals rely on detritus as a food resource and therefore play a role in influencing rates of decay.

## The Future

With the processes of decomposition linked to essentially all elemental cycles and under the control of biotic and environmental conditions there are a huge number of fruitful research avenues for the future. Here, just two areas are mentioned related to the release of carbon from the massive pools stored in terrestrial ecosystems and implications for global carbon cycling. First, with climate change affecting both temperature and water availability there has been a great deal of interest in whether (how) dynamics of soil carbon pools might be affected. Overall, there is recognition that carbon mineralization is almost certain to increase as soils warm, with the most dramatic effects in regions of thawing permafrost (Dorrepaal et al. 2009; von Lutzow and Kogel-Knabner 2009). The precise mechanism leading to higher respiration and implications for linked element cycles (nitrogen in particular) are perhaps less clear and with variable response strengths (Groffman et al. 2009; Chapin et al. 2009), but the fact of significant change seems inevitable.

Second, there are numerous reports that dissolved organic carbon export from terrestrial ecosystems has recently increased (Findlay 2005), and there is good evidence that this DOC supports heterotrophic metabolism in many surface waters (Roehm et al. 2009). The exact mechanism driving this increase is still uncertain; a response of soils to reduced acidic deposition has been put forward as one such mechanism (Evans et al. 2008). In any case, this increased flux of carbon must draw down terrestrial storage and represents a potential for additional $CO_2$ release during transport in aquatic ecosystems. In essence, any environmental change, whether small scale or global, has the potential to alter decomposition of organic matter. Such effects will ramify throughout the ecosystem, affecting trophic pathways and element cycling.

# References

Acuña, V., Wolf, A., Uehlinger, U., Tockner, K., 2008. Temperature dependence of stream benthic respiration in an Alpine river network under global warming. Freshw. Biol. 53, 2076–2088.

Aerts, R., De Caluwe, H., 1997. Nutritional and plant-mediated controls on leaf litter decomposition of *Carex* species. Ecology 78, 244–260.

Ardon, M., Stallcup, L.A., Pringle, C.M., 2006. Does leaf quality mediate the stimulation of leaf breakdown by phosphorus in neotropical streams? Freshw. Biol. 51, 618–633.

Arsuffi, T.L., Suberkropp, K., 1984. Leaf processing capabilities of aquatic hyphomycetes: Interspecific differences and influence on shredder feeding preferences. Oikos 42, 144–154.

Austin, A.T., Vivanco, L., 2006. Plant litter decomposition in a semi-arid ecosystem controlled by photodegradation. Nature 442, 555–558.

Barlocher, F., 1982. The contribution of fungal enzymes to the digestion of leaves by *Gammarus fossarum* (Koch) (Amphipoda). Oecologia 52, 1–4.

Bartz, K.K., Naiman, R.J., 2005. Effects of salmon-borne nutrients on riparian soils and vegetation in southwest Alaska. Ecosystems 8, 529–545.

Bell, T., Newman, J.A., Silverman, B.W., Turner, S.L., Lilley, A.K., 2005. The contribution of species richness and composition to bacterial services. Nature 436, 1157–1160.

Benfield, F., 2006. Decomposition of leaf material. In: Hauer, F.R., Lamberti, G.A. (Eds.), Methods in stream ecology. Academic Press, New York, pp. 711–720.

Benstead, J.P., Rosemond, A.D., Cross, W.F., Wallace, J.B., Eggert, S.L., Suberkropp, K., et al., 2009. Nutrient enrichment alters storage and fluxes of detritus in a headwater stream ecosystem. Ecology 90, 2556–2566.

Berg, M.P., Bengtsson, J., 2007. Temporal and spatial variability in soil food web structure. Oikos 116, 1789–1804.

Boulton, A.J., Boon, P.I., 1991. A review of methodology used to measure leaf litter decomposition in lotic environments: Time to turn over an old leaf? Australian Journal of Marine and Freshwater Research 42, 1–43.

Canton, S.P., Martinson, R.J., 1990. The effect of varying current on weight loss from willow leaf packs. J. Freshw. Ecol. 5, 413–415.

Cebrian, J., 1999. Patterns in the fate of production in plant communities. Am. Nat. 154, 449–468.

Cebrian, J., Lartigue, J., 2004. Patterns of herbivory and decomposition in aquatic and terrestrial ecosystems. Ecol. Monogr. 74, 237–259.

Chapin, F.S., McFarland, J., McGuire, A.D., Euskirchen, E.S., Ruess, R.W., Kielland, K, et al., 2009. The changing global carbon cycle: Linking plant-soil carbon dynamics to global consequences. J. Ecol. 97, 840–850.

Cummins, K., 1974. Structure and function of stream ecosystems. BioScience 24, 631–641.

Cummins, K.W., Klug, M.J., 1979. Feeding ecology of stream invertebrates. Annu. Rev. Ecol. Syst. 10, 147–172.

Dang, C.K., Schindler, M., Chauvet, E., Gessner, M.O., 2009. Temperature oscillation coupled with fungal community shifts can modulate warming effects on litter decomposition. Ecology 90, 122–131.

del Giorgio, P.A., Cole, J.J., 2000. Bacterial energetics and growth efficiency. In: Kirchman, D. (Ed.), Microbial ecology of the oceans. Wiley-Liss, pp. 289–325.

Dorrepaal, E., Cornelissen, J.H.C., Aerts, R., Wallen, B., Van Logtestijn, R.S.P., 2005. Are growth forms consistent predictors of leaf litter quality and decomposability across peatlands along a latitudinal gradient? J. Ecol. 93, 817–828.

Dorrepaal, E., Toet, S., van Logtestijn, R.S.P., Swart, E., Weg, M.J., Callaghan, T.V., et al., 2009. Carbon respiration from subsurface peat accelerated by climate warming in the subarctic. Nature 460, 616–619.

Enriquez, S., Duarte, C.M., Sandjensen, K., 1993. Patterns in decomposition rates among photosynthetic organisms: The importance of detritus C-N-P content. Oecologia 94, 457–471.

Evans, C., Goodale, C., Caporn, S., Dise, N., Emmett, B., Fernandez, I., et al., 2008. Does elevated nitrogen deposition or ecosystem recovery from acidification drive increased dissolved organic carbon loss from upland soil? A review of evidence from field nitrogen addition experiments. Biogeochemistry 91, 13–35.

Ferreira, V., Graça, M., de Lima, J., Gomes, R., 2006. Role of physical fragmentation and invertebrate activity in the breakdown rate of leaves. Archiv für Hydrobiologie 165, 493–513.

Findlay, S.E.G., 2005. Increased carbon transport in the Hudson River, NY: Unexpected consequence of nitrogen deposition? Front Ecol. Evol. 3, 133–137.

Findlay, S., Meyer, J., Smith, P.J., 1986. Incorporation of microbial biomass by Peltoperla sp. (Plecoptera) and Tipula sp. (Diptera). J. North Am. Benthol. Soc. 5, 306–310.

Findlay, S., Carreiro, M., Krischik, V., Jones, C., 1996. Effects of damage to living plants on leaf litter quality. Ecol. Appl. 6, 269–275.

Findlay, S.E.G., Tank, J., Dye, S., Valett, H.M., Mulholland, P.J., McDowell, W.H., et al., 2002a. A cross-system comparison of bacterial and fungal biomass in detritus pools of headwater streams. Microb. Ecol. 43, 55–66.

Findlay, S., Dye, S., Kuehn, K.A., 2002b. Microbial growth and nitrogen retention in litter of Phragmites australis and Typha angustifolia. Wetlands 22, 616–625.

Findlay, S.E.G., Sinsabaugh, R.L. (Eds.), 2003. Aquatic ecosystems: Interactivity of dissolved organic matter. Academic Press, New York.

Findlay, S., 2010. Stream microbial ecology. J. North Am. Benthol. Soc. 29, 170–181.

Groffman, P.M., Hardy, J.P., Fisk, M.C., Fahey, T.J., Driscoll, C.T., 2009. Climate variation and soil carbon and nitrogen cycling processes in a northern hardwood forest. Ecosystems 12, 927–943.

Gulis, V., Suberkropp, K.F., 2006. Fungi: Biomass, production, and sporulation of aquatic hyphomycetes. In: Hauer, F.R., Lamberti, G.A. (Eds.), Methods in stream ecology, second ed. Academic Press, New York, pp. 311–325.

Hattenschwiler, S., Vitousek, P.M., 2000. The role of polyphenols in terrestrial ecosystem nutrient cycling. Trends. Ecol. Evol. 15, 238–243.

Heemsbergen, D.A., Berg, M.P., Loreau, M., van Haj, J.R., Faber, J.H., Verhoef, H.A., 2004. Biodiversity effects on soil processes explained by interspecific functional dissimilarity. Science 306, 1019–1020.

Hendrix, P.F., Parmelee, R.W., Crossley, D.A., Coleman, D.C., Odum, E.P., Groffman, P.M., 1986. Detritus food webs in conventional and no-tillage agroecosystems. Bioscience 36, 374–380.

Hieber, M., Gessner, M.O., 2002. Contribution of stream detritivores, fungi and bacteria to leaf breakdown based on biomass estimates. Ecology 83, 1026–1038.

Jonsson, M., Malmqvist, B., 2000. Ecosystem process rate increases with animal species richness: Evidence from leaf-eating, aquatic insects. Oikos 89, 519–523.

Kaushik, N.K., Hynes, H.B.N., 1971. The fate of dead leaves that fall into streams. Archiv für Hydrobiologie 68, 465–515.

Langhans, S.D., Tiegs, S.D., Gessner, M.O., Tockner, K., 2008. Leaf-decomposition heterogeneity across a riverine floodplain mosaic. Aquatic Sciences 70, 337–346.

Leal, I.R., Silva, P.S., Oliveira, P.S., 2011. Natural history and ecological correlates of fungus-growing ants (Formicidae: Attini) in the neotropical Cerrado Savanna. Ann. Entomol. Soc. Am. 104, 901–908.

Lecerf, A., Risnoveanu, G., Popescu., C., Gessner, M.O., Chauvet, E., 2007. Decomposition of diverse litter mixtures in streams. Ecology 88, 219—227.

Leroy, C.J., Marks, J.C., 2006. Litter quality, stream characteristics and litter diversity influence decomposition rates and macroinvertebrates. Freshw. Biol. 51, 605—617.

Lichter, J., Billings, S.A., Ziegler, S.E., Gaindh, D., Ryals, R., Finzi, A.C., et al., 2008. Soil carbon sequestration in a pine forest after 9 years of atmospheric $CO_2$ enrichment. Global Change Biology 14, 2910—2922.

Mateo, M.A., Romero, J., 1997. Detritus dynamics in the seagrass *Posidonia oceanica*: Elements for an ecosystem carbon and nutrient budget. Mar. Ecol. Prog. Ser. 151, 43—53.

Mitsch, W.J., Gosselink, J.G., 1993. Wetlands, second ed. Van Nostrand Reinhold, New York.

Naiman, R.J., Bilby, R.E., Schindler, D.E., Helfield, J.M., 2002. Pacific salmon, nutrients, and the dynamics of freshwater and riparian ecosystems. Ecosystems 5, 399—417.

Niyogi, D.K., Cheatham, C.A., Thomson, W.H., Christiansen, J.M., 2009. Litter breakdown and fungal diversity in a stream affected by mine drainage. Fundam. Appl. Limnol. 175, 39—48.

Pace, M.L., Cole, J.J., Carpenter, S.R., Kitchell, J.F., Hodgson, J.R., Van de Bogart, M.C., et al., 2004. Whole-lake carbon-13 additions reveal terrestrial support of aquatic food webs. Nature 427, 240—243.

Reice, S.R., 1977. The role of animal associations and current velocity in sediment-specific leaf litter decomposition. Oikos 29, 357—365.

Rier, S.T., Tuchman, N.C., Wetzel, R.G., Teeri, J.A., 2002. Elevated-$CO_2$-induced changes in the chemistry of quaking aspen (Populus Tremuloides Michaux) leaf litter: Subsequent mass loss and microbial response in a stream ecosystem. J. North Am. Benthol. Soc. 21, 16—27.

Robinson, C.T., Gessner, M.O., 2000. Nutrient addition accelerates leaf breakdown in an alpine springbrook. Oecologia 122, 258—263.

Roehm, C.L., Giesler, R., Karlsson, J., 2009. Bioavailability of terrestrial organic carbon to lake bacteria: The case of a degrading subarctic permafrost mire complex. Journal of Geophysical Research-Biogeosciences 114, G03006.

Sanderman, J., Amundson, R., 2005. Biogeochemistry of decomposition and detrital processing. In: Schlesinger, W.H. (Ed.), Biogeochemistry. Elsevier, Boston, pp. 249—316.

Schindler, M.H., Gessner, M.O., 2009. Functional leaf traits and biodiversity effects on litter decomposition in a stream. Ecology 90, 1641—1649.

Srivastava, D.S., Cardinale, B.J., Downing, A.L., Duffy, J.E., Jouseau, C., Sankaran, M., et al., 2009. Diversity has stronger top-down than bottom-up effects on decomposition. Ecology 90, 1073—1083.

Stark, S., Julkunen-Tiitto, R., Kumpula, J., 2007. Ecological role of reindeer summer browsing in the mountain birch (*Betula pubescens* ssp. *czerepanovii*) forests: Effects on plant defense, litter decomposition, and soil nutrient cycling. Oecologia 151, 486—498.

Suberkropp, K., Chauvet, E., 1995. Regulation of leaf breakdown by fungi in streams: Influences of water chemistry. Ecology 76, 1433—1445.

Suberkropp, K., Gulis, V., Rosemond, A.D., Benstead, J.P., 2010. Ecosystem and physiological scales of microbial responses to nutrients in a detritus-based stream: Results of a 5-year continuous enrichment. Limnol. Oceanogr. 55, 149—160.

Swan, C.M., Palmer, M.A., 2004. Leaf diversity alters litter breakdown in a Piedmont stream. J. North Am. Benthol. Soc. 23, 15—28.

Swan, C.M., Palmer, M.A., 2006. Preferential feeding by an aquatic consumer mediates non-additive decomposition of speciose leaf litter. Oecologia 149, 107—114.

Teodoru, C.R., del Giorgio, P.A., Prairie, Y.T., Camire, M., 2009. Patterns in $pCO_2$ in boreal streams and rivers of northern Quebec, Canada. Global Biogeochemical Cycles 23, GB2012, 10.1029/2008GB003404.

von Lutzow, M., Kogel-Knabner, I., 2009. Temperature sensitivity of soil organic matter decomposition—What do we know? Biology and Fertility of Soils 46, 1—15.

Wallace, J.B., O'Hop, J., 1985. Life on a fast pad: Water lily leaf beetle impact on water lilies. Ecology 66, 1534—1544.

Wallace, J.B., Webster, J.R., Cuffney, T.F., 1982. Stream detritus dynamics: Regulation by invertebrate consumers. Oecologia 53, 197—200.

Wetzel, R.G., Tuchman, N.C., 2005. Effects of atmospheric $CO_2$ enrichment and sunlight on degradation of plant particulate and dissolved organic matter and microbial utilization. Archiv für Hydrobiologie 162, 287—308.

Zhang, D.Q., Hui, D.F., Luo, Y.Q., et al., 2008. Rates of litter decomposition in terrestrial ecosystems: Global patterns and controlling factors. J. Plant Ecol. 1, 85—93.

# BIOGEOCHEMISTRY

# Element Cycling

*Kathleen C. Weathers*[1] *and Holly A. Ewing*[2]

[1]Cary Institute of Ecosystem Studies, Millbrook, NY
[2]Bates College, Lewiston, ME

Element cycling is the transport and transformation of chemicals within and among eco-systems, and as such is a major focal area for ecosystem scientists. Elements are required by all life, and element cycles thus link the living and nonliving parts of ecosystems. Nutrient cycles are an important subset of elemental cycles because they represent elements that are especially important to living organisms (e.g., the plant macronutrients nitrogen (N), potassium (K), calcium (Ca), magnesium (Mg), phosphorus (P), and sulfur (S)) or are the building blocks of life (carbon, C). Because the pathways of nutrient cycling are those traveled by all elements, whether beneficial or harmful to life, our understanding of nutrient cycling informs nearly all other areas of ecosystem science. Indeed, we cannot understand primary production without understanding the availability of nutrients and the pathways by which those nutrients are transformed in food webs, liberated through decomposition, and again used for primary production. Nearly every process you might consider in an ecosystem is linked in some way to nutrient cycling.

Many environmental management issues arise from too much or too little of particular elements within a system. Not surprisingly, given how essential nutrient cycling is to primary production and food webs in ecosystems, and to our need to harness large amounts of primary and secondary production for human food (Vitousek et al. 1986), whole areas of study examine the elemental requirements for and deterrents to growth of organisms. Much of this focus is on important macronutrients in agricultural systems: nitrogen, phosphorus, calcium, and potassium. However, some elements that are needed for growth in trace amounts, often because of their presence in enzymes, also garner attention, although often because they are not only essential but may be toxic in high concentrations. For example, copper is a micronutrient required for plant growth, but it has been used extensively in high concentration as a toxin to control both parasites and algae in freshwater and marine systems (e.g., as copper sulfate). Other elements, such as the heavy metals (e.g., lead, cadmium, chromium), are highly toxic to organisms, but important in modern industry, even in what we think of as "green" technologies (e.g., the use of cadmium in some kinds of rechargeable batteries and solar panels). Still other elements are redistributed in large quantities as a by-product of industrial activity (e.g., mercury from coal-burning or waste incineration) and are problematic to organisms when in high concentration (see Chapter 15).

Human use of materials for fertilizer and industry, the changes we have made in land cover, and our combustion of large amounts of fossil fuels have led to profound changes in many element cycles (Vitousek 1994). We have affected element cycles through activities that lead to loss, retention, or redistribution of materials. For example, land-use changes often result in soil erosion, increased retention time of water and sediment in reservoirs, and movement of materials contained in crops from fields to cities. Globally, we have doubled the amount of nitrogen fixed from the atmosphere into reactive forms (see Chapter 7), and annually, humans mine more phosphorus for agricultural use than is weathered from rocks (see Chapter 8). For both elements this has greatly increased the transport from terrestrial to aquatic systems. Both the distribution and abundance of elements have taken on completely new geographical patterns as a result of human activity. These changes ripple throughout ecosystems and across continents as we will see in the next three chapters.

## WHAT IS AN ELEMENT CYCLE?

Element cycles involve the movement and transformation of biotic and abiotic forms of elements—particularly the elements that are essential to life—as they make their way through ecosystems. There are numerous pathways that both organic and inorganic materials follow, and generally they can be described as transformation between abiotic and biotic pools, within biotic pools, within abiotic pools, or physical movement while in any pool (Figure 5.1). Nearly all elements may be taken up by organisms and incorporated

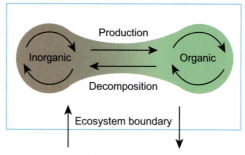

**FIGURE 5.1** Inorganic and organic materials follow many pathways as they move through ecosystems, but in general they flow between abiotic and biotic pools as they are taken up by organisms and incorporated into living biomass (production) and broken down (decomposition). They also move within inorganic pools (e.g., through soil weathering) and within organic pools (e.g., in trophic transfer). Materials may be added or lost from these pools as elements are transferred across ecosystem boundaries.

into living biomass (i.e., production). When organisms die, these organically bound forms are exposed to decomposers, which break down the organic material (i.e., decomposition) and either incorporate, liberate, or leave behind the elements that were previously part of other living organisms. Liberated elements may be used by other organisms—for example, uptake of inorganic nitrogen by plants—or may be bound in inorganic forms in the soil, as in potassium associated with clay minerals in the soil. Elements in the abiotic pool may be taken up by organisms or precipitate from solution as secondary minerals. And then there is weathering, which breaks down the physical and chemical structure of minerals, often in the presence of organic acids. The soluble products of weathering may be taken up by organisms or participate in further geochemical reactions.

Individual nutrient cycles are thus, not surprisingly, much more complex than this brief generalized view and are invariably linked to each other (Box 5.1; Figure 5.2). The spiraling of nutrients in streams provides an excellent example of how cycling can work in an

---

## BOX 5.1

## LINKED ELEMENTAL CYCLES

Both the living and nonliving world are mixtures of many elements. In the biotic world, there are over 20 elements essential for plant growth and reproduction, and another dozen or so that frequently occur in organisms (Schlesinger 1997). In the mineral world, oxygen, silicon, aluminum, and iron are the most abundant elements, but minerals may be composed of anywhere from 1 to more than 10 elements, depending on the size of the sample considered and the number of impurities in the crystal structure. So although we are used to thinking about element cycles separately, this is a convenience, not a common reality, and there is considerable interest in understanding the linkages among elemental cycles (Schlesinger et al. 2011 and other articles in *Frontiers in Ecology and the Environment* 2011, 9(1)).

There are many ways that elemental cycles can be linked, but two useful categories of linkage are those that have to do with (1) structural stoichiometry and (2) the functions of chemical reactivity and material and energy flow. On the structural side, stoichiometry describes the ratio of elements that are present as part of the fundamental structure of a material or organism, and linkages occur because structures need to be built with particular ratios of elements. Alternatively, element cycles can be linked because materials may move together down physical gradients or through chemical reactions where the "product" of the reaction is not itself an organism or mineral of interest. These two kinds of linkages are inevitably related to each other since much of the flow of material and energy goes to building the structure of organisms in ecological time, or minerals over geologic time, and these structures always involve stoichiometry. Nevertheless, the distinction can be useful in clarifying our thinking about the reasons for linkages across element cycles.

In an ecological setting, the most common linkages in elemental cycles occur because organisms contain roughly constant ratios of some elements. Redfield (1958) reported that marine phytoplankton typically contained carbon, nitrogen, and phosphorus atoms in the ratio 106:16:1. He also observed that ocean water, though variable from place to place, had those same three elements in the ratio of 105:15:1, and he went on to argue that the abundance of those elements in ocean water was controlled by the synthesis and decomposition of organic matter. He thus began a scientific conversation about the ways in which the abundance of elements in biotic and abiotic pools might be linked because of the structural requirements of organisms. Building on this idea, Sterner and Elser (2002) explored the stoichiometric requirements of primary producers and consumers and the ways in which these requirements influence consumption patterns of organisms and adaptations to different environments. They also developed further Redfield's ideas about the ways in which the stoichiometric structure of organisms, communities, and ecosystems are linked to ecological processes such as decomposition.

Linkages among elements also occur via chemical reactivity and material and energy flow. Redox reactions (appendix) are one of the most straightforward ways that element cycles are linked through chemical reactions. For example, the oxidation of carbon requires an electron acceptor, and if an environment is anoxic, but rich in free manganese, it can be used as an electron acceptor, thus linking the manganese cycle to that of carbon. While Redfield (1958) is often cited for his recognition of structural stoichiometry, he also calculated the amount of oxygen and sulfate that might be consumed to oxidize organic matter and compared this to observations about the abundance of oxygen and sulfate in the ocean. He then discussed the importance of linkages among decomposition, oxygen

availability, and redox reactions involving sulfur in regulating the oxygen concentration of the atmosphere. Thus, his work pointed out not only the linkages of carbon, nitrogen, and phosphorus cycles across ecosystem pools, but also the connection between those cycles and those of oxygen and sulfur both within the ocean and atmosphere.

Element cycles can also be linked because of chemical changes that occur as material moves through an ecosystem. For example, when acidic precipitation percolates through the soil, a variety of elemental cycles are brought together as the water moves through different environments. Water from the atmosphere may be rich in hydrogen, sulfur, and nitrogen, but it enters the soil where the elements most easily exchanged might include calcium, potassium, and sodium in much greater concentrations than in the atmosphere. Because the water encounters chemical gradients that include a different array of ions that are more or less tightly held than those entering in solution—and yet must maintain charge balance, the equivalency of positive and negative charges—there will be some ions left behind while others move into solution (Figure 5.2). Thus, the movement of water through the soil environment will result in a change in the water's chemical composition—and new associations of elements. Notice here that there are many other chemical reactions that can occur—for example, the precipitation of calcium carbonate or the chelation of metals with organic material—that bring new assemblages of elements into association: the linkage of biogeochemical cycles through move, stick, and change.

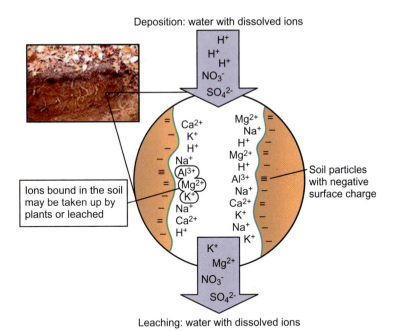

**FIGURE 5.2** Element cycles are linked as materials flow through ecosystems. Water transports elements such as hydrogen, sulfur, and nitrogen from the atmosphere to soil, where new elements such as calcium, potassium, sodium, and aluminum are encountered in the soil solution on the soil exchange complex. Interactions among these elements may result in a different assemblage of elements in soil solution—some of which may be taken up by plants or lost via leaching—thereby altering the chemical composition of water and changing what is retained in biotic and abiotic pools in the ecosystem.

ecosystem, and it reminds us that nutrient cycling is not static in space despite our attempts to picture such cycles in textbooks (Box 5.2; Figures 5.3 and 5.4).

## THE IMPORTANCE OF CHEMICAL PROPERTIES

Reactions of elements within nutrient cycles and the forms an element will take in various pools are controlled largely by their chemical properties—something that can be generalized in part from an element's position within the periodic table (Figure 5.5). Elements in the first two columns of the periodic table tend to give up electrons easily and so are commonly cations (ions with a positive charge) when free in ecological systems. They are also likely to be associated with negatively charged exchange sites in soils. In contrast, elements in the second-from-right column of the periodic table commonly acquire electrons and are usually present as anions (ions with a negative charge) in ecological systems. Elements in the farthest-right column, the noble gases, are highly unreactive, and they

## BOX 5.2

## NUTRIENT SPIRALING

In streams, currents move materials downstream at the same time that they are cycling between compartments. Stream ecologists think of this combination of processes as drawing out a nutrient cycle into a coil or spiral (Figure 5.3; see also Chapter 16) and have developed a formal framework to analyze nutrient spiraling, the combination of transport and cycling.

Three parameters are commonly calculated to describe nutrient uptake and transport in this framework. Areal uptake ($U$) is the rate at which a dissolved nutrient is removed from stream water, per area of streambed (in units of mass per area per time). This uptake could be biotic or abiotic.

Uptake length ($S_w$) is the distance that a dissolved nutrient travels before it is taken up by the streambed or the biota. $S_w$ obviously depends on both the intensity of nutrient uptake and the velocity of water flow; a short uptake length could result from rapid nutrient uptake, slow water flow, or both. Uptake velocity ($v_f$) is the apparent vertical velocity at which the nutrient is lost from the water column (as if it were sinking out from the water). Because $U$ and $v_f$ do not depend directly on the discharge or water velocity of a stream, they can be especially useful in removing the effects of these variables when comparing stream ecosystems. The spiraling parameters are related

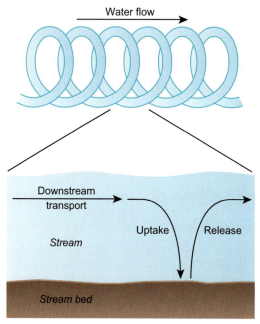

FIGURE 5.3    Nutrient spiraling, in which downstream transport draws out nutrient cycles into spirals.

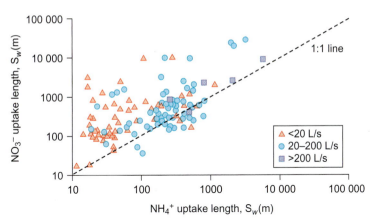

**FIGURE 5.4** Uptake length of two forms of dissolved inorganic nitrogen in streams of different sizes, synthesized from 54 published studies by Tank et al. (2008). Symbol colors and shapes differentiate streams by their discharge, the volume of water moving downstream per unit time. Streams with greater discharge tend to be larger. This analysis suggests several conclusions: (1) that ammonium is taken up much more rapidly (shorter uptake lengths) than nitrate, especially in small streams (those with lower discharge); (2) that uptake length increases with discharge (which is a function of current velocity and the cross-sectional area of the stream, so either or both of these factors can be important); (3) that there is a lot of variation in uptake length among streams; and (4) that there is a paucity of research on nutrient dynamics in larger (high discharge) streams (which are logistically difficult to study).

to one another by the following equations (Webster and Valett 2006):

$$U = v_f C$$
$$S_w = uzC/U$$
$$v_f = uz/S_w$$

where $u$ is the average current speed, $C$ is the nutrient concentration, and $z$ is the average water depth. In practice, spiraling parameters usually are estimated by adding nutrients (sometimes labeled with a stable isotope) along with a conservative (unreactive) tracer

such as chloride or bromide to a stream for several hours and then analyzing the changes in concentrations over time along the course of the stream (Tank et al. 2006; Webster and Valett 2006).

This framework has allowed stream ecologists to make rigorous comparisons of nutrient dynamics across streams (Figure 5.4 shows an example). Although this framework was developed for and has been applied almost exclusively to streams, it could be applied to any system in which transport is large compared to uptake.

have accumulated in the atmosphere. The most abundant highly electronegative element (an element with a strong affinity for electrons), oxygen, is likely to serve as an electron acceptor in redox reactions (appendix). Additionally, carbon, nitrogen, and sulfur—nonmetals in the interior of the periodic table that are essential nutrients for organisms—occur in ecological systems in many different oxidation states and hence take many forms within

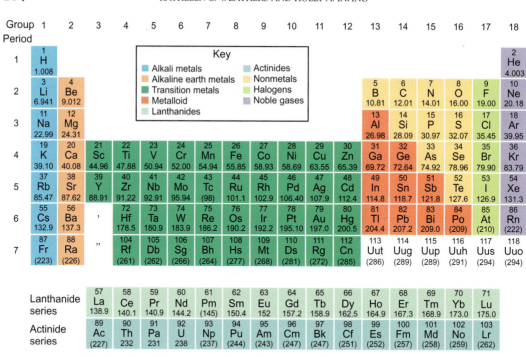

**FIGURE 5.5**  Periodic table of elements. An element's reactivity—determined in part by its chemical structure and hence position within the periodic table—is important in element cycling because it affects reactions within cycles and variety of forms an element will take as it moves among different pools in an ecosystem. *(From http:// periodic.lanl.gov/index.shtml.)*

ecosystems. The ecological importance of multiple oxidation states is illustrated by both carbon and nitrogen, and stands in contrast to phosphorus, as will be seen in the following chapters.

## MOVE, STICK, AND CHANGE: A SIMPLE FRAMEWORK FOR ELEMENTAL CYCLING

Much of the complexity of various element cycles and the movement and fate of materials in ecosystems can be encompassed by a simple three-part framework: *move, stick,* and *change.* Ecosystem scientists frequently ask what controls the *movement* of materials within or between pools or what mechanisms result in materials *sticking* within systems. The balance between these mechanisms will determine whether systems are gaining, losing, or in steady-state with respect to the material of interest. Understanding transformations— *changes* in materials from one chemical state or form to another—is also very important since an entity's state will often determine whether it moves or sticks.

Material *moves* both within and between systems. For example, carbon dioxide can move both through mixing within a lake and by flux from lake to atmosphere. Soil erosion can be described in terms of loss from a field or movement downstream in a river. In any case, the relevant questions are about the quantities of material that move and the mechanisms that move them. The vectors that move materials may be physical, chemical, or biological. Movement may occur down physical or chemical gradients (e.g., insect frass falling out of trees onto soil or diffusion of carbon dioxide away from areas of respiration in the soil). Biological vectors sometimes move materials against physical or chemical gradients (e.g., migrating salmon carry large amounts of nutrients upstream, against the current; Helfield and Naiman 2001). Biological vectors can also result in the increase in the concentration of toxins as they are transferred up trophic levels (e.g., bioaccumulation of mercury in small fish and its transfer to predatory fish or birds).

When an element *sticks* it is temporarily held in place somewhere within an ecosystem—for example, in the soil, a stream, an organism, or even the atmosphere. Since there is usually some kind of resistance to movement out of such a place, sticking is important in limiting losses from systems. Retention may occur on time scales ranging from fractions of seconds to millennia or more. Examples include sedimentation of organic material in a lake, precipitation of iron and sulfur as iron sulfide at the bottom of a lake, or retention of allochthonous carbon from a watershed through consumption by in-lake bacteria that are themselves consumed and eventually become part of fish biomass. As these examples illustrate, sticking, like movement, can be driven by physical, chemical, or biological mechanisms.

In the case of sticking, however, we are also often interested in how long something will remain (i.e., its residence time) and its availability within a system. For example, elemental mercury ($Hg^0$) has a residence time between five months and a year in the atmosphere (i.e., the average $Hg^0$ atom emitted will remain in the atmosphere for the better part of a year) and can be globally distributed. In contrast, reactive gaseous mercury (in the $Hg^{2+}$ form) is much more soluble. It has a residence time in the atmosphere of less than five days and usually is deposited within 300 km (and often much less) of its emission source. In a terrestrial example, a calcium ion associated with charged soil particles (i.e., the soil exchange complex; Figure 5.2) is more available for plant uptake than one that precipitates as calcium carbonate, so the former is more likely to cycle within the system or be lost sooner than the latter. In general, properties such as solubility, charge, size, reactivity, and specific gravity influence the stickiness of a substance.

Transformations—*changes* in materials from one chemical state or form to another—are important since an entity's state will often determine whether it moves or sticks, as well as its availability to the biota. Some of these changes are phase changes driven by energetic gains or losses from a system—for example, when snow melts. In other cases, there are changes in how an element is chemically bound—for example, whether iron is bound with phosphate or is free in solution at the sediment-water interface at the bottom of a lake. Some of these chemical changes may involve a switch between biotic and abiotic binding, say when potassium is released from plant roots and binds on the soil exchange complex. Alternatively, changes from one chemical form to another (either with or without a phase change) can be biologically mediated—for example, when sulfate is reduced to hydrogen sulfide by microbes using sulfur as an electron acceptor in metabolic processes (see appendix). Such changes in form are often coupled with changes in mobility. For example, liquid water is more easily lost from a watershed than snow, and calcium precipitated with phosphorus is much less likely to leach from the soil than when loosely bound on the soil exchange complex. These changes also can be important in storage or release of energy in the system, as with changes in latent heat as water moves among solid, liquid, and gas phases. Within a system, repeated changes that involve both abiotic and biotic binding are often thought of as cycling or spiraling—that is, the repeated transformation from inorganic to organic and from organic back to inorganic (Figures 5.1 and 5.3; Box 5.2).

To illustrate move, stick, and change, we use an example of (simplified) sulfur cycling in a northern hardwood watershed ecosystem, from atmospheric deposition through leaching loss to stream water (Figure 5.6). Sulfur, more specifically, sulfate ($SO_4^{2-}$), has been used as a tracer of atmospheric deposition (e.g., Weathers et al. 2006), because it moves from atmosphere to the forest floor, and into ground and stream water with little sticking, especially where acidic deposition is prevalent. However, the largest long-term pools of sulfur in these northeastern ecosystems are in the biomass and soils. Hence, when a forest is our frame of reference, we can see sulfur *moving* as sulfate from atmosphere to

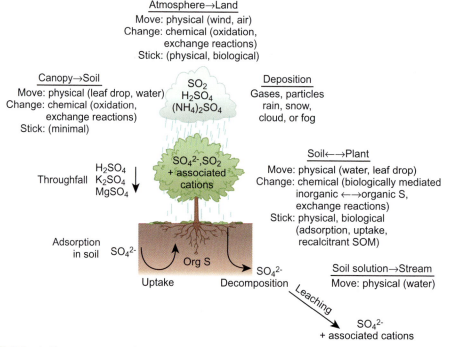

FIGURE 5.6   Sulfur *moves*, *sticks*, and *changes* as it cycles through a northern hardwood ecosystem. Sulfur may enter a forest through atmospheric deposition of, for example, gaseous sulfur dioxide ($SO_2$), dissolved sulfuric acid ($H_2SO_4$), or dissolved or particulate ammonium sulfate (($NH_4$)$_2SO_4$). In the canopy, ions such as potassium ($K^+$) and magnesium ($Mg^{2+}$) may be more abundant than in the atmosphere, so these may be picked up and become associated with sulfate ($SO_4^{2-}$) in solution as water moves through the canopy. Sulfate moves readily from atmosphere to forest, soil, and stream water with little sticking and usually few chemical changes. Sulfur sticks when taken up by plants and adsorbed in soils, and this may or may not involve a change in form. Sulfur can change between abiotic and biotic forms when it is taken up by plants or later when organic material is mineralized from organic to inorganic forms during decomposition (SOM = soil organic matter). The loss of sulfur from a forested ecosystem is most often as sulfate in solution, although in anoxic soils sulfate reduction can lead to the production of hydrogen sulfide gas (appendix).

forest, soil, and stream water, but *sticking* when sulfate is taken up by plants and incorporated into biomass (also a *change*). Later *changes* in the chemical form of sulfur—from organic to inorganic—as litter decomposes allows the sulfur to be more easily lost from the system. Thus, a description of the sulfur cycle in a forest includes movement among pools (atmosphere, soil, plant, water), sticking within the system (particularly in organic forms here), and transformation between inorganic and organic forms.

## WHAT KINDS OF QUESTIONS ARE ASSOCIATED WITH ELEMENT CYCLES?

Ecosystem scientists ask many kinds of questions about element cycles and make comparisons among elements and across ecosystems. For example, we might be interested in whether two systems retain potassium in the same way or whether differences in soils or crops lead to one farm field being "leakier" than another. Alternatively, a scientist might be interested in the length of time an element spends in a system—its residence time. Residence time questions are particularly important in studies of element transport and sequestration, say, how long carbon arising from fossil fuel burning might be retained in terrestrial ecosystems or in the ocean. As you will see in the following chapters, a great deal is already known about how ecologically important the cycle of elements within and between systems is, but there are important fundamental questions remaining—for example, the interplay between biotic and abiotic factors in the release of phosphorus from lake sediment. Some of these questions, as well as others that might be asked in a management context, have implications for our actions as individuals and communities, as well as the policies we make to mitigate disturbances within ecosystems that arise from anthropogenic stressors (see Chapters 12–16).

The next three chapters focus on carbon, nitrogen, and phosphorus cycling. We chose these three elements because they are critical to life. They also provide important contrasts in their sources, reactivity, and linkages to each other and across ecosystems. We encourage readers to explore how other elements move, stick, and change in and among ecosystems in Schlesinger and Bernhardt (2013). In fact, before you launch into the next chapters, we encourage you to consider a hypothetical example: suppose a new element—fogidium—has been discovered and your task is to research its importance in ecosystem science. Take 10 minutes to identify what you need to know about fogidium to assess its importance in the context of ecosystem science. Keep this list in mind when reading about carbon, nitrogen, and phosphorus (below is a list of what other students have identified).

## SOME CHARACTERISTICS IMPORTANT FOR UNDERSTANDING AN ELEMENT'S ROLE IN ECOSYSTEMS

- Number of oxidation states
- Whether it is involved in oxidation-reduction reactions

- Reactivity
- Whether it is commonly a cation or anion (or neither) in solution
- Whether it is a metal or nonmetal
- Electronegativity
- Half-life
- Toxicity
- Ability to bind with common elements
- Kind of bonding that is common (e.g., ionic, covalent)
- Importance in biological processes
- Phase (solid, liquid, or gas) at Earth surface temperature and pressure
- Solubility in water—for elemental and ionic forms
- Solubility in organic solvents
- Volatility
- Whether it has industrial applications (affects human extraction and dispersion)
- How common it is
- The locations where it is found in high concentrations without human alteration of its cycle
- Likelihood of its incorporation into living organisms
- Likelihood of its binding with organic matter
- Likelihood of its chelation and stability of chelates
- Whether it bioaccumulates or biomagnifies

# References

Helfield, J.M., Naiman, R.J., 2001. Effects of salmon-derived nitrogen on riparian forest growth and implications for stream productivity. Ecology 82, 2403—2409.

Redfield, A.C., 1958. The biological control of chemical factors in the environment. Am. Sci. 46, 205—221.

Schlesinger, W.H., Bernhardt, E.S., 2013. Biogeochemistry: An analysis of global change, third ed. Academic Press, San Diego.

Schlesinger, W.H., Cole, J.J., Finzi, A.C., Holland, E.A., 2011. Introduction to coupled biogeochemical cycles. Fron. Ecol. Environ. 9, 5—8.

Sterner, R.W., Elser, J.J., 2002. Ecological stoichiometry: The biology of elements from molecules to the biosphere. Princeton University Press, Princeton, NJ.

Tank, J.L., Bernot, M.J., Rosi-Marshall, E.J., 2006. Nitrogen limitation and uptake. In: Hauer, F.R., Lamberti, G.A. (Eds.), Methods in stream ecology, second ed. Academic Press, Amsterdam, The Netherlands, pp. 213—238.

Tank, J.L., Rosi-Marshall, E.J., Baker, M.A., Hall, R.O., 2008. Are large rivers just big streams? A pulse method to quantify nitrogen demand in a large river. Ecology 89, 2935—2945.

Vitousek, P.M., 1994. Beyond global warming: Ecology and global change. Ecology 75, 1861—1876.

Vitousek, P.M., Ehrlich, P.R., Ehrlich, A.H., Matson, P.A., 1986. Human appropriation of the products of photosynthesis. BioScience 36, 368—373.

Weathers, K.C., Simkin, S.M., Lovett, G.M., Lindberg, S.E., 2006. Empirical modeling of atmospheric deposition in mountainous landscapes. Ecol. Appl. 16, 1590—1607.

Webster, J.R., Valett, H.M., 2006. Solute dynamics. In: Hauer, F.R., Lamberti, G.A. (Eds.), Methods in stream ecology, second ed. Academic Press, Amsterdam, The Netherlands, pp. 169—185.

# 6

# The Carbon Cycle
## With a Brief Introduction to Global Biogeochemistry

*Jonathan J. Cole*

**Cary Institute of Ecosystem Studies, Millbrook, NY**

## WHY STUDY THE CARBON CYCLE?

There are multiple reasons to study the carbon cycle. For one, carbon (C) is the major building block of all known life and is the second-most important element by mass (after oxygen) in organisms. Further, C is chemically versatile and can form a diverse array of organic and inorganic compounds. In the atmosphere, two carbon compounds, carbon dioxide and methane, are potent greenhouse gases that are on the rise due to human activity. In many ways the study of climate change is the study of the global C cycle.

In this chapter we will examine the C cycle starting at the global scale at several time frames and then focus on the C cycle in a few exemplar ecosystems to illustrate certain aspects. First, let us review the biogeochemistry of C and what a biogeochemical cycle is.

## BIOGEOCHEMISTRY OF CARBON

In a biogeochemical cycle, an element can cycle between chemical forms; between major global reservoirs (e.g., biosphere, lithosphere, and atmosphere); between smaller ecosystems (forest to river in a landscape); or between reservoirs within an ecosystem (soil to plant, etc.). The chemical forms can cycle among physical states (gas, solid, liquid) or redox states. No element cycles in isolation. Rather, there are a number of simultaneous interacting cycles of multiple elements. When we discuss the cycle of an individual element, we are just choosing to focus on one member of an interacting set of parts. Although focusing on the biogeochemical cycle of a single element is a useful heuristic tool, we should keep in mind that this cycle is a small part, or a narrow view, of many coupled biogeochemical cycles involving multiple elements (Schlesinger et al. 2011). As biogeochemical transformations are partly mediated by oxidation-reduction reactions, before proceeding it may be helpful to review the section on redox chemistry (appendix).

# THE CARBON ATOM AND ITS CHEMISTRY

Carbon can exist in various compounds in different oxidation states: all states from $-4$ to $+4$ are possible. From the point of view of a C atom, the oxidation state increases (becomes more positive or less negative) if that atom is bound to either more O atoms, fewer H atoms, or both. For example, $CH_4$ is a highly reduced form of C (oxidation state is $-4$), whereas $CO_2$ is highly oxidized (oxidation state is $+4$). Organic matter is always substantially more reduced than $CO_2$ and moderately more oxidized than $CH_4$. To move C from a more oxidized to a more reduced state requires the input of energy; to move it to a more oxidized state releases energy (as long as an appropriate chemical oxidant, also called an *electron acceptor,* is present). With sufficient activation energy, reduced forms of C (e.g., $CH_4$, oil, sugars) will be oxidized in the presence of $O_2$ and some other electron acceptors (e.g., $SO_4^{-2}$, $NO_3^-$, $Fe^{+3}$). Biological enzymes, by reducing the amount of activation energy required for certain redox reactions to occur, catalyze many very important biogeochemical fluxes that would otherwise occur at much slower rates.

## Key Biologic Reactions in the Carbon Cycle

The reduction of $CO_2$ to organic matter using light energy (photosynthesis) or chemical energy (chemosynthesis) is the source of essentially all organic matter on Earth (see Chapter 2). The oxidation of inorganic compounds in chemosynthesis generates the energy that some organisms use to reduce $CO_2$ to organic C compounds. The oxidation of organic C (catabolic processes) provides the energy for most heterotrophic organisms.

Carbon is involved in nearly every energy-generating and most energy-consuming reactions in biology. Outlined next are some of the most important energetic reactions in the biosphere.

### Oxygenic Photosynthesis

This is the major photosynthetic pathway for modern plants and photosynthetic microorganisms. In oxygenic photosynthesis, $O_2$ is generated and $CO_2$ is reduced to organic compounds; light is the energy source and water is the electron (hydrogen) donor. Oxygenic photosynthesis first appeared on Earth about 2 billion years before present (YBP) with the evolution of the cyanobacteria. A general stoichiometric scheme for oxygenic photosynthesis is:

$$CO_2 + H_2O + light \longrightarrow (CH_2O) + O_2 \qquad (6.1)$$

where $CH_2O$ represents the initial carbohydrate products of photosynthesis.

### Anoxygenic Photosynthesis

Anoxygenic photosynthesis creates organic C from $CO_2$ without generating $O_2$. This was the earliest type of photosynthesis on Earth and is present today in major bacterial groups such as the purple sulfur bacteria. This is another form of $CO_2$ fixation, in which light is again the energy source but compounds other than water (e.g., $H_2$ or $H_2S$) are the electron donors. On modern Earth, anoxygenic photosynthesis is restricted to environments such as the oxic-anoxic interface in stratified lakes, where there is both the necessary reduced inorganic compounds (e.g., $H_2$ or $H_2S$) and light. As an example, the stoichiometry for the photosynthetic sulfur bacteria is:

$$CO_2 + 2H_2S + light \longrightarrow (CH_2O) + H_2O + 2S \qquad (6.2)$$

### Chemosynthesis

This is another form of $CO_2$ fixation in which the energy for reducing the $CO_2$ to organic matter comes not from light but from the oxidation of reduced chemical compounds (e.g., $NH_4$, $CH_4$, $H_2S$, $Fe^{+2}$) from the environment. Most, but not all, chemosynthesis requires $O_2$ to oxidize these compounds. Thus, $H_2S$ is oxidized by $O_2$ to elemental sulfur, thiosulfate, or sulfate, and $CO_2$ is reduced to organic C. There are a few examples of chemosynthesis in the absence of $O_2$, such as *Thiobacillus ferrooxidans*, which gets energy under anoxic conditions by oxidizing reduced iron using sulfate as the electron acceptor.

In most cases of chemosynthesis the reduced inorganic compound involved was ultimately produced by photosynthesis, so chemosynthesis is not necessarily independent from photosynthesis from the point of view of energy. However, some reduced sulfur and iron compounds are present in minerals and have been produced geothermally. In deep-sea hot (hydrothermal) vents, entire ecosystems are supported by the oxidation of geothermal sulfides by chemosynthetic bacteria, some of which are endosymbionts in invertebrates (Stewart et al. 2005). Some examples of chemosynthesis follow. The part of the equation shown is just the part that generates energy. This energy is used to reduce $CO_2$ to carbohydrate in a way similar to the energy generated from photosynthesis; we do not show the reduction of $CO_2$ to organic C for simplicity.

| Common Name | Exemplar Organism | Equation |
|---|---|---|
| Sulfide oxidation | *Thiobacillus* | $H_2S + 0.5O_2 \longrightarrow S^{\circ} + H_2O$ |
| Sulfur oxidation | *Thiobacillus* | $S^{\circ} + 1.5\,O_2 + H_2O \longrightarrow H_2SO_4$ |
| Nitrification has two parts, ammonium oxidation and nitrite oxidation | | |
| Ammonium oxidation | | |
| | *Nitrobacter* | $NH_4^+ + 1.5\,O_2 \longrightarrow NO_2^- + 2H^+ + 2H_2O$ |
| Nitrite oxidation | | |
| | *Nitrosomonas* | $NO_2^- + 0.5\,O_2 \longrightarrow NO_3^-$ |

### Oxic Respiration

Oxic respiration is the major energy-generating reaction in aerobic organisms. This is the most modern form of biological oxidation of organic matter in which $O_2$ is the oxidant and organic matter the reductant. Oxic respiration is the form of respiration that we humans and all metazoans use. $CO_2$ and $H_2O$ and energy are the end products. It is oxygenic photosynthesis in reverse. Oxic respiration did not occur until about 2 billion YBP when significant oxygen had accumulated in the atmosphere, following the evolution of oxygenic photosynthesis (Kennedy et al. 2006). The basic stoichiometry for oxic respiration is:

$$C_6H_{12}O_6 + 6O_2 \longrightarrow 6CO_2 + 6H_2O + \text{energy output} \qquad (6.3)$$

## Anaerobic Respiration

This is the oxidation of organic matter using something other than $O_2$ as the electron acceptor. With the exception of fermentations and some reports of the use of nitrate as an electron acceptor in protozoa and diatoms (see Kamp et al. 2011; Pina-Ochoa et al. 2010), these pathways are restricted to prokaryotes. Anaerobic respiration is extremely common in anoxic environments such as wet soils, sediments, and stratified water bodies. About half of all modern decomposition goes through anaerobic respiration (Howarth and Teal 1991). The most important electron acceptors are $SO_4$, $NO_3$, and $Fe^{+3}$. The end products are inorganic C ($HCO_3^-$ or $CO_2$), energy, and more reduced forms of the electron acceptor (e.g., sulfide [or elemental S or thiosulfate], nitrite [or nitrous oxide or $N_2$], or $Fe^2$).

| Common Name | Exemplar Organism | Equation |
|---|---|---|
| Denitrification | *Pseudomonas, Bacillus,* many others | $5[CH_2O] + 4NO_3^- + 4H^+ \longrightarrow 5CO_2 + 2N_2 + 7H_2O$ |
| Sulfate reduction | *Desulfovibrio* | $CH_3COO^- + 2H^+ + SO_4^{2-} \longrightarrow 2CO_2 + 2H_2O + HS^-$ |
| Methanogensis | | |
| (1) acetoclastic | *Methanosarcina* | $CH_3COOH \longrightarrow CO_2 + CH_4$ |
| $H_2/CO_2$ | *Methanococcus* | $4H_2 + CO_2 \longrightarrow CH_4 + 2H_2O$ |
| (2) Glucose fermentation | Many yeasts, some bacteria | $C_6H_{12}O_6 \longrightarrow 2CH_3CH_2OH + 2CO_2$ |

Fermentative decomposition is familiar in the making of cheese and wine, but it is also a key decomposition pathway. It is like anaerobic respiration in that oxygen is not required. Unlike aerobic or anaerobic respiration, there is no external electron acceptor. Rather, an organic molecule is split such that one portion becomes more oxidized and one portion more reduced. There are a number of different biochemical variations of the fermentation process using different organic substrates and producing different organic end products. Glycolysis is a common type of fermentation in which glucose is fermented to pyruvate and protons. Glycolysis occurs in the cells of most higher organisms (including yeasts and humans) as a precursor to both aerobic and anaerobic respiration.

Methane ($CH_4$) is most often formed by the fermentative oxidation of acetic acid into $CH_4$ (more reduced) and $CO_2$ (more oxidized). This is the acetoclastic (e.g., formation of methane from the fermentation of acetate) pathway mentioned previously. Methane can also be formed by the reduction of $CO_2$ using $H_2$ as the electron donor (called $H_2/CO_2$ methanogenesis previously). This latter type of methanogenesis fits the description of anaerobic respiration rather than a fermentation. Methanogenesis is restricted to a narrow taxonomic group of bacteria but is a very common process in anaerobic environments, particularly in freshwaters and wetlands.

## INORGANIC CARBON

The amount of inorganic C far exceeds the amount of organic C on Earth (Table 6.1; Figure 6.1) and also participates in a number of chemical transformations. The major molecules in the inorganic part of the carbon cycle are $CO_2$, a gas that readily dissolves in water; $HCO_3^-$ (bicarbonate), which exists only as a dissolved form; and $CO_3^=$ (carbonate), which can be dissolved or solid and forms major mineral deposits in the ocean and in uplifted marine sediments on land (limestones and dolomites).

## INORGANIC CARBON IN WATERS

Dissolved inorganic carbon (DIC = dissolved $CO_2 + HCO_3^- + CO_3^=$) is present in all natural waters. Dissolved $CO_2$ actually consists of two pools, free $CO_2$ and $H_2CO_3$. At equilibrium with each other, which is extremely rapid, $H_2CO_3$ is about 1/1000 of the concentration of free $CO_2$. Neither $CO_2$ nor $H_2CO_3$ is charged; they interchange readily and behave as one pool in chemical reactions. Thus, we treat $CO_2 + H_2CO_3$ as a single pool and refer to it as either $H_2CO_3^*$ or simply as $CO_2$. $H_2CO_3^*$ is also known as carbonic acid because it can behave as a proton ($H^+$) and a bicarbonate ion ($HCO_3^-$). It is a weak acid but very prevalent in the biosphere and extremely important in processes like weathering and ocean acidification (follows).

The concentration of DIC varies from less than 0.24 mg C/L (20 μM) in acidic, poorly buffered waters to more than 60 mg C/L (5000 μM) in highly alkaline hard waters, but ranges between about 1.2 and 120 mg C/L (100 to 10,000 μM) in most freshwater and averages about 29 mg C/L (2400 μM) in the ocean. DIC is usually the most abundant form of C in water. Although $CO_2$, like other gases, readily exchanges with the

TABLE 6.1 Major reservoirs of C on Earth. Units are in Pg C (1 Pg = $10^{15}$ g and is the same as 1 billion metric tons).

| Reservoir | C Mass (Pg) | Comments | Reference |
|---|---|---|---|
| Earth | 100,000,000 | Poorly known | Schlesinger (1997) |
| Sedimentary rocks—carbonate | 65,000,000 | | Schlesinger (1997) |
| Sedimentary rocks—organic compounds | 16,000,000 | | Schlesinger (1997) |
| Marine dissolved carbonates (DIC) | 38,000 | Sum of dissolved $CO_2$, $HCO_3^-$, and $CO_3^=$ | Sundquist and Viser (2005) |
| Large lake sediments | 19,510 | Most in African rift lakes | Alin and Johnson (2007) |
| Fossil fuel (coal, oil, natural gas) | 5200 | Known plus likely reserves | Sundquist and Viser (2005) |
| Terrestrial soils | 2150 | | Sundquist and Viser (2005) |
| Atmospheric $CO_2$ | 750 | Modern, industrial, rising | Houghton (2005) |
| Reactive marine organic C | 650 | | Sundquist and Viser (2005) |
| Terrestrial vegetation | 560 | | Houghton (2005) |
| Marine biota | 2 | | Houghton (2005) |

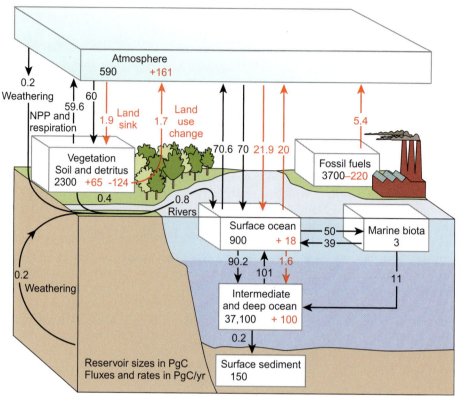

**FIGURE 6.1** Simplified diagram of some of the key fluxes in the global carbon cycle. The values inside the boxes are standing stocks (in Pg C); the arrows represent annual fluxes (Pg C/y). The black arrows and numbers show the preindustrial values of standing stocks and fluxes; the red arrows and numbers indicate the changes due to anthropogenic activity. Note there are some differences in the values shown on this figure and in Table 6.1 due to different levels of aggregation and different time periods for the estimates. *(The diagram is redrawn from Climate Change (2007): The Physical Scientific Basis, Intergovernmental Panel on Climate Change.)*

atmosphere, even the surface waters of most inland waters are usually greatly supersaturated with respect to the atmosphere. A number of factors cause this disequilibrium, including respiration in excess of photosynthesis, $CO_2$ inputs from ground water, or the precipitation of $CaCO_3$, which releases $CO_2$ (see Cole et al. 1994).

Inorganic C is intimately involved in many of the acid-base reactions in soils and water. Bicarbonate and carbonate constitute the major buffers in most natural waters and thus account for most of the acid-neutralizing capacity (ANC; also called alkalinity). Free $CO_2$ is the most dynamic of the constituents of DIC and is the dominant acid in most natural waters. The ratio of $CO_2$ to $HCO_3^-$ and $CO_3^=$ is the major control of pH in most natural waters.

## INORGANIC CARBON ON LAND AND SEDIMENTS

Solid-phase carbonate-bearing minerals on land are found principally in limestones and related dolomite rocks, as well as some soils in arid regions (caliche; Schlesinger 1982). Most of these terrestrial rocks are of marine origin. The amount of carbonate in rocks and soils is 60 to $100 \times 10^6$ Pg, the planet's largest reservoir of C (Table 6.1; Figure 6.1). The amount of fossil fuels is trivial in comparison (about $4-6 \times 10^3$ Pg). Shallow-water marine sediments contain large amounts of carbonate in so-called carbonate ooze, which originated in the plankton as the carbonate shells of phytoplankton (principally coccolitho-phorids) and animals that make calcite or aragonite (an alternative mineral form of calcium carbonate) shells. Thus, much of the inorganic C deposits were formed biologically.

## INORGANIC CARBON IN THE ATMOSPHERE

The only abundant form of inorganic carbon in the atmosphere is $CO_2$. The modern atmosphere contains about 750 Pg of C as $CO_2$ and this quantity is on the rise (Table 6.1; Figure 6.1). Carbon dioxide comes principally from decomposition of organic matter and the burning of organic matter, with much smaller amounts from the formation of carbonate shells by corals and other marine organisms. Humans contribute to the formation of $CO_2$ by combusting fossil fuels, converting forests to cleared land (which is often accompanied by burning and accelerated decomposition; Houghton 1995), and by making cement from carbonate rock (Worrell et al. 2001).

## KEY REACTIONS FOR INORGANIC CARBON

*Chemical weathering*: Dissolved bicarbonates are formed principally by the dissolution of carbonate and aluminosilicate minerals (e.g., andalusite or kyanite) by $CO_2$ and water. The $CO_2$ involved in these reactions comes largely from biological respiration. When $CO_2$ dissolves in water it forms carbonic acid, which is the major acid that dissolves carbonates (earlier).

Carbonate weathering:

$$CO_2 + H_2O + CaCO_3 \longrightarrow Ca^{++} + 2HCO_3^- \qquad (6.4)$$

$$CaMg(CO_3)_2 \longrightarrow Ca^{++} + Mg^{++} + 4HCO_3^- \qquad (6.5)$$

Silicate weathering:

$$2CO_2 + 3H_2O + CaSiO_3 \longrightarrow Ca^{++} + 2HCO_3^- + H_4SiO_4 \qquad (6.6)$$

$$2CO_2 + 3H_2O + MgSiO_3 \longrightarrow Mg^{++} + 2HCO_3^- + H_4SiO_4 \qquad (6.7)$$

## REVERSE WEATHERING AND CARBONATE FORMATION

The weathering reactions generate bicarbonate from clays and limestones. Reverse weathering creates clays and limestones (Michalopoulos and Aller 1995; MacKenzie and Kump 1995). Chemically these reverse weathering reactions can be written as Eqs. 6.4 through 6.7 running in reverse.

## CLAY FORMATION

Although carbonate precipitation (see below) is relatively fast (seconds) the formation of alumino-silicate clays (reverse weathering) is very slow (millions of years). The net reaction is comparable to Eqs. 6.6 and 6.7 in reverse: An $HCO_3^-$ ion from solution becomes incorporated as an $OH^-$ in the clay and causes a $CO_2$ to be released. This reverse weathering is a major control of atmospheric $CO_2$ on long (e.g., millions of years) time-scales (Berner and Kothavala 2001). The combination of weathering and reverse weathering of alumino-silicate minerals is a major way that the silica and C cycles intersect (Conley 2002). Another way that silica affects the global C balance is through its effect on primary production in the ocean (Dugdale and Wilkerson 1998).

## CARBONATE PRECIPITATION

When carbonates are formed, either biotically or abiotically (the reverse of Eqs. 6.4 and 6.5), $CO_2$ is released. These reactions take place mostly in the ocean, but also in some freshwaters. The building of coral reefs is basically this same process and is a source of $CO_2$ to the water column. Over time there can be chemical changes in the cations associated with anions from a domination of $Ca^{++}$ to a mixture of $Ca^{++}$ and $Mg^{++}$. The replacement of $Ca^{++}$ by $Mg^{++}$ causes limestones to become dolomites, which have significantly different biogeochemical properties and different uses by humans. Dolomite is harder than calcite limestone and weathers more slowly. Hence, dolomite is preferred over limestone in many construction applications.

In summary, C is found in both organic and inorganic forms and is involved in all aspects of photosynthesis and both aerobic and anaerobic respiration. C is also controlled by a number of abiotic reactions including chemical precipitation and weathering. The inorganic C system is the major buffer in the sea and in most freshwaters; dissolved $CO_2$ is an important acid in weathering reactions.

# THE PRESENT-DAY GLOBAL CARBON CYCLE AND THE GREENHOUSE EFFECT

You probably know quite a bit about the modern global C balance because of its connection to climate change. As we pointed out in the beginning of this chapter, the global C cycle is most often looked at from the point of view of Earth's atmosphere as the response. Because $CO_2$ is a greenhouse gas (GHG), its rising concentration in the atmosphere traps heat and leads to global warming and other interrelated climatic changes (Houghton and Woodwell 1989). Concern about GHGs has led to a great deal of research about what actually controls atmospheric $CO_2$ (IPCC 2007). We will not discuss climate change in this chapter but we will look in detail about the global C cycle from the perspective of atmospheric $CO_2$. Figure 6.2(a) shows the concentration of $CO_2$ measured on a high mountain in Hawaii, Mauna Loa (Keeling et al. 1995; Tans and Keeling 2012). This site provides a reasonably accurate sample of the atmosphere of the Northern Hemisphere. Two important patterns are apparent in the time trend: mean atmospheric $CO_2$ has increased by about 30% since measurements began in 1958, and there is an annual cycle in $CO_2$ concentrations. The seasonal oscillation is caused by the seasonal variation in the balance between photosynthesis and respiration in the Northern Hemisphere. During the growing season the net uptake of $CO_2$ by photosynthesis is larger than the net release by respiration; in the winter the reverse is true. Thus, $CO_2$ is higher in the winter than in the summer. This oscillation in atmospheric $CO_2$ is a profound example of the influence of biology on elemental cycles. The long-term increasing trend is the result of anthropogenic activities,

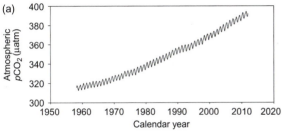

(a)

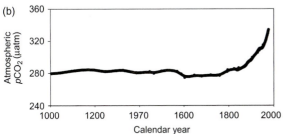

(b)

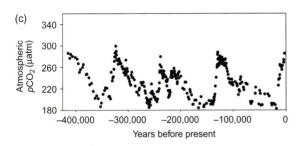

(c)

FIGURE 6.2 Variation in atmospheric $CO_2$ over three timescales. Panel (a) shows direct measurements of atmospheric $CO_2$ at Mauna Loa, Hawaii. The data for panels (b) and (c) come from ice cores for (b) the Law Dome ice core in Antarctica and (c) the Vostok ice core in Antarctica. The x-axis for panel (c) is in years before present; for panels (a) and (b) the x-axis is the calendar year. *((a) is drawn from data available at Dr. Pieter Tans, NOAA/ESRL (www.esrl.noaa.gov/gmd/ccgg/trends/) and Dr. Ralph Keeling, Scripps Institution of Oceanography (scrippsco2.ucsd.edu/); (b) is drawn from data available at http://cdiac.ornl.gov/trends/co2/lawdome.html (Etheridge et al. 1996); and (c) is drawn from data available at http://www.ncdc.noaa.gov/paleo/icecore/antarctica/vostok/vostok.html (Petit et al. 1999).)*

mostly the combustion of fossil fuel. There are several lines of evidence that, together, underscore this fact; two are described as follows (see IPCC for further reading at http://www.ipcc.ch/):

1. Global mass balance. In Table 6.2 we show the major inputs and output of $CO_2$ to and from the atmosphere for the decade of 1990 to 2000. We chose this decade because the numbers were published in a peer-reviewed journal (Schimel et al. 2001) and have been well vetted. Newer sources list larger anthropogenic inputs (Field and Raupach 2004), but the basic story has not changed. In Table 6.2 we see that the combustion of fossil fuel puts about 5.5 Pg of C/y as $CO_2$ into the atmosphere, with an additional ~1 Pg of C/y from land-use changes (basically the cutting of forests, mostly in the tropics; Dixon et al. 1994). This 6.5 Pg C/y anthropogenic source is larger than the observed rate of increase in the atmosphere (3.1 Pg C/y), so there is more than enough anthropogenic $CO_2$ to account for the atmospheric increase. The difference between $CO_2$ emissions and the gain in storage in the atmosphere represents C that is either

TABLE 6.2   Balance of atmospheric $CO_2$ during the 1990s.

| Flux of $CO_2$ Category | Rate (Pg C/y) | Comments |
|---|---|---|
| Fossil fuel plus forest clearing emissions to the atmosphere | 6.5 | Estimated from national records and additionally confirmed by changes in $^{13}C$ and $^{14}C$ of the atmosphere. |
| Measured increase in atmosphere | 3.1 | Direct measurement. Known well from Mauna Loa and other observatories. |
| Ocean $CO_2$ uptake | −1.5 | Semidirect measurement based on both DIC concentrations and the penetration of bomb $^{14}C$ into the ocean. Largely a physical-diffusion sink. |
| Net "terrestrial sink" | −1.9 | Estimated by difference between the other terms. Poorly constrained. Must be biological if on land. |

Positive values are inputs into the atmosphere; negative values are losses from the atmosphere. The net "terrestrial sink" sometimes called the "missing sink" is inferred by the difference among the other sources and sinks. (*Data from Schimel et al. 2001.*)

sequestered into the oceans (1.5 Pg C/y) or on the continents (1.9 Pg C/y). The estimates of both fossil fuel combustion and oceanic uptake are considered to be relatively precise. The sequestration on the continents is basically estimated by difference and not considered to be very precise. In fact, this net terrestrial sequestration in literature published in the 1980s and 1990s is referred to as the "missing C sink" largely because it has proven difficult to locate where on land or by what processes this sequestration occurs (Hobbie et al. 1985; Woodwell et al. 1998; Fan et al. 1998). While there is active research into the missing sink, the processes causing it have not yet been resolved but the sink is likely on land (Tans et al. 1990).

2. The changes in C isotopes ($^{13}C$, a stable isotope, and $^{14}C$, a radioactive isotope) in the atmosphere. The isotopic make-up of atmospheric $CO_2$ provides a second line of evidence (Tans et al. 1979). Photosynthetic uptake strongly favors the lighter isotope of C ($^{12}C$). Thus, any plant biomass or subsequent product is depleted (depleted here means has less of the particular isotope) in both $^{13}C$ and $^{14}C$ compared to $CO_2$ in the atmosphere. The decline over time of $^{13}C$ in the atmosphere shows that the new source of $CO_2$ ultimately had a photosynthetic origin (Bacastow et al. 1996). Radioactive decay of $^{14}C$ further depletes this isotope from material that was produced by photosynthesis in an earlier time (Jain et al. 1995). With a half-life of 5780 years, material that is many millions of years old, such as oil and coal, has essentially no remaining $^{14}C$. The decline over time of $^{14}C$ in the atmosphere tells us that the source of the increased $CO_2$ was highly depleted in $^{14}C$, which points to fossil fuel as the likely source. The isotopic changes in atmospheric $CO_2$ over time, first reported by Suess (1980), are also in quantitative agreement with the mass balances of total $CO_2$.

## The Role of the Oceans

The sequestration of $CO_2$ on land and in the ocean are dominated by fundamentally different processes. On land the major sink is storage or export of organic matter ultimately from photosynthesis. What remains after plant, animal, and microbial respiration (e.g., NEP; see Chapter 2) is either exported to the sea or stored in biomass, soils, or freshwater sediments. Both the export and storage terms are part of terrestrial C sequestration, and in both cases the material is organic C.

In the ocean, nearly all the GPP of phytoplankton is respired within the mixed zone of the ocean. Additional decomposition occurs as particles sink through the deep-water column. Only about 0.12 Pg C/y is stored (long term) as organic C in marine sediments, which is less than 10% of the oceanic total $CO_2$ sink. This part of the oceanic sink is called the *biological pump* because organisms are actively involved. The larger oceanic $CO_2$ sink is predominantly a physical-chemical one, called the *diffusion pump* because it is caused by physical and chemical processes. Rising atmospheric $CO_2$ concentrations create a gradient causing $CO_2$ to diffuse into the ocean. There it meets two major fates. Downwelling ocean water brings newly equilibrated surface water into the deep ocean where it is isolated from the atmosphere for about 1000 years (the mixing time of the oceanic water column). Seawater also has high concentrations of bicarbonate and carbonate. Dissolved $CO_2$ reacts with $CO_3^=$ to form two ions of $HCO_3^-$:

$$CO_2(aq) + H_2O + CO_3^= = 2HCO_3^- \qquad (6.8)$$

Seawater is well buffered, meaning that it can absorb a lot of $CO_2$ with little change in pH and little change in the concentration of free $CO_2$. Depending on location and temperature, surface seawater needs to absorb about 10 moles of $CO_2$ for the $CO_2$ concentration to increase by 1 mole. So the total DIC increases much faster than does dissolved $CO_2$. You learned earlier that dissolved $CO_2$ is an acid. When the carbonate system is the dominant buffer, as it is in the ocean, the pH is proportional to the ratio of $CO_2$ to the sum of bicarbonate plus carbonate. As more and more $CO_2$ enters the ocean from the atmosphere, the oceanic pH also declines (=ocean acidification; Doney et al. 2009), as does the capacity of seawater to absorb more atmospheric $CO_2$ (Thomas et al. 2007). The pH in the ocean is now measurably reduced as a result of anthropogenic $CO_2$. There is great interest in ocean acidification (Orr et al. 2005) and there are already some reports of negative biological effects (Balch and Fabry 2008) as a result of increasing ocean acidification. On land there are also abiotic sinks for $CO_2$ in the weathering of carbonate and silicate minerals but these are small in comparison to storage in the organic products of terrestrial photosynthesis (see Raymond and Cole 2003).

To summarize the present-day C cycle, atmospheric concentrations of $CO_2$ are rapidly rising; both the ocean and the continents are net sinks for this excess $CO_2$ but the dominant processes are different. Biological processes dominate on land and physical-chemical ones dominate in the ocean. The astute reader will have noticed something odd about the terrestrial C balance in that it is treated both as an anthropogenic C source (e.g., forest clearing and burning) and as a C sink (forest regrowth). What is the rationale for this?

## THE HOLOCENE PREINDUSTRIAL GLOBAL CARBON BUDGET

From the start of the last interglacial period, some 10,000 to 12,000 YBP, until 200 years ago, the concentration of atmospheric $CO_2$ was relatively constant (Figure 6.2b). Since the atmosphere is dynamic, this near constancy implies a near steady state for $CO_2$. That is, the inputs to and outputs from the atmosphere were very close to balanced for these 10,000 years. Since some organic C accumulated in sediments and on land, the question remains: Where did the $CO_2$ come from to keep atmospheric concentrations from falling?

Geological sources resulting from plate tectonics (including volcanism and diffuse degassing) supply the long-term (hundreds of thousands of years) source, which balances long-term storage. While individual volcanic eruptions can occasionally put large amounts of $CO_2$ into the atmosphere, the long-term average tectonic input is small. Williams et al. (1992) estimate that 65 Tg of C as $CO_2$ (0.07 Pg) is emitted each year. This estimate is close to but smaller than the long-term burial rate of C in the oceans of 0.12 Pg/y. Clearly, tectonic inputs were too small to balance both sedimentation in the ocean and NEP on land. Further, some estimates of long-term tectonic inputs are an order of magnitude lower than those of Williams (Morner and Etiope 2002).

NEP on land is positive; that is, GPP $> R$ (see Chapter 2). The fates of this NEP are increases in terrestrial biomass or organic matter in soils, or export in rivers to lakes or the ocean. Including the export term in rivers (a major fate for terrestrial NEP), terrestrial NEP (at 1 to 4 Pg C $y^{-2}$) is much larger than volcanism. The inference is that NEP on land, during this period, was supported by the degassing of $CO_2$ from the oceans. Since the oceans were not declining in DIC (nor was the pH increasing), this degassed marine $CO_2$ should be looked at as part of a terrestrial-marine loop. That is, much of the NEP on land over this 10,000-year period was exported to the ocean (some 0.5 Pg/y) where it was decomposed in surface waters and returned to the atmosphere as $CO_2$. This cycle implies that the overall ocean was "net heterotrophic" ($R >$ GPP) and is a source of $CO_2$ to the atmosphere during the pre-Anthropocene era following the last glaciations about 12,000 YBP.

The present-day ocean is still most likely net heterotrophic (del Giorgio and Williams 2005) but is clearly no longer a net source of $CO_2$ to the atmosphere. It is a major sink (Quay et al. 1992). This apparent paradox is easy to resolve by looking at the organic C balance of the ocean.

The organic C inputs to the ocean are gross primary production (GPP) in the ocean, and import from land ($I$) largely from rivers. The outputs are respiration ($R$) and long-term burial in the sediments ($B$), and any long-term trended change in the standing stock of POC (particulate organic carbon) or DOC (dissolved organic carbon) in the water column ($\Delta S$). Since inputs and outputs must be equal:

$$GPP + I = R + B + \Delta S \tag{6.9}$$

Since $\Delta S$ in the water column is negligible in comparison to the other terms, we can dismiss it in comparison to the other terms and rearrange:

$$GPP - R = B - I \tag{6.10}$$

We learned in Chapter 2 that GPP$-R =$ NEP, which is a measure of the net biological $CO_2$ or $O_2$ balance for an ecosystem, in this case the global ocean. Thus,

$$NEP = B - I \tag{6.11}$$

For the global ocean $B$ is estimated at about 0.12 Pg/y; rivers deliver about 0.5 Pg/y of organic C (combining POC and DOC; Cole et al. 2007 and references therein). Thus, total oceanic NEP would be negative and equal to about $-0.38$ Pg/y. So the modern ocean is a biological source of $CO_2$ to its water column. The very rapid rise in atmospheric $CO_2$ over the past 100 years, along with the reactions that this $CO_2$ has with the carbonate system, allows the ocean to be a net sink of atmospheric $CO_2$ while being simultaneously slightly net heterotrophic (del Giorgio and Williams 2005). Note that this net dominance of respiration over primary production is very small in comparison to either GPP or $R$, both of which is near 50 Pg/y.

## The Global Carbon Balance at Longer Timescales

There is considerable variation in atmospheric $CO_2$ and $CH_4$ over long periods of time. The primary evidence for this variation comes from the analysis of bubbles of air trapped in glacier ice (Figure 6.2). There are excellent records going back to about 400,000 YBP at multiple sites around the globe (Figure 6.2c). Over this time frame (excluding the modern Anthropocene period), atmospheric $CO_2$ varied between about 190 and 280 ppm. While this variation is small compared to the changes during industrial times, it is intriguing. Atmospheric $CO_2$ was lowest during glacial times and highest during periods between glaciations (interglacials). Since the mass of both terrestrial vegetation and soil organic matter was also lowest during glacial times, the expansion and contraction of the terrestrial biosphere should have had an effect on atmospheric $CO_2$ opposite to what was actually observed. The explanation for the interglacial $CO_2$ pattern probably reflects changes in the oceanic C cycle. Decreased delivery of terrestrial C during glacial times deprived the ocean of external supplies of both inorganic and organic C, but this was probably too small and too short-lived to explain the atmospheric pattern. Martin et al. (1990), in a very influential paper, argued that the low atmospheric $CO_2$ during glacial periods was driven by high net primary production in the southern ocean, which was stimulated by iron-rich dust. Martin et al. (1990) calculated that the drier terrestrial soils during glacial periods would have supplied 50 times more iron in windblown dust than during the interglacial. The present Southern Ocean, while rich in nitrogen and phosphorus, has very low supplies of iron that limit primary production. Martin and colleagues intriguing hypothesis led to a series of open-ocean iron additions, which demonstrated that the Southern Ocean phytoplankton could be greatly stimulated by iron (Coale et al. 2004). These experiments are at least consistent with Martin's hypothesis.

At the timestep of tens of millions of years, the coarse variation in atmospheric $CO_2$ and the rest of the global C cycle is easier to visualize as being linked to the cycles of oxygen and sulfur. Prior to about 2.5 billion years ago there was effectively no free oxygen in the atmosphere. The oldest fossils of cyanobacteria, the first organisms capable of oxygenic photosynthesis, are about 3.5 billion years old. The time lag between the possible advent of oxygenic photosynthesis and free oxygen in the atmosphere has multiple causes. It took considerable time for cyanobacteria to become abundant, and reduced compounds (e.g., $Fe^{+2}$ and sulfides) were so abundant that they consumed the photosynthetically produced oxygen for many years (Kennedy et al. 2006). By 2 billion YBP the atmosphere had about 1% of its present level of $O_2$; by 0.7 BYA, 10%; and by 0.35 BYA, 100% (Berner and

Kothavala 2001). At the coarse timestep atmospheric oxygen has been roughly at its present level, near 20% (or 0.2 atm), for the past 350 million years (Figure 6.3). The production of organic matter by oxygenic photosynthesis consumes $CO_2$ and releases $O_2$, so the $O_2$ in the atmosphere represents the net balance between the production and consumption of oxygen. The graph in Figure 6.3 suggests that for the past 500 million years (Phanerazoic time), the processes that produce and consume $O_2$ have been about equal. During the rapid rise in $O_2$ from about 2 to 0.7 billion YBP, the production of $O_2$ exceeded its consumption. The mass balance is simplified by recalling that (1) at the scale of the entire Earth, there is no significant import or export of either organic matter or oxygen; (2) we can use $O_2$ as a proxy for organic matter, because it is produced and consumed mostly by the same processes (e.g., photosynthesis and respiration). Thus, the change in the amount of $O_2$ is approximated by:

$$\Delta O_2 = GPP - R = NEP \qquad (6.12)$$

$$NEP = B \text{ (since } I \text{ and } E \text{ are 0)} \qquad (6.13)$$

This means that for the past 2 billion years or so, to a first approximation, the accumulation of atmospheric $O_2$ is equal to the burial (or preservation in rock) of organic matter. In fact, the net preservation of organic matter and the accumulation of $O_2$ in the atmosphere are in some sense the same process. If organic matter had not been protected from decomposition, there would not be oxygen in the atmosphere. The long-term sink for organic matter on Earth is in marine sediments and, more important, in uplifted sedimentary rocks derived from marine sediments. There is a surprisingly large amount of organic matter at low concentration in sedimentary rocks (Falkowski and Godfrey 2008). While this organic matter is potentially available to bacteria when it is released from the rocks (Petsch et al. 2001; Schillawski and Petsch 2008), its release requires special conditions that are rare. The long-term preservation (hundreds of millions years) of organic matter in these rocks caused Paul Falkowski to write, "Were it not for the continents, the atmosphere would never have oxidized" (Falkowski and Godfrey 2008). What he means here is that the really long-term sink for organic C (and hence the net production of oxygen) is in uplifted sediments now on continents that have escaped from the cycle of subduction and volcanism.

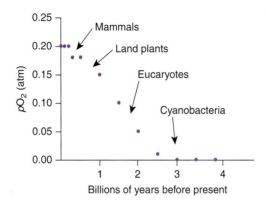

FIGURE 6.3  Rough diagram of the long-term (4 billion year) record of oxygen in Earth's atmosphere. Arrows show the appearance of major groups of the biota. (*Modified from Berner and Kothavala 2001.*)

This balance is missing an important feature. For the past 700 million years atmospheric $O_2$ has been roughly at a steady state. Setting $\Delta O_2$ to zero would cause $B$ to also be zero. At about 0.1 to 0.2 Pg/y $B$ is very small in comparison to GPP or $R$ (each about 100 Pg/y) but it is not zero. Clearly, we are missing a small global sink for $O_2$ that does not involve the oxidation of organic matter. This sink is the microbial and abiotic oxidation of iron sulfide (pyrites) in rock (Garrels et al. 1976). The oxidation of sulfide or other reduced compounds that were produced during the anaerobic decomposition of organic matter would not affect this long-term balance. Rather, these simply reflect intermediate states. Sulfate is reduced to sulfide at the expense of the oxidation of organic matter; any sulfide that is eventually reoxidized simply consumes the oxygen that would have been consumed had the organic matter been directly oxidized by oxygen. Thus, the oxygen sink in the long-term global balance has to be a reduced compound that is present on Earth independent of modern primary production and respiration, such as mineral pyrite.

## Summary of the Global Carbon Cycle

We have learned that the concentration of $CO_2$ in the atmosphere is the end result of a number of linked physical and biogeochemical cycles and that oxygen, sulfur, and iron are key regulators of this cycle. While the terrestrial system tends to be a small but consistent net sink for $CO_2$, largely as a result of biological processes, the ocean has at times been a source and is presently a sink for $CO_2$. The modern oceanic sink for $CO_2$ is largely a physical chemical process. Given the complexity of the C cycle and its coupling to other cycles, it is remarkable how slowly atmospheric $CO_2$ concentrations have changed in the past, and that these changes have been in a relatively narrow range, at least during the past 500 million years. The combustion of fossil fuel, a very small reservoir of C on Earth, has led to increases in atmospheric $CO_2$ at rates much faster than anything in the geological record. Because $CO_2$ is a greenhouse gas, the temperature of Earth increases as its concentration in the atmosphere increases. It is not a warmer Earth that worries climate scientists so much as the unprecedented rapidity of this temperature rise and the ability of natural and human systems to adapt to this pace (IPCC 2007; MEA 2005).

In summary, in the pre-Anthropocene part of the Holocene (since the retreat of the last glacier) $CO_2$ in the atmosphere increased slightly at very slow rates. Processes that removed $CO_2$ from the atmosphere (photosynthesis, weathering, etc.) were in near-perfect balance with those that added it back to the atmosphere (respiration, precipitation of $CaCO_3$, etc.). Over longer timescales we see that $CO_2$ has varied with the phases of the glaciations. Although there are pronounced differences in atmospheric $CO_2$ over these longer timescales, the rate of increase of atmospheric $CO_2$ is much slower than in the present.

# THE CARBON CYCLE IN SELECTED ECOSYSTEMS

In this section we will look at some key aspects of the C cycle at a smaller spatial scale: in forest, river, and large-river-forest complex ecosystems. We will look mostly at the ecosystem-level aspects of the C cycle.

# A Temperate Hardwood Forested Ecosystem

Except for being remarkably well studied, the small, forested watersheds at the Hubbard Brook Experimental Forest are quite typical of forests in northeastern North America. This forested landscape had a history of cutting and clearing that ended in the early 1900s. For the past century the forest has been growing back, or aggrading, and in the most recent years the net growth of trees has ceased (Fahey et al. 2005). As with many upland forests there is little import of organic C into the ecosystem: Rainfall, the only significant input, which typically has DOC concentrations of approximately 1 mg C/L, contributes $1.6 \text{ g C m}^{-2}\text{y}^{-1}$ (McDowell and Likens 1988; Likens 1992). The major input to this system is from gross photosynthesis, about $1230 \text{ g C m}^{-2}\text{y}^{-1}$ (Fahey et al. 2005). A little more than half of GPP ($645 \text{ g C m}^{-2}\text{y}^{-1}$) is consumed by the respiration of the plants themselves ($R_a$). Thus, NPP (NPP $=$ GPP $- R_a$) is $585 \text{ g C m}^{-2}\text{y}^{-1}$. NPP is the organic C that is potentially available to consumers. Fahey et al. (2005) estimate that the lion's share of heterotrophic respiration at Hubbard Brook occurs within the soil, and the lion's share of this is attributable to soil microbes ($460 \text{ g C m}^{-2}\text{y}^{-1}$ or 79% of NPP). Above-ground insects, birds, and mammals respire only about $10 \text{ g C m}^{-2}\text{y}^{-1}$, less than 2% of NPP. The portion of NPP that is not respired by heterotrophs ($R_h$) is either stored in new biomass in the system, stored as detritus in the soils, or exported. If we take these numbers at face value, NPP $- R_h = 115 \text{ g C m}^{-2}\text{y}^{-1} =$ NEP. Export in stream flow as DOC ($1.7 \text{ g C m}^{-2}\text{y}^{-1}$) and POC ($0.56 \text{ g C m}^{-2}\text{y}^{-1}$) accounts for only 2.5% of this NEP. Thus, about $112 \text{ g C m}^{-2}\text{y}^{-1}$, more than 90%, is sequestered in this forest either as new biomass or soil detritus. As there has been essentially no net addition in the biomass of living trees in the past 20 years at this site, the inference is that sequestration must occur either on the forest floor or in the soil. Direct measurements of the organic matter in the surface organic horizons of the soil ($O_{ie}$ and $O_a$ layers) show no net change in repeated measurements since 1975 (Fahey et al. 2005), leading to the inference that the deeper, mineral soil is the location of most of the C sequestration.

Clearly, NEP is small in comparison to GPP and most sequestration is into detrital rather than living pools. The soil organic C pool is very large, about $15,740 \text{ g C/m}^2$, and varies with both depth and space. One thing that is important to note is that it is not possible to detect an annual or even decadal increment to this pool.

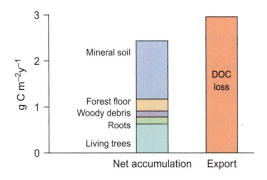

**FIGURE 6.4** Carbon storage and export for the past 12,000 years at the Hubbard Brook Experimental Forest. (*Redrawn from Cole and Caraco 2001.*)

Looking at a longer time frame (e.g., 10,000 years ago), we can glean some interesting information about the C balance at Hubbard Brook. Assuming that the soils and rock surfaces were free of organic C at the retreat of the glacier some 12,000 to 10,000 years ago, we can look at the total sequestration of organic C in soils and biomass (Figure 6.4). All the NEP during this time is either stored in biomass or soil, burned, or was fluvially exported. This simplifies the problem of estimating rates of C sequestration because all we need to do is take the total standing stock and divide by elapsed time. We can also roughly estimate the fluvial export. At the millennial timestep NEP is roughly evenly divided between storage in the soil and fluvial export (Figure 6.4). The major storage is in the mineral soil, rather than in the organic horizons or in biomass. On the other hand, this long-term, direct estimate of C sequestration (about $2.5 \, g \, C \, m^{-2}y^{-1}$) is 45 times lower than the current estimate that we arrived at by difference. Further, this sequestration estimate is probably an upper bound since it is likely that the material in the soils was not entirely C-free when the glacier receded. Over the millennial time step, NEP would be equal to the sum of long-term C accumulation in soils plus biomass (about $3.5 \, g \, C \, m^{-2}y^{-1}$) plus fluvial export (about $3 \, g \, C \, m^{-2}y^{-1}$) minus DOC import in rain ($1.7 \, g \, C \, m^{-2}y^{-1}$), or about $4.8 \, g \, C \, m^{-2}y^{-1}$. This net result at the millennial time step does not imply anything about short-term variations in the C balance. There are times of rapid storage and rapid loss.

There are intriguing features about C cycling at Hubbard Brook that are not captured by looking only at the ecosystem-level fluxes. Despite the high rates of photosynthesis in this forest, the organic C leaving the stream water as DOC has about the same concentration found in incoming rainwater, thus inputs balance outputs on an annual basis. This is made even more intriguing by looking at the changes in DOC concentrations as water moves from rain, to tree canopy, to soil, and out in stream water (Figure 6.5). As this rain passes through the forest canopy (called throughfall) the concentration increases 10-fold. In the upper (organic) soil horizons DOC collected in lysimeters (soil water collection devices) is even higher, three to four times what it was in throughfall. So as water moves through the forest and soil it increases in DOC concentration by about 30-fold. However, as this water passes through the mineral horizons, its DOC concentration decreases dramatically (Figure 6.5). The concentration as water leaves the lower B horizon and enters

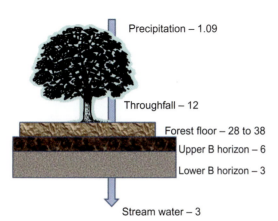

Precipitation – 1.09

Throughfall – 12

Forest floor – 28 to 38

Upper B horizon – 6

Lower B horizon – 3

Stream water – 3

FIGURE 6.5 Changes in the concentration of dissolved organic C as it passes through a forest. Values are mg C/L. Precipitation has low concentrations of DOC, but as this water moves through the forest canopy it acquires DOC from the trees (throughfall) and even more in the rich organic layers of the forest floor. DOC concentrations are reduced due to both decomposition and sorption in the mineral layers of the soil (upper and lower B horizons). As water exits the system in stream water it has concentrations much lower than in throughfall or forest floor soils. *(Redrawn from the data in McDowell and Likens 1988.)*

the stream is about equal. Two main processes reduce the DOC concentration in the soil-sorption to minerals and respiration by microbes (McDowell and Wood 1984; Bernhardt and McDowell 2008).

## A Tidal, Freshwater River

The Hudson River originates at Lake Tear of the Clouds in the Adirondack Mountains of New York state. The Mohawk River, which drains part of central New York, joins the Hudson near Troy, NY. After flowing over a small dam at Green Island, basically on the site of the original fall line of this river, the Hudson estuary flows south 240 km where it joins the sea at the southern tip of Manhattan Island. The Hudson estuary is navigable and at sea level for its length and is influenced by tides up to the dam at Green Island. Only the final southern 40 km of the river contain brackish (meaning salinity from 0.5 to 30 psu) water most the time. Occasionally, during dry summers, the salt front is pushed farther north, but most of the time the upper 150 to 200 km of the Hudson is tidal, fresh-water, and relatively well mixed top to bottom in the 8 to 9 m deep (on average) water column (Cole et al. 1992).

Unlike the forest at Hubbard Brook, the C inputs to the Hudson River from its watershed ($650 \, \text{g C m}^{-2}\text{y}^{-1}$; Howarth et al. 1996; Caraco and Cole 2004) dominate the organic C balance and exceed riverine primary production by about two-fold. The major primary producers within this system are phytoplankton and macrophytes. Phytoplankton GPP (prior to the recent introduction of the exotic zebra mussel) was about $330 \, \text{g C m}^{-2}\text{y}^{-1}$ and a large fraction of this ($280 \, \text{g C m}^{-2}\text{y}^{-1}$ or 85%) was respired by the phytoplankton themselves. So the net input (or NPP) of phytoplankton was about $50 \, \text{g C m}^{-2}\text{y}^{-1}$ and co-equal to the NPP of the two dominant macrophytes (*Vallisneria* and *Trapa*) of 30 to $40 \, \text{g C m}^{-2}\text{y}^{-1}$. Bacteria dominated the respiratory output ($116 \, \text{g C m}^{-2}\text{y}^{-1}$) and actually respired more organic C than the combined inputs from NPP of phytoplankton and macrophytes. Benthic invertebrates (again prior to the zebra mussel invasion) accounted for only about 10% of bacterial respiration ($9 \, \text{g C m}^{-2}\text{y}^{-1}$). NEP for this ecosystem was negative, $-43 \, \text{g C m}^{-2}\text{y}^{-1}$, and there was a large export of the organic C not consumed by respiration ($607 \, \text{g C m}^{-2}\text{y}^{-1}$).

The appearance of the invasive zebra mussel (*Dreissena polymorpha*) in 1992 had a large effect on the C balance. The respiration of zebra mussels added some $83 \, \text{g C m}^{-2}\text{y}^{-1}$ to $R_h$ and greatly reduced, by its huge filtration rates, the standing stock and primary production of phytoplankton (to NPP of about $12 \, \text{g C m}^{-2}\text{y}^{-1}$ if we correct for 24-hour algal respiration). Thus, following the zebra mussel invasion in 1982, NEP of the Hudson became even more negative (to $-153 \, \text{g C m}^{-2}\text{y}^{-1}$) and downstream export somewhat smaller ($497 \, \text{g C m}^{-2}\text{y}^{-1}$; Caraco et al. 1997; Caraco and Cole 2004).

In summary, compared to the Hubbard Brook Experimental Forest, this river has much less autochthonous primary production and much larger allochthonous inputs. Further, to a first approximation the river does not store C in its sediments, apart from some small depositional areas covering much less than 1% of the river's bottom. The forest is net auto-trophic; GPP $> R$ and some organic C is sequestered and net exported. The river is

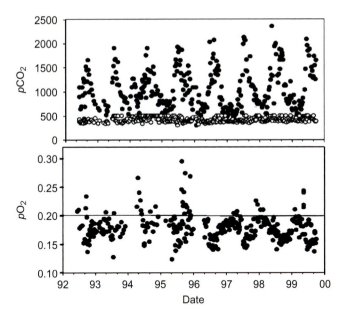

FIGURE 6.6 An eight-year record of the partial pressures in the tidal, freshwater Hudson River. Upper panel: $CO_2$ in the water (closed symbols) and air (open symbols); lower panel: $O_2$ in the water; the solid line $pO_2 = 0.2$ represents $O_2$ in air. *(Modified from Raymond et al. 1997 and Cole and Caraco 2001.)*

strongly net heterotrophic; GPP $< R$, and a large fraction of $R_h$ is supported by external inputs. The river exports less organic C than it imports.

In this river, as with most rivers, heterotrophic organisms are subsidized by organic C inputs from the watershed. GPP produces $O_2$ and consumes $CO_2$; $R$ does the reverse. Because GPP $< R$, the Hudson and most large rivers tend to be supersaturated in $CO_2$ and undersaturated in $O_2$ with respect to the atmosphere (Cole and Caraco 2001; Cole et al. 2007; Figure 6.6). Since gases equilibrate according to their partial pressures in air and water, these systems are net sources of $CO_2$ to the atmosphere and net sinks for atmospheric $O_2$. The Hudson has some area of anoxic sediments and is also a source of $CH_4$ to the atmosphere (about 2 g C $m^{-2}y^{-1}$; de Angelis and Scranton 1993).

An interesting feature of the Hudson C budget is how much it changed in response to the zebra mussel over just 20 years. Many rivers, including the Hudson, are turbid and well mixed. This means that the phytoplankton spend a lot of time in water with too little light for photosynthesis. Their physiologic balance can easily be tipped because they already respire a great deal of their own photosynthesis, more so than in well-lit environments (Cole et al. 1992). Thus, even a modest increase in grazing pressure from zebra mussels caused the phytoplankton to crash (Caraco et al. 1997, 2006). The zebra mussel effect was also far from modest. Prior to that invasion, the water column of the Hudson was filtered by organisms about once every 50 days. Following the invasion the zebra mussel alone filtered the water about once every 2 to 3 days depending on the location and year. The biomass of the phytoplankton decreased by about 80% with the onset of the zebra mussel (Caraco et al. 1997; Strayer et al. 1999). The Hudson example illustrates the substantial effect that a single species, either native or introduced, can sometimes have on the food web structure and patterns of biogeochemical cycling in an ecosystem.

## A Temperate Grassland

The Great Plains covers about $2.6 \times 10^6$ km$^2$, making it the second largest ecozone in North America. The vast size of the North American Great Plains and those of other grasslands around the world make them important for the global C budget. Some have argued that grasslands, globally, might account for as much as 0.5 Pg C/y of the so-called missing terrestrial C sink (Scurlock and Hall 1998). Because of the large values of both GPP and $R$ in grasslands, small changes in the balance between GPP and $R$ can affect C sequestration into soils at a globally significant scale (Schimel et al. 1994). Physically, grasslands are well suited for measurement of gas exchange with the atmosphere because of their relatively uniform plant height. The use of net ecosystem gas exchange (NEE) was discussed as a technique for measuring primary production in Chapter 2 as is particularly suited to this kind of ecosystem. NEE is for nearly all purposes identical to NEP (see Chapter 2). NEE would include both the biotic (respiration and photosynthesis) as well as abiotic (weathering, carbonate precipitation) reactions, and so it is slightly different from NEP.

Several grasslands are part of a network of ecosystems with exchange towers called Ameriflux (http://public.ornl.gov/ameriflux/). At one of the network sites (in Alberta, Canada), the dominant grasses are in the genus *Agropyron* and the dominant forb, *Tragopogon* (Flanagan et al. 2002). Using eddy covariance during both daylight and night, researchers were able to calculate GPP and total ecosystem respiration ($R$) nearly continuously for a several-year period (Figure 6.7). As in many grassland regions, rainfall is highly variable and exerts profound controls over plant biomass, gross productivity, and respiration. In this system leaf area index (the total area of leaves above a unit area of ground) ranged from 0.2 m$^2$/m$^2$ when soil moisture was low, to as much as 8 m$^2$/m$^2$. Both GPP and NEE were tightly correlated to leaf area index. The system was a small net source of $CO_2$ to the atmosphere when soil moisture was low and a sink for $CO_2$ when moisture was high (Figure 6.7). In 1999, a year with average precipitation, NEE showed a net loss of 18 g C/m$^2$; the system achieved a peak, above-ground biomass of 51.2 g C/m$^2$; and stored 4.9 g C/m$^2$ in below-ground pools. For the driest year, 2000, NEE was a much smaller net gain (21 g C/m$^2$); peak biomass was much smaller (39.4 g C/m$^2$); and the system lost 16.5 g C/m$^2$ from below-ground pools. Studies of the export term are uncommon for grassland environments: typically, runoff is very low due to relatively low precipitation (40 cm/y at this site) and high evaporation. We can say only that export is probably small. The import term would be entirely by DOC in rainfall, which we did not consider. Assuming a DOC content of 1 mg C/L, the input would be about 0.4 g C m$^{-2}$y$^{-1}$. Averaging the two years, NEE was 1.5 g C m$^{-2}$y$^{-1}$ (Figure 6.7).

## Small Mesotrophic Lakes

In lakes, whole-system changes in dissolved gases are used in much the same way that eddy covariance is used in terrestrial systems. In the aquatic system, we measure the

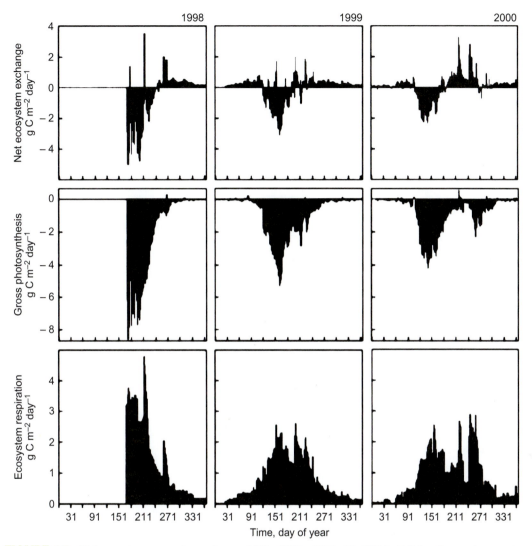

**FIGURE 6.7** Net ecosystem gas exchange (upper; NEE = NEP = GPP − R); GPP (middle) and ecosystem respiration (R; lower) in a temperate grassland in Alberta, Canada. Shown are three years of data based on eddy flux towers. Negative values represent the uptake of $CO_2$ by the system; positive values represent the net release of $CO_2$. In this system GPP is almost always larger than R, leading to negative values (net uptake) of $CO_2$ for the system as a whole (NEE) during the growing season. (*Data from Flanagan et al. 2002.*)

concentrations of the dissolved gases ($CO_2$ and $O_2$) directly and continuously, and model the gas flux across the air—water interface (see Chapter 2). From these measurements we can calculate whole-system GPP, R, and NEP. Paul, Peter, and Tuesday Lakes in the Upper Peninsula of Michigan, near Land O'Lakes, Wisconsin, are typical of the small (1 to

5 ha), deep (mean depth 5 to 8 m), and colored systems of much of the northern United States, Canada, and Scandinavia (Carpenter and Kitchell 1993). These lakes receive terrestrial runoff as ground-water seepage that is usually darkly stained with colored DOC (CDOC). The external loading of terrestrial DOC can equal or exceed primary production in these and many other types of lakes (Caraco and Cole 2004). While total phosphorus and chlorophyll-a concentrations are not extremely low in the surface waters, the photic zone is quite shallow due to light extinction from the CDOC (Carpenter et al. 1998). Thus, autochthonous primary production is limited to the shallow pelagic photic zone and a relatively narrow band of active periphyton on the shallow benthic areas. Using a variety of approaches, including whole-lake additions of inorganic $^{13}C$, the following view of the C balance of several of these was arrived upon (Table 6.3; Cole et al. 2000, 2006; Houser et al. 2001, 2003; Carpenter et al. 2005): For Paul Lake, the combined gross primary production of the upper mixed layer plus benthic littoral zone is $165 \, g \, C \, m^{-2} y^{-1}$; pelagic (upper mixed layer) plus benthic respiration (including both autotrophs and heterotrophs) is about $195 \, g \, C \, m^{-2} y^{-1}$. Thus, R exceeds GPP by about $30 \, C \, m^{-2} y^{-1}$, which is coequal with $CO_2$ efflux from this lake. Allochthonous loading, which includes DOC, POC, and the influx of terrestrial insects, adds up to about $72 \, C \, m^{-2} y^{-1}$. Export, largely in the form of outseeping DOC, accounts for about $16 \, C \, m^{-2} y^{-1}$, and sediment burial about $19 \, C \, m^{-2} y^{-1}$. Because Paul Lake, and many like it, has anoxic sediments and bottom water, $CH_4$ is produced and some is released to the atmosphere. This release is nontrivial in the C budget of this lake (about $7 \, g \, C \, m^{-2} y^{-1}$). In these lakes, actually a great deal of $CH_4$ is released from the sediments to the water column but most is oxidized in the water column by methanotrophic bacteria. Were it not for these bacteria, the atmospheric methane flux would be much larger (Bastviken et al. 2008).

The Paul Lake C budget shows an interesting thing about aquatic ecosystems. Because they are subsidized by terrestrial C inputs, these systems can both sequester C in their sediments and be net sources of $CO_2$ and $CH_4$ to the atmosphere. The dual role of lakes and other subsidized aquatic ecosystems is widespread (Pace and Prairie 2005). The budgets for Peter and Tuesday Lakes are broadly similar to that of Paul Lake. Peter Lake was experimentally fertilized by adding nitrogen and phosphorus. Under this eutrophication the C balance is quite different (Peter + N + P in Table 6.3). Both GPP and R increase greatly and the balance between GPP and R is altered. Under the fertilization regime Peter Lake becomes net autotrophic and NEP becomes positive (Table 6.3).

## The Case of the Amazon

The world's largest river, the Amazon, accounts for about 20% of the total flow of freshwater to the ocean. Its drainage basin, $6.9 \times 10^6 \, km^2$, is covered by moist tropical forest belonging to nine different nations. As one of the largest forests on Earth, the Amazon basin may affect the global atmospheric $CO_2$ budget. The value of wood and the need for pastureland has resulted in a great deal of deforestation and burning in the Amazon basin. This practice results in less C storage on land and a release to the atmosphere of most of the C once contained in biomass (Houghton 2003).

**TABLE 6.3**  Organic C inputs and respiratory losses in three lakes in northern Michigan.

| | Paul | Tuesday | Peter | Peter (+ N and P) |
|---|---|---|---|---|
| *Autochthonous inputs* | | | | |
| GPP phytoplankton | 130.7 | 131.4 | 101.9 | 313.6 |
| GPP benthic algae | 34.2 | 2.2 | 20.2 | 55.8 |
| Total autochthonous inputs | **165.2** | **133.9** | **122.8** | **369.4** |
| *Allochthonous inputs* | | | | |
| T-DOC | 78.8 | 178.9 | 112 | 76 |
| T-POC | 16.9 | 56.9 | 22.3 | 16.9 |
| T-prey | 0.7 | 2.7 | 0.2 | 0.6 |
| Total allochthonous inputs | **99.7** | **238.7** | **136.8** | **124.6** |
| *Respiratory outputs* | | | | |
| R of autotrophs | 34.9 | 16.9 | 24.8 | 47.9 |
| R of pelagic heterotrophs | 84.2 | 57.6 | 72.7 | 155.5 |
| benthic R | 75.6 | 54.7 | 30 | 94.3 |
| Total respiratory outputs | **194.8** | **129.2** | **127.4** | **299.2** |

Peter Lake is shown in different years, one in its ambient state (Peter) and one during which nutrients (N and P) were added to stimulate primary production. Shown are estimates of GPP and respiration ($R$) along with the major external inputs of organic C (allochthonous inputs). GPP is divided into phytoplankton and benthic algae. T-DOC, T-POC, and T-prey are the external inputs of DOC, POC, and terrestrial prey items (largely insects), respectively. Respiration is divided into that by autotrophs, and pelagic and benthic heterotrophs. Note that allochthonous loading is about as large as total GPP in most cases and larger than net primary production (NPP = GPP−(auotrophic $R$) in all cases except Peter with added nutrients. *(Modified from Cole et al. 2006.)*

There are two very different ways to assess the C balance of large terrestrial ecosystems, so called "bottom-up" and "top-down" (Houghton 2003). Top-down approaches look at large-scale spatial and temporal changes in atmospheric $CO_2$ (sometimes with $O_2$ and C isotopes as well) and use modeling to infer the magnitudes of the sources or sinks from land. Bottom-up approaches use changes in inventories of C in plants and soils, and sometimes gas exchanges at the scale of small watersheds. Based on both approaches regrowing forests in northern latitudes are a large net sink for $CO_2$ and store 2 Pg C/y in new biomass and soil. The role of tropical forests in the atmospheric $CO_2$ balance is less clear. Inverse models of atmospheric $CO_2$ and C isotopes for the tropics suggest that these forests now release 1.5 Pg C/y to the atmosphere (Houghton 2003). On the other hand, eddy flux towers deployed in the Amazon forest suggest that the forest is a large to very large sink for $CO_2$, implying that the effect of forest cutting and land use change is overwhelmed or at least offset by forest regrowth (Grace et al. 1995).

How can the remaining Amazon forest be a large sink for $CO_2$ while the Amazon basin as a whole system is a net source of $CO_2$ to the atmosphere? Taking a cue from work at smaller scales that showed that rivers and lakes tend to emit $CO_2$ to the atmosphere, Richey et al. (2002) calculated the loss of $CO_2$ from the entire Amazon River, its tributaries, and its flooded flood plain. They estimate that about 0.5 Pg C/y is released as $CO_2$ from the "wet" parts of the Amazon basin. Scaling up to all tropical forests, Richey et al. (2002) put the estimate at 0.9 Pg C/y. This loss of gaseous C from the aquatic parts of the terrestrial system is 10-fold larger than the fluvial export of DOC plus DIC to the ocean. The $CO_2$ evaded to the atmosphere could explain the difference between the top-down and bottom-up estimates of the Amazon basin C balance.

Recall that the fates of NEP are burial plus export. The $CO_2$ evaded from the aquatic systems arises either because terrestrially derived organic C is metabolized in the river (e.g., this came from terrestrial export, $E$), or because soil $CO_2$ is transported into the river directly. It is important to note that a local flux tower on land misses both of these processes. Soil $CO_2$ that was transported in water is terrestrial $R$ that never made in into the local atmosphere of the forest. So, for the Amazon, local flux towers might measure NEP that is 0.5 Pg C/y larger than would be seen by large-scale atmospheric modeling that included these lateral losses. There are many other possible explanations for the discrepancy. For example, Lloyd et al. (2007) suggest that eddy flux towers underestimate terrestrial $R$ in the Amazon for aerodynamic reasons. The point here is that at large spatial scales, the lateral, aquatic fluxes in DOC, DIC, and $CO_2$ can affect the apparent C balance of terrestrial ecosystems.

# CONCLUDING REMARKS

The answer to the question, "What factors regulate the carbon cycle?" is complex for several reasons. First, there are many interrelated factors, some of which are biological (tree growth), physical (diffusion of $CO_2$ into the ocean), or both (the preservation of organic matter in sediments, or the transport of DOC into a lake). Second, what we mean by regulation depends on both the temporal and spatial boundaries of the system. Over short timescales (minutes), the physiology of stomates affects the local atmosphere that is in contact with a forest. Over decadal timescales, drought, fire, land clearing, and the use of fossil fuels affect the concentration of $CO_2$ in the entire atmosphere. Over geologic timescales, the long-term preservation of organic C in sediments and rocks and the return of $CO_2$ during subduction, volcanism, and reverse weathering are the major controls. The ecosystem approach allows the scientist to set temporal and spatial boundaries that make a particular problem tractable and offer different insights into "the answer."

# References

Alin, S.R., Johnson, T.C., 2007. Carbon cycling in large lakes of the world: A synthesis of production, burial, and lake-atmosphere exchange estimates. Global Biogeochem. Cycles 21. doi: 10.1029/2006GB002881.

Bacastow, R.B., Keeling, C.D., Lueker, T.J., Wahlen, M., Mook, W.G., 1996. The [13]C Suess effect in the world surface oceans and its implications for oceanic uptake of $CO_2$: Analysis of observations at Bermuda. Global Biogeochem. Cycles 10, 335–346.

Balch, W.M., Fabry, V.J., 2008. Ocean acidification: Documenting its impact on calcifying phytoplankton at basin scales. Mar. Ecol Prog Ser 373, 239–247.

Bastviken, D., Cole, J.J., Pace, M.L., van de Bogert, M.C., 2008. Fates of methane from different lake habitats: Connecting whole-lake budgets and $CH_4$ emissions. J Geophys Res-Biogeosciences 113, G02024. doi: 10.1029/2007JG000608.

Berner, R.A., Kothavala, Z., 2001. GEOCARB III: A revised model of atmospheric $CO_2$ over Phanerozoic time. Am. J. Sci. 301, 182–204.

Bernhardt, E.S., McDowell, W.H., 2008. Twenty years apart: Comparisons of DOM uptake during leaf leachate releases to Hubbard Brook Valley streams in 1979 versus 2000. J. Geophys. Res-Biogeosciences 113, G03032. doi: 10.1029/2007JG000618.

Caraco, N.F., Cole, J.J., Raymond, P.A., Strayer, D.L., Pace, M.L., Findlay, S., et al., 1997. Zebra mussel invasion in a large turbid river: Phytoplankton response to increased grazing. Ecology 78, 588–602.

Caraco, N.F., Cole, J.J., 2004. When terrestrial organic matter is sent down the river: Importance of allochthonous C inputs to the metabolism in lakes and rivers. In: Polis, G.A., Power, M.E., Huxley, G.R. (Eds.), Food webs at the landscape level. University of Chicago Press, Chicago, pp. 301–316.

Caraco, N.F., Cole, J.J., Strayer, D.L., 2006. Top-down control from the bottom: Regulation of eutrophication in a large river by benthic grazing. Limnol. Oceanogr. 51, 664–670.

Carpenter, S.R., Cole, J.J., Kitchell, J.F., Pace, M.L., 1998. Impact of dissolved organic carbon, phosphorus and grazing on phytoplankton biomass and production in experimental lakes. Limnol. Oceanogr. 43, 73–80.

Carpenter, S.R., Cole, J.J., Pace, M.L., Van de Bogert, M., Bade, D.L., Bastviken, D., et al., 2005. Ecosystem subsidies: Terrestrial support of aquatic food webs from $^{13}C$ addition to contrasting lakes. Ecology 86, 2737–2750.

Carpenter, S.R., Kitchell, J.F., 1993. The trophic cascade in lakes. Cambridge University Press, Cambridge, MA.

Coale, K.H., Johnson, K.S., Chavez, F.P., Buesseler, K.O., Barber, R.T., Brzezinski, M.A., et al., 2004. Southern ocean iron enrichment experiment: Carbon cycling in high- and low-Si waters. Science 304, 408–414.

Cole, J.J., Caraco, N.F., Peierls, B., 1992. Can phytoplankton maintain a positive balance in a turbid, freshwater, tidal estuary? Limnol. Oceanogr. 37, 1608–1617.

Cole, J.J., Caraco, N.F., Kling, G.W., Kratz, T.K., 1994. Carbon dioxide supersaturation in the surface waters of lakes. Science 265, 1568–1570.

Cole, J.J., Caraco, N.F., 2001. Carbon in catchments: Connecting terrestrial carbon losses with aquatic metabolism. Mar. Freshw. Res. 52, 101–110.

Cole, J.J., Caraco, N.F., McDowell, W.H., Tranvik, L.J., Striegl, R.G., Duarte, C.M., et al., 2007. Plumbing the global carbon cycle: Integrating inland waters into the terrestrial carbon budget. Ecosystems 10, 171–184.

Cole, J.J., Carpenter, S.R., Pace, M.L., Van de Bogert, M.C., Kitchell, J.L., Hodgson, J.R., 2006. Differential support of lake food webs by three types of terrestrial organic carbon. Ecol. Lett. 9, 558–568.

Cole, J.J., Pace, M.L., Carpenter, S.R., Kitchell, J.F., 2000. Persistence of net heterotrophy in lakes during nutrient addition and food web manipulations. Limnol. Oceanogr. 45, 1718–1730.

Conley, D.J., 2002. Terrestrial ecosystems and the global biogeochemical silica cycle. Global. Biogeochem. Cycles. 16. doi: 10.1029/2002GB001894.

de Angelis, M., Scranton, M.I., 1993. Fate of methane in the Hudson River and estuary. Global Biogeochem. Cycles 7, 509–523.

del Giorgio, P.A., Williams, P.J. le B., 2005. Respiration in aquatic ecosystems. Oxford University Press, Oxford, UK.

Dixon, R.K., Brown, S., Houghton, R.A., Solomon, A.M., Trexler, M.C., Wisniewski, J., 1994. Carbon pools and flux of global forest ecosystems. Science 263, 185–190.

Doney, S.C., Balch, W.M., Fabry, V.J., Feely, R.A., 2009. Ocean acidification: A critical emerging problem for the ocean sciences. Oceanography 22, 16–25.

Dugdale, R.C., Wilkerson, F.P., 1998. Silicate regulation of new production in the equatorial Pacific upwelling. Nature 391, 270–273.

Etheridge, D.M., Steele, L.P, Langenfelds, R.L., Francey, R.J., Barnola, J.-M., Morgan, V.I., 1996. Natural and anthropogenic changes in atmospheric CO2 of the last 1000 years from air in Antarctic ice and firn. J. Geophys. Res. 101, 4115–4128.

Fahey, T.J., Siccama, T.G., Driscoll, C.T., Likens, G.E., Campbell, J., Johnson, C.E., Battles, J.J., 2005. The biogeochemistry of carbon at Hubbard Brook. Biogeochemistry 75, 109–176.

Falkowski, P.G., Godfrey, L.V., 2008. Electrons, life and the evolution of Earth's oxygen cycle. Philos. Trans. R. Soc B, Biol. Sci. 363, 2705–2716.

Fan, S., Gloor, M., Mahlman, J., Pacala, S., Sarmiento, J., Takahashi, T., et al., 1998. A large terrestrial carbon sink in North America implied by atmospheric and oceanic carbon dioxide data and models. Science 282, 442−446.

Field, C.B., Raupach, M.R., 2004. The global carbon cycle. Integrating humans, climate, and the natural world. SCOPE 62. Island Press, New York, NY.

Flanagan, L.B., Wever, L.A., Carlson, P.J., 2002. Seasonal and interannual variation in carbon dioxide exchange and carbon balance in a northern temperate grassland. Glob. Change Biol. 8, 599−615.

Garrels, R.M., Lerman, A., MacKenzie, F.T., 1976. Controls of atmospheric $O_2$ and $CO_2$: Past, present and future. Am. Sci. 64, 306−315.

Grace, J., Lloyd, J., McIntyre, J., Miranda, A.C., Meir, P., Miranda, H.S., et al., 1995. Carbon-dioxide uptake by an undisturbed tropical rain-forest in southwest Amazonia 1992 to 1993. Science 270, 778−780.

Hobbie, J.E., Cole, J.J., Dungan, J., Houghton, R.A., Peterson, B.J., 1985. Role of biota in global $CO_2$ balance: The controversy. BioScience 34, 492−498.

Houghton, R.A., 1995. Land-use change and the carbon-cycle. Glob. Change Biol. 1, 275−287.

Houghton, R.A., 2003. Why are estimates of the terrestrial carbon balance so different? Glob. Change Biol. 9, 500−509.

Houghton, R.A., 2005. The contemporary carbon cycle. In: Schlesinger, W.H. (Ed.), Biogeochemistry. Elsevier, New York, pp. 473−514.

Houghton, R.A., Woodwell, G.M., 1989. Global climate change. Sci. Am. 260, 36−44.

Houser, J.N., Bade, D.L., Cole, J.J., Pace, M.L., 2003. The dual influences of dissolved organic carbon on hypolim-netic metabolism: Organic substrate and photosynthetic reduction. Biogeochemistry 64, 247−269.

Houser, J.N., Carpenter, S.R., Cole, J.J., 2001. Food web structure and nutrient enrichment: Effects on sediment phosphorus retention in whole lake experiments. Can. J. Fish. Aquat. Sci. 57, 1524−1533.

Howarth, R.W., Schneider, R., Swaney, D., 1996. Metabolism and organic carbon fluxes in the tidal freshwater Hudson River. Estuaries 19, 848−865.

Howarth, R.W., Teal, J.M., 1991. Energy flow in a salt marsh ecosystem: The role of reduced inorganic sulfur com-pounds. Am. Nat. 116, 862−872.

IPCC, 2007. Fourth Assessment Report: Climate Change 2007 (AR4).

Jain, A.K., Kheshgi, H.S., Hoffert, M.I., Wuebbles, D.J., 1995. Distribution of radiocarbon as a test of global carbon cycle models. Global Biogeochem. Cycles 9, 153−166.

Kamp, A., de Beer, D., Nitsch, J.L., Lavik, G., Stief, P., 2011. Diatoms respire nitrate to survive dark and anoxic conditions. Proc. Natl. Acad. Sci. 108, 5649−5654.

Keeling, C.D., Whorf, T.P., Wahlen, M., Vanderplicht, J., 1995. Interannual extremes in the rate of rise of atmo-spheric carbon-dioxide since 1980. Nature 375, 666−670.

Kennedy, M., Droser, M., Mayer, L.M., Pevear, D., Mrofka, D., 2006. Late Precambrian oxygenation: Inception of the clay mineral factory. Science 311, 1446−1449.

Likens, G.E., 1992. The ecosystem approach: Its use and abuse. Ecology Institute, Oldendorf.

Lloyd, J., Kolle, O., Fritsch, H., de Freitas, S.R., Dias, M., Artaxo, P., et al., 2007. An airborne regional carbon bal-ance for Central Amazonia. Biogeosciences 4, 759−768.

MacKenzie, F.T., Kump, L.R., 1995. Reverse weathering, clay mineral formation, and oceanic element cycles. Science 270, 586−587.

Martin, J.H., Gordon, R.M., Fitzwater, S.E., 1990. Iron in Antarctic waters. Nature 345, 156−158.

McDowell, W.H., Likens, G.E., 1988. Origin, composition, and flux of dissolved organic-carbon in the Hubbard Brook Valley. Ecol. Monogr. 58, 177−195.

McDowell, W.H., Wood, T., 1984. Podzolization-soil processes control dissolved organic-carbon concentrations in stream water. Soil Sci. 137, 23−32.

Michalopoulos, P., Aller, R.C., 1995. Rapid clay mineral formation in Amazon delta sediments—Reverse weather-ing and oceanic elemental cycles. Science 270, 614−617.

Millenium Ecosystem Assessment (MEA), 2005. Ecosystems and human well-being: Health synthesis: A report of the Millennium Ecosystem Assessment. Core writing team: C. Corvalan, S. Hales, and A. McMichael.

Morner, N.A., Etiope, G., 2002. Carbon degassing from the lithosphere. Glob. Planet. Change 33, 185−203.

Orr, J.C., Fabry, V.J., Aumont, O., Bopp, L., Doney, S.C., Feely, R.A., et al., 2005. Anthropogenic ocean acidification over the twenty-first century and its impact on calcifying organisms. Nature 437, 681−686.

Pace, M.L., Prairie, Y.T., 2005. Respiration in lakes. In: del Giorgio, P.A., Williams, P.J. le B. (Eds.), Respiration in aquatic systems. Oxford University Press, Oxford, UK, pp. 103−121.

Petit, J.R., Jouzel, J., Raynaud, D., Barkov, N.I., Barnola, J.M., Basile, I., et al., 1999. Climate and atmospheric history of the past 420,000 years from the Vostok ice core, Antarctica. Nature 399, 429−436.

Petsch, S.T., Eglinton, T.I., Edwards, K.J., 2001. $^{14}C$-dead living biomass: Evidence for microbial assimilation of ancient organic carbon during shale weathering. Science 292, 1127−1131.

Pina-Ochoa, E., Hogslund, S., Geslin, E., Cedhagen, T., Revsbech, N.P., Nielsen, L.P., et al., 2010. Widespread occurrence of nitrate storage and denitrification among foraminifera and *Gromiida*. Proc. Natl. Acad. Sci. 107, 1148−1153.

Quay, P.D., Tilbrook, B., Wong, C.S., 1992. Oceanic uptake of fossil fuel $CO_2$: Carbon-13 evidence. Science 256, 74−78.

Raymond, P.A., Caraco, N.F., Cole, J.J., 1997. $CO_2$ concentration and atmospheric flux in the Hudson River. Estuaries 20, 381−390.

Raymond, P.A., Cole, J.J., 2003. Increase in the export of alkalinity from North America's largest river. Science 302, 88−91.

Richey, J.E., Melack, J.M., Aufdenkampe, A.K., Ballester, V.M., Hess, L.L., 2002. Outgassing from Amazonian rivers and wetlands as a large tropical source of atmospheric $CO_2$. Nature 416, 617−620.

Schillawski, S., Petsch, S., 2008. Release of biodegradable dissolved organic matter from ancient sedimentary rocks. Global Biogeochem. Cycles 22, GB3002. doi: 10.1029/2007GB002980.

Schimel, D.S., Braswell, B.H., Holland, E.A., McKeown, R., Ojima, D.S., Painter, T.H., et al., 1994. Climatic, edaphic, and biotic controls over storage and turnover of carbon in soils. Global Biogeochem. Cycles 8, 279−293.

Schimel, D.S., House, J.I., Hibbard, K.A., Bousquet, P., Ciais, P., Peylin, P., et al., 2001. Recent patterns and mechanisms of carbon exchange by terrestrial ecosystems. Nature 414, 169−172.

Schlesinger, W.H., 1982. Carbon storage in the caliche of arid soils—A case study from Arizona. Soil Sci. 133, 247−255.

Schlesinger, W.H., 1997. Biogeochemistry, second ed. Academic Press, San Diego.

Schlesinger, W.H., Cole, J.J., Finzi, A.C., Holland, E.A., 2011. Introduction to coupled biogeochemical cycles. Front Ecol. Environ. 9, 5−8.

Scurlock, J.M.O., Hall, D.O., 1998. The global carbon sink: A grassland perspective. Global Change Biol. 4, 229−233.

Stewart, F.J., Newton, I.L.G., Cavanaugh, C.M., 2005. Chemosynthetic endosymbioses: Adaptations to oxic-anoxic interfaces. Trends Microbiol. 13, 439−448.

Strayer, D.L., Caraco, N.F., Cole, J.J., Findlay, S., Pace, M.L., 1999. Transformation of freshwater ecosystems by bivalves: A case study of zebra mussels in the Hudson River. BioScience 49, 19−27.

Suess, H.E., 1980. The radiocarbon record in tree rings of the last 8000 years. Radiocarbon 22, 200−209.

Sundquist, E.T., Visser, K., 2005. The geologic history of the carbon cycle. In: Schlesinger, W.H. (Ed.), Biogeochemistry. Elsevier, New York, pp. 425−472.

Tans, P.P., Dejong, A.F.M., Mook, W.G., 1979. Natural atmospheric $^{14}C$ variation and the Suess effect. Nature 280, 826−827.

Tans, P.P., Fung, I.Y., Takahashi, T., 1990. Observational constraints on the global atmospheric $CO_2$ budget. Science 247, 1431−1438.

Tans, P.P., and R. Keeling. 2012. Dr. Pieter Tans, NOAA/ESRL (www.esrl.noaa.gov/gmd/ccgg/trends/) and Dr. R. Keeling, Scripps Institution of Oceanography (scrippsco2.ucsd.edu/).

Thomas, H., Prowe, A.E.F., van Heuven, S., Bozec, Y., de Baar, H.J.W., Schiettecatte, L.S., et al., 2007. Rapid decline of the $CO_2$ buffering capacity in the North Sea and implications for the North Atlantic Ocean. Global Biogeochem. Cycles 21, GB4001. doi: 10.1029/2006GB002825.

Williams, S.N., Schaefer, S.J., Calvache, M.L., Lopez, D., 1992. Global carbon-dioxide emission to the atmosphere by volcanoes. Geochim. Cosmochim. Acta 56, 1765−1770.

Woodwell, G.M., Mackenzie, F.T., Houghton, R.A., Apps, M., Gorham, E., Davidson, E., 1998. Biotic feedbacks in the warming of the earth. Clim. Change. 40, 495−518.

Worrell, E., Price, L., Martin, N., Hendriks, C., Meida, L.O., 2001. Carbon dioxide emissions from the global cement industry. Annu. Rev. Energy Environ. 26, 303−329.

# The Nitrogen Cycle

*Peter M. Groffman and Emma J. Rosi-Marshall*

**Cary Institute of Ecosystem Studies, Millbrook, NY**

## INTRODUCTION

Nitrogen (N) limits primary production over large areas of the earth, especially in temperate forest and saltwater ecosystems, and has a particularly complex and interesting series of biological transformations in its cycle. Human manipulation of the N cycle is intense, as large amounts of reactive[1] N are needed for crop production and are produced as a by-product of fossil fuel combustion. This manipulation leads to an excess of N in the environment that cascades through ecosystems, leading to problems with air and water quality and ecosystem integrity (Galloway and Cowling 2002; Galloway et al. 2003; Driscoll et al. 2003; Vitousek et al. 1997).

In this chapter, we first present a global perspective on the N cycle and how humans have altered it. We then discuss the processes and transformations that make up the N cycle and describe how these processes are expressed and regulated in terrestrial and aquatic ecosystems.

## THE GLOBAL PICTURE

The largest pool of N on Earth is in the atmosphere as dinitrogen ($N_2$), a very stable (not available to most organisms) molecule that accounts for 79% of the atmosphere. Nitrogen is unique among the elements that are essential for primary production in that it is not a component of the common rocks that make up Earth's crust. Use of N by primary producers thus depends on conversion of $N_2$ into soluble forms.

---

[1]Reactive nitrogen has no standard definition but generally refers to forms of nitrogen capable of combining with other chemicals in the environment and/or that have biological effects. The vast reservoirs of stable nitrogen in the atmosphere ($N_2$ gas) and in soil organic matter are not reactive.

Conversion or "fixation" of atmospheric nitrogen has been deliberately altered by humans for the production of fertilizer to stimulate crop production and inadvertently via the combustion of fossil fuels. Natural fixation results from lightning and the activities of specialized organisms (discussed later). Human activities have doubled global N fixation, mostly since 1950 (Figure 7.1). The increase has been driven by increases in fertilizer use to support food production and by increases in fossil fuel combustion, which inadvertently converts (or fixes) $N_2$ into reactive N (Figure 7.2). The increase in human nitrogen use has occurred more recently and quickly than other major human alterations of global processes (Figure 7.1). A major technological advance facilitating human nitrogen use was the development of the Haber-Bosch process for chemically fixing nitrogen to the atmosphere. In this process, $N_2$ is reacted with hydrogen gas ($H_2$) over an iron or ruthenium catalyst to produce ammonia. The process was originally developed to facilitate the production of explosives early in the twentieth century and was adopted for fertilizer use decades later. Widespread increases in the cultivation of N-fixing crops have also facilitated the increase in human nitrogen use. Because food production and fossil fuel combustion are high in the United States, the alteration of the U.S. N cycle is much more dramatic than the global average. Changes in the nitrogen cycle are currently much more dynamic in the developing world, for example China and India, which is experiencing rapid increases in both fertilizer use and fossil fuel combustion.

Extra reactive N added to the atmosphere by humans via fossil fuel combustion and as fertilizer cascades through the environment and causes a series of biological, chemical, and physical changes in ecosystems (Figure 7.3). For example, some of the fertilizer that is applied to agricultural fields leaves those fields in surface runoff or ground-water flow. This N becomes a drinking water pollutant and cascades through the environment in streams, rivers, estuaries, and eventually in the sea. This N stimulates the productivity of primary producers in aquatic ecosystems just as it does in crop fields leading to eutrophication (a process where water bodies receive excess nutrients that stimulate excessive plant and algal growth), especially in coastal ecosystems. As the excessive growth decays in the bottom waters of these ecosystems, oxygen is consumed, leading to hypoxic dead zones in ecosystems across the world, from the Gulf of Mexico to the Chesapeake Bay to the Baltic and South China seas.

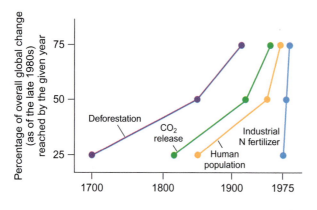

FIGURE 7.1  The time course of selected human actions that have effects at the global scale. Note that human manipulation of the global N cycle has been the most recent and drastic component of global change. *(From Vitousek et al. 1997.)*

Extra reactive N in the atmosphere also cascades through the environment creating a series of untoward effects. Some forms of excess N in the atmosphere are precursors to tropospheric ozone and particulate matter (PM) that are detrimental to human health. Other forms of atmospheric N contribute to the greenhouse effect and to the destruction of ozone in the stratosphere. Some of the reactive N added to the atmosphere is deposited on terrestrial ecosystems, where it can increase the productivity of vegetation, but can also cause N saturation (extra N beyond what the biology can use) of ecosystems that developed under low N conditions (Aber et al. 1989, 1998). N saturation can lead to changes in plant community composition, nutrient imbalances (e.g., with phosphorus or base cations), and delivery of excess N to lakes, rivers, and estuaries.

In summary, two concepts that are helpful to keep in mind as we think about the environmental impacts of N are (1) the idea that N added to one place will often move to other

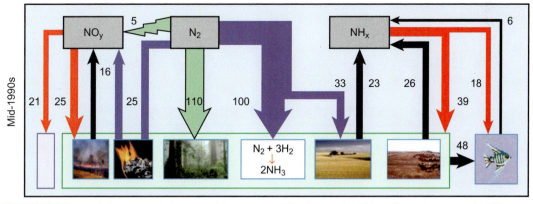

FIGURE 7.2    Global nitrogen budget for 1860 and mid-1990s. Data in Tg N/yr. The emissions to the NOy box from the coal reflect fossil-fuel combustion. Those from the vegetation include agricultural and natural soil emissions, and combustion of biofuel, biomass (savannah and forests), and agricultural waste. The emissions to the $NH_x$ box from the agricultural field include emissions from agricultural land and combustion of biofuel, biomass (savannah and forests), and agricultural waste. The $NH_x$ emissions from the cow and feedlot reflect emissions from animal waste. *(From Galloway and Cowling 2002.)*

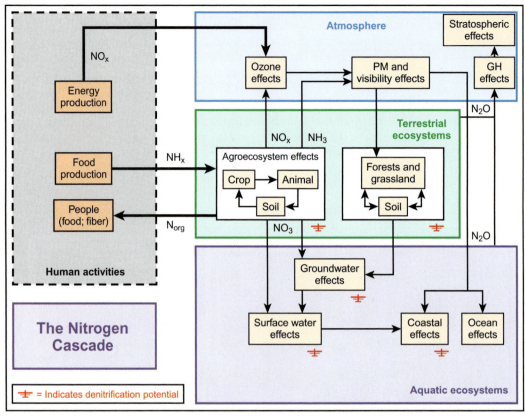

**FIGURE 7.3**   The nitrogen cascade. Nitrogen added to the environment by human activity "cascades" through the atmosphere and terrestrial and aquatic ecosystems causing a series of air- and water-quality problems. *(From Galloway 2003.)*

places, and (2) this extra N can be "too much of a good thing" and cause a wide variety of environmental problems.

## NITROGEN CYCLE PROCESSES

As stated earlier, the N cycle is one of the more complex nutrient cycles. In the following sections we define and describe the controls on each of the processes shown in Figure 7.4. Table 7.1 is a handy "cheat sheet" listing the dominant forms and processes of the N cycle.

### Nitrogen Fixation

Pathways:

$$N_2 \longrightarrow NH_3$$
$$N_2 \longrightarrow \text{various forms of reactive N in the atmosphere } (NO_y)$$

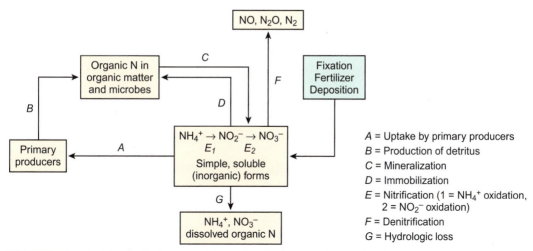

FIGURE 7.4   The N cycle. Each process indicated in the figure is discussed in the text.

N fixation refers to the conversion of dinitrogen ($N_2$) into ammonia ($NH_3$) or to various forms of reactive N in the atmosphere, generally referred to as NOy. The process requires a great deal of energy as the $N_2$ molecule is extremely stable. As a result, N fixation occurs only in situations where there is ample energy. Physical/chemical fixation takes place during lightning discharges in the atmosphere, in $NH_3$ manufacturing plants where large quantities of natural gas are used to convert $N_2$ to $NH_3$, and when fossil fuels are combusted, for example, in an internal combustion engine. Biological N fixation occurs in situations where relationships between primary producers and microbes with the enzymes necessary to convert $N_2$ to $NH_3$ allow for an energetic subsidy of the N-fixing microbes, in cyanobacteria (blue-green algae) that are primary producers with the ability to fix N, or in specific niches with abundant energy and low N availability, like rotting logs.

The energetics of N fixation have a powerful influence on the ecology of this process. The N-fixation enzyme (nitrogenase) is present only in a few genera of soil bacteria (e.g., *Rhizobia*, *Frankia*) and in blue-green algae (cyanobacteria). Use of the enzyme can consume more than half of the energy that the bacteria obtain from their normal consumption of substrates. Organisms that devote half of their energy to one process tend to grow more slowly and/or have reduced metabolic capacity compared to other organisms with which they compete for space and substrate in the environment. As a result, "free-living" N fixation activity is usually quite low, and is restricted to environments where the ability to fix N conveys a strong competitive advantage, for example, on substrates with high energy but low N content such as decaying logs.

The vast majority of biological N fixation in terrestrial ecosystems occurs in the context of symbiotic relationships between primary producers and N-fixing microbes. In terrestrial ecosystems, examples are plants in the legume family and the genus *Alnus* that have developed symbiotic relationships with *Rhizobia* and *Frankia* bacteria. The bacteria live in specialized nodules attached to plant roots: the plant sends energy in the form of sugars to the nodules, and the bacteria fix N in the nodules and share this N with the plant.

**TABLE 7.1**   A "cheat sheet" for the nitrogen cycle.

| Pools/Chemical Forms | | Importance |
|---|---|---|
| **Gases** | | |
| $N_2$ | Dinitrogen | Dominant global pool, 79% of atmosphere. |
| $N_2O$ | Nitrous oxide | Greenhouse gas, destroys stratospheric ozone. |
| NO | Nitric oxide | Toxic, precursor of tropospheric ozone. |
| $NH_3$ | Ammonia | Plant available (soluble), can be toxic, rapidly deposited. |
| $NO_y$ | Diverse reactive forms of N in the atmosphere produced by combustion of fossil fuels and/or atmospheric chemical reactions | Plant available (soluble), component of acid rain, rapidly deposited. |
| **Ions/Soluble Forms** | | |
| $NH_4^+$ | Ammonium | Available to plants. |
| $NO_2^-$ | Nitrite | Toxic, rarely found at high levels in nature. |
| $NO_3^-$ | Nitrate | Available to plants, highly leachable. |
| DON | Dissolved organic nitrogen | Mixture of many different chemical forms. |
| **Processes** | | |
| $N_2 \longrightarrow NH_3$ | Biological N fixation | See text. |
| $N_2 \longrightarrow NO_y$ | Abiotic N fixation | See text. |
| Organic N $\longrightarrow NH_4^+$ | Mineralization | See text. |
| $NH_4^+$ or $NO_3^- \longrightarrow$ Organic N | Immobilization | See text. |
| $NH_4^+ \longrightarrow NO_2^- \longrightarrow NO_3^-$ | Nitrification | See text. |
| $NO_3^- \longrightarrow NO_2^- \longrightarrow NO \longrightarrow N_2O \longrightarrow N_2$ | Denitrification | See text. |
| $NO_3^- \longrightarrow NH_3$ | Dissimilatory nitrate reduction to ammonia (DNRA) | See text. |
| $NH_4^+ + NO_2^- \longrightarrow N_2$ | Anaerobic oxidation of ammonium (anammox) | See text. |

In aquatic ecosystems, specific species of cyanobacteria fix N in specialized structures (heterocysts) that enclose nitrogenase, which is fed by sugars produced elsewhere in the organism. Other aquatic N fixers, especially in marine systems, do not have specialized structures, but all have some energetic subsidy to facilitate fixation.

Symbioses with N fixers have powerful effects on the ecology of the primary producers involved in these relationships. These organisms can send up to 50% of the energy that they fix from the sun to their N-fixing symbionts, reducing the amount of energy available for growth, chemical defense, and other functions. As a result, legumes and *Alnus* plants tend to live in specialized temporal or spatial niches where their ability to fix N gives them a competitive advantage and/or their slow growth is not a hindrance, for example, in the early phases of succession, or on substrates very low in N such as recent lava flows or sand dunes. Cyanobacteria tend to thrive in water bodies with low N:P ratios where their ability to fix N gives them a selective advantage.

## Nitrogen Mineralization and Immobilization

Pathways:

$$\text{Mineralization: Organic N} \longrightarrow NH_4^+$$
$$\text{Immobilization: } NH_4^+ \text{ or } NO_3^- \longrightarrow \text{Organic N}$$

In addition to N fixation, the other main natural source of soluble reactive N in ecosystems is N mineralization. In this transformation, N contained in organic matter is converted to an inorganic form as ammonium ($NH_4^+$). The mineralization process is sometimes referred to as *ammonification*.

At the molecular level, N mineralization is a by-product of the microbial degradation of N-containing compounds such as proteins. Microorganisms degrading these compounds convert the carbon components into biomass or carbon dioxide and either convert the N components into their own biomass (e.g., proteins) or release them to the environment. In the case of proteins, this results in the release of an amino group ($NH_2$), which is rapidly converted to $NH_4^+$ in the environment (although $NH_3$ can be released as a gas under high pH conditions). Mineralization thus depends on microbial needs for N. If the microbes are degrading compounds with lots of N, such as proteins, their needs for N are readily satisfied and excess N is released to the environment (mineralized). If the microbes are degrading compounds low in N (e.g., oak leaves or sawdust), they become N limited and need to take up (immobilize) inorganic N (either $NH_4^+$ or nitrate ($NO_3^-$)) from some other environmental source (see Chapter 4). It is energetically preferable for microbes to take up $NH_4^+$ because $NO_3^-$ has to be reduced to $NH_4^+$ (which requires energy) before it can be used to construct proteins or other compounds in microbial cells.

It is useful to distinguish between "gross" and "net" mineralization and immobilization. Given that these are molecular-scale processes, we can observe only the net balance by measuring net changes in inorganic N pools over time. For example, if gross mineralization is 10 mg N m$^{-2}$ d$^{-1}$ and gross immobilization is 11 mg N m$^{-2}$ d$^{-1}$, conventional methods detect only a net immobilization of 1 mg N m$^{-2}$ d$^{-1}$. However, using stable isotope methods (see Chapter 1), gross processes can be inferred. The two processes of gross production and consumption of inorganic N have been shown to exist in a dynamic balance such that gross fluxes are often 10 or 100 times the net fluxes.

Many microorganisms, including all heterotrophic (nutrition obtained by digesting organic compounds) microbes, carry out mineralization and immobilization. Thus, these processes go on under aerobic and anaerobic conditions, and at extremes of temperature, pH, salinity, water availability, and other environmental conditions.

Recent research showing that plants can take up simple, soluble amino acids (a type of dissolved organic N) has motivated discussion about expanding the concept of mineralization to include not just the production of $NH_4^+$, but any simple, soluble, N-containing compound available to plants. Such a redefinition would not alter the basic concept that mineralization involves simplification of organic compounds into forms available to plants.

The balance between mineralization and immobilization regulates the size of the soluble N pool and is thus a critical regulator of N availability to primary producers and for hydrologic losses. If immobilization dominates over mineralization, the soluble pool decreases and vice versa. A good predictor of this balance is the C:N molar ratio of the substrate being decomposed. If microbes are degrading substrates (a molecule upon which an enzyme acts) rich in N, their needs for N are easily met and mineralization dominates. As a general rule, substrates with molar C:N of 25:1 or lower lead to net mineralization, while substrates with C:N greater than 25:1 lead to net immobilization (Table 7.2). Thus, it is easy to understand why adding materials such as manure stimulates plant growth whereas adding materials such as sawdust inhibits plant growth (See Figure 4.8 in Chapter 4). Some materials, such as soil organic matter, have low C:N ratios but do not lead to increases in the soluble N pool because they are extensively degraded and chemically altered (humified) and are therefore not susceptible to microbial use.

In addition to switching from mineralization to immobilization to meet their N needs, microbes have the ability to produce N-acquiring enzymes in response to N limitation of their growth and activity. Thus, addition of N-poor substrates will stimulate production of such enzymes as chitinase, which releases N from chitin (N-acetylglucosamine) or

TABLE 7.2  Molar C:N ratios in various organic materials.

| Organic Material | C:N Ratio |
| --- | --- |
| Soil microorganisms | 8:1 |
| Sewage sludge | 9:1 |
| Soil organic matter | 10:1 |
| Alfalfa residues | 16:1 |
| Farmyard manure | 20:1 |
| Corn residue | 60:1 |
| Grain straw | 80:1 |
| Oak | 200:1 |
| Pine | 300:1 |
| Crude oil | 400:1 |
| Conifer sawdust | 625:1 |

*From Tisdale et al. 1993; Hyvönen et al. 1996.*

peptidases that liberate N from proteins. This enzymatic flexibility extends to other nutrients, for example, production of phosphatase increases when phosphorus is limiting to microbial growth or activity.

## Nitrification

Pathway:

$$NH_4^+ \longrightarrow NO_2^- \longrightarrow NO_3^-$$

Nitrification refers to two transformations that take place within the soluble inorganic N pool: the conversion of $NH_4^+$ to nitrite ($NO_2^-$), followed by the conversion of $NO_2^-$ to $NO_3^-$. The transformations are carried out by two different groups of chemoautotrophic (get their energy from inorganic compounds and carbon to make their cells from carbon dioxide) microbes that derive energy from these oxidations. Nitrite is highly reactive (both chemically and biologically) and is usually present for very short periods and thus is in vanishingly small quantities in the environment, making $NO_3^-$ the dominant product of the nitrification process.

Nitrification has great ecological importance. Due to its negative charge, $NO_3^-$ is much more mobile than $NH_4^+$. This is because soil and sediment particles generally carry a negative charge to which positively charged ions such as $NH_4^+$ are attracted. Therefore, rates of nitrification are key controllers of hydrologic losses of N. Production of $NO_2^-$ and $NO_3^-$ by nitrifiers feeds the denitrification process (discussed later) and thus fosters gaseous losses of N, cycling of N between the atmosphere and the biosphere, and the production of trace gases that affect the chemistry and physics of the atmosphere. If nitrification did not exist, N limitation of terrestrial production and N-related water and air pollution would be rare.

Like N fixation, the ecology of nitrification is strongly influenced by energetic constraints. The substrates used by nitrifiers ($NH_4^+$, $NO_2^-$) are not rich in energy relative to the substrates used by heterotrophic microbes (see the Appendix), and as a result, nitrifiers grow slowly and compete poorly with heterotrophs and plants for oxygen, $NH_4^+$, and other resources. The competition for $NH_4^+$ with plants and immobilizing heterotrophs is a particularly strong regulator of nitrification activity. Thus, we expect to find high nitrification activity in situations with high levels of $NH_4^+$, for example, crop fields fertilized with $NH_4^+$, heavily manured crop fields, N-rich sediments, or ecosystems with some disturbance that reduces plant uptake, such as clear-cutting of a forest.

The microbiology and physiology of nitrification are more complex than they first appeared. For many decades, it was assumed that $NH_4^+$ oxidation was carried out dominantly by one genus of bacteria, *Nitrosomonas*, and that $NO_2^-$ oxidation was carried out by another single genus, *Nitrobacter*. Recent molecular analysis has shown that there are several other genera of $NH_4^+$- and $NO_2^-$-oxidizing bacteria, as well as newly discovered $NH_4^+$-oxidizing Archaea. Other recent studies have identified several heterotrophic nitrification pathways whereby organic N is converted directly to $NO_3^-$.

Even more interesting than the discovery of multiple nitrifying genera and pathways is the developing understanding of nitrifier physiology. It was originally thought that these organisms could use only their primary substrates ($NH_4^+$ or $NO_2^-$), but it turns out that the ammonia monoxygenase enzyme is capable of oxidizing methane as well as a series of carbon compounds including propane and a series of chlorinated aliphatic compounds of great environmental concern (e.g., trichloroethylene). Nitrifiers were originally thought to be strict aerobes, but it turns out that they are capable of growing facultatively under anaerobic conditions as denitrifiers (discussed later). They were also thought to be highly sensitive to low pH, and incapable of growth at pH less than 5, yet nitrification has been found to be vigorous in acid soils (pH 4) in many locations. The relative importance of these diverse physiologies in both the distribution and abundance of ammonia oxidizers is an area of active research.

## Denitrification

Pathway:

$$NO_3^- \longrightarrow NO_2^- \longrightarrow NO \longrightarrow N_2O \longrightarrow N_2$$

Denitrification is a form of anaerobic respiration carried out by bacteria that use $NO_3^-$, $NO_2^-$, nitric oxide (NO), or nitrous oxide ($N_2O$) as electron acceptors producing progressively reduced products, ending in $N_2$. Most denitrifiers are facultative anaerobes; that is, they normally respire oxygen, but in its absence use N-oxides. There are many heterotrophic denitrifiers; the ability is widely distributed among hundreds of genera. There are also chemoautotrophic denitrifiers that use compounds such as $NH_4^+$ (nitrifier denitrification) or sulfur compounds as electron donors, and the N-oxides as electron acceptors.

The ecology of denitrification is strongly controlled by the fact that it is an anaerobic process. Therefore, we expect rates to be high in wetlands, in anaerobic sediments of aquatic ecosystems, and in deep oceanic oxygen minimum zones. Denitrification is also strongly regulated by the availability of $NO_3^-$ and is often transient in response to pulses of $NO_3^-$ input or production. For example, inputs of $NO_3^-$ to wetlands from surrounding agricultural fields can create high rates of denitrification that will be sustained only as long as the supply of $NO_3^-$ continues. Alternating periods of drying and wetting in wetland soils can lead to increases of $NO_3^-$ production by nitrification during the dry periods, followed by denitrification during the wet, anaerobic periods. In sediments, $NO_3^-$ production by nitrification can be vigorous in an aerobic surface layer and can support high denitrification in anaerobic sediment layers just below the surface (see later and Figure 7.5).

Denitrification is important in several applied contexts. Originally, denitrification was seen as a threat to soil fertility because it directly removes N from the plant-available pool. More recently, there has been interest in the role of denitrification in maintaining water quality, as it can prevent the movement of N into aquatic ecosystems sensitive to N-induced eutrophication. Efforts are active in many areas of the world to protect, restore, and/or create ecosystems that facilitate denitrification of excess N from agriculture, sewage, and atmospheric deposition. These range from riparian zones in agricultural watersheds, to highly engineered systems to treat sewage wastewater, to small wood-chip bioreactors to directly process N leaving agricultural fields in subsurface drainage pipes, to specialized anaerobic tanks adjacent to individual sewage disposal systems (septic systems).

Denitrification also influences air quality, as NO is a precursor to ozone formation in the troposphere (where ozone is a pollutant) and $N_2O$ is a greenhouse gas and contributes

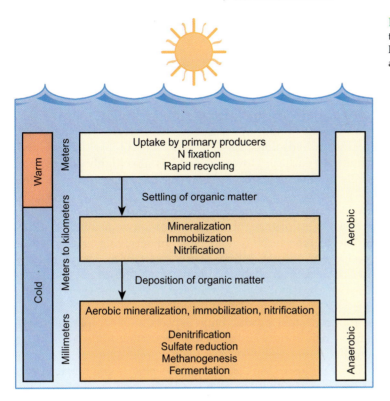

**FIGURE 7.5** The N cycle in the water column and sediment layers of a thermally stratified aquatic ecosystem such as a lake.

to destruction of ozone in the stratosphere (where ozone absorbs UV radiation). The factors controlling the distribution of the gaseous end products of denitrification are complex and variable, making relative assessment of the water quality benefits and atmospheric chemistry problems associated with denitrification very difficult.

## Other Dissimilatory Processes (DNRA and Anammox)

In addition to denitrification, there are other anaerobic processes where N-oxides serve as electron acceptors to facilitate the dissimilation of energy. In the process of dissimilatory nitrate reduction to ammonia (DNRA), $NO_3^-$ serves as an electron acceptor and $NH_3$ is the end-product. This process is thought to be favored over denitrification in environments where the ratio of energy sources to electron acceptors is high because DNRA consumes more electrons than denitrification. Recent work has focused the ability of different energy sources (e.g., reduced sulfur) to favor one pathway over the other.

In anaerobic oxidation of ammonia (anammox), the oxidation of ammonia as an energy source is coupled to reduction of $NO_2^-$ as an electron acceptor, with $N_2$ as the end-product. This process was originally discovered in sewage waste treatment plants, but has been found to be important in the ocean and more generally in highly anaerobic environments that have low supplies of organic energy sources.

## Hydrologic Losses

As mentioned earlier, the need for primary producers to take up simple, soluble forms of nutrients greatly complicates nutrient cycling in ecosystems as it creates the possibility of hydrologic losses. For N, interest in hydrologic losses centers on $NO_3^-$, which is highly mobile due to its negative charge (see earlier). However, $NH_4^+$ is also highly soluble and can be lost at high rates, especially in flowing waters, which have less opportunity to interact with positively charged soil particles. There is also interest in loss of dissolved organic N (DON), which consists of a wide range of compounds produced during the decomposition of organic matter or synthesized by primary producers. Some components of DON are highly labile and can degrade to release $NH_4^+$ and $NO_3^-$ in receiving waters, while others are highly humified (products of decomposition, highly resistant to decay) and stable. Because most DON may not be directly available to plants, it may represent an uncontrollable form of hydrologic loss that contributes to N limitation of ecosystem productivity over the long term.

Given the importance of N for ecosystem productivity, especially in temperate terrestrial ecosystems, there has been extensive study of the factors regulating hydrologic losses of N. Many studies have focused on how disturbance of plant uptake by clear-cutting of forests leads to increases in hydrologic losses and on the plant, soil, and microbial factors that control the magnitude of these losses. Other research has focused on the ability of terrestrial ecosystems to absorb increasing amounts of N deposition from the atmosphere, which has increased along with fossil fuel combustion, and prevent its movement into downstream waters sensitive to N-induced eutrophication. And a vast body of research has focused on minimizing hydrologic losses from intensively fertilized agricultural fields, including efforts to use wetlands as denitrification "sinks" for excess N moving out of fields in surface runoff or ground-water flow (Mitsch et al. 2001).

# NITROGEN CYCLING IN TERRESTRIAL ECOSYSTEMS

## Pools and Fluxes

In nearly all terrestrial ecosystems, the largest pool of N is in the soil (Table 7.3). Most of this N is tied up in recalcitrant soil organic matter (the long-term residual by-product of decomposition) and plays little role in N cycling between plants and the soluble, available pool. The available pool is very small and dynamic over the timescale of days, with mineralization constantly adding N to this pool and plant uptake and immobilization constantly removing N. Plant biomass (living and dead) represents the next largest pool of N in

TABLE 7.3 Pools and fluxes of N in an aggrading (55-year-old) northern hardwood forest (Hubbard Brook, New Hampshire) and an ungrazed tallgrass prairie (Konza Prairie, Kansas)

| Pools (kg N/ha) | Hubbard Brook[1] | Konza Prairie[2] |
|---|---|---|
| Soil organic matter | 4700 | 6250 |
| Inorganic N pool in soil | 26 | 2–6 |
| Plant biomass | 532 | 60–250 |
| **Fluxes (kg N ha$^{-1}$ y$^{-1}$)** | | |
| Atmospheric deposition | 10 | 10–20 |
| N fixation | 1 | 1–5 |
| Net mineralization | 70 | 10–40 |
| Net nitrification | 15 | ? |
| Hydrologic losses | 4 | 0.1–0.3 |
| Denitrification | 0–10 | 0–10 |
| Plant uptake | 80 | 40–50 |
| Litterfall | 54 | 5–20 |

[1]Values from Bormann et al. (1977), Likens and Bormann (1995), and Melillo (1977).
[2]From Blair et al. (1998).

terrestrial systems, especially in systems with woody biomass (e.g., tree trunks) that represent another relatively large pool of N that is not actively cycling.

The dominant cycling fluxes in intact native terrestrial ecosystems are plant uptake, litterfall, and mineralization, which roughly balance each other in an ecosystem that is not growing (adding new biomass). Inputs in fixation and atmospheric deposition are low (roughly 10-fold less) relative to these internal fluxes, even though deposition has been roughly doubled by anthropogenic additions of reactive N to the atmosphere near many densely populated regions. Hydrologic and gaseous outputs are also low relative to internal fluxes, reflecting the intense demand for N as a critical resource by plants and microbes.

## Ecosystem Development

A useful way to think about N cycling in terrestrial ecosystems is to think about changes that occur during ecosystem development or plant succession following a disturbance that removes most of the living plant biomass, like clear-cutting a forest. Following such a disturbance, plant uptake is reduced and microbial mineralization and nitrification often increase as the loss of plant biomass (and uptake) leads to increases in soil moisture and temperature. The stimulation of nitrification and lack of plant uptake creates larger pools and hydrologic losses of $NO_3^-$. As vegetation begins to grow back following disturbance, hydrologic losses decrease, often to levels lower than before the disturbance, as the young, actively growing vegetation creates a strong demand for water and nutrient uptake. Once biomass stops increasing, nutrient losses then increase and should come into rough balance with inputs (Figure 7.6). While the patterns of N cycling with ecosystem development described earlier are a useful way to think about N cycling in terrestrial ecosystems, there is much variation in response to disturbance from site to site due to differences in inherent site fertility (e.g., nutrient-rich sites lose more nutrients following disturbance), hydrologic conditions (e.g., high precipitation, permeable soils facilitate nutrient losses), and the details of the disturbance (e.g., just how are trees cut and removed from the system).

There are two interesting unresolved nitrogen mysteries that have arisen over the past couple of decades. The first mystery is the persistence of N limitation of above-ground net primary production (ANPP) over long (millions of years) time frames. Even though pools of N in soils and vegetation become very large over time, additions of N in fertilizer still lead to increases in ANPP. Persistent N limitation is likely due to uncontrolled gaseous and hydrologic N losses. A second mystery, which somewhat contradicts the first mystery, is low hydrologic losses of N even in mature (nonaggrading) ecosystems in regions with relatively high atmospheric N deposition. This high N retention is likely due to storage of excess N in dead wood, soil pools that increase over time, or poorly quantified and underestimated gaseous fluxes.

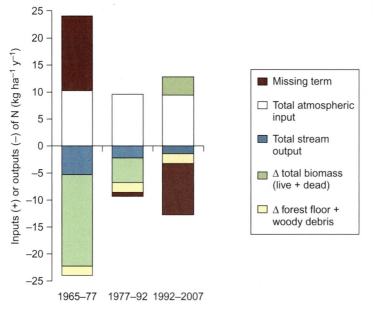

FIGURE 7.6 The watershed-scale mass balance of nitrogen at Hubbard Brook Experimental Forest Watershed 6 (New Hampshire) is shown for a 37-year period. This northern hardwood forest was aggrading (building up) biomass until about 1982. During the aggrading period, there were "missing inputs" to support the large accumulation in biomass, and in the nonaggrading period, there were "missing outputs" as stream output, which is measured very accurately at Hubbard Brook, and is much lower than atmospheric input. These missing outputs must be either to gases or accumulation in soil organic matter. (From Yanai, R.D., S.P. Hamburg, M.A. Arthur, M.A. Vadeboncoeur, C.B. Fuss, and T.G. Siccama, unpublished.)

# Site Controls

Much of the variation in N cycling among terrestrial ecosystems can be understood by considering how inherent site resources control interactions between water, plant community composition, and N dynamics (e.g., Pastor et al. 1984; Pastor and Post 1986). Within any given region, soil texture exerts strong control over water availability as coarse-textured (sandy) soils hold less water than more fine-textured soils. Water stress favors the development of plant communities with leaves containing compounds (e.g., waxes) that contribute to the retention of water. These compounds increase the C:N ratio of the leaves, which shifts the balance between N mineralization and immobilization toward immobilization, leading to low inorganic N availability for plant uptake or hydrologic losses. The decrease in available N creates positive feedback toward plant species with high C:N ratios, leading to further decreases in N availability (Figure 7.7). Thus over time, marked patterns in plant community composition and N cycling across the landscape develop and persist. A major

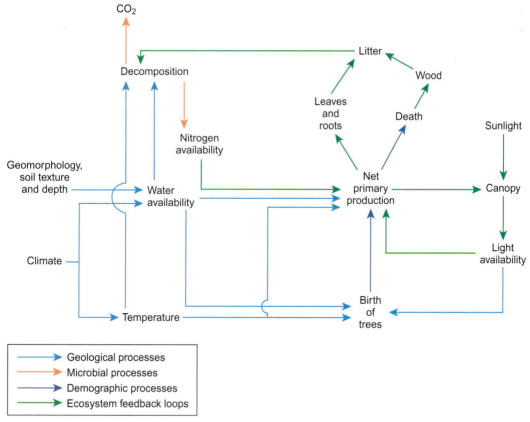

FIGURE 7.7  Conceptual model showing how site characteristics (geomorphology, soil texture, and depth) influence water availability, which in turn influences litter quality and nitrogen availability in temperate forests. *(From Pastor and Post 1986.)*

area of current research is if these inherent site controls can be overwhelmed by increases in atmospheric deposition and invasions by exotic plant species.

## Agriculture

Conversion of native ecosystems to cultivated fields and pasture is one of the most widespread and intensive global alterations of terrestrial N cycling and is a major source of air and water N pollution. If we revisit Figure 7.4, it is easy to see how agriculture alters the N cycle and increases hydrologic and gaseous N losses. Fertilizer, which usually consists of ammonium salts or urea ($CON_2H_4$ or $(NH_2)_2CO$, which rapidly decomposes to ammonium), is a direct addition to the soluble, available pool, which increases the flow of N to plants (the intended target), but also increases the potential for hydrologic and gaseous losses that arise from these pools. Harvest, which removes the plant community, also increases the potential for losses as the flow of N to plants ceases. Harvest also decreases the flow of organic matter to soil pools, which alters the balance between mineralization and immobilization toward mineralization, leading to further increases in the soluble pool. Soil organic matter pools are also reduced by tillage, which stimulates decomposition. There is great interest in developing agricultural systems with "tighter" N cycles by altering management to sustain plant uptake and soil organic matter pools, for example, through the use of winter "cover crops" to maintain plant uptake for a larger portion of the year and to increase soil organic matter pools. There is also interest in evaluating agricultural ecosystems in a landscape context, using downstream or downslope wetlands or other ecosystem types with high capacity for absorbing excess N moving from agricultural areas and converting this excess N into gases, plant biomass, or soil organic matter.

## NITROGEN CYCLING IN AQUATIC ECOSYSTEMS

### Lakes and Oceans

In aquatic ecosystems, N is often an important limiting nutrient for both aquatic primary production and decomposition (see Chapters 2 and 4). In lakes, there are typically distinct zones with different forms and concentrations of N and dominant cycling pathways. Thermal stratification of the water column creates these distinct zones; warmer water is less dense than colder water, thereby resulting in distinct density zones within a lake that do not mix for extended periods of time. Understanding ecosystem-level N dynamics requires exploring these distinct zones independently and understanding when these zones mix (Figure 7.5). In lakes, uptake of N by primary producers (phytoplankton) occurs in the top of the water column where light availability is highest. In this photic zone (the epilimnion), N cycling is dominated by uptake by primary producers (e.g., algae, diatoms, and cyanobacteria), and a fraction of the N is excreted as DON by primary producers. Zooplankton consume algae and excrete dissolved inorganic N and heterotrophic bacteria mineralize particulate and dissolved organic matter, releasing inorganic N into the epilimnion, which can be rapidly taken up by primary producers. This can result in rapid and tight N cycling in the epilimnion. This zone is where most consumers are found as well (e.g., zooplankton and fishes).

In lakes, as algae and other organisms die and settle to the bottom some N leaves the epilimnion and is no longer available for N cycling in the top layers. The dark bottom water layers of the lake (hypolimnion) and sediments are net heterotrophic and processes such as decomposition, mineralization, immobilization, nitrification, and denitrification dominate. As a result, the dark, cold, and often anoxic conditions promote different pathways of N cycling. The decomposition of organic matter and lack of photosynthesis drives down oxygen concentrations in the water column and some lakes may have anoxic hypolimnia. The concentrations of dissolved nutrients in the bottom layers can be much higher than in the surface layers because of high mineralization rates and low uptake rates. In anoxic hypolimnia, concentrations of ammonium can be high because the low oxygen conditions block nitrification. In aerobic hypolimnia, N transformations in the sediments are controlled by the flow of oxygen and detritus from the water column, which leads to a marked layering of redox conditions within the sediments. The surface layer of the sediment may be aerobic, with high rates of decomposition, mineralization, and nitrification. High rates of oxygen consumption combined with low rates of diffusion can lead to the development of anaerobic layers below the surface aerobic layer. If nitrification rates are high, a supply of $NO_3^-$ can support a vigorous denitrification layer just below the surface aerobic layer. This coupled nitrification–denitrification layering can make aquatic sediments significant "sinks" for N in the landscape, since much of the N that enters these systems is returned to the atmosphere. Beneath the denitrification layer, other anaerobic processes (e.g., sulfate reduction, methanogenesis) dominate (see the Appendix). In stratifying lakes, the layers of water can mix completely during seasons when thermal stratification of the layers breaks down (typically spring and fall). During these times, the bottom nutrient-rich waters mix with the nutrient-poor surface waters and act to "reset" the system, which can promote seasonal increases in primary production.

In oceans, similar depth-driven changes in light, settling, and decomposition can lead to variable N transformations in different zones. In oceans, rates of primary production are often N limited and the sources of N are fixation, runoff of N from rivers, zones of upwelling, and internal cycling. The sunlit surface waters of the ocean (euphotic zone) contain primary producers (e.g., phytoplankton) and many heterotrophic organisms such as zooplankton, fishes, marine mammals, and birds. Because particulate carbon (e.g., phytoplankton, marine snow, and fecal pellets) produced in the euphotic zone sinks, the supply of nitrogen is greater than can be supplied by internal cycling alone (Eppley and Peterson 1979). The nitrogen available for primary producers in the euphotic zone comes from internal recycling and external inputs such as upwelling, N-fixation, and nitrogen from terrestrial landscapes via river flow. In addition, ocean shelf sediments and oxygen minimum zones associated with the decomposition of settled organic matter can promote higher levels of anoxic N transformations (e.g., denitrification). The sinking of particulate matter from the euphotic zone fuels heterotrophic activity and is a source of nitrogen to the deep ocean. Movements of organisms that feed at depth and come to the surface (e.g., whales) can also bring nutrients from deep zones to the photic zone.

Cycling of N in standing-water ecosystems can vary, and be disrupted by human activities in several ways. Stimulation of primary production by addition of nutrients (typically phosphorus in freshwater, N in saltwater, but also often colimited by both N and phosphorus) can lead to algal blooms and altered ecosystem properties. For example, increases in phosphorus in lakes and estuaries (associated with phosphates in detergents and fertilizers) can stimulate high rates of population growth by N-fixing blue-green algae (cyanobacteria). These N-fixers are often unpalatable to zooplankton, and despite high rates of primary production, this shift in algal species composition can lead to less available edible food for consumers. In oceans, increases in N from riverine inputs associated with fertilizer application and human wastewater can lead to algal blooms as well. When these algal blooms die and sink to deeper layers and decompose, the increased decomposition can lead to very low concentrations of oxygen, which can be harmful to fishes and other aquatic organisms. Loss of the aerobic conditions above the sediments also cuts off the coupled nitrification−denitrification process that operates in sediments with an aerobic surface layer. Loss of this process creates a positive feedback as ammonium produced by mineralization (which occurs under both aerobic and anaerobic conditions) diffuses back into the water column where it can contribute to further increases in primary production. This switch from aerobic to anaerobic conditions can occur seasonally; in summer, decomposition of organic material produced during spring "bloom" conditions can deplete oxygen at depth in the water column leading to completely anaerobic sediments (Figure 7.8). Sediments can also be made anaerobic by direct additions of organic matter to open water

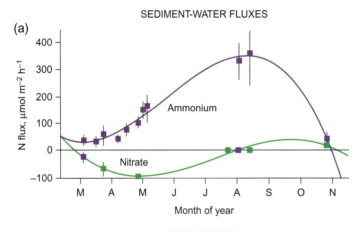

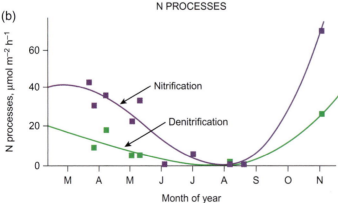

FIGURE 7.8 Sediment N dynamics in the mesohaline portion of the Chesapeake Bay. (a) Seasonal variation in net fluxes of ammonium and nitrate across the sediment−water interface. (b) Seasonal variation in net nitrification and denitrification in sediments. Nitrogen dynamics are driven by oxygen availability, which is low in summer. *(From Kemp et al. 1990.)*

bodies, such as when untreated sewage or waste from pulp mills is discharged. This organic matter settles to the sediments, stimulates decomposition, creates anaerobic conditions, and cuts off coupled nitrification−denitrification.

## Streams and Rivers

Streams and rivers are both the kidneys of the continents (e.g., they can remove significant amounts of N from the water column) and the delivery system moving nutrients from continents to the sea. Typically, the coupling between the water column and sediments is much stronger in small streams than in large water bodies because the water column is in close contact with the sediments. As streams get larger and depth increases, the interactions between the water column and the sediment may diminish.

In rivers and streams, directional water flow creates additional complexity in N cycling. The downstream movement of water and solutes results in N being pulled downstream as it cycles and is referred to as nutrient spiraling (see Box 5.2 in Chapter 5). Streams and rivers are both spatially and temporally heterogeneous with respect to N cycling and are composed of patches of aerobic and anaerobic environments. For example, shallow areas of rapid flow (riffles) are well oxygenated and support high rates of mineralization and nitrification, while quiescent pool areas and accumulations of organic matter behind obstructions in the stream channel can be anaerobic "hotspots" of denitrification. In addition, zones of upwelling, downwelling, and ground-water interactions in a stream can strongly influence N transformations. Explorations of hotspots and hot moments (when N transformations are maximized in time) are currently an area of fruitful research.

Small headwater streams have the capacity to remove N from the water column via assimilation and denitrification, but this capacity is influenced by human activities such as land-use change in the watershed and runoff of N. For example, streams draining agricultural watersheds can have high rates of uptake and denitrification, but can only remove a small fraction of large amounts of N entering the systems from fertilizer. In contrast, streams draining forested catchments do not have high rates of N removal, but can remove a larger fraction of the total N load entering the stream. The extent to which large rivers process and retain N needs further research, as these systems are less frequently studied.

## Ground Water

There is great interest in nitrogen dynamics in ground water, because as noted earlier, nitrate is readily transported through the soil profile into ground water. Nitrate is the most commonly detected drinking water pollutant in ground water in the United States, although it is usually below the regulatory threshold of 10 mg N/L. Ground-water contamination with nitrate is widespread in agricultural landscapes and in rural/suburban landscapes serviced by septic systems.

Much of the interest in ground-water nitrate dynamics focuses on the potential for denitrification to convert the nitrate into nitrogen gases, removing the water quality concerns. Ground water can be anaerobic (necessary for denitrification) if there is sufficient microbial respiration to consume the oxygen present. Relatively low rates of respiration (10 times less than surface soil) can be sufficient to make ground water anaerobic because ground-water often flows very slowly (months to years per km). It is also important to note that respiration can be fueled by reduced inorganic compounds (e.g., iron, sulfur) that can be common in the subsurface (see the Appendix). These compounds are often important sources of energy for subsurface microbes because organic carbon (the energy source for heterotrophs) is often very low in the subsurface.

## NITROGEN BALANCES: THE ENIGMA OF MISSING NITROGEN

It is generally assumed that the N cycle is balanced globally by equal movements of N out of the dominant atmospheric pool by fixation (both natural and anthropogenic) and into the atmospheric pool by denitrification. This assumption is supported by the fact that the concentration of $N_2$ in the atmosphere is relatively stable (although small changes in the concentration of this dominant gas are hard to detect). Mechanistically, the balance is facilitated by the movement of excess anthropogenic N from land to the ocean, which has a vast potential for denitrification.

In addition to the global balance, it is also useful to consider N mass balances at smaller (1 to > 1,000,000 ha) scales, comparing inputs from atmospheric deposition and fertilizer to hydrologic outputs in stream flow, allowing for the calculation of ecosystem "N retention." These balances are useful tools for addressing questions about the fate of anthropogenic N, eutrophication of coastal waters, and changes in atmospheric chemistry.

A common feature of nearly all N mass balances is a high "retention" (calculated as inputs minus hydrologic outputs; Figure 7.9). Given that the balances do not specify just

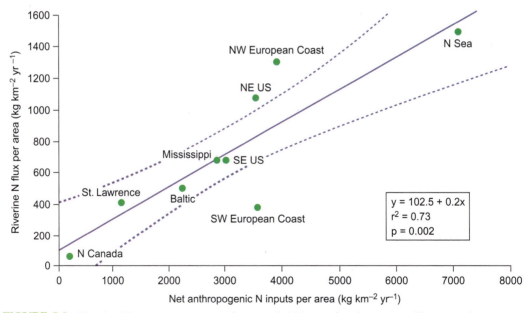

**FIGURE 7.9**   Riverine N export versus net anthropogenic N inputs for nine regions. The regression suggests that 75% of input is "retained" in soils or vegetation or lost as gas somewhere within these large watersheds. *(From Howarth et al. 1996.)*

TABLE 7.4  Fates of fertilizer N added over 22 years in an Iowa watershed with continuous corn.

| Fate | % of Input |
|------|-----------|
| Grain | 50 |
| Leaching | 16 |
| Runoff | 1 |
| Missing (unaccounted for); must be either stored in the soil or denitrified | 31 |

*From Steinheimer et al. (1998).*

where this retention is taking place (soil storage, vegetation storage, gaseous loss) there is a great quantity of "missing" or unaccounted-for N in these balances (Boyer et al. 2002). At the regional scale, it is easy to assume that this unaccounted-for N is being stored in soil or vegetation somewhere in the watershed, or perhaps being denitrified in wetland "hotspots" of denitrification (McClain et al. 2003). At smaller scales (Table 7.4), where it is possible to account for these possible fates of N with more precision, the "missing N" represents a fundamental challenge to our understanding of ecosystem N cycles that will likely continue to be the focus of much research over the next several decades.

# References

Aber, J.D., McDowell, W.H., Nadelhoffer, K.J., Magill, A., Berntson, G., Kamakea, M., et al., 1998. Nitrogen saturation in temperate forest ecosystems: Hypotheses revisited. BioScience 48, 921−934.

Aber, J.D., Nadelhoffer, K.J., Steudler, P., Melillo, J.M., 1989. Nitrogen saturation in northern forest ecosystems. BioScience 39, 378−386.

Blair, J.M., Seastedt, T.R., Rice, C.W., Ramundo, R.A., 1998. Terrestrial nutrient cycling in tallgrass prairie. In: Knapp, A.K., Briggs, J.M., Hartnett, D.C., Collins, S.L. (Eds.), Grassland dynamics: Long-term ecological research in tallgrass prairie. Oxford University Press, New York, pp. 222−243.

Bormann, F.H., Likens, G.E., Melillo, J.M., 1977. Nitrogen budget for an aggrading northern hardwood forest ecosystem. Science 196, 981−983.

Boyer, E.W., Goodale, C.L., Jaworski, N.A., Howarth, R.W., 2002. Anthropogenic nitrogen sources and relationships to riverine nitrogen export in the northeastern USA. Biogeochemistry 57, 137−169.

Driscoll, C., Whitall, D., Aber, J., Boyer, E., Castro, M., Cronan, C., et al., 2003. Nitrogen pollution in the northeastern United States: Sources, effects and management options. BioScience 53, 357−374.

Eppley, R.W., Peterson, B.J., 1979. Particulate organic matter flux and planktonic new production in the deep ocean. Nature 282, 677−680.

Galloway, J.N., Aber, J.D., Erisman, J.W., Seitzinger, S.P., Howarth, R.W., Cowling, E.B., et al., 2003. The nitrogen cascade. BioScience 53, 341−356.

Galloway, J.N., Cowling, E.B., 2002. Reactive nitrogen and the world: Two hundred years of change. Ambio 31, 64−71.

Howarth, R.W., Billen, G., Swaney, D., Townsend, A., Jaworksi, N., Lajtha, K., et al., 1996. Regional nitrogen budgets and riverine N & P fluxes for the drainages to the North Atlantic Ocean: Natural and human influences. Biogeochemistry 35, 75−139.

Hyvönen, R., Agren, G.I., Andren, O., 1996. Modeling long-term carbon and nitrogen dynamics in an arable soil receiving organic matter. Ecol Appl 6, 1345−1354.

Kemp, W.M., Sampou, P., Caffrey, J., Mayer, M., Henriksen, K., Boynton, W.R., 1990. Ammonium recycling versus denitrification in Chesapeake Bay sediments. Limnol Oceanogr 35, 1545–1563.

Likens, G.E., Bormann, F.H., 1995. Biogeochemistry of a forested ecosystem, second ed. Springer-Verlag, New York.

McClain, M.E., Boyer, E.W., Dent, C.L., Gergel, S.E., Grimm, N.B., Groffman, P.M., et al., 2003. Biogeochemical hot spots and hot moments at the interface of terrestrial and aquatic ecosystems. Ecosystems 6, 301–312.

Melillo, J.M., 1977. Mineralization of nitrogen in northern hardwood forest ecosystems, Ph.D Dissertation. Yale University, New Haven, CT.

Mitsch, W.J., Day Jr., J.W., Gilliam, J.W., Groffman, P.M., Hey, D.L., Randall, G.W., et al., 2001. Reducing nitrogen loading to the Gulf of Mexico from the Mississippi River basin: Strategies to counter a persistent ecological problem. BioScience 51, 373–388.

Pastor, J., Aber, J.D., McClaugherty, C.A., Melillo, J.M., 1984. Aboveground production and N and P cycling along a nitrogen mineralization gradient on Blackhawk Island, Wisconsin. Ecology 65, 256–268.

Pastor, J., Post, W., 1986. Influence of climate, soil moisture, and succession on forest carbon and nitrogen cycles. Biogeochemistry 2, 3–27.

Steinheimer, T.R., Scoggin, K.D., Kramer, L.A., 1998. Agricultural chemical movement through a field size watershed in Iowa: Surface hydrology and nitrate losses in discharge. Environ. Sci. Technol. 32, 1048–1052.

Tisdale, S.L., Nelson, W.L., Beaton, J.D., Havlin, J.L., 1993. Soil fertility and fertilizers, fifth ed. Macmillan, New York.

Vitousek, P.M., Aber, J.D., Howarth, R.W., Likens, G.E., Matson, P.A., Schindler, D.W., et al., 1997. Human alteration of the global nitrogen cycle: Sources and consequences. Ecol. Appl. 7, 737–750.

# 8

# The Phosphorus Cycle

*Elena M. Bennett[1] and Meagan E. Schipanski[2]*
[1]McGill School of Environment and Department of Natural Resource Sciences,
McGill University, Canada; [2]Plant Sciences Department, Pennsylvania State University,
University Park, PA

## INTRODUCTION

Phosphorus (P) is essential for all organisms since it is an important component of DNA, RNA, ATP, and the phospholipids that form cell membranes. Relative to its biological importance, P is present in only small quantities on Earth (Filippelli 2008). P plays a crucial role in limiting or colimiting primary production in many ecosystems, including agricultural ecosystems where it is needed for production of crops and livestock. It also plays an important role in the productivity of inland waters and estuaries. Inland waters with low P concentrations generally have not only low primary production, but also low secondary production of invertebrates and fish. Consequently, inland waters are extremely sensitive to increases in P concentrations that often lead to eutrophic (high productivity) conditions associated with low water clarity, decline of rooted plants, anoxic bottom waters, fish kills, and algal blooms. Phosphorus' critical role in agricultural production as well as eutrophication has triggered much of the ecological research on P over the past 50 years.

In this chapter, we present information about the key processes in P cycling in terrestrial and aquatic systems, followed by a discussion of the interactions between terrestrial and aquatic P cycles at the global, watershed, and local scales. We conclude with a discussion of human management of the P cycle.

## BACKGROUND

Literally, phosphorus means "bearer of light"; elemental P ($P^o$) glows in the presence of oxygen and is easily combustible. In 1669, the German alchemist Henning Brandt discovered P, isolating $P^o$ from urine. By the 1800s, $P^o$ was being used to make matches and weapons. The interest in and utility of $P^o$ led to many studies of P abundance in tissues of animals and plants and to methods to extract P from these tissues, particularly P-rich bone. By the mid- to late 1800s, the extraction of P moved from these tissues to rock P. These rocks, especially apatite (a term that refers to a variety of tri-calcium phosphate minerals) are still the major source of P for human use. The P extracted from rocks is now primarily used in the oxidized form (phosphates) in fertilizer, feed additives, and detergent additives. These human uses of P have profoundly influenced P cycling on the planet.

P is rarely found in its elemental form. Instead, it typically exists as some form of phosphate, including $PO_4^{3-}$, $HPO_4^{2-}$, $H_2PO_4^-$, and $H_3PO_4$. Phosphorus has a number of potential oxidation states ranging from $-3$ to $+5$ ($P^o$ is, of course, 0). However, unlike nitrogen, carbon, and sulfur, the cycles of which could not occur in the absence of changes in oxidation state, P exists almost exclusively in its most oxidized form, $PO_4^{3-}$. This is true whether P is dissolved or particulate, organic or inorganic. That is, whether in apatite deposits, soils, sediments, bones, living organisms, or detrital organic matter, P is in the $+5$ (oxide) form. Another difference between P and many other biologically important elements is that the gaseous phase is extremely rare in nature.

Despite the fact that P does not itself have an active redox cycle and has only a minor gaseous form (phosphine), the cycling of P in both terrestrial and aquatic systems can be complex due to the large number of biotic, physical, and chemical pathways controlling its movement and form. Phosphorus readily binds to siliceous clays, humic material, and iron and aluminum oxides. This chemical binding is sufficient under many conditions to strongly inhibit phosphorus release from soils and sediments; thus, P often moves physically within and across ecosystems attached or incorporated into soils and sediment particles (see Chapter 5). The chemical reactivity of P, combined with rapid biotic uptake, partly explains the low concentration of P in most ground water and surface water.

# THE IMPORTANCE OF PHOSPHORUS IN TERRESTRIAL ECOSYSTEMS

Soil P is an important plant nutrient that plays a critical role in limiting productivity in terrestrial environments. A recent meta-analysis by Elser et al. (2007) summarized patterns of P limitation developed through fertilization experiments conducted in over 1000 sites, including nearly 200 terrestrial ecosystems. Contrary to expectations that nitrogen supply typically limits plant growth in temperate forests, grasslands, and the coastal ocean while P limits freshwater ecosystems and tropical forests, Elser et al. (2007) found the mean effect of P (added alone) to be substantial—similar to that of nitrogen added alone—across terrestrial ecosystems. Most P in terrestrial ecosystems is derived from weathering of parent material, and is affected by climate, topography, time, and biota (Jenny 1941). Ecosystems are ultimately limited by the amount of P available in the local parent material. Because of its role in productivity, P is particularly important to people as an important fertilizer in agricultural ecosystems.

# THE IMPORTANCE OF PHOSPHORUS IN AGRICULTURAL ECOSYSTEMS

Phosphorus plays a critical role in food production. It is needed for all aspects of plant growth, including root growth, flowering, fruiting, and seed formation (Smil 2000). As crops grow, they take up P from the soil. Increasing crop yields means that some crops remove double or even triple the P they did 50 years ago. To maintain yields, this P must be replenished. Before widespread use of commercial fertilizers, P was replenished by manure from livestock grazing, flooding, or shifting cultivation. Availability of mineral P fertilizers has enabled additions of P to come from far away. This, in turn, means that consumption of food can happen far from where it is produced and far from local sources of P (such as manure) since P and other minerals no longer need to be locally recycled. This ultimately can lead to specialization and high-density production of livestock, often beyond what the surrounding land can sustain (Schroder et al. 2009). However, mineral inputs of P have also improved human food security through the massive increases in yield achieved through the Green Revolution.

# THE IMPORTANCE OF PHOSPHORUS IN AQUATIC ECOSYSTEMS

## The Importance of Phosphorus in Freshwater Systems

Phosphorus limits primary production in many freshwater systems. Phosphorus additions in these systems can stimulate growth of aquatic primary producers, including phytoplankton, macroalgae, and epiphytes. This limitation has been demonstrated experimentally by adding P alone or in conjunction with nitrogen, which results in significant and sometimes very large increases in production and biomass of phytoplankton (Schindler 1977; Figure 8.1). Conversely, declines in P input can result in dramatic declines in phytoplankton production and biomass. This control of P input on phytoplankton production has been particularly well demonstrated in clear, temperate lakes. For other inland waters, the strong link between P status of the aquatic system and phytoplankton production is less obvious and may occur only seasonally, in some parts of the system, or not at all. For example, in a number of estuaries P concentrations are high relative to nitrogen concentrations (e.g., atomic N:P ratios are substantially lower than 16:1), and a substantial stimulation of primary production may occur by nitrogen additions alone.

Primary production occurs on the sediments as well as in the water column of aquatic ecosystems. This benthic primary production includes both algal production and plant production. Benthic primary production generally dominates total system primary production in wetlands, shallow lakes and estuaries, and streams. Although benthic primary producers require P to grow, P additions to the ecosystem sometimes can have negative impacts on these producers. For well-lit streams, a number of studies have shown that benthic algal biomass and production increase with increased P inputs. However, in shallow lakes and some estuaries, declines in benthic production may occur with

FIGURE 8.1    An aerial photo of Lake 226 (Ontario, Canada), divided at the narrows by a nylon curtain and treated on one side (right in this photo) with carbon, nitrogen, and phosphorus, and on the other (left in this photo) with only carbon and nitrogen. The photo clearly shows the resulting algal blooms in the side where phosphorus was included in the fertilization mix. *(From Schindler 1977.)*

increased P inputs. This decline occurs when phytoplankton production is stimulated to such a large degree that light levels reaching the benthos become too low to sustain primary production. Interestingly, once a system has lost benthic plants due to nutrient enrichment it can be difficult to restore the system's benthic plants and the system may remain phytoplankton-dominated even after nutrients decline (see Chapter 11).

Phosphorus concentrations may select for specific types of primary producers. As just noted, aquatic systems can switch from domination of benthic producers to planktonic producers. Additionally, the specific benthic or planktonic producer that dominates can be altered through changes in P inputs. Of particular interest is the switch to dominance by cyanobacteria (blue-green algae) that can occur within the phytoplankton community when P inputs are large. This switch has received a great deal of attention as some cyanobacteria produce toxins that can kill or sicken animals, including humans and livestock that ingest the water (Carey et al. 2012). Additionally, many cyanobacteria can fix nitrogen, which can be a significant input to some inland waters (see Chapter 7).

Phosphorus can also limit production of consumers (secondary production), including bacteria, fungi, and animals, which use organic P created by primary producers to meet their P requirements. Both bacteria and fungi can supplement this organic P with inorganic P taken up directly from the environment. In fact, bacteria can compete effectively with phytoplankton for inorganic P. Despite their two possible modes of P uptake, heterotrophic bacteria are P-limited in many aquatic systems. This limitation can translate into lower bacterial production as well as lower decomposition rates of organic matter in low-P systems.

There is some evidence that grazers (e.g., crustacean zooplankton, benthic invertebrates) in aquatic systems can also be P-limited. Lower growth rates and lower reproductive rates can result when their food has very low P content compared to the P content of the consumer (see Box 3.1 in Chapter 3). Phytoplankton P content varies substantially with the severity of P limitation; thus, the low P content in inland waters may lead to lower grazer abundance both due to lower overall primary production and lower P content of this production.

## The Importance of Phosphorus in Marine Systems

In many ways, the importance of P in marine systems echoes its role in freshwater systems. While there remains active debate about whether estuaries are limited by P, nitrogen, or colimited by both nutrients, P clearly plays an important role in stimulating primary production in these systems. Not only is P important for biological productivity of the oceans, but it controls the long-term carbon cycle via its role as a limiting nutrient. The main P source in the ocean is runoff from rivers, which delivers annually about 1.5 Mt of dissolved P and more than 20 Mt of suspended P into the ocean.

## THE GLOBAL PHOSPHORUS CYCLE

The P cycle is one of the slowest biogeochemical cycles on Earth. While P can cycle relatively quickly through plants and animals, its movement from rock through soils to the oceans is extremely slow (500 million years; Figure 8.2). Unlike many other biogeochemical cycles, the atmosphere does not play a significant role in the movement of P, because P-based compounds are usually solids at the typical ranges of temperature and pressure found on Earth. (See Box 8.1 for definitions of the key terms in this section.)

The global P cycle follows the new inputs of P into ecosystems from *weathering* of rocks, through burial in the ocean, to rock formation from pressure and heat, and eventual uplift to terrestrial environments. Weathering of primary minerals is the major source of P to terrestrial ecosystems and is controlled by both biological and geochemical processes. Weathering involves both chemical and physical breakdown of P-bearing minerals, primarily apatite, to release phosphates. The rate of P release due to weathering is affected by mineral type, topography, climate, and biota (Cross and Schlesinger 1995). Weathering rates tend to increase with increasing temperature, precipitation, and slope. Acids produced from reactions of rainwater and soil $CO_2$ and organic acids produced by plants and microbes increase the dissolution of apatite through chemical weathering. The weathering of primary minerals is nonreversible.

Once released from rock, P can be *adsorbed*, or chemically adhered, to soil or sediment particles, moving with erosion or other processes that cause movement of soils. This process varies with soil type: Each soil has a P "fixation" capacity determined by the number of positively charged sites that can bind phosphate ions. Adsorption reactions are usually

---

## BOX 8.1

### FORMS OF PHOSPHORUS

Phosphorus in natural waters is divided into three operational parts: soluble reactive phosphorus (SRP), soluble unreactive phosphorus (SUP), and particulate phosphorus (PP; Rigler 1973). The sum of all phosphorus components is termed *total phosphorus (TP)*.

*Soluble phosphorus (SP)* is all filterable forms of P, both organic and inorganic. (Organic P is P that is bound to living or dead tissues or dissolved biological molecules (such as ATP and DNA) of organisms, and inorganic P is P that is not associated with organic material.) Soluble and particulate phosphorus are differentiated by whether or not they pass through a 0.45 μm filter. SP is divided into two parts: SRP and SUP.

*Soluble reactive phosphorus (SRP)* is filtered P (not captured by a 0.45 μm membrane) that reacts with certain reagents used to measure it. It is usually primarily inorganic orthophosphate ($PO_4$), the form directly taken up by plant cells.

*Soluble unreactive phosphorus (SUP)* is filterable P that does not readily react with reagents and is typically measured as the difference between SP and SRP. It is made up of organic P and chains of inorganic P molecules called polyphosphates.

*Particulate phosphorus (PP)* is all P captured by a 0.45 μm filter, including organic and inorganic particles and colloids.

---

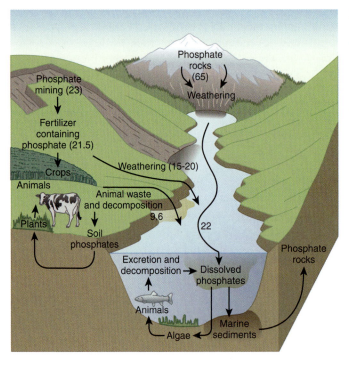

FIGURE 8.2 Summary of the phosphorus cycle in the modern world. Standing stocks in rocks given in billions of metric tonnes (petagrams); other fluxes and stocks given in millions of metric tonnes (teragrams). *(Based on Cordell et al. 2009, MacDonald et al. 2011, and FAO 2007.)*

reversible. Phosphorus can also be *dissolved*, in which case it moves with surface and subsurface flows of water on its way to the ocean. Dissolved P cycles through terrestrial and aquatic ecosystems, being *assimilated* into plants and algae as they take up P from soils and water through their roots. This P can move into herbivores that eat plants containing P, and into carnivores that eat these herbivores. P taken up by plants and animals is returned to the soil through the excretion of urine and feces as well as the *mineralization* that happens upon death and decomposition as fungi and decomposers break down tissues, releasing phosphate back into the soils.

While this shorter cycle-within-a-cycle of P movement through organisms is happening, P is completing a long journey from the place of initial weathering to the oceans, where, over geologic timescales, it will be reformed into rocks and uplifted to terrestrial settings. A P atom might cycle for hundreds of thousands of years among soils, water, plants, and animals before it finally reaches the bottom of the ocean. Inland running waters play an obvious role in this cycle by being conduits of terrestrial P to coastal oceans through other aquatic systems such as lakes and wetlands. Wetlands, lakes, and, more recently, reservoirs can add a substantial time-lag to this delivery as a substantial part of the P being weathered can be stored temporarily in sediments of these inland waters rather than being delivered immediately to coastal waters. The P carried by rivers to the oceans consists of both *dissolved* and *particulate* forms. In general, particulate forms make up the majority of the P being transported. Much of this P is very low reactivity and may never enter the biotic cycle before being buried in deltaic and coastal sediments. Once in the oceans, P can remain in sediments for hundreds of millions of years before being lifted by geological forces to Earth's surface, where the cycle will continue, beginning anew with weathering.

# HUMAN ALTERATION OF THE GLOBAL PHOSPHORUS CYCLE

Today's P cycle is dominated by human activity, especially agriculture (Figure 8.2). Obvious human impact on the P cycle comes from mining P and distributing it around the world in the form of fertilizers, animal feeds, and detergents. There is also international movement of P in traded feed and food crops as well as traded livestock and animal products. Less obvious, but still important, alterations are in the form of increased soil erosion, and therefore increased P movement, due to land use change, as well as locally increased movement of P from terrestrial to aquatic ecosystems through sewage release and septic tank leaks. Thus, human activities impact many parts of the P cycle, and have resulted in the redistribution of P. In fact, there is a concern that P supplies may become limited in the future (Box 8.2). The human-dominated P cycle (Figure 8.2) releases more P into the cycle annually (approximately triple the prehuman-dominated cycle; see Bennett et al. 2001) and speeds the delivery of P to the oceans.

Humans directly mine P from rocks to make fertilizers and other compounds. In 2010, we mined approximately 23.5 Tg ($10^{12}$ g) P, about 22.6 Tg of which was added to agricultural systems in the form of fertilizers and animal feeds (MacDonald et al. 2011). Weathering likely adds 15–20 Tg P/year to the soils, meaning that mining is currently a

## BOX 8.2

# WILL WE RUN OUT OF PHOSPHORUS?

The supply of P available for human use is limited, P is essential to grow crops and feed people, and there are no known substitutes. Increasingly, people are aware of the issue of peak oil, typically defined as the point in time when the maximum rate of petroleum extraction is reached, after which extraction will decline. Yet, known substitutes for fossil fuels are many, including solar energy, biofuels, and wind energy. And unlike nitrogen, which can be fixed from vast atmospheric reservoirs (see Chapter 7), we cannot manufacture P. Among these major constituents upon which human life depends, it is only P for which there are no known substitutes *and* a limited supply.

At the same time, consumption of P is increasing at about 3% annually, an increase that is expected to expand (Cordell et al. 2009). More P will be needed to meet increased demands for agricultural production, which will have to double by 2050 to meet demands posed by a growing human population and increased demand for meat in rapidly developing countries. Add to this expanding biofuel enterprises that also raise P demand. Approximately 10% of fertilizer use in the United States is applied to corn used to produce ethanol (Childers et al. 2011). Prices of P rock are beginning to fluctuate wildly in response to changes in our estimates of how much we have, global politics, and so on.

These facts increasingly bring us to consider the issue of peak P and to wonder when limited P supplies will become a critical issue in food supply and how this will affect global politics. Working with the 2009 United States Geological Survey (USGS) P reserve estimates, sustainability scientist Dana Cordell and colleagues used a Hubbert, "peak oil"—type analysis to forecast a date for "peak P" production of approximately 2030 (Cordell et al. 2009). Currently, perspectives on emerging P scarcity are in flux following a revision of the global P reserve estimate by economic geologist Steven Van Kauwenbergh of the International Fertilizer Development Center (IFDC; Van Kauwenbergh 2010): The new figure is nearly 10 times higher than the 2009 USGS value and this new value has now been adopted by USGS. Importantly, these "new" reserves, which were identified largely based on Van Kauwenbergh's inclusion of some overlooked 25-year-old reports, lie entirely in one country: Morocco (and its disputed territory of Western Sahara).

To the extent that the IFDC estimates are accurate, the urgency of geological scarcity issues is perhaps pushed back by several decades, according to reanalysis by Cordell and colleagues. However, politics may trump geology in this case. The geographic distribution of P reserves is hyper-concentrated—five countries control 90% of estimated reserves, with Morocco obviously in the driver's seat. Since major regions of the world have diminishing (USA), few (India), or no (northern Europe) P reserves of their own, without diversification of fertilizer supplies (via internal recycling) many of the world's food producers will become completely dependent on trade with Morocco.

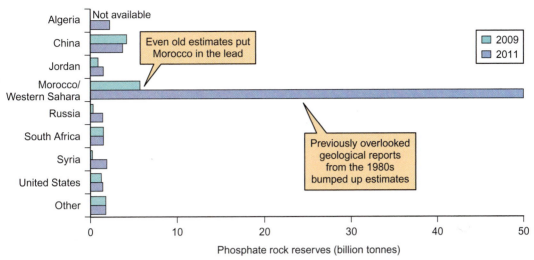

FIGURE 8.3    Global distribution of world phosphate rock reserves (in billion metric tons, BMT). Blue indicates the assessment of USGS in 2009 and the purple indicates the adjustment made by Van Kauwenbergh (2010) after comprehensive analysis of available industry and government reports, gray literature, and published studies. It is important to note that a "reserve" is a geological deposit of a material that can be economically and legally extracted or produced at the time of the determination. The USGS has now adopted the new estimates in its official phosphate reports. *(Reprinted from Elser and Bennett 2011.)*

larger source of P than weathering to the world's soils. Large deposits of mineable apatite are located in China, Morocco, South Africa, Jordan, and parts of the United States (Figure 8.3). These five countries control approximately 85% of the P mined globally, with implications for geopolitical stability. There are ongoing debates about the amount of P remaining in reserves (Box 8.2).

Figure 8.4 shows the amount of P "leakage" or waste that occurs as it moves through the food system from mined phosphate rock to human waste. Of all P mined for food production, only one-fifth is consumed by people (Cordell et al. 2009). Along the way, 8 million tonnes are lost in erosion from agricultural land each year, and 7 million tonnes in runoff from animal manure. About 3 million tonnes are forgone in crop losses (e.g., wild animal consumption, disease). There are postharvest losses, too: 0.2 million tonnes before crops become food products, 1 million tonnes in food chain losses (including distribution, retail, and household losses), and 2.7 million tonnes lost as landfill or sewage.

People have also altered the transfer of P around the world in products such as fertilizers, animal feed crops, and food crops. We remove P from mines in only a few places, spread it around the world on agricultural soils, then trade the crops produced using—and now containing the P from—those fertilizers. While global crop production has nearly tripled over the past 50 years, crop trade has increased much more rapidly (and the quantity of P in traded crops increased more than six-fold for most countries over this same time period; Schipanski and Bennett 2012). Because a large fraction of traded crops are destined for livestock feed and most P consumed by livestock ends up in

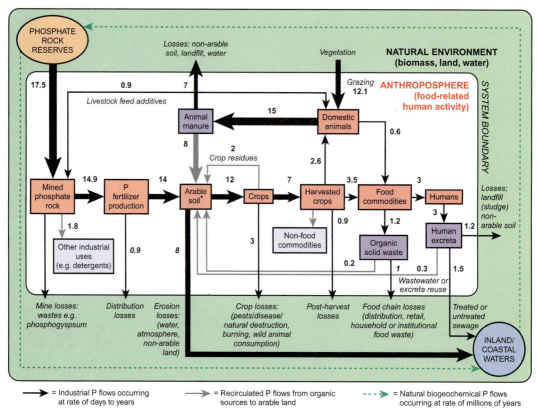

**FIGURE 8.4** Phosphorus flows through the global food production and consumption system (in Mt/year). *(From Cordell et al. 2009.)*

manure, crop trade has facilitated the concentration of livestock production in regions without enough land to grow the livestock feed or, therefore, enough land to assimilate the resulting P-rich manures. Thus, moving P around the planet in fertilizers and agricultural products has the effect of overfertilizing some soils while leaving others without the nutrients required to grow crops.

Global P budgets, which subtract P uptake by crops and animals from P input in manures and fertilizers, have shown that P is accumulating in agricultural areas due to the use of fertilizers and animal feeds, increasingly so in some developing countries (Bennett et al. 2001). More recent global P budgets (MacDonald et al. 2011) have been able to examine the build-up and decline in soil P in a more spatially explicit manner, finding P surpluses on 70% of the world's cropland and P deficits on 30%, with both surpluses and deficits found on every continent (Figure 8.5). Areas of surplus P are likely to have issues with eutrophication and water quality because the excess P is available to runoff or leach into nearby freshwaters. On the other hand, areas of deficit indicate regions that may have reduced agricultural production. The largest imbalances are spatially concentrated—just 10% of the global cropland area with the largest deficits contributes 65% of the cumulative

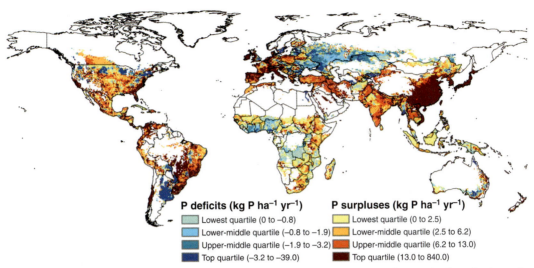

**P deficits (kg P ha⁻¹ yr⁻¹)**

- Lowest quartile (0 to −0.8)
- Lower-middle quartile (−0.8 to −1.9)
- Upper-middle quartile (−1.9 to −3.2)
- Top quartile (−3.2 to −39.0)

**P surpluses (kg P ha⁻¹ yr⁻¹)**

- Lowest quartile (0 to 2.5)
- Lower-middle quartile (2.5 to 6.2)
- Upper-middle quartile (6.2 to 13.0)
- Top quartile (13.0 to 840.0)

**FIGURE 8.5** Global map of agronomic P imbalances for the year 2000 expressed per unit of cropland area in each 0.5° grid cell. Inputs to each cell are fertilizers and manures applied. Outputs are crops harvested. The difference between inputs and outputs is the change-in-storage. The P surpluses and deficits shown here are each classified according to quartiles globally (0−25th, 25−50th, 50−75th, and 75−100th percentiles). *(Reprinted from MacDonald et al. 2011.)*

global P deficit. Similarly, 10% of the cropland area with the largest surpluses contributes 45% of the cumulative global P surplus.

Agricultural areas with surplus P often face issues of runoff due to loss of P with eroded soil or dissolved in water runoff. Dissolved P in soil solution travels in ground water to running waters and standing waters. Particulate forms of P are transferred by stream-bank erosion and overland flow of water. Particulate P transfer in erosion is usually thought to encompass the vast majority of P runoff in agricultural areas. Ultimately, this P ends up in the oceans. The net input of dissolved P to the oceans is 4−6 Tg P/year (Filippelli 2008), a doubling of prehuman inputs. Estimates of particulate P inputs range from 6 Tg P/year (Seitzinger et al. 2010) to 20 Tg P/year (Meybeck 1982). Reconstructions of human-caused P inputs from land to the oceans, and projections into the future indicate that sustained and significant eutrophication can be expected over the next two millennia (Figure 8.6). This figure shows the reconstructions and projections of anthropogenic P delivery to the oceans as a result of fertilization, deforestation, and soil loss. The fertilizer drop-off in about 2100 coincides with estimates of the date of expected depletion of known reserves.

Cities are playing an increasingly important role in the global P cycle. The food requirements of urban areas are supplied from agricultural areas that may be thousands of kilometers away. The import of food is generally the primary P input to urban areas although P in cleaning products can also be significant. Both these P imports generally end up in sewage treatment plants. In the 1960s, essentially all the P in sewage was pumped into rivers, lakes, and estuaries. Today the extent of P removal in these plants varies dramatically. Some sewage treatment plants still remove little to no P. Even those

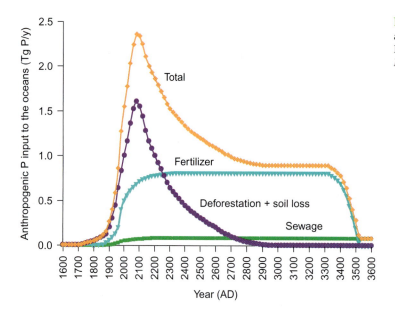

FIGURE 8.6 Reconstructions and projections of anthropogenic P delivered to the oceans. *(From Filippelli 2008.)*

with relatively advanced secondary treatment can remove as little as 10% of the P in wastewater. Still others use biological or chemical treatment to remove up to 95% of the P. Whatever the case, the resulting P (in bacterial biomass or in sludge) can be landfilled or resold for use in fertilizer. In general, developed countries have more P removal than do developing countries, but even in rich countries, not all P is removed at water treatment.

P removal from sewage has been associated with clear declines in soluble reactive P and even total P in a number of lakes and rivers. For example, P concentration in a number of rivers including the Thames and the Rhine have decreased to less than 50% of the maximum values observed in the 1970s, coincident with changes in sewage treatment. Concentrations are still high compared to most pristine watersheds because of high nonpoint loads that persist. At present, the net balance of these reactions on the global scale is a tripling of the P in rivers compared to preindustrial flows (Bennett et al. 2001).

The global influence of human action on P cycling raises questions about the amount of change in global processes that can be accommodated while maintaining or improving human well-being. Rockström et al. (2009) introduced the concept of planetary boundaries to define a safe operating space for humanity on Earth. These boundaries are intended to define key thresholds, critical values for one or more control variables that, if crossed, could generate unacceptable environmental change on Earth. They identified nine processes for which planetary boundaries should be defined, including interference with the global P cycle. These authors set the planetary boundary for P as the quantity of P flowing into the oceans that would avoid major ocean anoxic events for over 1000 years, or about 11 million tonnes of P per year entering the oceans. Recent reexamination of the planetary boundary for P based on maintaining freshwater systems in a noneutrophic state indicates that we have already gone beyond acceptable levels of P in terms of input to freshwater systems, input to soils, and overall mass in soils (Carpenter and Bennett 2011). We address possible strategies to tackle the issue of human alteration of the P cycle, and the problems caused by that alteration, in the final section of this chapter.

## THE PHOSPHORUS CYCLE AT THE WATERSHED SCALE

Nested within the global cycle of P are smaller (spatial)-scale P cycles. For relatively pristine forested and grassland systems, the inputs of P include weathering and (limited) atmospheric inputs in the form of dust, but also P transferred by animal movement and migration. Organisms feeding in the terrestrial environment or in the coastal oceans can transfer P directly from one ecosystem to another. For some lakes, geese have been shown to be important in the transfer of P from grasslands to aquatic systems and salmon are well cited as an example of transfer from coastal oceans and estuaries to rivers, lakes, and even terrestrial systems. In the case of Pacific salmon, more than 95% of their body mass is accumulated in the marine environment, yet this material is deposited in freshwater systems where the salmon return to spawn and die. This represents an important nutrient subsidy from marine to freshwater systems (Naiman et al. 2002). These same transfers can happen in terrestrial systems. For example, roe deer that graze on crops and then defecate in nearby forests may bring a significant source of nutrients to those forest patches (Abbas et al. 2012).

The P transferred from terrestrial to aquatic ecosystems is of particular interest because of the extreme sensitivity of many aquatic systems to P inputs. The P cycling in inland waters and the supply from the watershed are controlled by the interaction of hydrology, chemistry, and biology. Phosphorus typically enters aquatic systems from terrestrial ones bound to soil particles carried there by erosion or via air as dust. However, P can also enter water bodies from sewage, manure runoff, industrial wastes, seepage from septic tanks, and other sources. Table 8.1 shows the relationship of lake productivity to P concentrations as well as typical P concentrations in pristine and human-impacted lakes.

The amount of P transferred to aquatic systems from pristine watersheds depends on a number of factors including soil texture and chemistry, the slope of the watershed, and the amount and pattern of precipitation and water runoff. Human-induced climate change can alter P outputs through its impact on water runoff. Additionally, atmospheric pollution may alter these transfers. In particular, acid precipitation is thought to decrease soil pH and increase binding of P to soils and, hence, decrease P transfer from terrestrial

TABLE 8.1  Relationship between lake productivity and average epilimnetic total P concentrations.

| Lake Productivity | Total P |
| --- | --- |
| Oligotrophic | $<5 \, \mu g/L$ |
| Mesotrophic | $5-30 \, \mu g/L$ |
| Eutrophic | $30-100 \, \mu g/L$ |
| Hypereutrophic | $>100 \, \mu g/L$ |

to aquatic systems. This decrease in P transfer coupled with changes in P cycling within lakes has been thought to be responsible for decreases in primary production in some poorly buffered lakes in Europe and North America of which the watersheds are subject to high inputs of acid in precipitation. This decline in production has been termed *oligotrophication*.

The transfers of P to aquatic systems from agricultural watersheds are often accelerated compared to transfers from intact forests or grasslands. Annual crop production can dramatically increase erosion, primarily during periods when soils are not vegetated. Additionally, fertilizer P is often applied in excess of P removed in crops. Over decades, this can lead to increased P in soils that can leach or be moved by erosion of P-rich soil particles into surface waters. In many areas these relatively diffuse (nonpoint) P inputs are sufficient to cause eutrophication of streams, lakes, and wetlands located within agricultural watersheds. To allay this increased P transfer best management practices (BMPs) can be applied. These measures include decreasing fertilizer application, altering timing of fertilizer and manure application, and constructing riparian buffer strips that can capture P leaving croplands before reaching streams.

# THE PHOSPHORUS CYCLE AT THE LOCAL SCALE

## Terrestrial Systems

Within terrestrial ecosystems, most P is in soil pools that are effectively unavailable for plant uptake (see Box 8.3 for a discussion of P pools throughout soil development). As a result, plants have developed multiple strategies for accessing limited, but critical, pools of soil P. As for nitrogen, P moves to plant roots via diffusion. Diffusion involves movement along a gradient from high concentrations to low concentrations. The rate of phosphate movement via diffusion is typically much slower than nitrate, and soil solution concentrations of phosphate tend to be very low due to the numerous different processes, such as soil adsorption and chemical precipitation, that take phosphate out of solution. The most common plant strategy to access more soil P is through symbiotic relationships with fungi. Certain types of fungi can colonize roots either by growing between root cells, or penetrating and growing within root cells. The relationship is generally mutualistic under conditions of low soil P availability. Plants supply carbon, an important energy source, to fungi, and fungi increase P availability for the plant. Fungi increase P availability by excreting phosphatase enzymes to mineralize organic P, and acids that increase weathering and dissolution of primary and secondary mineral P (and chelated P). The long, filamentous mycorrhizal fungal hyphae also effectively increase the root surface area of a plant, increasing the soil volume from which P can be accessed. It is estimated that more than 80% of terrestrial plants form mycorrhizal symbioses. The development of this symbiosis was likely a critical step in the evolution of land plants.

Within the small number of plants that do not form mycorrhizal symbioses, many have developed alternative strategies for accessing P. One example is the development of cluster roots. The production of root clusters (prolific root growth) in areas of high P and high acid exudation rates result in greater P availability and uptake. Organic acids can

# BOX 8.3

## RESEARCH TOOLS: CHRONOSEQUENCES AND PHOSPHORUS POOLS

Soil P content and bioavailability is influenced by the soil-forming factors of parent material, climate, topography, time, and biota (see Chapter 11; Jenny 1941). Walker and Syers (1976) presented a model for the changes in soil P pools over time during soil development (Figure 8.7). This figure shows that at the start of soil development, primary mineral P (apatite) is the dominant soil P pool. Phosphate released through apatite weathering is relatively bioavailable. Over time, total and bioavailable soil P decrease due to inorganic P leaching and mineralogical changes that increasingly bind P into less available, or even occluded, pools.

Ecosystem processes that occur on timescales of hundreds to thousands of years can be difficult to study. Chronosequences can be used to develop and test the Walker and Syers model of soil development. A chronosequence is a set of separate physical sites that vary in age or time since disturbance. The challenge is to find locations that are similar in all soil-forming factors besides age, such as climate, parent material, and topography.

The Hawaiian Islands have been used effectively for chronosequence studies of many different ecosystem processes. This volcanic chain of islands is formed by the slow movement of the ocean floor over a deep source of volcanic lava. Islands build up over "hot spots" of lava. As they shift away from these "hot spots" they begin to age without inputs of new lava flows. The islands range in age from a few hundred to more than 4 million years. Through careful site selection, a chronosequence of sites can be selected that have similar parent material, climate, topography, and vegetation.

Walker and Syers synthesized results from several chronosequence studies ranging in age from 10,000 to 130,000 years to develop their model of soil P fraction development over time. Crews et al. (1995) used the Hawaiian Islands as a chronosequence

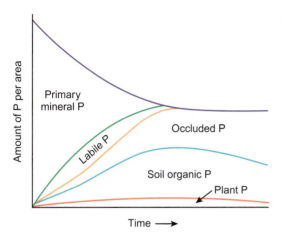

FIGURE 8.7 Shifts in P pools and total quantity of P throughout the course of soil development. *(Based on Walker and Syers 1976 and adapted by Vitousek et al. 2010.)*

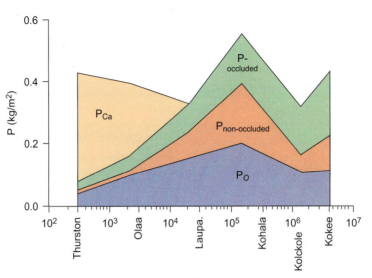

**FIGURE 8.8** Soil P fractions measured across the Hawaiian archipelago chronosequence provided general support for the Walker and Syers model of the relative shifts in P pools during soil development. $P_{Ca}$ = calcium phosphates and $P_O$ = P bound to organic matter. *(From Crews et al. 1995.)*

to test the Walker and Syers model of soil P transformations over time and its implications for ecosystem structure and function. Their results generally supported the Walker and Syers model as primary mineral P declined rapidly and P was increasingly incorporated into occluded P pools over Time.

increase P availability through multiple pathways. First, acids can increase chemical weathering of P-containing minerals as described earlier. Second, as with other organic matter, organic acids can compete with phosphates for sorption sites on clays, thereby reducing P binding sites.

## Aquatic Systems

Inland waters are active sites of storage and transformation of the P that enters these systems from point and nonpoint sources. There are three ultimate fates of all elements that enter a water body. The P can be stored in sediments (buried), exported downstream, or lost to the atmosphere. For P, there are very few examples where atmospheric loss is reported to be substantial. Thus, the two primary fates of P are hydrologic export and burial. The proportion of P that is lost to sediment burial and hence not transported downstream varies substantially between and within types of inland waters. Lakes have some of the highest retentions (approaching 100%) while retention is generally lowest in fast-moving streams and rivers. Variation in nutrient retention between and within inland water systems is related to a number of factors. Perhaps the most important factor is water residence time. Systems with long residence times, such as lakes, bury a higher percent of the P that enters the system and export a lower fraction of the P that enters.

Much of the P is delivered to sediments as sinking particles. These particles include organic matter originating from phytoplankton production or from plant production in the watershed, and inorganic particles (e.g., iron oxides). The size and density (i.e., specific gravity) of particles strongly influence sinking rates and hence the likelihood of particles reaching sediments. Phytoplankton, which can be an important component of P delivered to sediments, vary substantially in both size and density and also vary in mobility, adding to great variation in sinking rate. Diatoms are often dense (due to a silica shell) and relatively large and sink rapidly compared to low-density cyanobacteria with gas vacuoles or small and mobile plankton. The delivery of P in phytoplankton or other particles can be enhanced by zooplankton grazing, some of which can package small particles into larger relatively rapid-sinking fecal pellets. While pelagic grazers can alter the capacity of particles to sink to sediments, benthic grazers such as bivalves can increase P delivery more directly. These organisms filter and remove particles from the water column; some of the P is incorporated into their biomass and some is egested onto the sediment surface.

Particles that reach sediments can return to the water column, either in dissolved form or through resuspension. Resuspension is likely in high-energy environments, and in running waters can be a major fate of P previously deposited during floods. In lakes, wave action generated by winds, boating, or dredging can be a major cause of resuspension. Benthic organisms can either stabilize sediments and reduce resuspension or increase resuspension. Microbial and algal films can act as stabilizing elements as can macrophytes and bivalves that increase structural resistance at the benthic boundary and decrease hydrologic flow. On the other hand, benthic-feeding fish such as carp can greatly increase resuspension. Humans can also increase resuspension in shallows directly through the use of motorized vehicles and indirectly by eliminating benthic plants and animals that previously stabilized sediments.

The particulate P that is not resuspended is subject to decomposition and chemical reactions associated with pH and oxidation-reduction differences within sediments. These reactions change the form of P but only sometimes result in release of P to overlying waters. A classic example of these interactions takes P from particulate organic P to dissolved inorganic P in porewater to P bound to particulate iron oxides at the sediment surface, and finally to dissolved P released to bottom waters.

The link between oxygen concentrations in bottom waters and P release from sediments of many inland systems has the potential to generate a positive feedback between P loads and production. This positive feedback has been termed *accelerated eutrophication* and occurs in both lakes and estuaries. Briefly, P loads lead to greater primary production, which leads to greater sedimentation of organic matter. Decomposition of this material results in lower oxygen in bottom waters. This lower oxygen in turn can lead to higher release of P from sediments. In softwater lakes (low alkalinity), iron tends to control internal P dynamics. Iron binds with P, giving sediments a capacity to tightly bind P. However, in the low-oxygen conditions common in eutrophic lakes, iron in the sediments releases P that it had previously bound, meaning that eutrophic lakes that become anaerobic can actually release more P into the water column. The link between P release and oxygen in bottom waters and the potential for a positive feedback accounts for the fact that bottom water aeration has been used to try to manage eutrophication.

## MANAGING HUMAN INTERACTION WITH THE PHOSPHORUS CYCLE

Human activity dominates the P cycle (Figure 8.2). It is up to us to manage this cycle in a sustainable manner, one that protects critical aquatic resources while promoting food security worldwide. Currently, only one-fifth of all mined P makes it to our fork. Luckily, promising strategies exist to slow the one-way flow of P to the ocean by using it more efficiently and by keeping it cycling in the human food system (Childers et al. 2011). Some solutions require advanced technologies, but many are quite simple and readily available, even in poor countries.

By far the largest losses occur from farms. Over 7 Mt P is lost annually from animal manure (Childers et al. 2011). Strategies to recover P from livestock production (i.e., to return manure to the land that produced the feed used to grow the livestock) have the potential to retain a sizeable percentage of this P. Large farms with high livestock densities and little cropland, common in industrial agriculture, make recovery of manure relatively easy. However, cropland on which manure could be used as fertilizer may be distant and manure is heavy and expensive to move over long distances. Livestock can be genetically modified to increase P uptake and reduce P in manure. Likewise, researchers have recently engineered some crop plants to increase their ability to scavenge nutrients, including P, from poor soils (Gaxiola et al. 2011). Similarly, the Enviropig™ has been engineered to produce phytase in its salivary gland, allowing use of P in otherwise indigestible P-rich phytate molecules (Golovan et al. 2001). The result is a pig that can grow well on feed with lower P content and, in doing so, generate 30% to 65% less P in its manure.

Dietary and other food use changes may also help increase the efficiency with which we use P or reduce losses. Because the conversion of P inputs to dietary P is so much higher for crops than for livestock, shifts to a less meat-intensive diet can reduce demand for mineral P. For example, a vegetarian diet requires about one-third the amount of mined P of a meat-based diet (Cordell et al. 2009). Switching to grazed livestock, which requires less P inputs than livestock fed grain produced with fertilizers, can also be part of the solution. Food waste (distribution, retail, household, or institutional loss) comprises 1 Mt P annually (Cordell et al. 2009). Producing food closer to areas of high demand such as cities is one method to help reduce waste. Composting unavoidable wastes can allow P to be recovered for local reuse, especially for nearby urban farming.

We can even reduce losses and increase recycling at the very end of the food system. Human production of P in waste is about $1.8 \, \text{g person}^{-1} \, \text{day}^{-1}$; trapping all of this P globally would result in 4.5 Mt P available for reuse, an amount that is nearly one-third of global annual fertilizer consumption. Currently, only about 10% of the P in human waste is recovered. Recent technical innovations allow struvite (magnesium ammonium phosphate) recovery from sewage treatment pipes and development into a pellet form that can be used as fertilizer. And urine-separating toilets or those that allow urine to be recovered can not only return these valuable nutrients to the soil, but also help improve sanitation.

An even less expensive potential solution is The Peepoo®, a single use, self-sanitizing, bio-degradable bag that can be used to capture human waste, which can be used as fertilizer just two to four weeks later (http://www.peepoople.com/).

Some methods are being used to recover P that is normally considered too diffuse or too difficult to recapture. Algal turf scrubbers (ATS) are an engineered system for flowing water over surfaces with naturally seeded filamentous algae that can later be recovered and used as a nutrient source on farms (Adey et al. 2011). The fast growth of algae on ATS means that this technology has the potential to remove nutrients at high rates. A pilot study in the Florida Everglades recovered up to $0.14$ g P m$^{-2}$ day$^{-1}$, roughly two orders of magnitude greater than the P capture of managed wetlands in the same region. Other studies of using ATS flowways with dairy manure effluents indicate that these systems can capture 40% to 100% of input P, depending on the P loading rate (Mulbry et al. 2008).

Finally, consideration of how demand for P will change in the future is essential. Global demand for P is forecast to increase by about 3% to 4% annually, primarily in Asia (FAO 2007). This demand is affected by human diets, by trade, by methods of agricultural production, and by access to fertilizers. For example, increases in demand may come from growing crops for bioenergy. Approximately 10% of fertilizer use in the United States is applied to corn that will be used to produce ethanol (Childers et al. 2011). Other increases in P demand may come from increasing population, increased urbanization, or changing diets. In 2003, an estimated 2 billion people ate a meat-based diet, while an estimated 4 billion lived primarily on a plant-based diet (Pimentel and Pimentel 2003). Diets in rapidly developing countries such as China are now increasingly shifting toward a diet heavier in meat as people grow wealthier (World Resources Institute 2012).

## SUMMARY

Phosphorus is a critical element, playing an important role in limiting or colimiting primary production in many terrestrial and aquatic ecosystems. This importance has stimulated a great deal of recent research into P cycling in many ecosystems and the human impact on P cycling. As we face increased demand for P to fertilize agricultural crops and globally limited P supply, understanding how P moves within and across systems will become ever more important. Our current understanding involves factors that affect P movement at local, watershed, and global scales. The next steps will certainly be in the area of understanding interactions across scales.

## References

Abbas, F., Merlet, J., Morellet, N., Verheyden, H., Hewison, A.J.M., Cargnelutti, B., et al., 2012. Roe deer may markedly alter forest nitrogen and phosphorus budgets across Europe. Oikos 121, 1271–1278.

Adey, W.H., Kangas, P.C., Mulbry, W., 2011. Algal turf scrubbing: Cleaning surface waters with solar energy while producing a biofuel. BioScience 61, 434–441.

Bennett, E.M., Carpenter, S.R., Caraco, N., 2001. Human impact on erodable phosphorus and eutrophication: A global perspective. BioScience 51, 227–234.

Carey, C.C., Ewing, H.A., Cottingham, K.L., Weathers, K.C., Thomas, R.Q., Haney, J.F., 2012. Occurrence and toxicity of the cyanobacterium *Gloeotrichia echinulata* in low-nutrient lakes in the northeastern United States. Aquat. Ecol. (in press).

Carpenter, S.R., Bennett, E.M., 2011. Reconsideration of the planetary boundary for phosphorus. Environ. Res. Lett. 6, article 014009. doi: 1. 10.1088/1748-9326/6/1/014009.

Childers, D.L., Corman, J., Edwards, M., Elser, J.J., 2011. Sustainability challenges of phosphorus and food: Solutions from closing the human phosphorus cycle. BioScience 61, 117–124.

Cordell, D., Drangert, J.-O., White, S., 2009. The story of phosphorus: Global food security and food for thought. Glob. Environ. Change 19, 292–305.

Crews, T.E., Kitayama, K., Fownes, J., Herbert, D., Mueller-Dombois, D., Riley, R.H., et al., 1995. Changes in soil phosphorus and ecosystem dynamics across a long soil chronosequence in Hawai'i. Ecology 76, 1407–1424.

Cross, A.F., Schlesinger, W.H., 1995. A literature review and evaluation of the Hedley fractionation: Applications to the biogeochemical cycle of soil phosphorus in natural ecosystems. Geoderma 64, 197–214.

Elser, J.J., Bennett, E.M., 2011. A broken biogeochemical cycle. Nature 478, 29–31.

Elser, J.J., Bracken, M.E.S., Cleland, E.E., Gruner, D.S., Harpole, W.S., Hillebrand, H., et al., 2007. Global analysis of nitrogen and phosphorus limitation of primary producers in freshwater, marine and terrestrial ecosystems. Ecol. Lett. 10, 1135–1142.

FAO [Food and Agriculture Organization], (2007). Current world fertilizer trends and outlook to 2010/11. Food and Agriculture Organisation of the United Nations, Rome.

Filippelli, G.M., 2008. The global phosphorus cycle: Past, present, and future. Elements 4, 89–95.

Gaxiola, R., Edwards, M., Elser, J.J., 2011. A transgenic approach to phosphorus sustainability in agriculture. Chemosphere 84, 840–845.

Golovan, S.P., Meidinger, R.G., Ajakaiye, A., Cottrill, M., Wiederkehr, M.Z., Barney, D., et al., 2001. Pigs expressing salivary phytase produce low phosphorus manure. Nat. Biotechnol. 19, 741–745.

Jenny, H., 1941. Factors of soil formation: A system of quantitative pedology. McGraw-Hill, New York.

MacDonald, G.K., Bennett, E.M., Ramankutty, N., Potter, P., 2011. Too much or not enough: Agronomic phosphorus balances across the world's croplands. Proc. Nat. Acad. Sci. 108, 3086–3091.

Meybeck, M., 1982. Carbon, nitrogen, and phosphorus transport by world rivers. Am. J. Sci. 282, 401–450.

Mulbry, W., Kondrad, S., Pizarro, C., 2008. Treatment of dairy manure effluent using freshwater algae: Algal productivity and recovery of manure nutrients using pilot-scale algal turf scrubbers. Bioresour. Technol. 99, 8137–8142.

Naiman, R.J., Bilby, R.E., Schindler, D.E., Helfield, J.M., 2002. Pacific salmon, nutrients, and the dynamics of freshwater riparian ecosystems. Ecosystems 5, 399–417.

Pimentel, D., Pimentel, M., 2003. Sustainability of meat-based and plant-based diets and the environment. Am. J. Clin. Nutr. 78, 6605–6635.

Rigler, F.H., 1973. A dynamic view of the phosphorus cycle in lakes. In: Griffith, E.J., Beeton, A., Spencer, J.M., Mitchell, D.T. (Eds.), Environmental phosphorus Handbook. John Wiley and Sons, New York, NY., 539–572.

Rockström, J., Steffen, W., Noone, K., Persson, A., Chapin III, F.S., Lambin, E.F., et al., 2009. A safe operating space for humanity. Nature 461, 472–475.

Schindler, D.W., 1977. Evolution of phosphorus limitation in lakes. Science 195, 260–262.

Schipanski, M.E., Bennett, E.M., 2012. The influence of agricultural trade and livestock production on the global phosphorus cycle. Ecosystems 15, 256–268.

Schroder, J.J., Cordell, D., Smit, A.L., Rosemarin, A., 2009. Sustainable use of phosphorus. EU Tender ENV.B.1/ETU/2009/0025.

Seitzinger, S.P., Mayorga, E., Bouwman, A.F., Kroeze, C., Beusen, A.H.W., Billen, G., et al., 2010. Global river nutrient export: A scenario analysis of past and future trends. Global Biogeochem. Cycles. doi: 10.1029/2009GB003587 (24: article GB0A08).

Smil, V., 2000. Phosphorus in the environment: Natural flows and human interferences. Annu. Rev. Energy Env. 25, 53–88.

Van Kauenbergh, S.J., 2010. World phosphate rock reserves and resources. International Fertilizer Development Center, Muscle Shoals, AL.

Vitousek, P.M., Porder, S., Houlton, B.Z., Chadwick, O.A., 2010. Terrestrial phosphorus limitation: Mechanisms, implications, and nitrogen–phosphorus interactions. Ecol. Appl. 20, 5–15.

Walker, T.W., Syers, J.K., 1976. The fate of phosphorus during pedogenesis. Geoderma 15, 1–19.

World Resources Institute, 2012. EarthTrends: Environmental Information. www.wri.org/project/earthtrends/

# SYNTHESIS

In reading the previous chapters about ecosystem energetics and biogeochemistry, you may have noticed that some ideas and themes arose repeatedly. Examples of these cross-cutting subjects include the creative use of boundaries to analyze ecosystems over different scales of space and time; quantitative analysis, including mass balance; the use of multiple approaches and tools to solve a single problem; the importance of human controls on ecosystems; and so on. In the next three chapters, some of these important cross-cutting ideas will be discussed explicitly. We hope that the explicit discussion of the cross-cutting subjects that appeared implicitly in earlier chapters will make it easier for readers to understand the central ideas of modern ecosystem science.

In Chapter 9, Michael Pace revisits some of the basic attributes of the ecosystem concept that were introduced in Chapter 1, and shows how these simple attributes lend flexibility and strength to ecosystem science. Pace reminds us that the fact that ecosystems contain all living and nonliving materials within a boundary allows scientists to use the powerful tools of budgets and mass balance to analyze ecosystems. He further emphasizes that flexibility in choosing boundaries, formulating specific problems, and focusing on different components of ecosystems allows the creative scientist to efficiently answer important questions about ecosystem structure and function. Most importantly, Pace argues that this flexibility and subjectivity does not prevent the development of robust generalities about ecosystems, but rather speeds their development and testing.

In Chapter 10, Steward Pickett and Mary Cadenasso consider the implications of heterogeneity for ecosystems. Although most traditionally regarded as internally homogeneous and surrounded by a uniform or neutral matrix, ecosystems are in fact both markedly heterogeneous and surrounded by varied, changing, and interactive neighbors. This internal and external heterogeneity can have strong and varied effects on ecosystems. After describing the nature and origins of ecological heterogeneity, Pickett and Cadenasso provide a framework for describing and understanding heterogeneity in space and time. They also consider the central knotty question: when is heterogeneity important in ecosystems? It is clear from this chapter that heterogeneity is important to ecosystems, and that its effects are not yet satisfactorily understood.

Finally, Chapter 11 on the controls on ecosystem structure and function by Kathleen Weathers and her coauthors closes this section of the book. Understanding how ecosystems are controlled is important both for basic science and for management.

Unfortunately, but not surprisingly, ecosystem controls can be highly varied and complex. Weathers et al. remind us that ecosystems may be controlled both by abiotic factors and biotic factors. Especially in the last few centuries, human controls have become important in many ecosystems. Control can come from inside or outside the ecosystem, and from the bottom of the food web or the top. Weathers et al. suggest that feedbacks within the ecosystem are nearly always important. The mathematical relationships between the controlling variable and the ecosystem can be of many kinds, including thresholds and poorly reversible relationships with which it may be difficult for environmental managers to deal with.

# Revisiting the Ecosystem Concept: Important Features That Promote Generality and Understanding

*Michael L. Pace*

Department of Environmental Sciences, University of Virginia, Charlottesville

## INTRODUCTION

Having learned about fundamental topics such as production, energy flow, and elemental cycling, we now reconsider some of the important features of the ecosystem concept. Recall that the study of an ecosystem requires defining boundaries. Thus, ecosystems are places defined by investigators. Ecosystems can be as small as a culture flask in a laboratory or as large as the entire Earth. The size of an ecosystem is flexible ("one size does not fit all") and depends on the questions being asked and the feasibility of measuring flows across ecosystem boundaries. By placing boundaries on an ecosystem, a mass balance approach can be applied tracing inputs, outputs, and storage over time. Mass balance provides a constraint that structures many ecosystem studies and gives the approach power to resolve questions and problems through an accounting of fluxes. Because ecosystems include both biotic and abiotic components, ecosystem studies are inherently inclusive. This inclusive approach means that the ultimate goal of ecosystem research is not to reduce or isolate specific components but rather to understand the system that results from the interactions of the components as a whole. Boundary specification, mass balance, and inclusiveness are three of the most important features of the ecosystem concept, and provide flexibility, power, and synthesis.

Despite the apparent strengths of the ecosystem concept, we could object to the approach on a number of grounds. Does the flexibility of ecosystem specification make the analysis of ecosystems too dependent on investigator-defined units and thereby prevent generality? For example, a study of carbon cycling might be done in a flask or for the globe. Both are ecosystems, but they hardly seem comparable in that the flask results would seemingly have little relevance to global carbon cycling studies. A further concern is whether ecosystems are subject to repeatable investigation where suitably controlled experimental studies can be conducted. If not, then ecosystems might fall outside the norms of scientific study for testing questions and drawing conclusions.

These considerations lead to the thought that the ecosystem concept might be too abstract to be useful. Ecosystems are heterogeneous with varying sizes, structures, and components. Can we compare (and contrast) ecosystems like a forest and field in the same way as other forms of biological organization (e.g., populations, organisms, organs, tissues, cells)? Can we experimentally manipulate conditions in a forest or a field to test a response in the same way we can measure the responses of organisms or cells to an experimental manipulation? This chapter addresses these issues by evaluating aspects of the ecosystem concept. The focus is on boundaries that separate the internal from external, allowing the establishment of budgets, and on inclusiveness and flexibility in defining the internal components of ecosystems. Evaluation of these aspects of the ecosystem concept leads to a consideration of whether it is possible to generalize about ecosystems and to develop predictions about their responses both to internal and external changes.

## BUDGETS AND BOUNDARIES

By defining boundaries the investigator establishes an ecosystem. As noted earlier, ecosystems can be any size and so ecosystems are scale-independent, meaning they are not defined by a particular spatial scale. Boundaries are defined according to the question of interest. Frequently, boundaries are made at some convenient and easily identified location such as a shoreline or transition from one vegetation type to another (field to forest). Boundaries are also established to define cohesive units. For example, watersheds often serve as convenient boundaries as they enclose a hydrologically cohesive unit.

The establishment of a boundary separates what is external to the ecosystem from what is internal. Fluxes across the boundary are inputs and outputs (Figure 9.1) and the simplest ecosystem budget is:

$$\text{Inputs} = \text{Outputs} + \text{Storage} \tag{9.1}$$

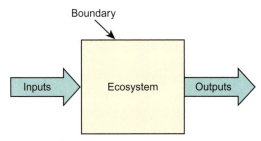

FIGURE 9.1   A simple input–output diagram for an ecosystem.

When storage is zero, then inputs equal outputs by definition, and the ecosystem is in a steady state. If storage is positive, inputs are accumulating in the system. If storage is negative, there is a net loss from the system, and outputs exceed inputs.

The calcium budget of a well-studied New Hampshire forested watershed provides an example of the power of boundaries and budgets (Likens et al. 1996, 1998). The boundaries of watersheds in the Hubbard Brook forest of New Hampshire are easily defined. The forest soil is underlain with bedrock and hence the watersheds are nearly watertight. There is no significant loss of water and solutes through deep ground-water flows (Likens and Bormann 1995). Thus, inputs and outputs in these watersheds can be readily measured. Calcium enters Hubbard Brook watersheds via atmospheric deposition and weathering reactions and exits the system in stream water. Within the system there is uptake, exchange, and cycling of calcium. The movements of calcium can be described as:

$$P + W = S + B \qquad (9.2)$$

where atmospheric inputs are represented by $P$ (precipitation); weathering inputs, meaning the mobilization of calcium from rocks via chemical reactions, are represented by $W$; $S$ is stream output; and $B$ is net storage in biomass. Equation 9.2 is analogous to the simple budget of Eq. 9.1. Precipitation ($P$) and weathering ($W$) represent new inputs of calcium to the system. Stream export ($S$) is the primary loss of calcium, while the primary storage of calcium is in the accumulation of biomass ($B$) in trees. The fluxes $P$, $W$, $S$, and $B$ in units of moles of calcium per watershed area per year were measured over a 30-year period at Hubbard Brook for specific watersheds. The combined rate of $S + B$ far exceeded $P + W$ (Figure 9.2). This apparent imbalance indicates how the constraint of mass balance in ecosystems can be particularly helpful and lead to important findings.

Where does the calcium come from to account for the excess of outputs over inputs? The "missing calcium" is mobilized from labile and exchangeable pools in the soil. This is essentially a new input of calcium that makes up for the shortfall in calcium measured in the budget of outputs relative to inputs. Precipitation at Hubbard Brook is acidic and this has caused soil calcium to dissolve to partially neutralize acid inputs (e.g., $CaCO_3$ dissolution leading to uptake of hydrogen ions, $H^+$, as for example in bicarbonate, $HCO_3$, and the consequent release of calcium). Acid inputs have declined over time because of air pollution controls and consequently the loss of soil calcium has also declined. However, the long-term net loss of calcium from the soil means that the total stock of calcium in the watershed has declined. One result of this net loss of calcium is that the system is more susceptible to acid precipitation. There is less calcium to neutralize acid, because less buffering capacity remains in the soil as calcium is exported at rates far faster than it is replenished (Likens et al. 1996). This long-term analysis of calcium would not have been possible without establishment of watershed (ecosystem) boundaries and measurement of the major inputs and outputs (i.e., fluxes across boundaries).

*Loading* is a term used to describe inputs across a boundary to an ecosystem. In the Hubbard Brook watershed example, the loading of calcium from outside the system comes via $P$, the precipitation inputs of calcium to the system. The calcium bound in rocks and minerals is not available for either chemical reactions or biological uptake. However, weathering defined as the dissolution of minerals by water releases the calcium and makes

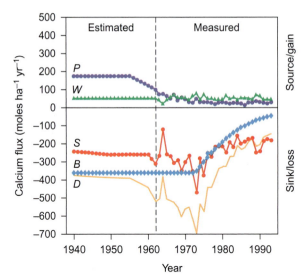

**FIGURE 9.2** Major fluxes of calcium for a watershed in the Hubbard Brook Experimental Forest in New Hampshire. Fluxes were measured in 1963–1994, and estimated for 1940–1963. $P$ is bulk precipitation input, $W$ is weathering release, $S$ is loss in stream water, $B$ is net storage in biomass, and $D$ is net release from labile soil pools (exchangeable + organically bound), which is estimated by difference. The decline in precipitation inputs ($P$) in the 1950s and 1960s is a result of better control of particulate air pollution from industrial sources. *(Redrawn from Likens et al. 1998.)*

it available. This flux is also "new" in that the calcium can begin to react with other components of the ecosystem. This type of flux is often called *internal loading* because the calcium was present in the system but not previously available. The loading of substances to ecosystems is a useful metric and often becomes important in analyzing and managing environmental problems. The loading of phosphorus to a lake, nitrogen to an estuary, and sulfate to a forest are measured fluxes across ecosystem boundaries that are often targeted for reduction by management.

Exports are the mirror image of loads. These are losses across ecosystem boundaries. Nitrate ($NO_3$) is an important constituent of river water and represents a major form of inorganic nitrogen loss from rivers to coastal ecosystems. Inputs of nitrate support primary production in estuaries and nearshore coastal waters and excesses contribute to eutrophication of the coastal zone (see Chapter 7). Concentrations of nitrate and exports of nitrate from watersheds vary for rivers as a function of human population density of the watershed (Figure 9.3). A relatively pristine river like the Yukon has a population density of only 0.4 people per $km^2$ and a correspondingly low nitrate concentration and low nitrate export of 62 $\mu$mol $sec^{-1}$ $km^{-2}$, whereas the Thames River has a much higher population density (400/$km^2$) and a very high nitrate export (> 4000 $\mu$mol $s^{-1}$ $km^{-2}$). The units of export in this case may seem strange but are quite straightforward. The units represent the loss of nitrate in micromoles each second from each square kilometer of the watershed. For the Thames watershed this translates to more than 1 billion moles of nitrate (> 17 million kg of N) exported from the Thames to the coastal zone every year.

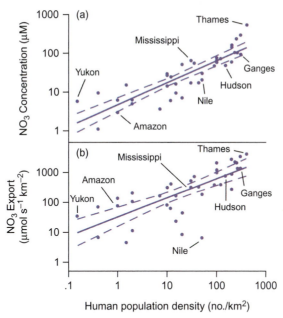

FIGURE 9.3 Relationship between human population density and (a) river nitrate concentration and (b) river nitrate export for major rivers throughout the world. *(Redrawn from Peierls et al. 1991.)*

Once fluxes across boundaries are quantified, a next question is often about sources. In the case of river nitrate what are the sources of export? Can sources be reduced by management? The primary sources of river nitrogen in developed areas include atmospheric deposition of nitrogen on the watershed, which is often enriched in nitrogen from air pollution, nitrogen from fertilizers, and point-sources such as sewage and industrial discharges (Caraco and Cole 1999). While there are other sources contributing to nitrogen export, atmospheric deposition, fertilizer use, and sewage plus industrial discharge are all potentially subject to management and regulation. Thus, the budgeting of inputs, outputs (exports), and sources provide critical insights needed to manage ecosystems. The understanding needed to apply management strategies derives from establishing ecosystem boundaries. Although rarely emphasized, this feature of the ecosystem concept is particularly significant.

The boundaries of ecosystems are set by investigators, not by independent structural definitions as for a cell or organism. At first glance the lack of specificity may seem troubling, especially in considering how to make generalizations across more than one ecosystem. Patterns of nitrate concentration and export in rivers throughout the world, however, provide an example of how it is possible to develop generalizations (Figure 9.3). The watersheds (i.e., the ecosystems) for the rivers presented in Figure 9.3 vary in size from 160 km$^2$ to over 7 million km$^2$. Yet, the exports of these river watersheds can be meaningfully compared. The differences among the rivers are largely determined by anthropogenic factors, not by geographic location, geochemical conditions, or watershed size.

Sizes, shapes, and spatial heterogeneity of ecosystems are important and may determine or influence important properties of ecosystems (Lovett et al. 2005). For example, the depth of the upper mixed layer for lakes that temperature-stratify is a key property. Mixed layer depth is influenced by the clarity of the water. Greater clarity leads to deeper light penetration and hence a deeper uniform heating of the surface waters. The upper mixed layer is deeper in clear lakes than in more turbid lakes. Water clarity is measured by light transmission (in units of inverse meters − m$^{-1}$) and so a relationship between percent light transmission (water clarity) and depth of the mixed layer is expected (Figure 9.4). The relationship, however, differs for small (< 500 ha) versus large (> 500 ha) lakes (Fee et al. 1996; Figure 9.4). It is possible to predict mixed layer depth from a measure of light transmission, but this important property of lake ecosystems is also scale-dependent. Mixing depth depends on the size of the lake. Large lakes differ from small lakes because of the differential effects of wind energy exerted over the greater length (fetch) of a large lake (Fee et al. 1996). In simple terms greater wind mixing in large lakes tends to promote deeper mixed layers and causes a different relationship between clarity and mixed layer depth.

The lake example represents two important outcomes. The first outcome is that generalizations about ecosystems are possible. This book contains many examples of patterns within and among ecosystems as well as explanations of these patterns. The development and evaluation of patterns is a fundamental scientific activity. Despite the abstract aspects of the ecosystem concept noted at the beginning of this chapter, the ability to generalize about ecosystems indicates this unit of nature is a worthy topic for scientific study. The second outcome is that variation in properties within and among ecosystems may be related to scale (see Chapter 17). Variation in ecosystem size in the lake example is directly

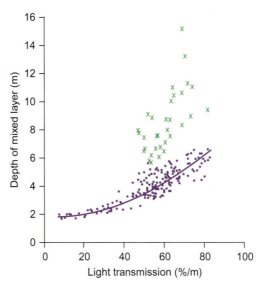

**FIGURE 9.4**　Relationship between water clarity (as % light transmission) and mixing depth in small (< 500 ha, closed circles) and large (> 500 ha, x's) lakes.

related to a physical property, mixing depth. A general model of this property must account for the scale of the system. In this sense then the heterogeneity of ecosystems is not a weakness, but instead leads to the development and application of scaling rules that help promote understanding of similarities and differences.

## INCLUSIVENESS AND FLEXIBILITY

Ecosystems include all biotic and abiotic components within—that's everything! Thus, ecosystems are inclusive. Biotic properties are not more important than abiotic properties. Mammals are not more important than microbes or vice versa. An ecosystem scientist may need to consider rocks, rainfall, and reindeer all in the same study. Ecosystem research seeks to integrate and synthesize knowledge about ecosystem components to arrive at a broad understanding (Likens 1992). The inclusiveness of ecosystem research seems, at first glance, to contrast with standard scientific approaches that seek to reduce the number of variables under consideration through isolation and control to study and understand mechanisms. The inclusive property of ecosystems might lead to the view that it is necessary to study everything in the system—an inherently difficult prospect and a poor scientific strategy.

The answer to this apparent contradiction is that ecosystem studies are not about everything. While an ecosystem is inclusive, research problems are specific and the investigator defines the components of an ecosystem to approach a question. In the simplest case, an ecosystem can be considered a "black box" with inputs and outputs and where no internal components are considered (Eq. 9.1). A study of carbon storage in an ecosystem might focus on only three internal components such as primary producers, heterotrophs, and the accumulation of organic carbon in long-term storage pools like sediments and wood. Another study of the carbon cycling might focus on energy flow and include a number of trophic groups such as producers, herbivores, decomposers, and predators, as well as a variety of biotic (e.g., respiratory) and abiotic (e.g., detrital sedimentation) flows. The definition of ecosystem components is particular to a study. This flexibility is a powerful feature of the ecosystem approach because of the potential for application to many problems and a variety of conceptual frameworks.

Consider the following hypothetical examples of possible questions and necessary components for an ecosystem study. One study asks for a set of lakes if these ecosystems are sinks for organic carbon—meaning, do the inputs of organic carbon to lakes exceed the outputs? The study lakes can be treated as a black box and the question resolved merely by measuring the balance of inputs and outputs (Figure 9.5a). A second study might ask if lakes are sinks for organic carbon and if the variation in sink strength among lakes is related to the efficiency of organic matter sedimentation and burial. In this study the inputs and outputs of organic carbon would need to be measured and internal processes that control sedimentation and burial would also need to be measured (Figure 9.5b). A third study, pursuing the same line of investigation, might ask if lakes are sinks for organic carbon and if the variation in sink strength among lakes is related to system respiration as well as sedimentation and burial processes. This study would need to consider the additional components controlling respiration (Figure 9.5c).

Each study asks a more refined question that in turn dictates the need to resolve additional components and processes of the ecosystem. The art of science in this case and others is to ask the question in the most interesting and creative way and to include the necessary components needed to resolve the question. In the early stages of understanding whether lakes are organic carbon sinks, the first study might be the most interesting and lead to results that in turn would indicate the second and third studies would be worth pursuing. The flexibility to include or not include particular components of an ecosystem is dependent on the state of understanding in a particular area and goals of the research effort.

The inclusive property of the ecosystem concept is not a weakness but a strength when scientific work is carried out with clear questions and objectives. This property forces investigators to consider both biotic and abiotic processes, as in the calcium study of Hubbard Brook watershed where purely chemical (weathering) and biological (calcium uptake and storage) processes are both critically important. Inclusiveness in ecosystem research also means that important inputs, outputs, or fluxes are considered and encompassed in a study and not ignored. Inclusiveness is sometimes associated with the mantra "everything is connected to everything," a saying often considered as a general lesson from ecology. Everything, however, is not equally important and effective research defines the most important entities and processes for a given scientific problem. Inclusiveness can become a difficulty when researchers specify too many potentially important entities and processes. The system is reduced into too many component parts making it very difficult to understand the interactions. The inclusive aspect of the ecosystem concept, however, when used well, promotes an integrated perspective. This perspective in the company of good questions and effective research strategies aids ecosystem research.

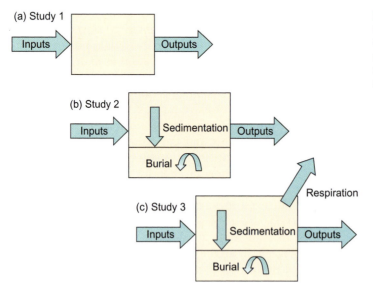

FIGURE 9.5 Illustration of three hypothetical studies that include different components for resolving questions related to the net loss of organic carbon in lake ecosystems.

# GENERALITY AND PREDICTION

One of the principal goals of science is to achieve generality through understanding. Ecosystem scientists seek to understand the workings of ecosystems and especially how these systems respond to external and internal drivers of change. One test of understanding is the ability to make and test predictions. For example, consider the simple hypothesis that nitrogen addition will increase forest productivity because nitrogen is the most limiting nutrient. A model could be developed to predict the actual increments of forest production that would result from given levels of nitrogen addition. The model predictions could be directly compared to data derived from an experiment. This type of predictive understanding, especially in the context of large-scale environmental change (e.g., climate change, losses of biodiversity), is a stated goal of many research efforts (Pace 2001).

While the goals of understanding, generality, and prediction are widely accepted by ecologists, the approaches to these goals vary depending, in part, on philosophical orientation. Pickett et al. (2007) characterize two philosophical perspectives that are important in ecology and science in general. The first perspective is synthetic. This approach evaluates multiple alternatives about ecosystems and places knowledge within larger integrated frameworks. Generality emerges readily from this approach as a consequence of synthesis and integration. The synthetic perspective often employs and evaluates alternative models. Choice among models is based on those that provide the best predictions in terms of the goodness of fit between models and data. Hence, model predictions feature prominently in the synthetic perspective. The second primary philosophical perspective of ecology and the one that has dominated much of the discussion concerning philosophical aspects of the science (Pickett et al. 2007) is deductive hypothesis testing or the deductive approach for short. The deductive approach attempts to eliminate explanations with a focus toward evaluating underlying causes of phenomena. Predictions arise via deduction from hypotheses and are either refuted or supported. Generality develops when a hypothesis becomes widely supported by various tests and becomes part of theory. The synthetic and deductive perspectives are important and complementary and both are typically represented in the approaches ecosystem scientists use to investigate questions (Carpenter 1998).

The aspects of the ecosystem concept described earlier—boundaries, budgets, inclusiveness, and flexibility—are all important in developing generality and predictions. Models related to the transport of materials across ecosystem boundaries are often a focus of research that leads to predictions. For example, the river nitrate loading model (Figure 9.3) provides estimates of transport across ecosystem boundaries in the form of the loading from the river watershed system to the downstream coastal zone. The model predictions are unambiguous—human density of the watershed tells you the expected loading of nitrate. The uncertainty associated with this prediction can be calculated with standard statistical methods.

This river nitrate model is simple and the predictions might prove wrong because the model is incomplete or does not apply in some situations. Using the deductive perspective we could imagine creating a more detailed model that delves into the mechanisms of nitrogen cycling, particularly processes associated with the production and consumption of nitrate, that result in the net flux of nitrate out of river watersheds. Such a model would include more entities (components) and processes (fluxes among the components) encompassing both biotic and abiotic interactions that influence nitrate. Such a model would probably be based on a mass balance. The inclusiveness aspect of ecosystem science promotes the deeper exploration of complex interactions that influence important system attributes like river nitrate.

The flexibility of the ecosystem concept allows one to boil down many interactions into a simple form that can be particularly useful for prediction and comparison. Similarly, flexibility allows us to focus on interactions and multiple contributing processes. Returning to the two philosophical perspectives, a deductive approach that developed a detailed nitrogen model for the river nitrate problem would provide hypotheses in the form of testable predictions. These predictions could be analyzed by experiments and/or measurement programs. A synthetic approach might pose a number of models of varying complexity and seek to develop a spectrum of model predictions that could be compared with existing data, new measurements, or experimental results.

There is no single path to generality. Students of ecology are advised to consider many models and varying approaches that together provide the means to investigate ecosystems (Carpenter 1998). The ecosystem concept provides a powerful framework for investigating many (but not all) ecological problems. The discipline of boundary setting and mass balance combined with inclusiveness and flexibility are key components of the concept that promote effective implementation of ecosystem studies.

# References

Caraco, N.F., Cole, J.J., 1999. Human impact on nitrate export: An analysis using major world rivers. Ambio 28, 167–170.

Carpenter, S.R., 1998. The need for large scale experiments to assess and predict the response of ecosystems to perturbation. In: Pace, M.L., Groffman, P.M. (Eds.), Successes, limitations, and frontiers in ecosystem science. Springer-Verlag, New York, pp. 287–312.

Fee, E.J., Hecky, R.E., Kasain, S.E.M., Cruikshank, D.R., 1996. Effects of lake size, water clarity and climatic variability on mixing depths in Canadian Shield lakes. Limnol. Oceanogr. 41, 912–920.

Likens, G.E., 1992. The ecosystem approach: Its use and abuse. Ecology Institute, Oldendorf/Luhe, Germany.

Likens, G.E., Bormann, F.H., 1995. Biogeochemistry of a forested ecosystem, second ed. Springer-Verlag, New York.

Likens, G.E., Driscoll, C.T., Buso, D.C., 1996. Long-term effects of acid rain: Response and recovery of a forest ecosystem. Science 272, 244–246.

Likens, G.E., Driscoll, C.T., Buso, D.C., Siccama, T.G., Johnson, C.E., Lovett, G.M., et al., 1998. The biogeochemistry of calcium at Hubbard Brook. Biogeochemistry 41, 89–173.

Lovett, G.M., Jones, C.G., Turner, M.G., Weathers, K.C. (Eds.), 2005. Ecosystem function in heterogeneous landscapes. Springer-Verlag, New York.

Pace, M.L., 2001. Prediction and the aquatic sciences. Can. J. Fish. Aquat. Sci. 58, 63–72.

Peierls, B., Caraco, N.F., Pace, M.L., Cole, J.J., 1991. River nitrogen export linked to human population density. Nature 350, 386–387.

Pickett, S.T.A., Kolasa, J., Jones, C.G., 2007. Ecological understanding, the nature of theory and the theory of nature, second ed. Academic Press, San Diego.

# Ecosystems in a Heterogeneous World

*Steward T.A. Pickett[1] and Mary L. Cadenasso[2]*

[1]Cary Institute of Ecosystem Studies, Millbrook, NY; [2]Department of Plant Sciences,
University of California, Davis

## INTRODUCTION

The ecosystem concept has few fundamental assumptions (Pickett and Cadenasso 2002). In fact, the core idea—that an ecosystem constitutes the interaction among a group of organisms with one another and with the physical environment within a specified area (Tansley 1935)—requires no additional assumptions (see Chapter 1). Yet, the history of ecology is rich with definitions of the ecosystem that assume such things as materially closed boundaries, equilibrium dynamics, or autotrophy (Golley 1993). Because the core definition is silent about such things, specific models are free to adopt any number of assumptions in their attempt to apply the concept to real or ideal situations. However, assumptions need to be identified as such, and clearly specified as attributes of models of ecosystems, not the core concept itself. Oddly, whether ecosystems are assumed to be spatially heterogeneous or homogeneous, and the relevance of heterogeneity outside their boundaries, have been among the largely unexamined features of ecosystem models.

As ecologists have been able to amass more data on how systems behave, they have seen the need to relax the restrictive assumption of internal homogeneity of ecosystems (Golley 1993). Empirical study has richly shown that ecosystems are internally heterogeneous, and that such patchiness could be significant to the functioning of ecosystems (Kolasa and Pickett 1991; Lovett et al. 2005). Similarly, as they have been able to observe systems over broader spatial contexts, they have abandoned the assumption that the external environment of an ecosystem is a uniform bath or quantitative field (Forman and Godron 1986).

The assumptions that ecosystems were homogeneous and embedded in uniform spatial contexts were very helpful in the early development of ecosystem science where the principal goal was to elucidate the fundamentals of how ecosystems worked. In fact, assessing input and output budgets or determining the controls on system metabolism made great progress under these assumptions (Likens 1992). However, as research on ecosystem structure and function has advanced, heterogeneity began to claim more attention from ecologists. Still, concerted focus on the implications of heterogeneity for ecosystem science is relatively new (Turner and Cardille 2007). Therefore, a body of empirical generalizations about heterogeneity and ecosystems does not yet exist. It is important, however, to have a clear way to guide the search for new knowledge about heterogeneity and ecosystems. This chapter outlines key features of a framework for addressing heterogeneity in and surrounding ecosystems.

## THE NATURE OF HETEROGENEITY

*Heterogeneity* is a technical term for the differentiation in structure or process over three-dimensional space or over time in any system. In more familiar terms, heterogeneity translates into such commonly observed spatial patterns as patchiness, or the variation across large landscapes (Figure 10.1). Such heterogeneity or patchiness has been used for a long time in some biological subjects and ecological subdisciplines. For example, because evolution uses the genetic differences among individuals as a key explanatory process, there are countless examples of studies of variation among individuals and its implications for selection and differential fitness (Futuyma 2009). Interest in variation has been important for a long time in population ecology as well, with its emphasis on within-population heterogeneity in age, sex, and size (Futuyma 2009). Heterogeneity in community ecology is illustrated by regional differences or differences along gradients in species composition (Scheiner and Willig 2005). The evolutionary and population ecologist's focus on differentiation between individuals and populations is beginning to be transferred to ecosystem science as the bridge between species biology and ecosystem science is increasingly explored (Jones and Lawton 1995).

The examples just mentioned expose an important aspect of heterogeneity. It can be identified within any kind of ecological unit, such as populations, communities, ecosystems, and individuals. Qualitative or quantitative differences among individual elements of each kind of unit result in heterogeneity (Figure 10.2). Heterogeneity can exist as (1) richness of entities of interest, (2) the frequency of those entities in a collection, or (3) the spatially or temporally explicit configuration of the entities. Population heterogeneity is expressed in the genetic or demographic differences mentioned earlier, for example. However, heterogeneity can also be identified as a matter of spatial arrangement at particular spatial or temporal scales. At a scale of hundreds of meters, an animal population in which bachelor males form separate herds will likely have different dynamics than unstructured herds. An additional example at the scale of many meters or kilometers is a set of plant communities that differ in such attributes as height, layering, or composition as a result of soil fertility or moisture differences.

Examples also exist at finer scales. Across only tens of meters, heterogeneity within plant communities can result from the biotic interactions among neighboring individuals. The examples of heterogeneity throughout this chapter can be differentiated based on whether they arise from differences expressed among the kinds of elements or patches of

FIGURE 10.1 Examples of spatial heterogeneity relevant to ecosystem science. Although these figures represent medium to coarse scales, spatial heterogeneity can exist on any scale, from intervals of millimeters to continental scope. (a) A treefall gap contrasting with the closed canopy of an old growth hemlock-oak forest on the grounds of Montgomery Place on the banks of the Hudson River. (b) A model of the surface elevation of the Dead Run watershed in metropolitan Baltimore, MD, based on LiDAR imagery. Both natural and modified surface features, such as roadbeds, leveled areas for large buildings and parking lots, culverts, and channelized drainages, are shown. Blue represents low elevations, and red represents higher elevations. (c) A mountainous landscape in Bhutan, showing cultivated and grazed fields, farmhouses, fallow field shrubland, and patches of intact and lightly managed forest ranging from lower-elevation pine, through oak, to coniferous dominance higher on the slopes of the Himalayan front range. (d) A vacant lot in an old rowhouse neighborhood in Baltimore, MD, that has been converted to a tidy lawn and flower garden by neighboring residents. *(Photos (a), (c), and (d) copyright S.T.A. Pickett. Photo (b) copyright Dr. Andrew Miller, University of Maryland, Baltimore County. All used by permission.)*

a system or differences expressed in arrangement of those elements. Of course, both aspects can play a role in a specific case of heterogeneity, because attention to kinds of elements and to arrangement of elements suggests a continuum of complexity in heterogeneity (Cadenasso et al. 2006).

Another stimulus for thinking about systems as spatially heterogeneous has affected ecosystem science. Since the mid-1970s, landscape ecology has emerged as a discipline

Baltimore city
land cover

🌳 Tree canopy
🌿 Grass/shrub
🟫 Bare earth
💧 Water
🏠 Buildings
▬ Roads
▱ Other paved
   surfaces

**FIGURE 10.2**   Differentiation of the elements of heterogeneity within patches, illustrated by coarse land cover types (left) present in human settlements. In this urban example, which is based on the aerial photograph on the right, the elements of terrestrial patchiness are dominant kinds of vegetation, including grass or woody, surfaces including bare or paved, and buildings. Water is also mapped. Patches can be discriminated either by computer algorithm or manually based on the clustering of the different kinds of elements in space, and the abruptness of shifts in distribution of the three kinds of elements. Principles of urban patch classification are described in Cadenasso et al. (2007). *(Image copyright M.L. Cadenasso and K. Schwarz, and used by permission.)*

**FIGURE 10.3**   A landscape ecology perspective on ecosystem heterogeneity. This landscape in Dutchess County, New York, combines terrestrial and aquatic patches; wild, cultivated, and built patches; and a transportation network. The landscape ecology perspective invites ecologists interested in populations, communities, and ecosystems to understand how patch composition, patch structure, patch adjacency, and the fluxes among patches, both above and below the surface, determine landscape and ecosystem function. *(Image copyright S.T.A. Pickett, and used by permission.)*

that takes heterogeneity as its core concern (Forman and Godron 1986). Landscape ecology takes a spatially extensive perspective, based on the technologies of aerial photography and remote sensing and on the accumulation of spatially distributed ecological samples (Figure 10.3). As the analytical tool of geographic information systems (GISs) has become readily available, use of such spatially extensive data has become commonplace in ecology, with a broadening of the ecosystem perspective to extend beyond the narrow focus carried over from the system science of the mid-twentieth century.

Before we outline a way of thinking about heterogeneity and ecosystems, we give some examples of ecosystem heterogeneity. Recall that the ecosystem concept requires that the boundaries be set by the researcher, so different ecosystems can have very different content and spatial extent (see Chapters 1 and 9). This explains why we can give such diverse examples of heterogeneity within and outside of particular ecosystems.

## Boreal Forest Fire Mosaics

Boreal forests cover wide expanses, and many retain aspects of the natural regimes of disturbance that have shaped them for centuries. One of the first such areas to be well documented was the 400,000-ha Boundary Waters Canoe Area in Minnesota. Myron Heinselman (1973) documented the pattern of burned areas over the landscape by examining scars on the trunks of trees that survived the catastrophic fires. The kinds of mosaics he documented have now become familiar through many studies elsewhere (Figure 10.4; Turner and Romme 1994). It is clear that spatial heterogeneity, expressed as the pattern of

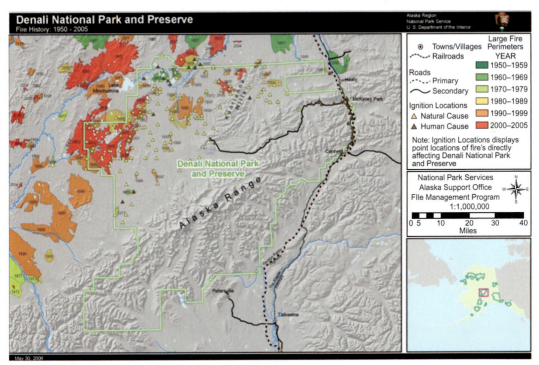

FIGURE 10.4    A fire mosaic in coniferous forest in the Denali National Park and Reserve, and adjacent areas of Alaska from 1950 through 2000. Ages of stands postfire are shown in decadal classes. In addition, whether a fire was set by people or ignited by natural forces is indicated. *(Image in the public domain.)*

trees that escaped fire, or were killed or damaged by fire, or newly established after fire, is a major feature in such regions. If it suits the interests of the researchers, a large landscape containing different patches of intact, burned, killed, or new trees can be considered a single ecosystem. Such a model might be appropriate to understanding the distribution of a large migrating herbivore. An alternative model would be to take the different burned and unburned patches as different ecosystems, assuming that their function would depend on the structure set by the fire history at each site. Sites representing different ages since fire will differ in key determinants of ecosystem functioning, such as nutrients, soils, light, temperature, and moisture.

## Pit and Mound Microtopography

In very old forests in moist temperate regions, a characteristic soil surface heterogeneity can be found. The forest floor is punctuated by mounds and nearby pits, often differing in elevation by 1 to 2 m from lowest to highest point. The pits were formed as root mats were wrenched from the ground when high winds blew down large trees. The adjacent mounds result from sloughing off of soil that was originally held in the web of exposed roots. Spatial heterogeneity in the topography created by pits and mounds is reflected in heterogeneity of moisture content, soil texture, stability, and organic matter (Peterson and Pickett 1990). Pits are subject to deep accumulations of plant litter, and of flooding during wet periods. These factors are all capable of affecting microbial activity, soil nutrient and water availability, and, therefore, the establishment dynamics of seedlings and saplings.

Pits and mounds in terrestrial systems are also created by animal burrowing or digging for below-ground storage organs of plants (Figure 10.5). For example, echidnas (*Tachyglossus aculeatus*) pits and mounds can have effects on ecosystem processes. An experiment by Eldridge (2011) found that increasing the proportion of an area disturbed increased the time for runoff to begin after rain, and increased the production of sediment

FIGURE 10.5   A pit dug by a foraging animal in Australian arid landscape. Such pits are common features in desert landscapes where animals dig to find the underground storage organs of perennial plants. Seeds, organic matter, and sediment accumulate in such pits, and the disruption of the microphytic soil crust permits enhanced water infiltration during rainfall events that are large enough to generate overland flow. Hence, pits are resource and regeneration hotspots. *(Photo copyright S.T.A. Pickett.)*

and the sediment concentration of runoff water. Movement of plant seeds from pit to pit, and from surface to pits was also increased by the proportion of disturbed surface.

## Plant Neighborhoods

A common feature in many ecosystems, ranging from deserts through savannas to moist forests, is the spatial heterogeneity created by nonuniform arrangement of individual plants. This is especially conspicuous when trees are the dominant growth forms. The conditions near or beneath various species often differ considerably. For example, in deserts, the area beneath shrubs may contain higher amounts of organic matter, and lack a soil microphytic crust that elsewhere generates an impervious surface (Schlesinger et al. 1996). In this case, heterogeneity reflects the presence or absence of a woody plant of any species (Figure 10.6). In other cases, the growth forms may be key differentials in heterogeneity. For example, in savannas, the understory grasses and grazing pressures beneath trees can differ substantially (Vetaas 1992). In other cases, the identity of the species is the key driver of heterogeneity. For example, in moist forests, soil nutrients, moisture, and litter dynamics can differ beneath different species of trees (Lavery et al. 2004). Thus, in many ecosystems, the heterogeneity of higher plant species can affect several ecosystem processes based on differences in nutrients, light, water, and microbes.

## Stream Patchiness

Heterogeneity is not restricted to terrestrial ecosystems; streams exhibit great heterogeneity as well (Fisher et al. 1998). Heterogeneity results when pools and riffles alternate with one another along a stream channel, and have contrasting sediments and current velocities. Heterogeneity in streams can also be created by natural dams formed by tangles of branches or large logs that accumulate fine sediments and organic matter on their upstream sides (Figure 10.7). Heterogeneity through time in stream channels also exists. The migration

**FIGURE 10.6** An arid landscape near Adelaide, Australia, showing the contrast between shrub-dominated patches and the mosaic dominated by microphytic soil crust. Shade, sediment, seeds, and leaf litter are among the factors that differ beneath the shrub-dominated patches compared to the crusted areas among shrubs. *(Photo copyright S.T.A. Pickett.)*

history of active channels across floodplains produces lakes or sloughs, and heterogeneous, patchy distributions of sediments in the stream itself, and in places now abandoned by active channels. Heterogeneity in the amount and rate of water penetration into soils, and of drainage and soil oxygenation of the patchy substrate, sets up different fluxes of nutrients as well as communities of microbes and plants within the stream bottom and adjacent floodplain. Stream and riparian patchiness sets up the template for nutrients, organic matter, and biological activity, all of which drive ecosystem metabolism (Naiman et al. 2005).

The productivity of stream ecosystems is widely held to be influenced by the existence and nature of any plant canopy that overhangs the stream channel. Usually the effects are assumed to be primarily the result of decomposition of leaf litter that falls into the stream. Experiments have shown that other aspects of heterogeneity can also be important (Lagrue et al. 2011). Although overarching canopies do add leaf litter, they also reduce stream temperature and input of sunlight. Together, these factors are associated with reduced decomposition in shaded reaches of streams.

## Marine Benthos

The spatial heterogeneity created by organisms in shallow marine and tidal habitats is well known. However, the attention to the ecosystem implications of such heterogeneity is of more recent origin. Spatially extensive assessments have documented that decreasing the heterogeneity in hard substrate marine sessile benthos decreases species richness in such waterscapes. The net result of patchiness is to increase coexistence regionally (Munguia et al. 2011). Such effects also appear in soft-bottomed areas. A model system in which species can preferentially select habitat patches alters the local composition of species and the distribution of organism density (Godbold et al. 2011). At the scale of individual patches, the intensity of bioturbation or burrowing in the soft substrate decreases, but across patches, the ecosystem nutrient concentration increases.

FIGURE 10.7  Spatial complexity in a small stream ecosystem (Black Creek in the Hudson Valley of New York state). In the background is an open canopy area above the stream, in which sunlight and temperature would be higher than elsewhere, while leaf litter input would be less. In the middle ground are two contrasting habitats, a pool of flowing water and a gravel bar through which subsurface or hyporheic flow would pass. In the foreground are downed logs, behind the submerged portions of which sediment and organic matter would accumulate. Each of these habitats will have different dynamics of material processing. *(Photo copyright S.T.A. Pickett.)*

## Boundary Effects

Boundaries between systems that are structurally or compositionally different are important aspects of heterogeneity (Cadenasso et al. 2004). Boundaries may act as barriers, may serve as distinctive habitat zones, or be areas of dynamic interaction between patches. For example, the wall of vegetation that exists between forests and open fields is an important boundary for wind, aerosols, and certain animals (Figure 10.8; Weathers et al. 2001). The movement of nutrients and organisms between the forest and field can be controlled by the structure of those boundaries. As a result of the physical environmental patterns and resource gradients, boundaries are likely to be locations of great contrast in ecosystem functions.

Boundaries rarely exist in landscapes and ecosystems in isolation. Indeed, different boundaries may interact. However, the interaction of multiple boundaries has rarely been investigated. Porensky (2011) provides a compelling example, based on research on abandoned livestock corrals in East Africa (Figure 10.9). Such patches can last for decades or centuries, and are nutrient-rich, treeless glades that influence the distribution of plants and animals. The areas between glades differed depending on whether other glades were less than 150 m away, or more than 250 m distant. Areas between close glades had double the number of trees, half the use by large herbivores, and less cover of open-site grasses. Even the ant species associated with *Acacia* trees differed between close and distant glades. Such a complex of differences may have many implications for ecosystem processes.

## Management and Built Patches

Few contemporary ecosystems lack signs of the activities of humans, and many are dominated by human activities and artifacts (Vitousek et al. 1997). Human activities and

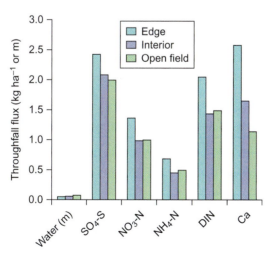

**FIGURE 10.8** Input of atmospheric nutrients and pollutants at a forest-field edge; DIN = dissolved inorganic nitrogen. Bulk water input in the open field represents the ambient nutrient flux from the atmosphere to the terrestrial ecosystem. Intact forest edge experiences higher inputs of sulfate, nitrate, and ammonium than do the forest interior or the open field. *(Data from Weathers et al. 2001.)*

FIGURE 10.9   Cattle corrals in Tanzania, East Africa. The corrals are the circular and irregular forms outlined by shrubs and small trees. Active corrals contain structures as well. An abandoned corral with a degenerating woody boundary appears near the center of the photograph. These systems are similar to those investigated by Porensky (2011). *(Photo copyright S.T.A. Pickett.)*

the associated buildings and infrastructure generate heterogeneity within or adjacent to ecosystems. Forest harvesting, whether by clear-cutting or by different patterns of thinning, generates patches that differ from those that are not harvested, or that were harvested at different times in the past. Similarly, the infrastructure that people insert into managed ecosystems is a source of heterogeneity. In managed forests, even small, one-lane unpaved roads alter surface water flow, local light availability, and access of new invaders (Gascon et al. 2000). A more extreme example is the heterogeneity that results from urban development and management of different properties or neighborhoods in cities and suburbs. Such heterogeneity combines biological elements, buildings and infrastructure, and a variety of surfaces, ranging from native to paved (Cadenasso et al. 2007). Urban spatial heterogeneity is conspicuously mosaic in form (Figure 10.2; McGrath et al. 2007). The question of how urban ecosystems function remains an important frontier for ecology (see Chapter 17). Metropolitan areas, consisting of cities, suburbs, and exurbs, are in fact ecosystems and their unique heterogeneous structures and associated functions require further elucidation (McGrath and Pickett 2011; Pickett et al. 2011).

These examples point to some basic ways of thinking about heterogeneity and ecosystems. Some point to parallels with population and evolutionary ecology, such as concern with biodiversity and genetic structure of populations. Some reflect the widely recognized distributions of organisms along local and regional gradients (Fox et al. 2011). Others connect with the continental and global gradients of diversity (Colwell 2011). Attention to heterogeneity, such as that of plant community composition, has been part of the core of ecology for a long time (Hutchings et al. 2000), but only recently has been applied in the ecosystem context. Other examples have relied on the newer disciplines of landscape ecology (Lovett et al. 2005; Dutilleul 2011) or ecological engineering (Jones et al. 1994). For all aspects of heterogeneity, however, empirical evidence about how heterogeneity affects ecosystems is still modest, and this ecological specialty is still too new to support confirmed generalizations (Turner and Cardille 2007). We can, however, provide a framework that suggests what to look for in understanding the relationships between ecosystems and heterogeneity. Ultimately, the question to be answered is, "How does heterogeneity affect ecosystem structure and function?"

# TOWARD A FRAMEWORK FOR SPACE AND TIME HETEROGENEITY

Constructing a way to think about heterogeneity in ecosystems can take many forms. Here, we summarize the fundamentals of spatial heterogeneity; link spatial to temporal heterogeneity, which can be summarized in the concept of patch dynamics; introduce some distinctive features of human-induced heterogeneity; and end with a pulse-press taxonomy of kinds of temporal events generating heterogeneity.

## Spatial Heterogeneity

Heterogeneity can appear as differentiation in either space or time. These two kinds of heterogeneity are linked conceptually and analytically (Dutilleul 2011), yet it is important to recognize their distinct characteristics. For example, spatial heterogeneity appears as three-dimensional patchiness or gradients such that different places are different from one another—the structure, composition, or processes underway at each place differ. Such heterogeneity may appear on fine scales, existing within a defined ecosystem, or on very coarse scales, encompassing what may be defined by researchers as several ecosystems. Spatial heterogeneity can take contrasting forms. In the case of patchiness, differentiation is abrupt at a given scale, while for gradients, differentiation at that same scale is gradual. Gradients are often detected directly and linearly through space. However, gradients may sometimes be abstracted from spatial mosaics, as in ordination, and do not necessarily appear as concrete, linear transects on the ground (Austin 2005). The principle of ecological differentiation along gradients is one of ecology's oldest ideas. It suggests that any area isolated for study on some part of a gradient would exhibit biotic differentiation within it that paralleled the environmental gradient, and would exhibit differences in composition, three-dimensional architecture, or process compared to adjacent areas along the gradient. Important exchanges of matter, energy, or influence may occur between the focal ecosystem and other ranges of the gradient. Most of the examples given in this chapter to this point have emphasized spatial heterogeneity.

## Patch Dynamics and the Linkage of Time and Space

Patch dynamics provides a way to both summarize spatial heterogeneity, and relate it to temporal heterogeneity. The time dimension of heterogeneity is incorporated in the concept of patch dynamics. Patch dynamics is a conceptual and modeling approach that recognizes the spatial patterning at a variety of scales and for various ecological criteria, including individuals, populations, communities, ecosystems, and landscapes (Pickett and Rogers 1997). Patches, as three-dimensional bodies, appear in aquatic systems as volumes of water that are formed and move differentially based on temperature, density, or chemical content. Even in streams, the movement of water interacts with the subsurface sediment in so-called hyporheic flow (Fisher and Welter 2005), or with debris dams in which some nutrient cycling processes are concentrated (Montgomery 2008). Burrowing in intertidal flats and shallow coastal habitats are examples of patch dynamics, and examples have been mentioned earlier in this chapter (Godbold et al. 2011).

The key insight of patch dynamics is that the spatial pattern of heterogeneity need not be constant through time. Therefore, the spatial heterogeneity of ecological systems can change as a result of changes within patches, or changes in surrounding patches. Entire mosaics of ecological patches, such as the fire mosaic in boreal forests (Figure 10.4) or the channel and sediment mosaics of alluvial floodplains, can change through time, with significant implications for ecosystem functioning and the fluxes between ecosystems. How temporal heterogeneity is generated and controlled is discussed in the following.

## Causes and Trends of Temporal Heterogeneity

There are many potential causes of temporal heterogeneity. It may appear as a result of disturbance, animal movement and activity, or the vegetation dynamics of succession (Pickett et al. 2000). For example, following disturbance, new plant species may invade or rise to dominance, and many abiotic features of the environment of an ecosystem may change as a result (Vitousek 2004). Consequently, the demand for and availability of light, nutrients, and water are all also subject to change. Primary productivity, respiration, litter production, and litter quality also differ through time as a result of the changes in resources and regulating factors altered by disturbance and succession. Its place in a successional sequence will determine many aspects of an ecosystem's material and energy budgets. In moist habitats, such successional differences can appear on new geological substrates over centuries to a few thousand years (Figure 10.10). In situations where

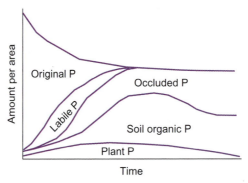

**FIGURE 10.10**  Generalized trends in phosphorus (P), a limiting nutrient over primary successions spanning millions of years. The total amount of P, an element with a geologic rather than a gaseous source (see Chapter 8), declines in the system over time. Labile P available to plants is a small and declining fraction of the total. Plant content is always low compared to insoluble or occluded P and that bound in soil organic matter is low, but peaks in middle ranges of the long succession. Trends redrawn from Vitousek (2004), who confirmed the applicability of this model to ancient volcanic succession across the Hawaiian Islands.

disturbances of geological substrates are rare or absent, substrates and soils may become quite old. Such old substrates, those on the order of several hundreds of thousands to millions of years since major geologic disruption, also differ based on age, just as they do in shorter successions. In both short and ancient successions, the interaction of the substrate and the organisms, modified by any input of nutrients or stress factors from elsewhere, determines the current biogeochemistry of the ecosystem (Vitousek 2004).

Past human actions can generate heterogeneity that determines an ecosystem's current metabolism. Human management adds or subtracts species from ecosystems, shifts the relative proportions and distributions of species, or adds or removes substrate and the nutrients it contains. Alternatively, management can add or remove disturbance or stress agents, or change the timing of disturbances. All of these kinds of human actions can have persistent effects, and their effects can change in intensity through time. Indeed, the action or management may be long past but still influence the current behavior of ecosystems (Foster et al. 2003). The past can echo into the present.

Other patterns of temporal heterogeneity and variation are relevant to ecosystems. Some temporal changes are not directional. Stochastic variation in weather and climate are examples of this sort of time dynamic. Wet versus dry years can appear unpredictably. Stream flow, migration or extirpation of populations, and the shift from denitrifying to nitrifying conditions can follow as the result of interposition of a very wet or dry year in riparian systems (Stanley and Fisher 1992). Wet versus dry years will experience different kinds of disturbances—for example, drought mortality, flooding, landslides, or fire.

Still longer-term shifts also occur in climate. Of course, the current anthropogenic shift in climate regimes is an example, with projected alterations in the distribution of temperature extremes and rainfall patterns. Both of these are major drivers of ecosystem function. Climate shifts likely will alter disturbance patterns as well because they change the energy and intensity of weather events, as well as the susceptibility of ecosystems through their effects on composition, productivity, and architecture.

Long climate excursions illustrate coarse-scale temporal heterogeneity (McKinzey et al. 2005). The "Little Ice Age" affected Europe and North America from at least 1650 to the middle of the nineteenth century. An average decrease in annual temperature of 1°C led to extreme winters, advance of mountain glaciers, and changes in success and then location of farming, and finally, shifts in human population distribution in some areas. Given the potential for persistent effects seen in long-lived trees and soils, such climate excursions are expected to have perceptible ecosystem signals. Climate scientists have been able to isolate the effects of this climate shift from the currently ongoing anthropogenic phase of global climate change (Jones and Mann 2004).

## Conceptual Refinements for Temporal Heterogeneity: Pulses and Presses

When considering temporal heterogeneity there are important refinements to consider. Temporal heterogeneity is recognized through the occurrence of ecologically relevant events. The mere passage of time is not really an environmental cause. It can be a useful proxy variable representing environmental mechanisms, but it is important to discover the actual causes or events that have ecological outcomes. Unpacking and operationalizing the concept of disturbance contributes to refining the understanding of temporal heterogeneity (Peters et al. 2011).

Refinement of translating time into actual events is facilitated by differentiating pulses from presses in ecological systems (Glasby and Underwood 1996). A pulse event is one that has a sudden onset, relative to the time window (or grain) and time span (or extent) under consideration. Pulse events also end soon after their onset. They may either repeat or not, and if they repeat, they may be irregular or cyclical. The specific events may include disturbance, in the strict sense of an alteration of the three-dimensional structure of an ecological system or part of the system, or the events may be stresses. Stresses, in contrast to disturbances that affect structure, directly affect the metabolism or functioning of systems. Stresses may be caused by introduction of toxins or by shift of environmental regulating factors to extremely high or low levels. Temperature and moisture are two of the most common environmental regulators that can cause stress when they reach extreme levels, and hence, generate heterogeneity in time.

Press events contrast with pulse events (Figure 10.11). Press events, once instigated, remain in place for a long time. A dry year is a pulse event, while climate shift to a different regime of temperature, moisture, or seasonality is a press event. Pulse events may be avoided by certain organisms, while press events can be avoided only by those with persistent dormant stages or ability to migrate. The complexity of ecosystem response to a mixture of press and pulse events can be considerable. It is important to recognize that ecological events are characterized by several things, and that pulse and press identify only a small subset of the logically complete set of kinds of ecological events (Reiners 2005). Ecological events are characterized by the relative suddenness of their onset, the length of their persistence, the suddenness or gradualness of their disappearance, and their effects (Figure 10.12). The effects of ecological events can also be temporary, persistent, or may reappear after a long dormant interval. So a more complete terminology might include pulses versus presses, long- versus short-lived, slow versus fast releasing, and effects that are immediate, temporary, slow, persistent, or echoes. A taxonomy of events through time has not been explored in ecosystem ecology, and suggests something

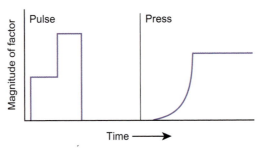

FIGURE 10.11  Diagrammatic representation of the contrast between pulse and press events. Pulse events, whatever the form of their onset, are relatively quick to appear as well as quick to dissipate, though they may have persistent effects. Press events, in contrast, represent persistent changes in the driving factors or structure of an ecological system. Pulse events are exemplified by fires, hurricanes, and floods. Press events include such things as climate shifts, persistent environmental stressors, the exposure of new surfaces by Earth movements, or the invasion of new dominant organisms into a region.

of the richness that remains to be accomplished in the study of temporal heterogeneity and ecosystems.

A final thought is necessary concerning the complexity of ecological events. What counts as an ecologically relevant event, and how the events are scaled, depends on the model of the system adopted by investigators. For one system model some environmental event may appear as a pulse, while for another system model, the same event might appear as a press. For example, a series of drought years may be represented in a long-term forest model as a pulse, while for a model of a salamander population in a vernal pool, the same drought may appear as a press. Therefore, the concepts of pulse and press, as well as the more complete lexicon of event onsets, persistence, and releases, are not absolutes. Rather, they are determined by the scale—grain and extent—used in models of particular systems.

## INTERNAL AND EXTERNAL HETEROGENEITY

The second dimension along which to consider the effects of heterogeneity identifies whether the heterogeneity of interest is inside or outside the focal ecosystem. Of course, an ecosystem study may well investigate both internal and external sources and effects of heterogeneity. These two, like temporal and spatial heterogeneity, are not mutually exclusive.

Internal heterogeneity is exemplified by such things as the pits and mounds within individual forest stands mentioned earlier, or the spatial arrangement of cut versus intact

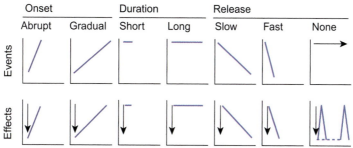

FIGURE 10.12  A conceptual alphabet illustrating the complexity of ecological events not represented by the simple pulse–press contrast. For each graph, the x-axis represents time and the y-axis represents the intensity of the event or of the effect. The top row shows different forms of onset, duration, or release of an ecological event, such as disturbance or imposition of stress. Specific real events can be described by combining the appropriate forms of onset, duration, and release. The bottom row indicates aspects of complexity in the responses to ecological events. Effects can be rapidly emerging, slowly emerging, short persistence, long persistence, gradually declining, or quickly declining. In the lower right panel, the existence of a peaked form of effect is shown by combining rapid emergence, no persistence, and rapid decline. This panel further illustrates the difference between immediately felt and lagged effects. The immediate effect arises directly after the event, and lagged effects are illustrated by the dashed line connecting the event with the right, delayed peak. Lags may exist for effects possessing any of the other combinations of emergence, duration, and decline as well. *(Figure courtesy of the Baltimore Ecosystem Study, Long-Term Ecological Research Project.)*

forest in a small watershed. Few such kinds of heterogeneity have been examined for their functional significance (Turner and Cardille 2007). However, examples do exist. An experiment in the high arctic showed that heterogeneity in depths of moss cover determined the soil temperature and duration of favorable thermal conditions for microbial activity. Deeper moss patches reduced the temperature and active season (Gornall et al. 2007). The thinner moss layers had higher levels of soil moisture and of plant-available nitrogen. A second example of the role of internal spatial heterogeneity, which also interacts with time, involves large woody debris left by extreme floods in the savanna landscape of Kruger National Park, South Africa (Pettit and Naiman 2007). Large woody debris, such as accumulations of uprooted trunks, large branches, and tangles of twigs, had two effects in the riparian zones. First, it permitted fire to occur closer to the river than usual, and resulted in unusually high mortality of large trees that were within 5 m of piles of debris. Second, plots supporting debris had higher levels of plant-available phosphorus in the soils, and higher levels of vegetation cover. Over 36 months of observation, the large woody debris piles and the patchy fire in the riparian zone resulted in alternative patterns of succession. The altered heterogeneity in the riparian ecosystems has the potential to cause long-lasting or permanent changes in the ecosystem functioning. Increased phosphorus availability can shift grazing patterns in the phosphorus-limited African savanna system. Increased nutrient availability is likely to favor exotic and weedy species (Foxcroft et al. 2009). Increased plant cover in the riparian zones, particularly of densely branched, upland shrubs, may enhance flammability and hence susceptibility to future fires. Together these changes may well increase mortality of the crucial large riparian trees, or inhibit their germination and establishment. Thus, the entire ecology of the riparian corridor may be sensitive to the pulsed input of coarse woody debris and new thresholds of resources, disturbance, and species composition.

External heterogeneity refers to the spatial pattern outside the boundaries selected for a particular ecosystem study. Traditionally ecologists were silent about even such contextual facts as what kinds of ecosystems were on the borders of a study site. Issues such as the identity of adjacent and nearby habitat types, and their arrangement on the landscape have not been much addressed in ecosystem ecology.

External heterogeneity may act on the focal ecosystem in several ways. Exactly how external heterogeneity functions depends on the nature of flows from outside the ecosystem (Cadenasso et al. 2003; Strayer et al. 2003). Flows may be by diffusion, by the mass movement of biota or advection of organisms and other materials, or movement along specific paths or networks. For organisms or propagules, or certain chemicals, mortality rate or decay rate will interact with the velocity of movement to determine the amount that arrives at a focal ecosystem from a distant source. Which pathway supports movement of a flow of interest determines how the focal ecosystem and its surrounding landscape interact. In the case of diffusion or mass movements, the mosaic structure of the surrounding environment will be crucial. How permeable the patches and their boundaries are to the mass flow is the determining factor, and this is modified by the spatial arrangement of patches.

Flows of water are an excellent example of how an altered external mosaic and imposition of a novel network affect a target ecosystem. Consider a stream in an unmanaged, forested watershed. The movement of water can be overland, in superficial layers, or in deep ground water, and will depend on slope, the transpirational activity of vegetation at different places, the soil texture and horizons, the current water content, and the temperature of the soil. With urban development, roads, pipes, and altered vegetation in the various patches through which the water flows directly and indirectly alter the amount, timing, and content of the water that arrives at the stream (Figure 10.13). Ground water and the riparian fringe become much less important, while piped flow and overland flow become more important. Urban riparian zones may, as a result, be much less effective in reducing stream nutrient pollution than those in unmanaged watersheds (Walsh et al. 2005; Cadenasso et al. 2008).

The interaction of atmospheric flow with a forest-field boundary exemplifies the control of an above-ground mass flow. Experimental reduction of the density of vegetation on the forest edge during the autumn peak for wind-dispersed field species demonstrated the efficient filtering effect of the edge on wind-borne seeds and nitrogen deposition to the forest (Cadenasso and Pickett 2001; Weathers et al. 2001). Both of these materials have the capacity to alter ecosystem function in the forest, the first by introducing species not currently present, and the second by increasing readily available soil nutrients.

Although we have spoken in terms of patchiness, which may imply discrete, homogeneous pattern in both landscapes and waterscapes, we intend the analysis to apply to all kinds of heterogeneity. First, patches may be either homogeneous or internally heterogeneous. It is not necessary for each patch to be homogeneous, but rather only to be heterogeneous in a way that distinguishes it from other patches at the same spatial scale of resolution. Furthermore, patches do not necessarily have to have hard and narrow boundaries. Boundaries may be zones across which gradients in the features that distinguish patches are pronounced (Cadenasso et al. 1997). At one extreme, entire landscapes or

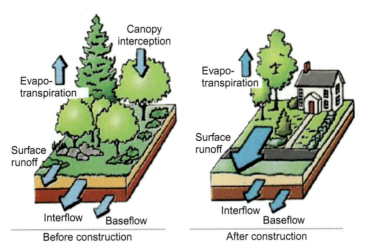

**FIGURE 10.13**   Contrast in water movement between nonurban and urbanized watersheds. Flow paths and magnitudes of flows across different flow paths are modified by development of human settlements. For example, gutters and curbs impose new headwater structures, storm drains redirect flow below surface layers and efficiently connect stream channels with rainfall, and alteration of vegetation type and cover changes infiltration and evapotranspiration rates. (*Diagram from the Maryland Department of Environment and in the public domain.*)

IV. SYNTHESIS

water bodies may exist as gradients, or as interacting gradients. In this case, a mosaic is better represented as a surface or mathematical field, analogous to a gravitational or radiation field, having continuous spatial variation.

# FIRST PRINCIPLES FOR ASSESSING
## HETEROGENEITY

Recognizing the kinds of fluxes and kinds of structures of heterogeneity prepares us to review the basic principles that suggest when heterogeneity would be important for ecosystems. Heterogeneity is now recognized to be a pervasive feature of ecosystems and the larger contexts in which they occur (Kolasa and Pickett 1991; Lovett et al. 2005). However, when might heterogeneity not be functionally important? Strayer (2005) suggests some first principles for making the decision about when to ignore heterogeneity.

Heterogeneity may be unimportant if its spatial size or temporal duration is much smaller than the extent in space or time over which the measurements of interest are taken. In such situations, the measurement integrates the finer-scale heterogeneity, and it becomes essentially invisible. Similarly, if the grain of heterogeneity is much larger than the study area, hierarchy theory assumes that heterogeneity is so inclusive or slowly changing relative to the size of the measurements that it can be taken to be a constant.

The second set of reasons to ignore heterogeneity deals with the functional connections it sets up (Strayer 2005). If the vectors across the patches or gradients are small relative to the spatial extent, or slow relative to the temporal duration of the study, then that heterogeneity is not likely to matter. Likewise, if the process dynamics across the heterogeneity are linear, then it can be ignored. A third functional exception is in situations where one patch type dominates the dynamics, allowing focus on that type to summarize the dynamics of the system. Note that understanding when to ignore heterogeneity still requires an empirical assessment of structures and transfers across the system of interest.

There are two situations in which it is especially unwise to ignore spatial heterogeneity: human origin of pattern and regional scope of study (Strayer 2005). Many authors have noted that anthropogenic heterogeneity has two conspicuous features (Forman and Godron 1986). First, anthropogenically generated edges in both built and managed landscapes tend to be linear, as compared to curvilinear or fractal patterns in less manipulated or natural systems. In nonurban systems that are subject to management, edges are often made more distinct and linear by fire, timber harvest, or construction of access roads.

The second practical situation in which heterogeneity is especially likely to be functionally significant is modeling regional and global scales (Strayer 2005). Management typically involves multiple patches or the interaction of different patches at these coarser scales (Knight and Landres 1998). Social processes may appear as a distinct matrix of pattern over a regional landscape. In addition, each kind of system is likely to have mixtures of attributes, sometimes even including built and biological components. For example, understanding the structure of urban systems requires assessing the combined covers of buildings, vegetation, and various kinds of surfaces (Cadenasso et al. 2007). The three spatial dimensions of each kind of attribute add additional complexity to the heterogeneity that exists in settled areas. Contrasts in the mixtures and details of these three major types of cover can result in different ecological functions.

# CONCLUSIONS: ECOSYSTEMS IN TIME AND SPACE

Understanding heterogeneity is an important frontier for ecosystem science. However, ecosystem ecology has come to focus on heterogeneity much more recently than the specialties of evolutionary, population, community, and landscape ecology. Heterogeneity can exist in both space and time. Spatial heterogeneity can appear as discrete patches with functionally important boundary zones, or as continuous gradients. Temporal heterogeneity appears as relatively short secondary successions, and as extraordinarily long primary successions on ancient substrates (Figure 10.10). Where an ecosystem is located on a successional gradient is an important aspect of its context, and can explain much about resource limitation, and whether disturbance—or management—will lead to dominance by organisms that demand more or fewer resources than current dominants. The ability of the resulting ecosystem to retain or acquire resources depends on its position along a successional gradient. Temporal variation important to ecosystems also includes short-term climate extremes, longer-term climate cycles, and now, the anthropogenic trajectory of global change, along with transient variation.

The two dimensions of heterogeneity can interact. Heterogeneity within ecosystems is broadly associated with successional status, and the external heterogeneity of an ecosystem will have different implications depending on its successional condition. This interaction is key to sorting out how readily invaded ecosystems can be, and thus has great practical significance. The essence of the ecosystem concept—the interaction between biota and the physical environment in a place—is embodied in understanding successional contexts. Indeed, the ecosystem concept was originally formulated to solve problems in succession theory.

Heterogeneity can be caused by multiple agents. Some agents and circumstances produce pulses of heterogeneity, while others act as persistent presses of altered conditions. The complexity of ecological events is only hinted at by the contrast between the press and pulse classes. Furthermore, both human causes and biophysical causes of heterogeneity are in play, often in the same ecosystems. Anthropogenic heterogeneity is often intentionally designed, and consequently has a relatively fine scale matching the spatial array of institutional and household controls of land, and straight or regular curvature based on efficiency of transport, property ownership, or on aesthetics.

Ecosystem heterogeneity can be important both within and outside of the ecosystem boundaries selected for a particular research question (Figure 10.14). Internal heterogeneity is currently less well understood than the effects of external heterogeneity. Both these kinds of ecological heterogeneity may exist at various scales. Indeed, both the study of ecosystems and the study of landscapes are less about a particular scale or location on some ideal, nested hierarchy from Earth to atom, and more about a research perspective or criterion. Landscape ecology asks about the reciprocal interactions among causes, nature, and effects of spatial and temporal heterogeneity. Its guiding question is applicable

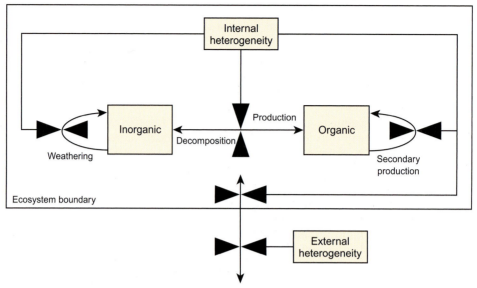

FIGURE 10.14   The general ecosystem heterogeneity framework introduced in Chapter 1, with the addition of interactions representing both internal and external sources of heterogeneity to reflect patterns and processes emphasized in this chapter. Bowties represent controls, and arrows represent flows.

at any scale that ecologists may choose to address (Allen 1998). Similarly, ecosystem ecology is about the interaction between biota and physical material and energy in specific locations, regardless of scale. Locking either of these two crucial concepts to a particular scale of analyses reduces their usefulness for explaining and understanding the structure, function, and change in ecological systems.

G. Evelyn Hutchinson (1965) conceived of a compelling idea, "the ecological theater and the evolutionary play," as the title for his pioneering book introducing the then-new field of evolutionary ecology. Hutchinson bears the distinction of being one of the few pioneering ecologists to have been a leader in both evolutionary and ecosystem approaches. His colleague, Raymond Lindeman (1942), was the first person to actually apply Tansley's (1935) definition of ecosystem to a field research problem. As ecosystem ecology increasingly recognizes the significance and potential of spatial and temporal heterogeneity, perhaps a translation of Hutchinson's idea to this realm would be helpful. Spatial and temporal heterogeneity encourage ecosystem ecologists to investigate the ecological theater and the biogeochemical play. The ecological theater is preeminently heterogeneous.

Of course, the postmodern, participatory interpretation of theater permits us to recognize that the play can feed back on the stage sets and on the physical arrangement of the audience relative to the actors. In other words, the feedbacks between the action of the play and the structure of the theater are a part of the new ecosystem ecology of heterogeneity.

The four benefits of the ecosystem approach identified by Pace (see Chapter 9)—mass balance, boundedness, inclusiveness, and flexibility—easily accommodate the insights of heterogeneity. Spatial and temporal heterogeneity are the context within which ecosystem mass balances and boundary dynamics must be understood. Conceptually, the inclusiveness of ecosystems must now accommodate heterogeneities within and outside them. The flexibility of the ecosystem concept is appropriate for understanding how specific ecosystems behave in heterogeneous contexts, and what each ecosystem contributes to the larger heterogeneity of the ecological world.

# References

Allen, T.F.H., 1998. The landscape "level" is dead: Persuading the family to take it off the respirator. In: Peterson, D.L., Parker, V.T. (Eds.), Ecological scale: Theory and applications. Columbia University Press, New York, pp. 35−54.

Austin, M.P., 2005. Vegetation and environment: Discontinuities and continuities. In: van der Maarel, E. (Ed.), Vegetation Ecology. Blackwell Science, Malden, MA, pp. 52−84.

Cadenasso, M.L., Pickett, S.T.A., 2001. Effects of edge structure on the flux of species into forest interiors. Conservat. Biol. 15, 91−97.

Cadenasso, M.L., Pickett, S.T.A., Weathers, K.C., Jones, C.G., 2003. A framework for a theory of ecological boundaries. BioScience 53, 750−758.

Cadenasso, M.L., Pickett, S.T.A., Weathers, K.C., 2004. Effects of boundaries and edges on flux of nutrients, detritus, and organisms. In: Polis, G.A., Power, M.E., Huxel, G. (Eds.), Food webs at the landscape level: The ecology of trophic flow across habitats. University of Chicago Press, Chicago, pp. 154−168.

Cadenasso, M.L., Pickett, S.T.A., Grove, J.M., 2006. Dimensions of ecosystem complexity: Heterogeneity, connectivity, and history. Ecol. Complexity 3, 1−12.

Cadenasso, M.L., Pickett, S.T.A., Schwarz, K., 2007. Spatial heterogeneity in urban ecosystems: Reconceptualizing land cover and a framework for classification. Front. Ecol. Environ. 5, 80−88.

Cadenasso, M.L., Pickett, S.T.A., Groffman, P.M., Brush, G.S., Galvin, M.F., Grove, J.M., et al., 2008. Exchanges across land-water-scape boundaries in urban systems: Strategies for reducing nitrate pollution. Ann. New York Acad. Sci. 1134, 213−232.

Cadenasso, M.L., Traynor, M.M., Pickett, S.T.A., 1997. Functional location of forest edges: Gradients of multiple physical factors. Can. J. Forest Res. 27, 774−782.

Colwell, R.K., 2011. Biogeographical gradient theory. In: Scheiner, S.M., Willig, M.R. (Eds.), The theory of ecology. University of Chicago Press, Chicago, pp. 309−330.

Dutilleul, P.R.L., 2011. Spatio-temporal heterogeneity: Concepts and analyses. Cambridge University Press, New York.

Eldridge, D.J., 2011. The resource coupling role of animal foraging pits in semi-arid woodlands. Ecohydrology 4, 623−630.

Fisher, S.G., Grimm, N.B., Marti, E., Holmes, R.M., Jones Jr., J.B., 1998. Material spiraling in stream corridors: A telescoping ecosystem model. Ecosystems 1, 19−34.

Fisher, S.G., Welter, J.R., 2005. Flowpaths as integrators of heterogeneity in streams and landscapes. In: Lovett, G.M., Jones, C.G., Turner, M.G., Weathers, K.C. (Eds.), Ecosystem function in heterogeneous landscapes. Springer, New York, pp. 311−328.

Forman, R.T.T., Godron, M., 1986. Landscape ecology. John Wiley and Sons, New York.

Foster, D.R., Swanson, F., Aber, J., Burke, I., Brokaw, N., Tilman, D., et al., 2003. The importance of land-use legacies to ecology and conservation. BioScience 53, 77−88.

Fox, G.A., Scheiner, S.M., Willig, M.R., 2011. Ecological gradient theory: A framework for aligning data and models. In: Scheiner, S.M., Willig, M.R. (Eds.), The theory of ecology. University of Chicago Press, Chicago, pp. 283−307.

Foxcroft, L.C., Richardson, D.M., Rouget, M., MacFadyen, S., 2009. Patterns of alien plant distribution at multiple spatial scales in a large national park: Implications for ecology, management and monitoring. Divers. Distribut. 15, 367−378.

Futuyma, D.J., 2009. Evolution, second ed. Sinauer Associates, Sunderland, MA.

Gascon, C., Williamson, G.B., da Fonseca, G.A.B., 2000. Receding forest edges and vanishing reserves. Science 288, 1356−1358.

Glasby, T.M., Underwood, A.J., 1996. Sampling to differentiate between pulse and press perturbations. Environ. Monit. Assess. 42, 241–252.

Godbold, J.A., Bulling, M.T., Solan, M., 2011. Habitat structure mediates biodiversity effects on ecosystem properties. Proc. Roy. Soc. B Biol. Sci. 278, 2510–2518.

Golley, F.B., 1993. A history of the ecosystem concept in ecology: More than the sum of the parts. Yale University Press, New Haven, CT.

Gornall, J.L., Jonsdottir, I.S., Woodin, S.J., Van der Wal, R., 2007. Arctic mosses govern below-ground environment and ecosystem processes. Oecologia 153, 931–941.

Heinselman, M.L., 1973. Fire in the virgin forests of the Boundary Waters Canoe Area, Minnesota. J. Quarter. Res. 3, 329–382.

Hutchings, M.J., John, E.A., Stewart, A.J.A. (Eds.), 2000. The ecological consequences of environmental heterogeneity. Blackwell Science, Malden, MA.

Hutchinson, G.E., 1965. The ecological theater and the evolutionary play. Yale University Press, New Haven, CT.

Jones, C.G., Lawton, J.H. (Eds.), 1995. Linking species and ecosystems. Chapman and Hall, New York.

Jones, C.G., Lawton, J.H., Shachak, M., 1994. Organisms as ecosystem engineers. Oikos 69, 373–386.

Jones, P.D., Mann, M.E., 2004. Climate over past millennia. Rev. Geophys. 42. doi:10.1029/2003RG000143RG2002.

Knight, R.L., Landres, P.B. (Eds.), 1998. Stewardship across boundaries. Island Press, Washington, DC.

Kolasa, J., Pickett, S.T.A. (Eds.), 1991. Ecological heterogeneity. Springer-Verlag, New York.

Lagrue, C., Kominoski, J.S., Danger, M., Baudoin, J.M., Lamothe, S., Lambrigot, D., et al., 2011. Experimental shading alters leaf litter breakdown in streams of contrasting riparian canopy cover. Freshwat. Biol. 56, 2059–2069.

Lavery, J.M., Comeau, P.G., Prescott, C.E., 2004. The influence of red alder patches on light, litterfall, and soil nutrients in adjacent conifer stands. Can. J. Forest Res. 34, 56–64.

Likens, G.E., 1992. The ecosystem approach: Its use and abuse. Ecology Institute, Oldendorf/Luhe, Germany.

Lindeman, R.L., 1942. The trophic-dynamic aspect of ecology. Ecology 23, 399–418.

Lovett, G.M., Jones, C.G., Turner, M.G., Weathers, K.C. (Eds.), 2005. Ecosystem function in heterogeneous landscapes. Springer, New York.

McGrath, B.P., Marshall, V., Cadenasso, M.L., Grove, J.M., Pickett, S.T.A., Plunz, R. (Eds.), 2007. Designing patch dynamics. Columbia University Graduate School of Architecture, Preservation and Planning, New York.

McGrath, B., Pickett, S.T.A., 2011. The metacity: A conceptual framework for integrating ecology and urban design. Challenges 2011 (2), 55–72. doi:10.3390/challe2040055.

McKinzey, K.M., Olafsdottir, R., Dugmore, A.J., 2005. Perception, history, and science: Coherence or disparity in the timing of the Little Ice Age maximum in southeast Iceland? Polar Rec. 41, 319–334.

Montgomery, D.R., 2008. Dreams of natural streams. Science 319, 291–292.

Munguia, P., Osman, R.W., Hamilton, J., Whitlatch, R., Zajac, R., 2011. Changes in habitat heterogeneity alter marine sessile benthic communities. Ecol. Appl. 21, 925–935.

Naiman, R.J., Décamps, H., McClain, M.E., 2005. Riparia: Ecology, conservation, and management of streamside communities. Elsevier, Academic Press, Amsterdam.

Peters, D.P.C., Lugo, A.E., Chapin III, F.S., Pickett, S.T.A., Duniway, M., Rocha, A.V., et al., 2011. Cross-system comparisons elucidate disturbance complexities and generalities. Ecosphere 2, art 81.

Peterson, C.J., Pickett, S.T.A., 1990. Microsite and elevational influences on early forest regeneration after catastrophic windthrow. J. Veget. Sci. 1, 657–662.

Pettit, N.E., Naiman, R.J., 2007. Postfire response of a flood-regenerating riparian vegetation in a semi-arid landscape. Ecology 88, 2094–2104.

Pickett, S.T.A., Cadenasso, M.L., 2002. Ecosystem as a multidimensional concept: Meaning, model and metaphor. Ecosystems 5, 1–10.

Pickett, S.T.A., Cadenasso, M.L., Jones, C.G., 2000. Generation of heterogeneity by organisms: Creation, maintenance, and transformation. In: Hutchings, M., John, E.A., Stewart, A.J.A. (Eds.), Ecological consequences of habitat heterogeneity. Blackwell, New York, pp. 33–52.

Pickett, S.T.A., Cadenasso, M.L., Grove, J.M., Boone, C.G., Groffman, P.M., Irwin, E., et al., 2011. Urban ecological systems: Scientific foundations and a decade of progress. J. Environ. Manag. 92, 331–362.

Pickett, S.T.A., Rogers, K.H., 1997. Patch dynamics: the transformation of landscape structure and function. In: Bissonette, J.A. (Ed.), Wildlife and landscape ecology: Effects of pattern and scale. Springer-Verlag, New York, pp. 101–127.

Porensky, L.M., 2011. When edges meet: Interacting edge effects in an African savanna. J. Ecol. 99, 923–934.

Reiners, W.A., 2005. Reciprocal cause and effect between environmental heterogeneity and transport processes. In: Lovett, G.M., Jones, C.G., Turner, M.G., Weathers, K.C. (Eds.), Ecosystem function in heterogeneous landscapes. Springer, New York, pp. 67–89.

Scheiner, S.M., Willig, M.R., 2005. Developing unified theories in ecology as exemplified with diversity gradients. Am. Nat. 166, 458–469.

Schlesinger, W.H., Raikes, J.A., Hartley, A.E., Cross, A.F., 1996. On the spatial pattern of soil nutrients in desert ecosystems. Ecology 77, 364–374.

Stanley, E.H., Fisher, S.G., 1992. Intermittency, disturbance, and stability in stream ecosystems. In: Robarts, R.D., Bothwell, M.L. (Eds.), Aquatic ecosystems in semi-arid regions: Implications for resource management. N.H.R.I. Symposium, Saskatoon, Canada, pp. 271–279.

Strayer, D.L., 2005. Challenges in understanding the functions of ecological heterogeneity. In: Lovett, G.M., Jones, C.G., Turner, M.G., Weathers, K.C. (Eds.), Ecosystem function in heterogeneous landscapes. Springer, New York, pp. 411–425.

Strayer, D.L., Ewing, H.A., Bigelow, S., 2003. What kind of spatial and temporal details are required in models of heterogeneous systems? Oikos 102, 654–662.

Tansley, A.G., 1935. The use and abuse of vegetational concepts and terms. Ecology 16, 284–307.

Turner, M.G., Cardille, J.A., 2007. Spatial heterogeneity and ecosystem process. In: Wu, J., Hobbs, R. (Eds.), Key topics in landscape ecology. Cambridge University Press, New York, pp. 62–77.

Turner, M.G., Romme, W.H., 1994. Landscape dynamics in crown fire ecosystems. Landscape Ecol. 9, 59–77.

Vetaas, O.R., 1992. Micro-site effects of trees and shrubs in dry savannas. J. Veget. Sci. 3, 337–344.

Vitousek, P.M., 2004. Nutrient cycling and limitation: Hawai'i as a model system. Princeton University Press, Princeton, NJ.

Vitousek, P.M., Mooney, H.A., Lubchenco, J., Melillo, J.M., 1997. Human domination of Earth's ecosystems. Science 277, 494–499.

Walsh, C.J., Roy, A.H., Feminella, J.W., Cottingham, P.D., Groffman, P.M., Morgan, R.P., 2005. The urban stream syndrome: Current knowledge and the search for a cure. J. North Am. Benthol og. Soc. 24, 706–723.

Weathers, K.C., Cadenasso, M.L., Pickett, S.T.A., 2001. Forest edges as nutrient and pollutant concentrators: Potential synergisms between fragmentation, forest canopies, and the atmosphere. Conservat. Biol. 15, 1506–1514.

# Controls on Ecosystem Structure and Function

*Kathleen C. Weathers[1], Holly A. Ewing[2], Clive G. Jones[1]*
*and David L. Strayer[1]*

[1]Cary Institute of Ecosystem Studies, Millbrook, NY
[2]Bates College, Lewiston, ME

What controls the character and functioning of ecosystems? In the previous chapters, we saw examples of how the energetics and biogeochemistry of ecosystems are controlled by a wide range of factors, such as inputs of nutrients and energy, disturbance, the activities of organisms (including people), and the shape and size of the ecosystem itself. The topic of controls over ecosystem structure and function turns out to be surprisingly complicated. There is no simple, comprehensive framework to explain the myriad factors that govern structure and function. Therefore, in this chapter, we offer some general observations about ecosystem controls that can be used both in scientific studies and management contexts.

## WHAT DO WE MEAN BY "CONTROL"?

In previous chapters, we described the components of ecosystems, the flows of energy and materials between those components, and the flows of energy and materials between ecosystems and the surrounding environment. In the broadest sense, we could say that a factor *controls* an ecosystem if a change in that factor changes the size or nature of any of these components or flows. In practice, we probably would reserve the term *control* for factors that have a large influence on the important components and flows (see Chapter 1 for a discussion of what ecosystem scientists usually consider to be "important"). Thus, we are much more likely to say that nitrogen inputs control a forest ecosystem if overall primary production doubles when we increase nitrogen inputs than if increased nitrogen merely enhances the flow of dissolved organic matter from a particular plant species to the soil by 5%. However, because ecologists may assign different values of importance to different components and flows, their views about the important controls on an ecosystem may likewise differ. Furthermore, as we will discuss in more detail later, the answer to the question of what controls an ecosystem depends on the scales of time and space at which the question is posed. As a result, it can be tricky to make general statements about the importance of different controls without specifying the components or flows of interest or the scales of time and space under consideration.

## WHY DO WE CARE ABOUT CONTROLS ON ECOSYSTEMS?

There are several reasons why the topic of controls occupies a central position in ecosystem science. First, understanding the factors that control an ecosystem is important to deciphering how and why different ecosystems work the way they do. Why are two adjacent forests so different with respect to nitrogen cycling? What determines how many fish are produced in a series of lakes? Knowing the forces that act on ecosystems allows us to address interesting questions such as these.

In a more applied sense, understanding how ecosystems are controlled allows us to predict or evaluate the consequences of various management actions. If we reduce inputs of nitrogen to Chesapeake Bay by 20%, will we see dramatic improvements in water quality, or just minor changes? How will forest-watershed ecosystems respond to timber cutting at different frequencies? The ability to predict consequences can be especially valuable if the proposed management actions are expensive or take a long time to implement, as often is the case.

Finally, with a good understanding of how ecosystems are controlled, we may be able to anticipate how they are likely to react to future changes in climate, land use, invasive species, and other large-scale changes in ecosystems. This capacity gives us the opportunity to implement management practices and policies to avoid or mitigate undesirable changes that may lie ahead. Obviously, the more complete and accurate our understanding of controlling factors, the better we will be able to recommend particular actions or policies.

## HOW ARE ECOSYSTEMS CONTROLLED?

Here, we review a few of the more important conclusions that ecosystem scientists have reached about how ecosystems are controlled.

### Both Abiotic and Biotic Control Are Important

Ecosystems may be controlled by abiotic or biotic factors, or interactions among these. Examples of abiotic controls are numerous and varied. Earlier, we learned that primary production may be limited—or controlled—by light, nutrients, and water. The texture of soils affects a terrestrial ecosystem's ability to retain water, nutrients, and other ions, which in turn affect nearly every aspect of terrestrial ecosystems. As an aquatic example, the clay content of marine sediments may control long-term rates of organic matter burial, with profound consequences for global biogeochemistry over long timescales (see Chapter 6).

Biotic control of ecosystems also is common and varied. Perhaps the best-known examples involve control through a food web. For example, the *trophic cascade* (Figure 11.1) is a mechanism by which top predators can control both lower trophic levels and abiotic properties of ecosystems (e.g., oxygen or nutrient concentrations), especially

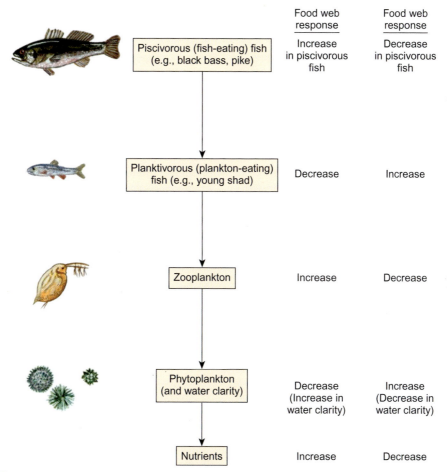

FIGURE 11.1    Biotic control of an aquatic ecosystem from the top of the food web. The trophic cascade hypothesis proposes that top predators may control the abundance of organisms lower in the food chain. By reducing the abundance of their prey (planktivorous fish), this in turn may allow an increase in the abundance or size of organisms among the prey's food source (zooplankton), which can lead to grazing down phytoplankton populations and increase water clarity and concentrations of dissolved nutrients *(Trophic cascade available at: http:// biology-forums.com/index.php?action = gallery;sa = view;id = 2029.)*

aquatic ecosystems. But biotic control is not always primarily about the food web; it may also be exercised through a variety of nontrophic pathways collectively often called *ecological engineering* (Box 11.1).

---

## BOX 11.1

## ECOSYSTEM ENGINEERS AND CONTROL ON ECOSYSTEM FUNCTIONING

Living organisms often control ecosystem functions such as productivity or nutrient cycling. How? One way is through energy and nutrient uptake and waste production—trophic processes that are universal to all organisms. Not all species exert significant control this way; it depends on their biomass, stoichiometry (ratio of elements present in their bodies; see Chapter 5), and rates of uptake and waste production.

This is not the sole means of organismal control, however. Consider beaver that clear-cut riparian zones and build dams forming ponds and wetlands that control hydrology, sedimentation, and biogeochemistry, simultaneously creating, maintaining, and destroying habitats for many species. Beaver control does not arise from how much they eat or the waste they produce (this is a small fraction of ecosystem energy and material budgets); it arises because beaver construction alters the physical template, changing abiotic resources and conditions that affect energy and material flows throughout the ecosystem. Or consider forest trees of which the canopies attenuate wind and cast shade creating habitat for understory species. This habitat depends on altered abiotic conditions caused by the physical properties of tree structure, not the carbon and nutrients taken up by the tree, even though these build the tree structure. Both beaver and forest trees are examples of physical ecosystem engineers

(Jones et al. 1994, 1997); they control energy and material flows via structurally mediated changes in resources and conditions.

Beaver are *allogenic* engineers—they cause structural change by altering extrinsic living or nonliving materials (a dam from felled trees and mud). In contrast, the forest tree example illustrates *autogenic* engineering—it is the physical structure of the tree itself that causes the abiotic changes. The same tree, through forming soil macropores that affect soil drainage via root growth, also illustrates allogenic engineering. Beaver and trees are not unique examples of ecosystem engineering by biota. A great variety of free-living organisms engineer ecosystems to varying degrees—from earthworms burrowing in soils, to coral and oyster reefs, to microbial crusts controlling runoff on desert soils (Figure 11.2). Humans are allogenic ecosystem engineers par excellence.

Physical ecosystem engineering has four cause-and-effect relationships (Figure 11.3):

1. An engineering species causes structural change.
2. Structural change causes abiotic change (resources and conditions).
3. Abiotic change and structural change (via living space) cause biotic change (i.e., other organisms and associated ecological processes).
4. Abiotic change, biotic change (via other interactions with the engineer such as

---

FIGURE 11.2  Autogenic (a, b, c) and allogenic (d, e, f) ecosystem engineering. (a) Oak (*Quercus rubra*) forest near Millbrook, NY, changes microclimate and affects soil biogeochemistry and understory species. (b) Smooth cordgrass, *Spartina alterniflora*, in a tidal marsh in the La Plata estuary near Playa Peninos, Uruguay. The marsh attenuates storm surges, increases sedimentation, and retains organic matter affecting biogeochemistry and creating protected habitat for other species. (c) Reefs of tube-building polychaetes, *Ficopomatus enigmaticus*, an exotic species in Mar Chiquita coastal lagoon, Argentina. The reef in the foreground is ca. 3 meters across, and it alters hydrodynamics and increases sedimentation, providing shelter for many invertebrates. (d) Riparian forest area transformed by the dam-building activity of beaver, *Castor canadensis*, in Tierra del Fuego, Chile, where it is an exotic species. The dam alters hydrology, sedimentation, and light levels and so affects biogeochemistry and species habitats. (e) Mound made by leaf-cutting ant, *Atta sexdens*, in the "blanqueal" area near Fray Bentos, Uruguay; ants bring saline soil from depth to the surface, eliminating most vegetation on the mound. (f) The Southwestern Atlantic burrowing crab, *Neohelice* (*Chasmagnathus*) *granulata*, in Mar Chiquita coastal lagoon, Argentina, buries litter in excavation mounds and prevents litter export as a nutrient subsidy to adjacent estuary. (*Photos: (a) Jorge Gutiérrez; (b) Cesar Fagúndez; (c) Martín Bruschetti; (d), (e) Clive Jones; (f) Pablo Ribeiro. From Gutiérrez and Jones 2008.*)

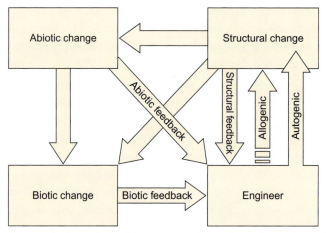

**FIGURE 11.3** Cause-and-effect relationships representing a physically engineered ecosystem. The solid arrow for autogenic engineering is the physical manifestation of organismal structure inserted into the abiotic milieu. The dashed arrow for allogenic engineering represents the action of the engineer on other living or nonliving structures. *(From Jones et al. 2010.)*

their food), and structural change (e.g., conspecific living space) may feed back to the engineer.

The magnitude of control by engineers depends on:

- The degree and type of structural change(s) they cause, which is a function of engineer density and *per capita* engineering activity (e.g., the number of dams per beaver, the amount of wind attenuation per tree).
- The persistence of these changes amidst physical and biological decay, which is a function of engineer maintenance (e.g., dam repair, tree growth and survival), intrinsic material durability (e.g., wood, mud), and destructive forces (e.g., floods, wind throw).

- The degree to which structural changes alter abiotic resources and conditions via interactions of structure, kinetic energy, and materials.
- The sensitivity of other species and ecological process to the structural and abiotic changes.

These variables are fundamentally different from those determining the degree of trophic control.

Extending the physics of organisms to ecosystems, along with the evolutionary ramifications of this kind of organism-environment coupling, is an active area in basic and applied research. Within the realm of policy and management, we need to understand the impacts of human ecosystem engineering to fully grasp our influence on ecosystem functioning.

Finally, abiotic and biotic factors often interact to jointly control ecosystem structure and function. One particularly useful framework that includes the interactions of abiotic and biotic factors is Jenny's (1941) state model of soil formation (Box 11.2). Beyond soil formation, however, there are many examples—across the full range of spatial and temporal scales—of interacting biotic and abiotic factors. To offer just one example, inputs of water to some ecosystems are determined by the architecture and morphometry of vegetation (biotic structure) and how it "captures" fog water from the air (abiotic flux; Figure 11.4). This captured fog water can influence ecosystem functions such as primary production, nutrient flow, and perhaps even soil development (Ewing et al. 2009). So our first lesson about control is that both abiotic and biotic factors are commonly involved, and that the details of these controls can be as varied as the abiotic and biotic contents of the world's ecosystems.

---

## BOX 11.2

### A BROAD PERSPECTIVE ON ECOSYSTEM CONTROLS: JENNY'S STATE FACTORS

The soil scientist Hans Jenny (1941) developed a well-known framework that defines the factors that account for much of the variation in the world's soils—a framework that can be extended easily to describe controls on variation in terrestrial ecosystems. Building from the work of Russian soil scientist Vasilii Dokuchaev, he identified a set of five *state factors* that control soil genesis. Jenny's list (often evoked by the ungainly mnemonic "clorpt") includes climate ("cl"), organisms ("o," that is, the biota), topography (or relief, "r"), parent material ("p," the material—usually geological—from which the soil formed), and time ("t"). Jenny's idea was that specifying values for these five factors for a site of interest would provide enough information to predict what kind of soil would occur on that site. No other information about the site would be required, but neither could any of the five state factors be omitted.

Although this framework was developed for soils, it is widely used to describe the factors that control terrestrial ecosystems, at least over broad scales of space and time.

That is, if we specify values for all five state factors for a site, we can predict a good deal about the ecosystem, as well as the soils, that would occur at the site. For example, consider a grassland site that has been developing on a steep limestone slope that has not been overrun by glaciers in at least the last 100,000 years and currently has a continental climate with hot, variably moist summers and cold, dry winters. An ecosystem ecologist with experience in a range of ecosystems would not have too much difficulty making general estimates about primary production, the types of grazers that might be present, and the likelihood that fire will be a part of the ecosystem's disturbance regime.

Nevertheless, there are limits to the applicability of Jenny's state factors for ecosystems. For example, it does not seem very useful if we are interested in controls over ecosystem function at short timescales (i.e., less than decades), as we often are. Short-term variation in variables such as weather or population dynamics may drive considerable variation in ecosystem function (see

Figure 2.6 in Chapter 2), and is not easily accounted for by Jenny's framework. In addition, although time is undoubtedly important to ecosystems, it is not always easy to offer an unambiguous definition of what exactly we mean by "time." Time since the underlying bedrock was formed? Time since the glaciers retreated? Time since the last fire or rainfall? Time since the last herbivorous insect outbreak? All of these are important to different aspects of ecosystem function, and they are not easily collapsed into a single value for "time."

One useful way to look at the utility of Jenny's state factors is to see them as the large-scale constraints within which the next-lower-level controls have to work. These in turn set the constraints within which the next-level controls have to operate, and so on.

In the end, the "best" framework depends on the scales on which the ecosystem is defined and the purposes for which the framework will be used. For example, terrestrial primary production at global and millennial scales is controlled primarily by latitude and altitude within the context of Earth's climatic history, while within regions at decadal scales Jenny's state factors are good predictors. Within an individual field or forest at daily scales, photosynthetically active radiation and soil water content are good predictors.

We know of no framework equivalent to Jenny's state factors for aquatic ecosystems, but the corresponding aquatic equivalents might be climate, organisms, hydrologic gradients, the physical and chemical characteristics of the fluid medium, and time. Can you apply these to an aquatic system you know? Are they sufficient, or do you need other state factors? As in terrestrial systems, these factors would be useful at some spatial and temporal scales and not at others.

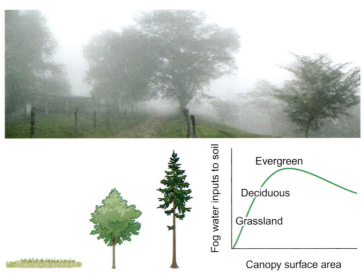

FIGURE 11.4   Biotic (vegetation structure) and abiotic (wind speed, cloud frequency, cloud liquid water content) factors interact to affect fog water capture. For a given elevation and climatic region, greater vegetation height and surface area will increase the fog capture.

## Control Can Be "Bottom-Up" or "Top-Down"

Historically, ecologists tended to think of ecosystems as being controlled from below—by inputs of nutrients, light, or water that set levels of primary production, which in turn control many other aspects of ecosystem function. Certainly, such "bottom-up" control is important in ecosystems: primary production in many ecosystems is controlled by inputs of energy or limiting materials (see Chapter 2), and many parts of ecosystems are controlled by the amount and quality of that primary production (see Chapter 3).

However, it has become increasingly apparent that not all control is from the bottom-up. As we have seen, ecosystems can be strongly controlled from the top-down through the trophic cascade (Figure 11.1) or by engineers at any point between the "top" and "bottom" of ecosystems (Box 11.1). Furthermore, ecosystems can just as easily be controlled by losses of key materials, such as nutrients and water, as by inputs. For instance, two forests receiving the same inputs of water and nutrients, but growing on soils with high and low abilities to retain nutrients and water, will develop very different structures and functions (Ewing 2002; see Chapter 7). Likewise, the activity of consumers in an ecosystem is tied to its ability to retain organic matter (see Chapter 3). Thus, although energy may flow from the bottom to the top of ecosystems, control may be exerted from the top, from the bottom, or from any point in between.

## Control Can Come from Outside or Inside the Ecosystem

All ecosystems are controlled by inputs from outside their boundaries. At the level of the planet, inputs of energy from the sun drive all of Earth's ecosystems, and variation in inputs of solar energy and resultant patterns in precipitation across the globe account for large structural differences in ecosystems (Figure 11.5a). At a more local level, we know that inputs of nutrients from outside the system control the character of ecosystems, for example, phosphorus loading from land to lake. Likewise, agents of disturbance such as hurricanes or lightning strikes that come in across ecosystem boundaries can play important roles in structuring ecosystems (see Chapter 10).

However, ecosystems also are controlled by their own internal structure. It is perhaps easiest to appreciate this by noting how much ecosystems can change following abrupt changes in biotic structure such as species invasions (Figure 11.5b) or overharvest, but there are many other examples of how the internal structure of an ecosystem controls how that ecosystem functions. Factors such as whether a lake is thermally stratified (i.e., water temperature varies with depth, with the warmest water at the top, and the coldest at the bottom) or mixes to the bottom, whether a river is clear or turbid with silt, or whether a forest soil is shallow or deep, clearly will affect primary production, decomposition, and other ecosystem functions. Thus, ecosystems are jointly controlled by their own internal structure and exchanges with the environment that surrounds them.

## Control Can Follow Various Mathematical Functions

Most of the examples of control mentioned in this book are simple linear functions, although some are presented on log-log scales (Figure 11.6a, b). Linear functions are

(a)
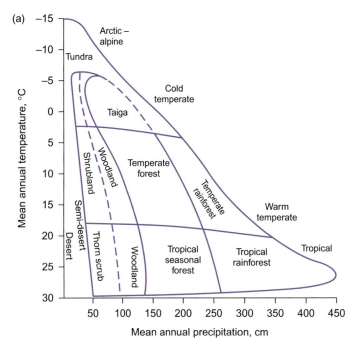

(b)
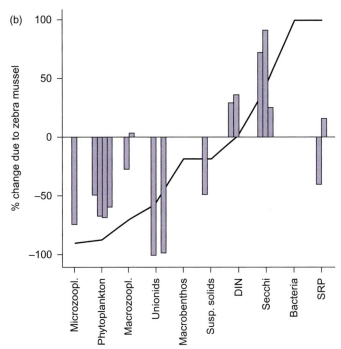

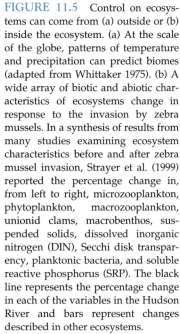

FIGURE 11.5 Control on ecosystems can come from (a) outside or (b) inside the ecosystem. (a) At the scale of the globe, patterns of temperature and precipitation can predict biomes (adapted from Whittaker 1975). (b) A wide array of biotic and abiotic characteristics of ecosystems change in response to the invasion by zebra mussels. In a synthesis of results from many studies examining ecosystem characteristics before and after zebra mussel invasion, Strayer et al. (1999) reported the percentage change in, from left to right, microzooplankton, phytoplankton, macrozooplankton, unionid clams, macrobenthos, suspended solids, dissolved inorganic nitrogen (DIN), Secchi disk transparency, planktonic bacteria, and soluble reactive phosphorus (SRP). The black line represents the percentage change in each of the variables in the Hudson River and bars represent changes described in other ecosystems.

simplest to fit to data, especially if data are scarce; they do describe the relationships between controller and response variable well in some cases. They also are easy to understand and apply—a given change in the controlling variable produces the same proportional response over the entire range of the controlling variable.

Nevertheless, relationships between controller and response in ecosystems can follow many different mathematical functions. A few nonlinear functions are of special interest. Increases in the controlling variable can lead to decelerating (Figure 11.6c) or accelerating responses (Figure 11.6d) in the ecosystem. Alternatively, the value of the response variable may be maximized or minimized at some intermediate value of the controlling variable, so that the sign of the relationship between the control and the response variable actually changes (Figure 11.6e). The relationship between the control and the response variable may include a threshold, at which the response of the system changes abruptly (Figure 11.6f). In all of these cases, the response of the ecosystem to a given change in the controlling variable depends critically on the position of the system along the $x$-axis.

Some especially important relationships in ecosystem science are hysteretic (Figure 11.6g). In such cases, the value of the response variable depends on the history of the system as well as on the present state of the controlling variable. Probably the best-known case of hysteresis in ecosystem science is the response of shallow lakes to phosphorus loading. Broadly speaking, shallow lakes can exist in two states: a clear-water state dominated by submersed plants when phosphorus loads are low, or a turbid-water state dominated by phytoplankton when phosphorus loads are high. These two states differ in many attributes, including biogeochemical cycling, habitat value for fish and water birds, and recreational value for people, so this transition is of considerable practical significance. Both states include a number of self-stabilizing mechanisms that resist change back to the alternative state. As a result, the transition from the turbid-water state back to the clear-water state occurs at a lower value of phosphorus loading than the reverse transition from clear water to turbid water, and it is not always possible to predict the state of the lake simply from current phosphorus loadings.

Knowing the shape of the mathematical function between controller and response is of great intellectual and practical importance. For instance, consider how you might respond to a proposal for a 25% increase in the controlling variable—say impervious surface in a watershed—if you were managing an ecosystem variable such as nuisance algal blooms. Knowing which of the forms given in Figure 11.6 that the response of the phytoplankton would take would allow you to give a much more robust and informed opinion.

## Feedbacks Are Almost Always Important

In highly connected systems such as ecosystems, interaction pathways often lead to feedbacks. That is, a change in one part of the system causes a change in another part of the system, which in turn comes back to affect the original component. Such feedback loops may be short or long, and may be negative (the response from the system opposes the initial change) or positive (the response from the system reinforces the initial change).

Feedbacks are almost always important in ecosystems, and untangling the effects of feedbacks can be critical to understanding system response or predicting how an

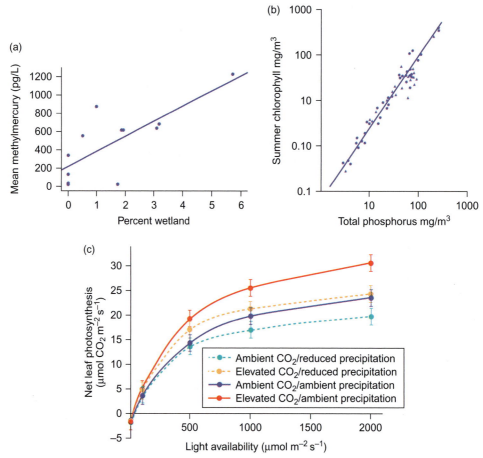

FIGURE 11.6   Examples of different kinds of functional relationships between controlling variables and ecosystem characteristics. (a) Linear relationship between the percentage of a stream's watershed occupied by wetlands and the concentration of methyl mercury (MeHg) in stream water. (*From Weathers et al. unpublished.*) (b) Linear relationship between the log of the total phosphorus concentration and the log of the chlorophyll-a concentration in lakes. (*From Dillon and Rigler 1974.*) (c) Decelerating relationship illustrated by the rate of photosynthesis in lupine as a function of light availability for plants grown under varying regimes of carbon dioxide and water availability in a Minnesota grassland experiment. Treatments were applied at BioCON, a free air carbon dioxide enrichment (FACE) study at Cedar Creek Ecosystem Science Reserve. (*From Lee et al. unpublished.*) (d) Accelerating relationship between the distance to the windward edge of the forest and throughfall from fog (fog water coming through the canopy to the forest floor) showing an exponential increase in the amount of water from fog that reaches the forest floor from leeward to windward forest edge. (*From Ewing et al. 2009.*) (e) Humpshaped relationship between species richness and latitude showing maximum species richness in equatorial regions. (*From Gaston 2000.*) (f) Threshold change in lake stability (a lake's resistance to mixing) following Tropical Storm Irene: percent change in stability (% change from before the storm to minimum value in the week following the storm) compared to proportion of the lake volume potentially replaced (the ratio of the water that fell on the catchment plus the lake relative to the volume of the lake) for nine lakes and reservoirs in northeastern North America. (*From Klug et al. unpublished.*) (g) Hysteretic relationship between the phosphorus concentration in Lake Veluwe (Netherlands) and turbidity (measured as the inverse of the Secchi depth, a measure of transparency) over a period that included eutrophication and then restoration. (*From Ibelings et al. 2007.*)

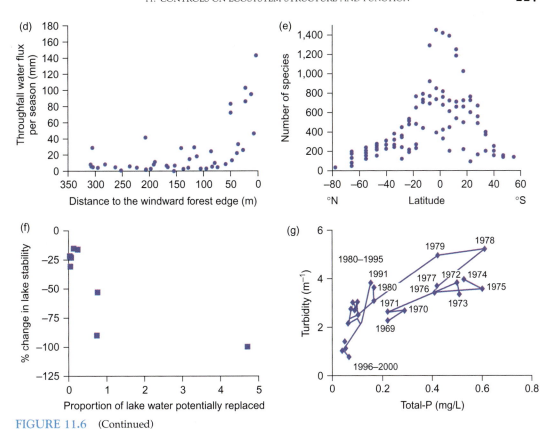

FIGURE 11.6    (Continued)

ecosystem might respond to future conditions, such as a warmer world. For example, climatic warming may have either positive or negative feedbacks to atmospheric carbon dioxide concentrations depending on whether warming leads to more soil respiration or more sequestration of carbon in plants and soil (Luo et al. 2001; Figure 11.7). Because feedbacks may operate on different timescales and yet the balance among them has profound consequences for further change, determining what kinds of feedbacks are present in a given system is one of the major foci in global change research.

## Human Activities Control Many Ecosystems

Human activities now control many ecosystems, both locally and globally. Human inputs of reactive nitrogen and phosphorus to the world's ecosystems are equivalent to those from nonhuman sources (see Chapters 7 and 8). We appropriate 24% of global terrestrial primary production (Haberl et al. 2007) and more than half of available runoff of water (Postel et al. 1996). Our changes to land cover result in billions of tons more

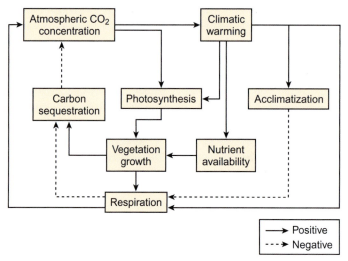

FIGURE 11.7   Both positive and negative feedbacks to climate, via atmospheric carbon dioxide, are possible with warming of a tallgrass prairie. An enhancement of root and soil respiration and a positive feedback to climate could result from stimulation of soil microbial activity associated with higher temperatures. This positive feedback would be weakened if there is acclimatization such that soil (root-plus-microbial) respiration does not continue to increase with increased warming. In contrast, if greater microbial activity leads to enhanced nutrient availability and plant growth, this could result in greater carbon sequestration in plants and soil—and a negative feedback to carbon dioxide concentrations in the atmosphere. *(From Luo et al. 2001.)*

sediment moving in rivers, but the overall sediment export to the ocean has decreased because of impoundments (Syvitski et al. 2005). We release toxins into air, water, and soil, and these reach every ecosystem on the planet (Weathers and Ponette-González 2011). We introduce, decimate, and even extirpate species in most ecosystems, radically change disturbance regimes in ecosystems around the world, and now, we are altering the planet's climate. As a result, it is hardly surprising that human population density (or some other measure of human activity) often now appears on the *x*-axis of graphs in ecosystem science. These human-mediated changes have altered the abiotic and biotic controls on ecosystems, and in turn, the structure and function of ecosystems around the world. As a result, we continuously need to expand our understanding of the structure, function, and controls on the world's ecosystems.

# COMPLICATIONS

One of the reasons that we have offered a brief list of useful generalizations rather than a comprehensive theory of ecosystem control is that the concept of control turns out to be slippery. For instance, suppose we ask the question about what controls primary production in a local lake. If bottle bioassays show that phosphorus limits algal production, we might conclude that phosphorus inputs to the lake control primary production, which would certainly be consistent with general knowledge about the phosphorus cycle (see Chapter 8). On the other hand, we just observed that human activities often control ecosystems, and a graph that relates primary production in the lake to human population along the lake shore over time might well show that primary production is well correlated with human population density. So we might answer that primary production is controlled by human population density. But an astute observer might notice that most of the lake frontage has green lawns. This observer might reasonably conclude that primary production in the lake is controlled by local economic growth or by social norms about having a green lawn. This example illustrates the familiar problem of proximate (P-loading) versus ultimate (social norms, technological capability, or economic growth) causes of a phenomenon, as well as the common situation where more than one "controlling" factor is important—all of which complicates our ability to identify "the" control over some aspect of ecosystem function.

A somewhat related issue is that "control" may imply different levels of mechanistic understanding of the problem. Sometimes, scientists and managers will be satisfied with a "black box" approach that does not explicitly consider any of the mechanistic pathways that link the controlling variable and the ecosystem (see Figure 1.3 in Chapter 1). For other purposes, a much more detailed understanding of mechanisms may be needed. Although much ink has been spilled over which of these interpretations of control is "correct," both approaches clearly can be useful, depending on the scientific or management issue at hand.

Finally, the answer to "What controls ecosystem function?" often depends on the scales of time and space over which the question is posed. Many ecosystem scientists are interested in knowing what controls denitrification (the conversion of nitrate to dinitrogen gas by certain bacteria), because this process leads to important losses of fixed nitrogen from ecosystems and can generate greenhouse gases (see Chapter 7). Denitrification occurs primarily under anaerobic conditions, and requires nitrate and labile organic carbon. Not surprisingly, if we are looking for controls on denitrification rates over the year at a single site, we often find that rates are controlled by soil moisture or flooding (which controls oxygen concentrations) or pulses of nitrate. However, if we are interested in what controls denitrification rates across a region, variables such as local topography, soil texture, and temperature may be better predictors. If we were interested in global denitrification rates at geologic timescales, we might find that atmospheric oxygen concentrations would be the best predictor. Consequently, two scientists studying the controls on the same ecosystem attribute may come up with different answers, and both may be right. Thus, "answers" should be given along with their spatio-temporal contexts.

Considering these complications, the great complexity of ecosystems, and the wide range of possible controls, it is perhaps surprising that we can say much at all about what controls ecosystems. Yet as the material in this chapter and throughout the rest of the book shows, scientists do understand a lot about what controls various aspects of ecosystem structure and function. This understanding underlies modern ecosystem management, and so is of great practical value. Ecosystem scientists of the future will be challenged to refine and extend this understanding, as well as to determine whether broad generalizations about ecosystem controls can be developed (see Chapter 17).

# References

Dillon, P.J., Rigler, F.H., 1974. The phosphorus-chlorophyll relationship in lakes. Limnol. Oceanogr. 19, 767–773.

Ewing, H.A., 2002. The influence of substrate on vegetation history and ecosystem development. Ecology 83, 2766–2781.

Ewing, H.A., Weathers, K.C., Templer, P.H., Dawson, T.E., Firestone, M.K., Elliott, A., et al., 2009. Fog water and ecosystem function: Heterogeneity in a California redwood forest. Ecosystems 12, 417–433.

Gaston, K.J., 2000. Global patterns in biodiversity. Nature 405, 220–227.

Gutiérrez, J.L., Jones, C.G., 2008. Ecosystem engineers. Encyclopedia of Life Sciences, Online. J. Wiley and Sons, Chichester, UK.

Haberl, H., Erb, K.H., Krausmann, F., Gaube, V., Bondeau, A., Plutzar, C., et al., 2007. Quantifying and mapping the human appropriation of net primary production in Earth's terrestrial ecosystems. Proc. Natl. Acad. Sci. 104, 12942–12947.

Ibelings, B.W., Portielje, R., Lammens, E.H.R.R., Noordhuis, R., van den Berg, M.S., Joosse, W., et al., 2007. Resilience of alternative stable states during the recovery of shallow lakes from eutrophication: Lake Veluwe as a case study. Ecosystems 10, 4–16.

Jenny, H., 1941. Factors of soil formation: A system of quantitative pedology. McGraw-Hill, New York.

Jones, C.G., Gutiérrez, J.L., Byers, J.E., Crooks, J.A., Lambrinos, J.G., Talley, T.S., 2010. A framework for understanding physical ecosystem engineering by organisms. Oikos 119, 1862–1869.

Jones, C.G., Lawton, J.H., Shachak, M., 1994. Organisms as ecosystem engineers. Oikos 69, 373–386.

Jones, C.G., Lawton, J.H., Shachak, M., 1997. Positive and negative effects of organisms as physical ecosystem engineers. Ecology 78, 1946–1957.

Luo, Y., Wan, S., Hui, D., Wallace, L.L., 2001. Acclimatization of soil respiration to warming in a tall grass prairie. Nature 413, 622–625.

Postel, S.L., Daily, G.C., Ehrlich, P.R., 1996. Human appropriation of renewable fresh water. Science 271, 785–788.

Strayer, D.L., Caraco, N.F., Cole, J.J., Findlay, S., Pace, M.L., 1999. Transformation of freshwater ecosystems by bivalves: A case study of zebra mussels in the Hudson River. BioScience 49, 19–27.

Syvitski, J.P.M., Vörösmarty, C.J., Kettner, A.J., Green, P., 2005. Impact of humans on the flux of terrestrial sediment to the global coastal ocean. Science 308, 376–380.

Weathers, K.C., Ponette-González, A., 2011. Atmospheric deposition. In: Levia, D.F., Carlyle-Moses, D.E., Tanaka, T. (Eds.), Forest hydrology and biogeochemistry: Synthesis of past research and future directions. Ecological Studies Series, No. 216. Springer-Verlag, Heidelberg, Germany.

Whittaker, R.H., 1975. Communities and ecosystems, second ed. Macmillan, New York.

# CASE STUDIES

Ecosystems, Tansley's (1935) "units of nature," are the fundamental ecological units supporting life on our planet. The complexity of ecosystems represents a strength for biotic survival and a challenge for human understanding. Case studies may be one of the best ways to illustrate the complexity of ecosystems, as well as to show the importance and relevance of the ecosystem approach. We present here five case studies, representing a spectrum of systems and approaches.

The initial case study by Pamela Matson presents an excellent example of how the complex biotic functions of ecosystems are intimately intertwined with the abiotic, and thereby drive the biogeochemistry of nitrogen. The agricultural ecosystems in the Yaqui Valley of Mexico are the focus of these studies. Nitrogen is a vital plant nutrient for these ecosystems, but when heavily fertilized for agriculture, they can become so enriched that they give off large amounts of nitrous oxide, an important "greenhouse" gas in the global atmosphere. Understanding these complicated relationships gives the fundamental information to describe this environmental problem and the guidance to regulate this unwanted flux of nitrogen.

Richard Ostfeld provides a clear example in the second essay of how the complexity of ecosystems needs to be understood to gain insight into the numerous, critical relationships among humans and the populations of plants and animals that they interact with daily. Although human disease is traditionally viewed as a medical problem, Ostfeld shows how the ecology and behavior of organisms and their relationships within an ecosystem are a primary determinant in the ecology of disease. Ostfeld uses Lyme disease, a common and serious tick-borne disease, as his example.

In the third essay, Emily Stanley presents an impressive story about the ecosystem effects that occur when flowing waters are dammed, a practice that has been done by humans for millennia. The removal of these dams, both experimentally and as a management intervention, provides a powerful opportunity to gain ecological insight into how streams and rivers function within a landscape.

The need for an ecosystem understanding of a major environmental problem to propose intelligent management interventions, including federal regulation of pollutant emissions, is the theme for the fourth essay on acid rain. Here, Gene Likens follows this story from the discovery of acid rain in North America in 1963 to its effects on aquatic ecosystems, to the passage of the U.S. Clean Air Act Amendments in 1990, to subsequent impacts on terrestrial ecosystems. Ecosystem complexity and interaction among various element cycles provide the grist for this essay.

Judy Meyer has done novel studies of the role and importance of stream and river ecosystems for decades. In the fifth essay, she elucidates the vital role and intimate interconnections that these fluvial ecosystems contribute to an integrated, functioning landscape. The "interactions between streams and their valleys"—ecosystems functioning separately and together—is the theme of her essay.

Many important lessons can be learned from the results as well as the scientific approaches underpinning these essays, including:

- Tackling ecosystem complexity provides increased knowledge about key ecological interactions.
- Experimental manipulation of entire ecosystems and long-term research and monitoring often yield new insights about how ecosystems are structured, function, and change with time.
- The result of ecosystem research, because often it is synonymous with a system of great human concern, typically has high management relevance in helping managers and decision-makers find solutions to environmental problems.
- Individual ecosystems are connected to other ecosystems of the biosphere through movements of air, water, and animals across their boundaries.
- The sum is greater than the parts in providing ecological understanding.

We trust that these five essays will help bring into focus the realities and value of research in the complex world of human interests and management needs. There are many other topics that could have been selected, but we hope that the diverse subjects presented here will entice you to explore further the multitudinous interfaces between ecosystem science and its applications to real-world, environmental problems. Enjoy!

## Reference

Tansley, A.G., 1935. The use and abuse of vegetational concepts and terms. Ecology 16, 284–307.

# From Global Environmental Change to Sustainability Science: Ecosystem Studies in the Yaqui Valley, Mexico

*Pamela A. Matson*
**Stanford University, Stanford, California**

The 1980s and early 1990s were exhilarating times for ecologists engaging in the analysis of global environmental change. We were just beginning to understand the global nature of environmental change, thanks to new tools such as remote sensing and global-scale mathematical models and perspectives. International programs such as the International Geosphere-Biosphere Program (IGBP) began bringing disciplines together—ecologists, atmospheric chemists, oceanographers, geographers, climatologists, and others—to learn each other's languages and work together to understand environmental change. Ecologists rejected the physical scientists' description of the biosphere as a homogeneous green carpet over the planet (the "green slime" model), and brought to bear ecologically based models that accounted for the spatial and temporal variability in ecosystem structure and function across the planet. Moreover, ecological understanding of the causes of that natural variation helped frame the analysis of the planetary system both in terms of measurements and models.

One of the emerging questions of the time had to do with change in the global nitrogen cycle and key components of the cycle such as emissions of the greenhouse gas nitrous oxide. With Peter Vitousek and other collaborators, our research team developed an ecological framework for studying emissions of nitrogen trace gases from ecosystems, explicitly using gradients of climate and soil development to estimate fluxes from tropical ecosystems and develop a global budget for the gas (Matson and Vitousek 1987, 1990;

Vitousek et al. 1989). In doing so, we began to identify the influences of land use change in the tropics on greenhouse gas emissions (Matson et al. 1987, 1990; Matson and Vitousek 1990), and the role of agricultural fertilization in driving the increase in nitrous oxide (Matson et al. 1996), the causes of which were in debate at that time. We explored the biogeochemical processes that regulated fluxes within and beyond tropical forest and agricultural ecosystems, and identified where and how management influenced the processes. And we helped articulate the global dimensions of changes in nitrogen, characterizing the enormous and rapid change driven largely by the use of industrial fertilizers (Vitousek and Matson 1993) and the consequences of that change for the global system. Altogether, it was an exciting time for ecosystem science, specifically biogeochemistry and global change science.

At some point in the early 1990s, our involvement in tracking change in the global nitrogen cycle and solving the puzzle of the increased nitrous oxide concentrations in the atmosphere moved beyond academic fascination: My view of the issues changed from "this is so (intellectually) fun" to "this is scary!" I began to want not just to study and understand and identify the causes and consequences of global changes, but to help do something about them. If land use change and fertilizer use were having significant impacts on the global atmosphere, climate, and species and ecosystems, what could we do about them?

In 1992, Roz Naylor, an economist at Stanford University, and I organized a session for the Aspen Global Change Institute called "Food, Conservation, and Environment: Is Compromise Possible?" Bringing together ecologists, agronomists, economists, geographers, atmospheric scientists, and others, we asked, among other things, how we might join forces to not just study change, but to develop approaches that would allow food production and other land use to proceed while reducing negative impacts on ecosystems and the environment. One outcome of that set of discussions was a rough research plan that eventually launched the Yaqui Valley study.

## THE YAQUI VALLEY CASE STUDY

In 1993, Roz Naylor, Ivan Ortiz-Monasterio (an agronomist working for the International Maize and Wheat Improvement Center (CIMMYT) in Sonora, Mexico), and I initiated a project centered on fertilizer use and nitrogen flows in the intensive wheat agricultural systems of the Yaqui Valley to (1) understand how and why farmers were managing their intensive cropping systems; (2) identify the resulting consequences for land, water, and atmosphere; and (3) also evaluate alternative management practices that could make sense economically, environmentally, and agronomically. From the beginning, our studies of fertilizer management straddled the worlds of global environmental change on the one hand and international agronomic systems and policies on the other. Over time, our focus evolved to include more cross-cutting themes such as vulnerability and knowledge systems issues, themes that are now emerging as crucial questions in sustainability science (Clark 2007). Likewise, our early innovation—the purposeful and at that time quite unusual focus on the integrated ecological–economic–agronomic system—evolved over time to a full-fledged focus on sustainability of human–environment systems.

## The Yaqui Valley

The Yaqui Valley is located on the northwest coast of mainland Mexico in the state of Sonora (Figure 12.1). Situated on a coastal strip along the Gulf of California, the Valley consists of an intensively managed agricultural region amidst a desert scrub forest and is bordered by estuarine ecosystems that provide critical habitat for migratory and resident water birds, marine mammals, and fish and shellfish populations (Flores-Verdugo et al. 1992). These coastal waters have long been an important center for both subsistence and the export fishing industry. More information on its history, climatic setting, and range of development issues (such as urbanization, coastal zone change, water resource supply and challenges, and population change) can be found in Matson et al. (2005) and in the synthesis volume, *Seeds of Sustainability* (Matson 2012). For this particular story, however, we'll focus primarily on intensive irrigated and fertilized agriculture in the Yaqui Valley.

The Yaqui Valley region is of vital economic importance to Mexico in terms both of its agricultural production and fish production. Today the Yaqui Valley consists of 235,000 ha of irrigated wheat-based agriculture, and is one of the country's most productive breadbaskets (Naylor et al. 2001). Using a combination of irrigation, high fertilizer rates, and modern

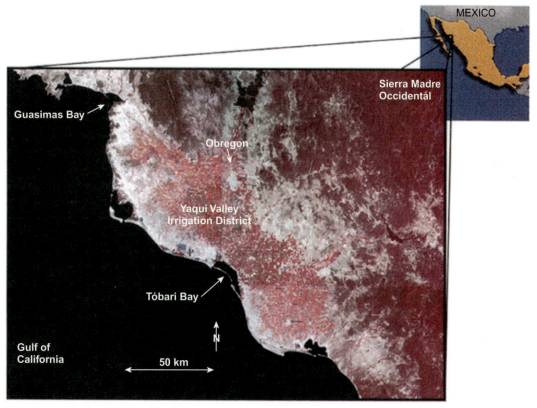

**FIGURE 12.1**    Satellite image of the Yaqui Valley irrigation district (in pink), bounded to the west by the Gulf of California and to the east by the Sierra Madres, in the state of Sonora, Mexico.

cultivars (Matson et al. 1998), valley farmers produce some of the highest wheat yields in the world (FAO 1997). The region also maintains the most productive fisheries in Mexico with sardines and shrimp being among the most important species (CONAPESCA 2002). In recent years the region also has developed the second largest shrimp aquaculture industries in Mexico (CONAPESCA 2002). However, in a world of globalized markets, reduced subsidies and price supports, drought, hurricanes, and other forces, many farmers and fishers in the region are concerned about maintaining production and household incomes.

In the mid-twentieth century, the Mexican government and the international development community identified the Yaqui Valley as an appropriate center for agricultural development. In 1943, Norman Borlaug, working for the Mexican government and the Rockefeller Foundation, launched a wheat research program that was the forerunner of the International Maize and Wheat Improvement Center (CIMMYT), which remains in the region today (Naylor et al. 2001). Later, a national agricultural experiment center (CIANO) also was established in the valley. Because the region is agro-climatically representative of 40% of the developing world's wheat growing areas, it was selected as an ideal place for the early wheat improvement program.

The use of fertilizer nitrogen has increased markedly in the past four decades; between 1968 and 1995 fertilizer application rates for wheat production increased from 80 to 250 kg N/ha, over a 200% increase. When we started the study, the most common agronomic practice for wheat production in the valley was a preplanting broadcast application of urea or injection of anhydrous ammonium (at the rate of 150–200 kg/ha), followed by irrigation (the preplanting irrigation is intended to aid in weed control by causing germination of weeds that can then be plowed under prior to planting). The causes and consequences of these management approaches were the first focus of our studies in the region.

## Fertilizer Use and Nitrogen Cycling in the Yaqui's Ecosystems

When we first tackled it in 1994, it seemed like an easy question: "Why do Yaqui farmers use so much nitrogen fertilizer, does it matter to yields or productivity of the crop, and to the environment, and if so, what can be done that makes sense economically and environmentally?" Irrigated wheat yields were about 5 tons per ha in the early 1990s and had held steady at that for almost two decades. Nevertheless, nitrogen applications had been dramatically increasing, the current rate of nearly 250 kg/ha seemed extraordinarily high, and the rate of increase in nitrogen use showed few signs of slowing down.

Given what we already understood about nitrogen cycling in any ecosystem, we expected dramatic losses of nitrogen through a variety of mechanisms (Figure 12.2). At the outset, the team carried out a series of experiments both on experimental station lands and in farmer fields that showed that the typical farmer's fertilization practice led to very high concentrations of ammonium and nitrate in soils following the fertilization and irrigation events, and large nitrous oxide and nitric oxide losses to the atmosphere—the highest fluxes ever measured (Matson et al. 1998, and others); ammonia flux was never quantified (despite several aborted attempts to do so), but comparative indicators suggested they too were extremely high. Levels of nitric oxide emissions were large enough to drive the serious air pollution that occurred during that time in Cuidad Obregón, a city just downwind of the valley. Deposition of nitrogen oxides certainly occurred in shrubland and forested

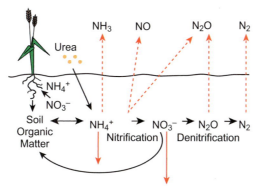

**FIGURE 12.2**    Expected pathways of nitrogen fertilizer transformations and losses. Most fertilizer nitrogen enters the system as urea, which is then rapidly hydrolyzed to ammonium. In the absence of plant uptake (the typical situation, given that most of the fertilizer is added before planting), ammonium ($NH_4$) is volatilized to ammonia ($NH_3$) or oxidized by nitrifying bacteria under aerobic conditions to nitrate ($NO_3$). During nitrification, some portion of nitrogen is lost in the trace gas forms of nitric oxide (NO) or nitrous oxide ($N_2O$). Nitrate in the soil can be leached in soil solution to depths below the rooting zone, or can be reduced to $N_2O$ or to dinitrogen ($N_2$) by denitrifying bacteria. All of these processes occurred in the Yaqui Valley soils.

ecosystems of the Sierra Madre, but our search for funding to study the amounts and consequences of the deposition was never successful.

Through a combination of measurements under varying soil conditions and with the use of $^{15}N$ analyses, we identified the biogeochemical pathways that controlled the loss of nitrogen from the fields to the atmosphere, showing clearly that a significant portion of the trace gases lost following fertilization is produced by nitrification rather than denitrification processes in these ecosystems (Panek et al. 2000). While microbial ecologists recognized the potential role for nitrification in emissions of both $NO_x$ and $N_2O$, most field-based studies assumed that $N_2O$ measured at the soil—air interface was related to denitrification. The discovery that nitrification could be an important source under some conditions carried implications for the management of gas fluxes in agricultural sites around the world.

We also tracked nitrogen losses through water systems. Lysimeter studies coupled with a multilayer biogeochemical model called NLoSS indicated high fluxes of nitrate though soil to below the rooting zone (Riley et al. 2001). While we wished to evaluate subsurface transport from fields through riparian areas to the "drainage canals" (natural streams and human-made drainage canals) that drain from the agricultural lands directly to the sea, we failed to get funding and thus never measured (or quantified) those fluxes. However, we did study transformations of nitrogen in the drainage canals themselves, measured extremely large fluxes of nitrous oxide (Harrison and Matson 2003), and uncovered the crucial role of extremely rapidly changing oxygen conditions in controlling them (Harrison et al. 2005). Moreover, we carried out a remote sensing-based study to illustrate the synchrony between irrigation and fertilization events on land and enormous phytoplankton blooms in the open waters of the Sea of Cortez (Beman et al. 2005), and delved deeply into the physical, chemical, and microbial controls on nitrogen processing and transport in the coastal waters. In the end, our research illustrated the land-to-sea movement of fertilizer nitrogen, and consequences of those fluxes for the oceans and

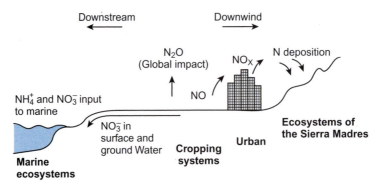

**FIGURE 12.3**   At the landscape scale, nitrogen moved from farmers' fields to atmosphere, water systems, oceans, and downwind terrestrial ecosystems.

atmosphere (Figures 12.3, 12.4). The integrated story of nitrogen transformations and transport from land to the sea is told in more detail in Ahrens et al. (2008).

While we pursued these exciting questions about nitrogen cycling and fluxes within the fields and across the valley, we did not lose sight of our original intention—to identify management alternatives that made sense for farmers and the environment. In addition to studying what happens in the farmers' fields, we also measured nitrogen cycling processes and crop dynamics in a set of comparative treatments that altered the timing and amount of fertilizer applied. These treatments were constrained by reality—we wanted to test options that could actually be practiced by farmers. One of the most important early articles to emerge from this research, published in *Science*, reported the consequences (in terms of nitrogen losses) of the mismatch between nitrogen needs of the wheat plant and the timing of large fertilizer applications by farmers (Matson et al. 1998). Its analyses of nitrogen losses, grain yields and quality, and farm budgets under a variety of alternative practices suggested that by changing the timing and amount of applications (removing the preplanting fertilization and applying (less of) it more closely timed to crop demand), farmers' profits could be increased and the negative externalities of fertilizer losses could be prevented. It also showed the benefits of a biogeochemist, an agronomist, and an economist attacking a problem from an ecosystem perspective.

## Beyond the Simple Answer

There was just one problem. Despite on-farm trials that generally confirmed our "best practice," even progressive farmers seemed unwilling to change application practices. That led to a series of new questions and hypotheses that engaged the research team for subsequent years. Team members David Lobell and Ivan Ortiz-Monasterio used remote sensing to demonstrate substantial spatial and temporal variability in wheat yields. Their work indicated that high applications of fertilizer in years of optimal weather—which farmers could not know in advance—could pay off for some farmers (Lobell et al. 2004). That result led to a search for new site-specific measurement technologies that could provide real-time estimates of fertilizer needs during the course of the growing season, a search that ultimately yielded the use of handheld radiometers to provide in situ information on nitrogen status

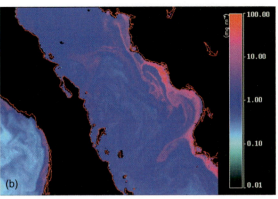

FIGURE 12.4  Irrigation water carried nitrogen from fields (a) and from other land sources to the ocean, resulting in (b) massive blooms of phytoplankton (here measured by SeaWiFS satellite imagery) that bloomed in synchrony with irrigation and fertilizer events on land. *(From Beman et al. 2005.)*

(Ortiz-Monasterio and Raun 2007). At the same time, however, we wondered why, in spite of climate uncertainties, farmers did not cut back on nitrogen use when fertilizer prices doubled following the removal of subsidies and again when petroleum prices spiked. We launched a new set of studies on the "knowledge system" of the valley, and uncovered the important role of credit institutions in controlling the fertilizer decisions made by farmers; credit union advisors tended to encourage all farmers toward application rates that were both uniform and very high (McCullough and Matson 2011), and could withhold credit if these practices were not followed. We realized that, if we hoped to get credit union managers to reduce unnecessary inputs, we needed to engage them in the research itself; through the influence of Ivan Ortiz-Monasterio and many of the more progressive farmers of the valley, many of the credit unions became involved to the extent that they helped buy the new site-specific management technology for their members.

Working in one ecosystem over a decade, of course, leads to an ever-changing set of questions. At the same time we were working toward improved fertilizer management, we engaged in research on sustainable use of water resources in the valley, and on the role of shrimp aquaculture in the loss of ecosystems and ecosystem services. And we began to worry about agriculture in the context of vulnerability to climate change, ultimately developing an index of vulnerability that suggested who among the farmers and farms of the valley were most vulnerable (or likely to suffer harm) to climate change and thus who might benefit most from management assistance (Luers et al. 2003). Research on these issues and others continue in the valley, thanks in large part to our graduate students and the Mexican collaborators on our team.

## LESSONS FROM THE YAQUI VALLEY ECOSYSTEMS STUDY

The fertilizer story is just one part of our interdisciplinary research in the valley, but it is illustrative. As viewed through this story, the Yaqui Valley is in transition to sustainability, in which their decisions make sense economically, socially, agronomically, and environmentally. They are not there yet and in fact may never be under current cropping systems, but the farmers' agenda has changed from one interested only in increasing yields to one focused on maximizing profits as well as social benefits by reducing environmental damages. Likewise, the story illustrates our transition as a research team, from one working from an ecological perspective focused on global environmental change to a sustainability perspective focused on meeting the needs of people while reducing negative impacts on the environment.

The Yaqui Valley case study has been useful in terms of identifying the dynamics of change in human–environment systems, and providing tools and approaches that can help the people of the Yaqui Valley in decision-making for human and environmental well-being. We did not fully design for the relevance of the work, at least not in the beginning. While the research was initially designed to provide useful information to farmers and decision makers, we only later began to learn how best to engage them fully in the work. We identified critical missing members of our research team as we went, often too late; having them at the beginning might have allowed us to answer additional critical questions. In hindsight, there is no doubt we would at times have done things quite differently. On the other hand, thanks to the involvement of collaborators who have practical and on-the-ground interests, the research is probably more directly useful than many such studies might be. There is no doubt that ecologists working alone would have done substantially different experiments and probably yielded far less useful information!

Our additional intent was to contribute information and knowledge that is useful not just in our place of study but beyond it as well. We believe that much of what we have learned in the Yaqui Valley is transportable (Matson 2012)—indeed, we selected the Yaqui Valley in part for its potential influence and relevance beyond its borders. Thus, the tools and metrics and models, some of which use remote sensing, can be applied in many places. Beyond that, the project has provided tremendous grist for general learning through a comparison with other case studies, a strategy that has yielded significant new knowledge in the past few years. And the Yaqui Valley project helped educate a new generation of researchers who understand ecosystems to be integrated "human–environment systems," who have learned what it means to be multi- or interdisciplinary in their perspectives or approaches, and who are committed to research for the sake of decision-making as well as for the sake of learning new things about how the world works. For this younger generation as well as for the older ones among us, the Yaqui Valley provided a real-life laboratory that allowed us to make serious contributions to the scientific knowledge base and to problem-solving as well.

# References

Ahrens, T.D., Beman, J.M., Harrison, J.A., Jewett, P.K., Matson, P.A., 2008. A synthesis of nitrogen transformations and transfers from land to the sea in the Yaqui Valley agricultural region of northwest Mexico. Water Resour. Res. 44, W00A05. doi: 10.1029/2007WR006661.

Beman, J.M., Arrigo, K.R., Matson, P.A., 2005. Agricultural runoff fuels large phytoplankton blooms in vulnerable areas of the ocean. Nature 434, 211–214.

Clark, W.C., 2007. Sustainability science: A room of its own. Proc. Natl. Acad. Sci. U.S.A. 104, 1737–1738.

CONAPESCA (Comisión Nacional de Acuacultura y Pesca), (2002). Available at http://www.conapesca.sagarpa.gob.mx/wb/.

Flores-Verdugo, F., Gonzalez-Farias, F., Zamorano, D.S., Ramirez-Garcia, P., 1992. Mangrove ecosystems of the Pacific coast of Mexico: Distribution, structure, litterfall, and detritus dynamics. In: Seeliger, U. (Ed.), Coastal plant communities of Latin America. Academic Press, San Diego, pp. 269–288.

Food and Agriculture Organization of the United Nations (FAO), 1997. FAOSTAT. On-line and Multilingual Database Time-Series Records Covering International Statistics. Food and Agriculture Organization, United Nations, Rome, Italy. Available at http://faostat.fao.org/.

Harrison, J.A., Matson, P.A., 2003. Patterns and controls of nitrous oxide emissions from waters draining a subtropical agricultural valley. Global Biogeochem. Cycles 17, 1080. doi: 10.1029/2002GB001991.

Harrison, J.A., Matson, P.A., Fendorf, S.E., 2005. Effects of a diel oxygen cycle on nitrogen transformations and greenhouse gas emissions in a eutrophied subtropical stream. Aquat. Sci. 67, 308–315.

Lobell, D.B., Ortiz-Monasterio, J.I., Asner, G.P., 2004. Relative importance of soil and climate variability for nitrogen management in irrigated wheat. Field Crops Res. 87, 155–165.

Luers, A.L., Lobell, D.B., Sklar, L.S., Addams, C.L., Matson, P.A., 2003. A method for quantifying vulnerability, applied to the agricultural system of the Yaqui Valley, Mexico. Glob. Environ. Change 13, 255–267.

Matson, P.A., 2012. Seeds of Sustainability: Lessons from the Birthplace of the Green Revolution in Agriculture. Island Press, Washington, D.C.

Matson, P.A., Billow, C., Hall, S., Zachariesson, J., 1996. Fertilization practices and soil variations control nitrogen oxide emissions from tropical sugar cane. J. Geophys. Res. 101 (D13), 18533–18546.

Matson, P.A., Luers, A., Seto, K., Naylor, R., Ortiz-Monasterio, I., 2005. People, land use and environment in the Yaqui Valley, Sonora, Mexico. In: Entwisle, B., Stern, P. (Eds.), Population, land use, and environment. National Research Council, Washington, DC, pp. 238–264.

Matson, P.A., Naylor, R.L., Ortiz-Monasterio, I., 1998. Integration of environmental, agronomic, and economic aspects of fertilizer management. Science 280, 112–115.

Matson, P.A., Vitousek, P.M., 1987. Cross-system comparisons of soil nitrogen transformations and nitrous oxide flux in tropical forest ecosystems. Glob. Biogeochem Cycles 1, 163–170.

Matson, P.A., Vitousek, P.M., 1990. Ecosystem approach for the development of a global nitrous oxide budget. BioScience 40, 667–672.

Matson, P.A., Vitousek, P.M., Ewel, J.J., Mazzarino, M.J., Robertson, G.P., 1987. Nitrogen transformations following tropical forest felling and burning on a volcanic soil. Ecology 68, 491–502.

Matson, P.A., Vitousek, P.M., Livingston, G.P., Swanberg, N.A., 1990. Sources of variation in nitrous oxide flux from Amazonian ecosystems. J. Geophys. Res. 95 (D10), 16789–16798.

McCullough, E.B., Matson, P.A., 2011. Evolution of the knowledge system for agricultural development in the Yaqui Valley, Sonora, Mexico. Proc. Natl. Acad. Sci. U.S.A. doi: 10.1073/pnas.1011602108.

Naylor, R.L., W.P. Falcon, Puente-González, A. 2001. Policy reforms and Mexican agriculture: Views from the Yaqui Valley. CIMMYT (International Maize and Wheat Improvement Center) Economics Program Paper No. 01-01. Mexico, DF: CIMMYT.

Ortiz-Monasterio, J.I., Raun, W., 2007. Reduced nitrogen and improved farm income for irrigated spring wheat in the Yaqui Valley, Mexico, using sensor based nitrogen management. J. Agric. Sci. 145, 215–222.

Panek, J., Matson, P.A., Ortiz-Monasterio, I., Brooks, P., 2000. Distinguishing nitrification and denitrification sources of $N_2O$ in a Mexican wheat system using $^{15}N$. Ecol. Appl. 10, 506–514.

Riley, W.J., Ortiz-Monasterio, I., Matson, P.A., 2001. Nitrogen leaching and soil nitrate, nitrite, and ammonium levels under irrigated wheat in Northern Mexico. Nutrient Cycling in Agroecosystems 61, 223–236.

Vitousek, P.M., Matson, P.A., 1993. Agriculture, the global nitrogen cycle, and trace gas flux. In: Oremland, R. (Ed.), Biogeochemistry of global change: Radiatively active trace gases. Chapman and Hall, New York, pp. 193–208.

Vitousek, P.M., Matson, P.A., Volkmann, C., Maass, M., Garcia, G., 1989. Nitrous oxide fluxes from seasonally dry tropical forests. Glob. Biogeochem. Cycles 3, 375–382.

# 13

# Ecology of Lyme Disease

*Richard S. Ostfeld*

Cary Institute of Ecosystem Studies, Millbrook, New York

## DISCOVERY

When two residents of Lyme, Connecticut, reported to the Connecticut State Health Department in 1975 that a number of children in their town were suffering from a recurrent, inflammatory disease of the knees and other joints, public health officials responded quickly. The local rate of this arthritic syndrome was 100 times greater than that of juvenile rheumatoid arthritis in the general population, suggesting a local cause. Some of the children had experienced a skin lesion about a month before the onset of joint pain and swelling.

Researchers from Yale University began to monitor the health of patients following the appearance of similar lesions, finding that many of them later developed arthritis as well as nervous system and heart disorders. These researchers were aware of previously described co-occurrences of similar skin lesions (called erythema migrans, or EM) with joint pain and neuritis in the European medical literature from the late nineteenth century. This European syndrome was associated with tick bites, and although the causative agent had never been identified, many patients responded well to treatment with penicillin, suggesting a bacterial etiology (reviewed by Stanek et al. 2002). The search for ticks in forested habitats near Lyme revealed abundant populations of what was then presented as a new species of ixodid tick, named *Ixodes dammini* (Spielman et al. 1979). Shortly thereafter it was discovered that cases of this new disease, named Lyme disease, were widespread in coastal New England and the upper Midwest of the United States, and in both regions were spatially correlated with abundant populations of this tick (Steere and Malawista 1979). The disease also occurred in California and Oregon associated with a closely related tick species, *I. pacificus*. Evidence was pointing toward a widespread, tick-borne bacterial agent as the cause of a newly named, but probably ancient disease characterized by multiple symptoms varying over time.

**243**

Meanwhile, on the north shore of Long Island, across Long Island Sound from Lyme, Connecticut, researchers surveying for the rickettsial agent of Rocky Mountain Spotted Fever, typically found in *Dermacentor* ticks, accidentally discovered spirochete bacteria in *I. dammini* ticks (Burgdorfer et al. 1982). Suspecting that they might have found the causative agent of Lyme disease, these researchers determined that Lyme disease patients indeed were infected with these spirochetes and were producing antibodies (Burgdorfer et al. 1982; Benach et al. 1983).

This newly discovered spirochete was named *Borrelia burgdorferi* (Johnson et al. 1984). Biomedical scientists now knew what caused Lyme disease, how the pathogen was transmitted, and where cases were clustered geographically. Spurred by a strong public health concern, biomedical researchers had discovered (or thought they discovered) a "new" tick species and a "new" spirochete species, both of which were shockingly widespread and abundant. But as new epidemiological and entomological information on this emerging zoonosis arose, it became apparent that tremendous spatial and temporal variation in Lyme disease existed. If the causes of this variation could be determined, mitigation strategies might be developed to benefit human health.

## IT'S THE DEER

The discipline of epidemiology is concerned with identifying risk factors for human disease. When an arthropod vector is known to be important, or even necessary, for a disease agent to infect humans, epidemiologists often collaborate with medical entomologists to study the life cycle, abundance, and distribution of the vector. A flurry of research on *I. dammini* ensued in the late 1970s and 1980s to advance an understanding of risk factors for Lyme disease and lay a foundation for preventative measures. Like other ixodid (hard) ticks, *I. dammini* was found to undergo two immature stages (larva and nymph) in addition to the adult stage. At each stage the tick takes a single blood meal from a vertebrate host to fuel transition to the next stage or, in the case of adults, for reproduction. Newly hatched larvae seek a host in midsummer, and following their blood meal, they molt into nymphs, which then overwinter on the forest floor before host-seeking the following late spring or early summer. After taking their blood meal, nymphs molt into adults, which seek a host in mid- to late fall. Adult females engorged with host blood overwinter before depositing an egg mass in spring, from which the next generation of larvae emerge in mid-summer. Thus, the tick life cycle lasts for two years and can involve three distinct vertebrate host species, with considerable time spent in a resting state on the forest floor.

The abundance and distribution of organisms with such complex life cycles are often assumed to be determined by a complex suite of biotic and abiotic factors, including availability of multiple hosts. However, even when first principles suggest that multiple factors are important in determining species abundances and temporal dynamics, such multifactorial approaches are rarely a part of initial research strategies (Lidicker 1978).

Medical entomologists working on islands off the coast of Massachusetts were so impressed with the large numbers of *I. dammini* ticks found on hunter-killed deer (Piesman et al. 1979) that the species was given the common name "deer tick." Early studies of the relationship between deer and tick abundances, again carried out on islands, found that the two were positively correlated (Wilson et al. 1985, Anderson et al. 1987). On the basis of these early studies and the common name "deer tick," it quickly became axiomatic that deer are indispensable for tick populations. Later studies by ecologists and medical entomologists have shown that the situation is much more complicated. Islands are known to have reduced faunal diversity, and on mainland sites where a number of other medium-sized to large mammals co-occur with deer, adult ticks commonly parasitize these nondeer hosts. Probably as a result of the effects of nondeer hosts, several studies of Lyme-disease ecology at mainland sites have found no relationship, either spatially or through time, between deer abundance and that of ticks (reviewed in Ostfeld et al. 2006). Several studies have even found that, when deer are excluded from areas less than a few hectares, the number of ticks *increases*, apparently owing to the use of other hosts that benefit from local exclusion of deer (Perkins et al. 2006). Studies in which the role of deer, compared to that of other hosts, is determined remain rare but are much needed for understanding the complex ecology of ticks.

Even the scientific name *Ixodes dammini* and associated moniker "deer tick" had to be discarded. Studies in the early and mid-1990s revealed that what had been considered a "new" species in fact was a northern population of the widespread species *Ixodes scapularis*, or blacklegged tick. The bases for this conclusion were (1) *I. dammini* from Massachusetts and *I. scapularis* from Georgia interbred readily in the lab and produced fertile offspring through several generations; (2) no discrete differences between the two groups existed in morphology, chromosomes, or isozymes; and (3) no discrete differences between the two groups existed in phylogenetically informative nucleotide sequences of either ribosomal or mitrochondrial loci (Oliver et al. 1993; Wesson et al. 1993; Norris et al. 1996). As a result of these studies, it is generally accepted that what was called *I. dammini* actually consists of northern populations of *I. scapularis*, which was described in 1821, and the correct common name for members of these populations is "blacklegged tick."

## It's the Mice

Even though deer were assumed to be essential for the occurrence of blacklegged tick populations, another key element is necessary for these ticks to pose a threat to human health—the ticks must be infected with *B. burgdorferi*. Because these spirochetes are not passed from mother ticks to eggs, each generation of ticks must acquire *B. burgdorferi* infections from hosts to be capable of transmitting infection to people. Deer were known to be highly inefficient at transmitting spirochetes to ticks, so this role must be served by other hosts. Early ecological studies (e.g., Donahue et al. 1987) demonstrated that larval ticks acquired *B. burgdorferi* more efficiently from white-footed mice (*Peromyscus leucopus*) than from any other host, and that this high "reservoir competence" in mice led to high prevalence of infection in the next generation of nymphs (Mather et al. 1989). Again, studies of the simplified ecology of island communities, where few nonmouse hosts for immature ticks occurred, led investigators to the paradigm that deer are required for the existence of a blacklegged tick population and mice are required for the ticks to be infected with Lyme disease spirochetes (Spielman et al. 1985). This paradigm has been highly resilient even in the face of considerable contradictory evidence and strong support for the role of nondeer, nonmouse hosts in determining numbers and infection prevalence of blacklegged ticks (see later).

## It's the Population Dynamics

In 1991, I established two large (2.25-ha) live-trapping plots within typical second-growth, eastern deciduous forest on the grounds of the Cary Institute of Ecosystem Studies in Millbrook, New York. Healthy populations of ticks had been discovered at Cary Institute several years earlier, and Lyme disease was an established problem for local residents. I had been trained as a population and community ecologist with a focus on the causes and consequences of fluctuating populations of small mammals. I knew that white-footed mice were likely to be the most abundant small mammal in this type of habitat, that these mice were known to be the most competent reservoir for *B. burgdorferi*, and that population size of these mice fluctuated dramatically through time. My purpose in establishing these trapping plots was to provide a monitoring baseline to pursue the impacts of fluctuating mice on the dynamics of their prey—particularly gypsy moths (*Lymantria dispar*) and tree seeds—and of their parasites—specifically blacklegged ticks and *B. burgdorferi*.

Because most of my prior studies of small mammals had been undertaken in grasslands, I was unprepared for the forest phenomenon I experienced during the fall of 1991, namely an extraordinary mast seeding event courtesy of red oaks (*Quercus rubrum*) and black oaks (*Q. velutina*). Personal observations indicated that the masting event extended throughout the eastern New York/western New England region. This impressive phenomenon (> 100 acorns per square meter in some places) prompted my colleague, Charles Canham, and me to establish seed traps to quantify the magnitude of acorn masting at our sites. It was well known that mice and other wildlife were voracious consumers of acorns, and it seemed possible that consumer populations could ebb and flow with variable acorn production. Indeed, live-trapping the following spring on these plots revealed abundant mouse populations, which then grew to extraordinary densities (> 100 individual per hectare) by late summer of 1992, after which they crashed to very low numbers (< 10 per hectare).

Another striking discovery my colleagues and I made the summer following the 1991 mast was that larval tick abundance had exploded in oak-dominated forest stands but not in maple-dominated stands that we were also monitoring. At about this time, I saw a presentation at a scientific meeting by William J. McShea showing that deer gravitate toward oak-dominated stands in the fall of a mast year to eat fallen acorns, but outside of mast years tend to avoid oak-dominated stands. Knowledge of this work (later published in McShea and Schwede 1993) led me to hypothesize that the burgeoning larval tick populations in 1992 in oak stands were a consequence of the heavy acorn crop in 1991, which attracted deer and their attached adult ticks to these sites and away from other habitat types. If so, we would expect that fed adult ticks would drop off deer largely in oak stands, ovipositing there, and leading to eruptions of larvae the following summer. The fact that very few acorns were produced in 1992 (heavy mast production is often followed by one or a few years of acorn failure) allowed us to assess this hypothesis. We expected that deer would avoid oak stands in the fall of 1992, that few fed adult ticks would occur there, and that consequently larvae would be sparse in oak stands in the summer of 1993 but abundant in maple-dominated sites. This pattern was exactly what we found (Ostfeld et al. 1996; Ostfeld 1997).

As described earlier, larval ticks hatch uninfected with Lyme disease spirochetes, so booms and busts in abundance of this life stage have no immediate impact on human health. But, larvae that feed on mice are highly likely to acquire a spirochete infection and become dangerous to us upon molting into nymphs. During the summer of 1992, following the 1991 masting event, both populations of mice and larval ticks had exploded as a result of two distinct responses by wildlife to acorn abundance. We predicted that abundant larvae with access to abundant mice would result in high densities of infected nymphal ticks in 1993, two summers following the masting event. And again, this is exactly what we found (Ostfeld et al. 1996; Ostfeld 1997). Similarly, our prediction that acorn failure in 1992 would lead to few mice and few larval ticks in 1993, and consequently to few infected nymphs in 1994, was confirmed.

## It's the Community Dynamics

Although mice were the best known of the many species that host immature ticks, and a well-established Lyme-disease reservoir, continued study at the Cary Institute sites revealed the existence of other equally important players. Extensive monitoring of acorns, small mammals, ticks, and spirochetes from the early 1990s to the present demonstrated that interannual variation in Lyme disease risk is not highly predictable based on the dynamics of any one host species, but is predictable from knowledge of the dynamics of the broader community of small mammals. Using maximum likelihood statistics and model comparison approaches, my colleagues and I found that the abundances of chipmunks and white-footed mice were equally important (and largely additive) in determining subsequent abundance of nymphal ticks. The infection prevalence of those nymphal ticks was influenced most strongly by acorn production two years earlier.

Although abundance and space used by deer affected local abundance of larval ticks the following summer, deer had essentially no influence on subsequent abundance of nymphs at our study sites. It appears that the abundance of larval ticks has a much weaker effect on subsequent nymphal abundance than does the availability of high-quality hosts for larval ticks (Ostfeld et al. 2006). Mice and chipmunks tend to fluctuate synchronously because both depend on acorn production for overwinter survival and reproduction. So, acorns are connected to Lyme disease risk through multiple pathways.

Demonstrating that acorns affect risk of human exposure to Lyme disease is only part of the puzzle. Whether variable risk, as measured by tick abundance and infection prevalence, results in parallel changes in numbers of reported cases of Lyme disease has seldom been addressed. To determine whether variable abundance of rodents or acorns has a direct public health impact, Eric Schauber, Andrew Evans, and I asked whether acorn density at the Cary Institute predicted per capita incidence of Lyme disease in human populations two summers later. Based on the expectation that acorn production is at least moderately synchronized over large geographic areas, we asked this question of human populations in Dutchess County, New York, where the Cary Institute is located, and also in surrounding states. We found that acorn production on two 2.25-ha plots at the Cary Institute predicts (detrended) incidence of Lyme disease in Dutchess County and the adjacent state of Connecticut (Schauber et al. 2005). Perhaps, not surprisingly, predictive power declined with distance from the Cary Institute.

Although mice and chipmunks play important roles as favorable hosts for ticks and competent reservoirs for the Lyme spirochete, many other mammals and birds also serve as hosts for ticks and could be involved in determining Lyme disease risk in humans. Recently, Dustin Brisson and I have found that two species of shrews (*Blarina brevicauda* and *Sorex cinereus*) together feed more larval ticks than do mice and chipmunks combined (Brisson et al. 2008). Even though the shrews are somewhat poorer reservoirs for the spirochete than are mice or chipmunks, the huge number of larval ticks they feed results in shrews being responsible for infecting about half of all the infected nymphs in the forest. Although it is difficult to monitor population dynamics of some shrews due to poor capture probabilities in standard live-traps, these shrews apparently do not fluctuate synchronously with mice and chipmunks. Whether the shrews and small rodents interact in other ways, for instance, via shared predators, is unknown.

## It's Biodiversity

Well over 100 years ago, medical entomologists suggested a connection between species diversity and transmission of vector-borne diseases of humans (reviewed in Service 1991). Researchers argued that malaria transmission might be reduced if alternative hosts for mosquito vectors (e.g., livestock) were placed around areas of human habitation, diverting vector meals away from humans, an idea termed *zooprophylaxis*. Recently, there has been renewed interest in the potential effects of biological diversity on disease risk, in large part because of interest in identifying and evaluating utilitarian functions of biodiversity (Loreau et al. 2001). Given the large number of host species involved in the Lyme disease system, with each host species potentially playing a distinct role as a tick host and pathogen reservoir, we might expect that variation in species diversity would strongly influence Lyme-disease transmission and risk. For instance, a low-diversity community composed largely of white-footed mice and deer might be expected to produce large numbers of infected nymphal ticks, owing to the high quality of mice as hosts for larval ticks and reservoirs for *B. burgdorferi*. In fact, such low-diversity communities exist and appear to be facilitated by human disturbances such as forest fragmentation and degradation. Under these conditions, mammalian and avian predators appear to be reduced or lost and white-footed mice thrive (references in Ostfeld and Keesing 2000). As vertebrate diversity increases, both the numbers of nymphal ticks and their infection prevalence with *B. burgdorferi* might decrease.

This response would be expected if the added species were poorer hosts for larval ticks, were to deflect tick meals away from mice, and/or were poorer reservoirs for *B. burgdorferi*. Evidence supports all of these expectations (LoGiudice et al. 2003; Keesing et al. 2006). We have used two general approaches to test these expectations. In one (LoGiudice et al. 2003; Ostfeld and LoGiudice 2003), we determined for each reasonably common host species the average population density, the average number of larvae fed, and the proportion of larvae that molt into infected nymphs. Together, these values allow us to estimate each species' individual contribution to producing infected nymphs. We then used computer simulation to create realistic "virtual" communities composed of different species compositions and to determine the expected proportion of nymphs that should become infected. We assessed these simulations by sampling natural nymph populations and determining whether observed values for infection prevalence matched those expected from our models. By examining both long-term data from our Cary Institute sites and shorter-term data from nymph populations distributed throughout Dutchess County, we found reasonably strong correlations between the infection prevalences predicted by our models and those observed in nature (LoGiudice et al. 2008).

Another important observation was that the roles played by individual species change with the ecological context. For example, adding shrews to a community consisting of only deer and mice resulted in a reduction of tick infection prevalence, but adding shrews to a community with many host species tended to increase tick infection prevalence. Consequently, the order by which species are added to or removed from communities (community assembly or disassembly rules) becomes crucial in determining natural patterns of change in disease risk with changes in host communities.

In the other approach, we compared nymphal tick abundance and infection prevalence in forest fragments that differ in size or in species richness. In both cases, we found that infection prevalence is higher in smaller fragments (Allan et al. 2003) and in fragments with fewer host species (LoGiudice et al. 2008). Results concerning nymphal tick abundance have been mixed. In general, knowledge of the specific identities of the host species provided considerably more predictive power over a simple accounting of the number of species in the host community. Interestingly, this same phenomenon, whereby species composition is a better predictor than species richness alone, has been found in other studies of the ecosystem functions provided by highly diverse communities compared with depauperate ones (e.g., Loreau et al. 2001).

## It's the Ecosystem

Lyme disease is typical of many zoonotic disease systems. The emergence of the disease is followed by hot pursuit of the species (pathogen, reservoir, host) responsible, which allows scientists (largely from health specialties) to produce a sketch of ecological sources of risk. These sketches are typically insufficient at best and inaccurate at worst. Their failings are a direct consequence of a reductionist focus on the minimum number of species that play what are assumed to be the strongest roles in producing a pool of pathogens. More holistic study of these systems tends to reveal that (1) predicting variable disease risk requires knowledge of a larger number of host species; (2) these hosts are embedded with communities and ecosystems in which unrelated processes (e.g., acorn masting or other resource pulses) can have profound effects; (3) individual host species can interact with one another, for example, with hosts "competing" for vectors or pathogens; (4) the aggregate of species that are good hosts/reservoirs and poor hosts/reservoirs can be crucial in determining disease dynamics; and (5) effects of individual host species can be highly context dependent, with even the qualitative effect of a species (increasing or decreasing risk) depending on the composition of the remaining community members.

On the basis of combining both relatively thorough case studies, such as Lyme disease, and basic epidemiological models (Rudolf and Antonovics 2005; Dobson 2004; Keesing et al. 2006), new theory is emerging that will guide the pursuit of general principles that allow the emergence of infectious diseases to be understood and even predicted. An ecosystem approach is an indispensable part of this pursuit.

The ways in which changes in the rates of ecosystem processes, such as nutrient cycling, nitrogen deposition, and primary production, might affect the zoonoses such as Lyme disease are unknown. Nitrogen or carbon dioxide "fertilization" of forest trees might influence the timing or magnitude of acorn masting, with potentially strong effects on Lyme disease risk. Climate warming might also stimulate acorn production and affect tick and host populations, although in ways that are difficult to predict. Warmer winters are likely to reduce winter mortality rates of ticks, and warmer summers might both increase summer mortality rates of ticks and change the seasonal timing of their host-seeking activity in ways that would affect Lyme disease risk.

Effects of winter and summer temperatures, as well as those of both the amount and pattern of precipitation, on tick population dynamics are poorly understood (Harvell et al. 2002). Pursuit of the effects of ecosystem processes and global climate change on zoonotic diseases represents a new research frontier.

New zoonotic diseases continue to emerge at a high rate, and old ones reemerge or invade new areas. An ecosystem approach to understanding the causes of emergence and possible preventive measures would include the following strategic elements. Interdisciplinary teams of researchers who specialize in pathogens, vectors, vertebrate hosts, population dynamics, community interactions, landscape ecology, and sociology of human interactions with ecological systems should be assembled. Research teams should explicitly incorporate spatial patterns and processes affecting disease, from the local scale of pathogen transmission events from one vector or host to another, to the important landscape features (e.g., edges, fragmentation, patch and matrix composition) influencing population dynamics of hosts and vectors, to regional land use and climatic characteristics that affect entire assemblages and vital rates.

Temporal dynamics, from the effects of seasonal phenology of vector-pathogen-host interactions to multiannual fluctuations in vector or host populations, must also be considered. The networks of taxa under study need to be expanded to include species other than the pathogen, vector, and primary host. For instance, dilution hosts—those that act as a "sink" for pathogen infections—often play crucial roles in disease dynamics, as do the species that act to regulate populations of important reservoir hosts. Research strategies that include such elements are likely to identify subtle but powerful factors affecting disease dynamics that might be amenable to intervention for the benefit of public health.

# References

Allan, B.F., Keesing, F., Ostfeld, R.S., 2003. Effects of habitat fragmentation on Lyme disease risk. Conservat. Biol. 17, 267–272.

Anderson, J.F., Johnson, R.C., Magnarelli, L.A., Hyde, F.W., Myers, J.E., 1987. Prevalence of *Borrelia burgdorferi* and *Babesia microti* on islands inhabited by white-tailed deer. Appl. Exp. Microbiol. 53, 892–894.

Benach, J.L., Bosler, E.M., Hanrahan, J.P., Coleman, J.L., Habicht, G.S., Bast, T.F., et al., 1983. Spirochetes isolated from the blood of two patients with Lyme disease. New Engl. J. Med. 308, 740–742.

Brisson, D., Dykhuizen, D.E., Ostfeld, R.S., 2008. Conspicuous impacts of inconspicuous hosts on the human lyme disease epidemic. Proceedings of the Royal Society of London, Series B, Biological Sciences 275, 227—235.

Burgdorfer, W., Barbour, A.G., Hayes, S.F., Benach, J.L., Grunwaldt, E., Davis, J.P., 1982. Lyme disease—A tick-borne spirochetosis? Science 216, 1317–1319.

Dobson, A.P., 2004. Population dynamics of pathogens with multiple host species. Am. Nat. 164, S64–S78.

Donahue, J.G., Piesman, J., Spielman, A., 1987. Reservoir competence of white-footed mice for Lyme disease spirochetes. Am. J. Trop. Med. Hyg. 36, 92–96.

Harvell, C.D., Mitchell, C.E., Ward, J.R., Altizer, S., Dobson, A., Ostfeld, R.S., et al., 2002. Climate warming and disease risks for terrestrial and marine biota. Science 296, 2158–2162.

Johnson, R.C., Schmid, G.P., Hyde, F.W., Steigerwaldt, A.G., Brenner, D.J., 1984. *Borrelia burgdorferi* sp.nov.: Etiological agent of Lyme disease. Int. J. Syst. Bacteriol. 34, 496–497.

Keesing, F., Holt, R.D., Ostfeld, R.S., 2006. Effects of species diversity on disease risk. Ecol. Lett. 9, 485–498.

Lidicker Jr., W.Z., 1978. Solving the enigma of microtine cycles. J. Mammal. 69, 225–235.

LoGiudice, K., Duerr, S., Newhouse, M., Schmidt, K., Killilea, M., Ostfeld, R.S., 2008. Impact of community composition on Lyme disease risk. Ecology 89, 2841—2849.

LoGiudice, K., Ostfeld, R.S., Schmidt, K.A., Keesing, F., 2003. The ecology of infectious disease: Effects of host diversity and community composition on Lyme disease risk. Proc. Natl. Acad. Sci., USA 100, 567–571.

Loreau, M., Naeem, S., Inchausti, P., Bengtsson, J., Grime, J.P., Hector, A., et al., 2001. Biodiversity and ecosystem functioning: Current knowledge and future challenges. Science 294, 804–808.

Mather, T.N., Wilson, M.L., Moore, S.I., Ribeiro, J.M.C., Spielman, A., 1989. Comparing the relative potential of rodents as reservoirs of the Lyme disease spirochete (*Borrelia burgdorferi*). Am. J. Epidemiol. 130, 143–150.

McShea, W.J., Schwede, G., 1993. Variable acorn crops, and the response of white-tailed deer and other mast consumers. J. Mammal. 74, 999–1006.

Norris, D.E., Klompen, J.S.H., Keirans, J.E., Black IV, W.C., 1996. Population genetics of *Ixodes scapularis* (Acari: Ixodidae) based on mitochondrial 16S and 12S genes. J. Med. Entomol. 33, 78–89.

Oliver Jr., J.H., Owsley, M.R., Hutcheson, H.J., James, A.M., Chen, C., Irby, W.S., et al., 1993. Conspecificity of the ticks *Ixodes scapularis* and *I. dammini* (Acari: Ixodidae). J. Med. Entomol. 30, 54–63.

Ostfeld, R.S., 1997. The ecology of Lyme-disease risk. Am. Sci. 85, 338–346.

Ostfeld, R.S., Canham, C.D., Oggenfuss, K., Winchcombe, R.J., Keesing, F., 2006. Climate, deer, rodents, and acorns as determinants of variation in Lyme-disease risk. PLoS Biol. 4, 1058–1068.

Ostfeld, R.S., Jones, C.G., Wolff, J.O., 1996. Of mice and mast: Ecological connections in eastern deciduous forests. BioScience 46, 323–330.

Ostfeld, R.S., Keesing, F., 2000. The function of biodiversity in the ecology of vector-borne zoonotic diseases. Can. J. Zool. 78, 2061–2078.

Ostfeld, R.S., LoGiudice, K., 2003. Community disassembly, biodiversity loss, and the erosion of an ecosystem service. Ecology 84, 1421–1427.

Perkins, S.E., Cattadori, I.M., Tagliapietra, V., Rizzoli, A.P., Hudson, P.J., 2006. Localized deer absence leads to tick amplification. Ecology 87, 1981–1986.

Piesman, J., Spielman, A., Etkind, P., Ruebush, T.K., Juranek, D.D., 1979. Role of deer in the epizootiology of *Babesia microti* in Massachusetts, USA. J. Med. Entomol. 15, 537–540.

Rudolf, V.H., Antonovics, J., 2005. Species coexistence and pathogens with frequency-dependent transmission. Am. Nat. 166, 112–118.

Schauber, E.M., Ostfeld, R.S., Evans, A., 2005. What is the best predictor of annual Lyme disease incidence: Weather, mice, or acorns? Ecol. Appl. 15, 575–586.

Service, M.W., 1991. Agricultural development and arthropod-borne diseases: A review. Revista de Saude Pública 25, 167–178.

Spielman, A., Clifford, C.M., Piesman, J., Corwin, M.D., 1979. Human babesiosis on Nantucket Island: Description of the vector *Ixodes (Ixodes) dammini*, n. sp. (Acarina: Ixodidae). J. Med. Entomol. 15, 218–234.

Spielman, A., Wilson, M.L., Levine, J.F., Piesman, J., 1985. Ecology of *Ixodes* dammini-borne human babesiosis and Lyme disease. Ann. Rev. Entomol. 30, 439—460.

Stanek, G., Strle, F., Gray, J., Wormser, G.P., 2002. History and characteristics of Lyme borreliosis. In: Gray, J.S., Kahl, O., Lane, R.S., Stanek, G. (Eds.), Lyme *borreliosis*: Biology, epidemiology and control. CABI Publishing, Oxon, UK, pp. 1–28.

Steere, A.C., Malawista, S.E., 1979. Cases of Lyme disease in the United States: Locations correlated with distribution of *Ixodes dammini*. Ann. Intern. Med. 91, 730–733.

Wesson, D.M., McLain, D.K., Oliver, J.H., Piesman, J., Collins, F.C., 1993. Investigation of the validity of species status of *Ixodes dammini* (Acari: Ixodidae) using rDNA. Proc. Natl. Acad. Sci., USA 90, 10221–10225.

Wilson, M.L., Adler, G.H., Spielman, A., 1985. Correlation between deer abundance and that of the deer tick *Ixodes dammini* (Acari: Ixodidae). Ann. Entomol. Soc. Am. 78, 172–176.

V. CASE STUDIES

# Understanding Ecosystem Effects of Dams

*Emily H. Stanley*

**University of Wisconsin, Madison**

As with most environmental problems, understanding the effects of dams on rivers, and how to manage these structures as they age, is a multifaceted challenge that moves well beyond the traditional bounds of ecological research. My involvement with this problem began with a strictly academic curiosity about how rivers and streams work. In particular, I have had a long-standing interest in how nutrients are transported and transformed as they move downstream, and saw dam removal as an opportunity to gain some new insights into this question. But this path led me into far broader environmental issues that included the practical challenges of dealing with dams that are getting old and literally falling apart, environmental policy debates, and the reactions of individuals and communities faced with the prospect of removing a dam from a river. In the end, the complexities of dam removal provided me with a remarkable experience that updated my personal definition of ecosystem science.

When I arrived in Wisconsin in 1998, I learned about a plan to remove a series of dams from the Baraboo River, a mid-sized river that travels through farmlands and a series of small towns and cities before flowing into the Wisconsin River. One dam had recently been removed, and the remaining three structures were to be taken out over the next three to five years. At the time, my research interests were being influenced by the nutrient spiraling concept (Webster and Patten 1979; Newbold et al. 1981; Box 5.2), which was the focus of enormous research in stream ecology at the time (e.g., LINX), as well as my graduate work in Sycamore Creek, Arizona. As a desert stream, ecological dynamics of Sycamore Creek are strongly affected by disturbances in the form of flash floods and drying (and later, we were to learn, also by the presence of cattle; see Fisher et al. 1982; Stanley et al. 1997; Heffernan 2008). As a recent arrival at University of Wisconsin and an "academic grandchild" of Gene Likens, I also had a strong appreciation for the power of whole-ecosystem experiments.

**253**

Forest cutting at Hubbard Brook and food web manipulations in Peter, Paul, and Tuesday Lakes were potent examples of simple but large-scale manipulations used to examine and develop core concepts in ecosystem science (nutrient cycling and the small watershed concept in the first case, the trophic cascade in the latter). These various influences came together in thinking about dam removal. I realized I could use the removal as a whole-ecosystem experiment to study disturbance and nutrient spiraling. My plan was to test the nutrient retention hypothesis of Vitousek and Reiners (1975)—that nutrient retention increased, then decreased over time following disturbance in forests as a function of changes in net biomass increment. This model had been successfully tested in Sycamore Creek by Nancy Grimm (1987), and I wondered if it would be a robust model that could fit a vastly different sort of disturbance.

This is where I started—all business about ecosystem concepts and experiments. But this single motivation did not stand alone for long. I quickly learned that rather than being a simple, elegant manipulation in a protected research setting, removing a dam was a complicated, emotional, and very public process. It became apparent that there was a real problem at hand—what to do with these old dams that were falling apart. The repair-or-remove decision needed to be informed by some knowledge of what happens following a removal, and that information simply was not available. I started getting phone calls from managers, advocacy groups, and concerned citizens asking me about the best course of action and what to expect if a dam was removed. It is probably not surprising to report that callers were not terribly interested in nutrient spiraling. They had much more practical questions about how the plants and animals in and around the river would be affected, and what the river would look like after the dam was extracted (Figure 14.1). At the same time, an adventurous graduate student from Purdue, Martin Doyle, who was also interested in dam removal as a whole-ecosystem experiment (in his case, for testing geomorphic concepts), called and asked if he could collaborate with me on planned removals in Wisconsin.

The collaboration between fluvial geomorphology and ecosystem science was, frankly, extremely fortuitous. The contribution of both perspectives was essential to the success of our research. Studying dam removal from a strictly ecological perspective would have provided an incomplete story, missing perhaps the most critical element: the fate of the sediments trapped in the reservoir and the changes in channel form above and below the dam. We learned that how the sediments moved not only determined the appearance of the river, it also shaped a wide range of ecological patterns playing out in the weeks and years after the removal. And over the long term, biotic (in particular, plant establishment and growth) and geomorphic processes are inextricably linked (Doyle et al. 2003a) and mutually influential. Studying only the physical changes following dam removal would have meant that many of the broader ecological changes of interest to managers and stakeholders would have been missed, and conversely, focusing purely on biological variables would have severely limited our ability to understand why the changes we observed were occurring.

While it is reasonable to say that my practice and perspective of ecosystem science matured substantially through this research to include interactions with other disciplines and attention to questions driven by practical needs, the basic strategy of using dam removals as whole-ecosystem experiments proved to be successful. This management

FIGURE 14.1  Changes in the reservoir of Koshkonong Creek before (a) and 24 hours (b), 2 months (c), and 8 months (d) after removal of the low-head dam. *(Modified from Doyle et al. 2003b.)*

action provided us with the planned (and later, by studying more removals, replicated) opportunity to examine changes in nutrient retention, as well as channel form following the removal disturbance. But instead of focusing on the Vitousek and Reiners hypothesis, we developed and tested a new model that emphasized how changing geomorphic form and process alters nutrient retention (Figure 14.2; Stanley and Doyle 2002; Doyle et al. 2003b; Orr et al. 2006). The geomorphology-nutrient retention relationship was massively amplified in the extreme case of dam removal, but we are learning that it also applies to less extreme cases, and can help explain differences in nutrient dynamics across different sites (e.g., see Lewis et al. 2006; Kaushal et al. 2008). No doubt there are any number of other similar whole-ecosystem "experiments" that are now under way that could provide basic ecological insights as well as practical information about ecosystem management.

Another concept from ecosystem science also provided us with important and unexpected inspiration for our dam removal research. One of the earliest lessons I had learned about studying ecosystems was the simple importance of looking at the big picture and figuring out what is and is not important. For example, in constructing nutrient budgets, we

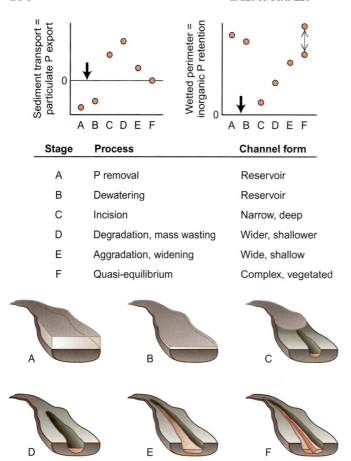

| Stage | Process | Channel form |
|-------|---------|--------------|
| A | P removal | Reservoir |
| B | Dewatering | Reservoir |
| C | Incision | Narrow, deep |
| D | Degradation, mass wasting | Wider, shallower |
| E | Aggradation, widening | Wide, shallow |
| F | Quasi-equilibrium | Complex, vegetated |

**FIGURE 14.2** Conceptual model of the stages of geomorphic adjustments in channel form within a reservoir following dam removal (left). Stages of channel adjustment are associated with predictable changes in sediment erosion and deposition (export) and cross-sectional channel form (wetted width; right). In turn, we hypothesized that these physical changes in process and form should dictate phosphorus retention or transport as water flows through the reservoir reach. Particulate phosphorus export should be tightly tied to sediment export, and the degree of sediment–water contact should affect dissolved inorganic phosphorus removal from the water column; i.e. phosphorus retention. (*Modified from Doyle et al. 2003b and Stanley and Doyle 2002.*)

can safely ignore some pools and fluxes if they are small without losing track of the larger picture of the budget. Put more generally, stepping back to look at the big picture leads us to ask the general question, how important is the process or phenomenon being studied? When we began our work, there was already a rich literature on the effects of dams on rivers, but the vast majority of these studies dealt with great huge dams, such as those that populate virtually all the rivers in the western United States. Yet dams in the more topographically challenged Midwest tend to be small structures, and these lesser dams and their reservoirs have attracted little attention from aquatic researchers. This led me to begin to try to figure out just how many dams there were in Wisconsin, where they were, how big they were, and whether dam removal was affecting the population of dams in the state.

One of the first things I learned in answering this question was that the abundance of what I now think of as "little dinky dams"—that is, small structures in small and midsized rivers—vastly outnumber the larger, grossly conspicuous structures that reach their extreme types in Hoover, Aswan, and Three Gorges dams. While there is no discounting of the immense consequences of these massive dams and their role in fundamentally altering large rivers, the ubiquity of these smaller dams suggests an equally large impact on running waters that we are only just now beginning to quantify. Put another way, this accounting of the dams in Wisconsin waterways emphasized how effective human engineering has been at reconfiguring flowing water systems, and how we as ecologists are still coming to terms with the actual structure of streams and rivers—not necessarily a linear feature in the landscape, but an interrupted series of channels and pools connected together to form complex networks that change shape over time. Doyle et al. (2008) took this analysis a step further to demonstrate that the amount of infrastructure across the United States, including dams and railroads, has grown rapidly since World War II, and is now aging; these structures are increasingly in need of repair or removal. The intersection of aging and environmental degradation may present an opportunity to kill two birds with one stone—that is, strategic removal of aging infrastructure may provide an excellent opportunity for ecosystem restoration (Doyle et al. 2008).

I think much of our success in studying dam removal, and providing some useful information to managers and stakeholders faced with the decision to keep or remove a dam, reflects the openness of ecosystem science to include anything, and the practical lesson that ecosystems are often best studied by collaborations of researchers from different disciplines. Finally, despite the fact that our research was strongly influenced by the need for practical answers to a pressing management problem, drawing on basic ecosystem concepts and blending physical and ecological perspectives provided the foundation for our best successes.

# References

Doyle, M.W., Selle, A.R., Stofleth, J.M., Stanley, E.H., Harbor, J.M., 2003a. Predicting the depth of erosion following dam removal using a bank stability model. Int. J. Sediment Res. 18, 128–134.

Doyle, M.W., Stanley, E.H., Harbor, J.M., 2003b. Hydrogeomorphic controls on phosphorus retention in streams. Water Resour. Res. 39, 1147. doi: 10.1029/2003WR002038.

Doyle, M.W., Stanley, E.H., Havlick, D., Kaiser, M.J., Steinbach, G., Graf, W., et al., 2008. Aging infrastructure and ecosystem restoration. Science 319, 286–287.

Fisher, S.G., Gray, L.J., Grimm, N.B., Busch, D.E., 1982. Temporal succession in a desert stream ecosystem following flash flooding. Ecol. Monogr. 52, 93–110.

Grimm, N.B., 1987. Nitrogen dynamics during succession in a desert stream. Ecology 68, 1157–1170.

Heffernan, J.B., 2008. Wetlands as alternative stable state in a desert stream. Ecology 88, 1261–1271.

Kaushal, S.S., Groffman, P.M., Mayer, P.M., Striz, E., Gold, A.J., 2008. Effects of stream restoration on dentrification in an urbanizing watershed. Ecol. Appls. 18, 789–804.

Lewis, D.B., Schade, J.D., Huth, A.K., Grimm, N.B., 2006. The spatial structure of variability in a semi-arid, fluvial ecosystem. Ecosystems 9, 386–397.

Newbold, J.D., Elwood, J.W., O'Neill, R.V., Van Winkle, W., 1981. Measuring nutrient spiraling in streams. Can. J. Fish. Aquat. Sci. 38, 860–863.

Orr, C.H., Rogers, K.L., Stanley, E.H., 2006. Channel morphology and P uptake following removal of a small dam. J. N. Am. Bentholog. Soc. 25, 556–568.

Stanley, E.H., Fisher, S.G., Grimm, N.B., 1997. Ecosystem expansion and contraction in streams. BioScience 47, 427–435.

Stanley, E.H., Doyle, M.W., 2002. A geomorphic perspective on nutrient retention following dam removal. BioScience 52, 693–701.

Vitousek, P.M., Reiners, W.A., 1975. Ecosystem succession and nutrient retention: A hypothesis. BioScience 25, 376–381.

Webster, J.R., Patten, B.C., 1979. Effects of watershed perturbation on stream potassium and calcium dynamics. Ecol. Monogr. 49, 51–72.

# 15

# Acid Rain

*Gene E. Likens*

**Cary Institute of Ecosystem Studies, Millbrook, New York**

I knew that the rain in the White Mountains of New Hampshire was acidic from the very first sample my colleague, Noye Johnson and I collected during the summer of 1963 at our research site at the Hubbard Brook Experimental Forest (HBEF). This rain sample had a pH of 3.7! But, I didn't know why the rain was so acidic—greater than 40 times more acidic than we thought it should have been (distilled water in equilibrium with $CO_2$ in the atmosphere would have a pH of 5.6)—or whether this finding was some unusual feature of the White Mountains, or whether it was unusual for the eastern United States. The samples of precipitation (rain and snow) that we continued to collect throughout the year for the next several decades as part of our larger research program on watershed ecosystems were similarly acidic. (The most acidic value we have measured for a rain storm at HBEF was pH 2.85).

This simple research finding formed the basis for a major conundrum that would have significant ramifications for ecosystem science and national policy related to air pollution. Setting out to measure the acidity of precipitation was not an original goal of my research, but was a serendipitous discovery emanating from a more comprehensive ecological and biogeochemical study of a forest landscape, which focused on quantifying all inputs and outputs to watershed ecosystems of the HBEF (Bormann and Likens 1967). Many important findings in science are the result of serendipity, which requires keeping your eyes, ears, and mind open to unusual events and then jumping quickly to find out what they mean.

It wasn't until I changed jobs in 1969, moving from a faculty position at Dartmouth College to one at Cornell University, and set up stations to collect precipitation around the Finger Lakes in New York state, that I discovered that the rainwater in New York had about the same acidity and chemistry as it did in New Hampshire (Likens 1989). This similarity was our first clue that acid precipitation might be a regional problem. There essentially were no other similar data for comparison. A serendipitous meeting and conversation with Svante Odén in Sweden during October 1969 greatly intrigued me and enriched my understanding of the potential for regional air pollution to affect precipitation chemistry (Likens 1989). Odén had begun investigations of how emissions of $SO_2$, from more urbanized and industrialized regions of Europe, were acidifying precipitation in Sweden. Sulfur dioxide, along with nitrogen oxides ($NO_X$), are major precursors for the strong acids, $H_2SO_4$ and $HNO_3$, found in anthropogenically-acidified precipitation. Both $SO_2$ and $NO_X$ emissions result from the combustion of fossil fuels, primarily coal and oil.

We published the first paper on acid rain in North America in 1972, entitling it "Acid Rain" after much thought and deliberation about the title and its potential impact (Likens et al. 1972). We didn't know at that time that R. A. Smith had referred to the acidity of rain around London some 100 years previously. We then published two papers in 1974 about the regional nature of acid rain, including one in *Science*, which was picked up by *The New York Times* for a front-page story. That visibility helped bring this environmental issue to be known around the world and helped to focus much of my subsequent research onto acid rain. This research has been sustained at the HBEF for more than four decades.

Initially, we considered acid rain to be the acidification of rain and snow from pollutant sources of $SO_2$, which acidified lakes and streams and killed fish and other aquatic organisms. It is now known that this serious environmental problem is much more complicated (Figure 15.1) and widespread, affecting ecosystems around the world. Acid rain has become a common and popular term for the mix of anthropogenically-acidified rain, snow, sleet, hail, fog, and cloud water, and the dry deposition of acidifying gases and particles. This definition makes clear that acid rain is more than just rain! Also, the increasing role of $NO_X$ emissions in contributing to nitric acid in precipitation has been growing in ecological importance. Indeed, recent data show that nitric acid could become the dominant acid in precipitation in eastern North America within the next 10 years or so.

As the problem of acid rain unfolded from those early days in the 1960s and 1970s, there were several simple, but fundamental, questions that needed to be answered, such as "What is the pH of unpolluted rain?" and "How long has rain been anthropogenically acidified?" Rain and snow are not distilled water; they contain a variety of dissolved and particulate substances. So, how do these impurities affect the pH?

To answer these questions, colleagues and I went to some of the most remote places on the planet to collect and analyze samples of rainfall to estimate what its chemistry might have been prior to the Industrial Revolution. Sites included Poker Flat, Alaska; Torres del Paine, Chile; Katherine, Australia; Amsterdam Island in the South Pacific Ocean; Cape Point at the southern tip of Africa; and interior China (Galloway et al. 1982; Likens et al. 1987). This research showed that unpolluted rain collected in these areas, remote from human activity, had a pH derived from mineral acids of about 5.1 (Likens et al. 1987).

In North America, using the few historical data that existed we deduced that acid rain, as a phenomenon, actually began in the mid-1950s (Cogbill and Likens 1974; Butler et al. 1984; Cogbill et al. 1984; Likens and Butler 1981). Certainly, anthropogenic emissions of $SO_2$ and $NO_X$ began to increase markedly with the Industrial Revolution, but apparently the inherent acid-neutralizing capacity of the atmosphere (dust particles, etc.) prevented any major change in the acidity of precipitation until the mid-1950s or so. Because of decreasing emissions of acid precursors, particularly $SO_2$, as a result of federal and state legislation designed to reduce emissions, the acidity of precipitation is now decreasing in eastern North America. Our long-term studies at the HBEF show this decrease, yet precipitation is still about two times more acid than it would be if the atmosphere were not

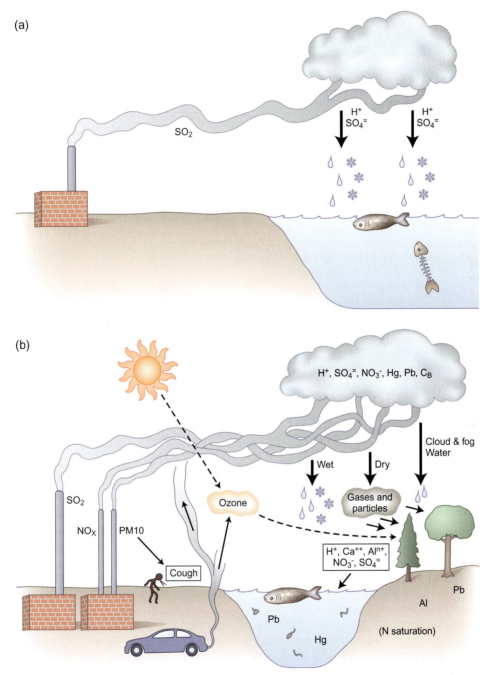

**FIGURE 15.1** Ecosystem response to acid rain. (a). The "simple" view of the early 1960s to early 1970s. (b). The increasingly complex view currently. (*From Likens 2001.*)

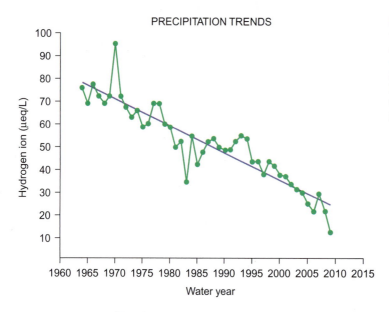

PRECIPITATION TRENDS

**FIGURE 15.2** Annual, volume-weighted hydrogen-ion concentration in bulk precipitation at the Hubbard Brook Experimental Forest, NH. The line represents a linear regression at $p < 0.05$. *(Updated from Likens 2006.)*

polluted (Figure 15.2). Studies of ice cores from glaciers in Greenland and elsewhere and paleoecological analyses of lake sediments have also shown these historical changes in precipitation chemistry.

In the early 1980s we began to study cloud- and fog-water chemistry, and found that it could be especially polluted, even more so than rain at a specific site, and that acidic fog events could be regional in extent (Weathers et al. 1988). One fog event collected near Bar Harbor, ME, was black in color and had a pH of 2.42 (Weathers et al. 1988).

In addition to increasing emissions of $SO_2$ and $NO_X$ with growing industrialization after World War II, another major factor affecting the regional pollution of the atmosphere and of precipitation was that during the 1950s the heights of chimneys and smokestacks increased dramatically (Likens 1984, 1991) carrying pollutants higher into the atmosphere, thereby reducing local pollution at ground level, but enhancing the potential for long-distance transport of pollutants in the atmosphere, affecting regions distant from the pollutant source. Indeed, $SO_2$ and $NO_X$ can be transported in the atmosphere for thousands of kilometers, allowing acid rain to cross political boundaries and impact ecosystems far downwind from where these acid precursors are generated and emitted. This transfer of pollutants through the atmosphere became highly charged politically, and ultimately led to regulations controlling emissions in the United States (1990 Clean Air Act Amendments), Canada, and Europe (see Likens 2010).

There are numerous ecological effects of acid rain on natural ecosystems, but they are greatly complicated by diverse abiotic and biotic interactions and ecosystem impacts (e.g., Driscoll et al. 2001). For example, acid rain can mobilize aluminum from the soil. When aluminum is bound in minerals of the soil, it is harmless to biota, but in the dissolved form it can be very toxic. Likewise, acid rain can leach calcium and magnesium from the soil, thereby reducing the buffering capacity of the soil (Likens et al. 1996, 1998; Likens

2010). Moreover, the acidification of surface waters can stress, or even kill, individual organisms such as mayflies, which may be sensitive to low pH. The acidification also can impact food webs by selective impact on different levels of the food chain, for example, on sensitive cladoceran zooplankton in lakes (e.g., Confer et al. 1983; Schindler et al. 1985).

Our long-term studies of forest, lake, and stream ecosystems during the past four decades have revealed findings about this complexity that are important to the understanding and management of acid rain as a major environmental problem:

- Changes in emissions of sulfur dioxide, $SO_2$, as a result of federal and state legislation, are strongly correlated with changes in sulfate concentrations in precipitation and in stream water at HBEF (Likens et al. 2002, 2005).
- Eighteen years of continuous study was required to verify that the acidity of precipitation had decreased significantly at HBEF (Figure 15.2). The volume-weighted, average, annual pH of precipitation has increased from about 4.1 in the mid-1960s to about 4.9 today (Figure 15.2).
- Nitric acid is increasing in importance in precipitation at HBEF and is predicted to be the dominant acid in precipitation in the near future without further changes in the controls on emissions of both $SO_2$ and $NO_X$.
- Calcium and other plant nutrients have been markedly depleted in the soils of the HBEF as a result of leaching by inputs of acid rain (Likens et al. 1996, 1998; Likens 2010).
  - As much as one-half of the pool of exchangeable calcium in the soil of the HBEF has been depleted during the past 50 years by acid rain (Likens et al. 1998).
  - As a result of losses in soil buffering, the forest ecosystem is currently much more sensitive to acid rain inputs than previously predicted (Likens et al. 1996, 1998; Likens 2010).

So, how did the ecosystem approach help to understand and manage the problem of acid rain? Understanding the sources and diverse effects of acid rain required me and other scientists to consider the quantitative flux of chemicals across ecosystem boundaries, as well as to evaluate the complicated exchanges and interactions among air, land, and water (e.g., meteorological analysis of air-mass trajectories from source to deposition, reactions in the atmosphere that made the pH less than 5.6, biogeochemical interactions in the watershed that led to accelerated weathering, and leaching of calcium from the soil and the dissolution of aluminum minerals). The expertise of biologists, geologists, hydrologists, meteorologists, chemists, foresters, limnologists, and humans (including their social institutions) was and is intricately entwined in understanding and managing the effects of acid rain on natural ecosystems and human-made structures; this problem is not just about chemistry! Understanding and managing acid rain requires careful consideration of boundaries. The low pH of precipitation in the White Mountains was not a unique consequence of local conditions, nor could it be solved solely by local action. Boundaries for airsheds, watersheds, lakes, and streams needed to be determined and evaluated, and political boundaries, although not recognized by pollutants moving in the atmosphere or water, were important to the political solutions.

Unfortunately, in spite of legislative controls and progress made in reducing emissions of $SO_2$ and $NO_X$, the acid rain problem persists in the White Mountains and in many other locations throughout the world (Rodhe et al. 2002; Likens et al. 2012). Because of the relentless impact of acid rain on sensitive forest soils, this environmental problem arguably is "worse" than it was in 1990. The varied questions about this complex environmental issue continue to intrigue, entice, and challenge me, so my long-term research on its causes and ecological effects continue.

# References

Bormann, F.H., Likens, G.E., 1967. Nutrient cycling. Science 155, 424–429.

Butler, T.J., Cogbill, C.V., Likens, G.E., 1984. Effect of climatology on precipitation chemistry. Bull. Amer. Meteorol. Soc. 65, 639–640.

Cogbill, C.V., Likens, G.E., 1974. Acid precipitation in the northeastern United States. Water Resour. Res. 10, 1133–1137.

Cogbill, C.V., Likens, G.E., Butler, T.J., 1984. Uncertainties in historical aspects of acid precipitation: Getting it straight. Atmos. Environ. 18, 2261–2270.

Confer, J.L., Kaaret, T., Likens, G.E., 1983. Zooplankton diversity and biomass in recently acidified lakes. Can. J. Fish. Aquat. Sci. 40, 36–42.

Driscoll, C.T., Lawrence, G.B., Bulger, A.J., Butler, T.J., Cronan, C.S., Eagar, C., et al., 2001. Acidic deposition in the northeastern United States: Sources and inputs, ecosystem effects, and management strategies. BioScience 51, 180–198.

Galloway, J.N., Likens, G.E., Keene, W.C., Miller, J.M., 1982. The composition of precipitation in remote areas of the world. J. Geophys. Res. 87, 8771–8786.

Likens, G.E., 1984. Acid rain: The smokestack is the "smoking gun." Garden 8 (4), 12–18.

Likens, G.E., 1989. Some aspects of air pollution on terrestrial ecosystems and prospects for the future. Ambio 18, 172–178.

Likens, G.E., 1991. Toxic winds: Whose responsibility? In: Bormann, F.H., Kellert, S.R. (Eds.), Ecology, economics, ethics: The broken circle. Yale University Press, New Haven, CT, pp. 136–152.

Likens, G.E., 2001. Ecosystems: Energetics and biogeochemistry. In: Kress, W.J., Barrett, G. (Eds.), A new century of biology. Smithsonian Institution Press, Washington, DC, and London, pp. 53–88.

Likens, G.E., 2007. Surprises from long-term studies at the Hubbard Brook Experimental Forest, USA. A better future for the planet earth, Vol. III—Commemorative book for Blue Planet prize winners. Asahi Glass Foundation, Tokyo, Japan, pp. 78–95.

Likens, G.E., 2010. The role of science in decision making: Does evidence-based science drive environmental policy? Front. Ecol. Environ. 8, e1–e8. doi: 10.1890/090132.

Likens, G.E., Bormann, F.H., Johnson, N.M., 1972. Acid rain. Environment 14, 33–40.

Likens, G.E., Butler, T.J., 1981. Recent acidification of precipitation in North America. Atmos. Environ. 15, 1103–1109.

Likens, G.E., Keene, W.C., Miller, J.M., Galloway, J.N., 1987. Chemistry of precipitation from a remote, terrestrial site in Australia. J. Geophys. Res. 92, 13,299–13,314.

Likens, G.E., Driscoll, C.T., Buso, D.C., 1996. Long-term effects of acid rain: Response and recovery of a forest ecosystem. Science 272, 244–246.

Likens, G.E., Driscoll, C.T., Buso, D.C., Siccama, T.G., Johnson, C.E., Lovett, G.M., et al., 1998. The biogeochemistry of calcium at Hubbard Brook. Biogeochemistry 41, 89–173.

Likens, G.E., Driscoll, C.T., Buso, D.C., Mitchell, M.J., Lovett, G.M., Bailey, S.W., et al., 2002. The biogeochemistry of sulfur at Hubbard Brook. Biogeochemistry 60, 235–316.

Likens, G.E., Buso, D.C., Butler, T.J., 2005. Long-term relationships between $SO_2$ and $NO_X$ emissions and $SO_4^{2-}$ and $NO_3^-$ concentration in bulk deposition at the Hubbard Brook Experimental Forest, New Hampshire. J. Environ. Monitoring 7, 964–968.

Likens, G.E., Butler, T.J., Rury, M.A., 2012. Acid rain. In: Anheier, H.K., Juergensmeyer, M. (Eds.), Encyclopedia of global studies. Sage Publications, Los Angeles, CA, pp. 17–19.

Rodhe, H., Dentener, F., Schulz, M., 2002. The global distribution of acidifying wet deposition. Environ. Sci. Technol. 36, 4382–4388.

Schindler, D.W., Mills, K.H., Malley, D.F., Finlay, D.D., Shearer, J.A., Davies, I.J., et al., 1985. Long-term ecosystem stress: The effects of years of experimental acidification on a small lake. Science 228, 1395–1401.

Weathers, K.C., Likens, G.E., Bormann, F.H., Bicknell, S.H., Bormann, B.T., Daube Jr., B.C., et al., 1988. Cloudwater chemistry from ten sites in North America. Environ. Sci. Technol. 22, 1018–1026.

# Streams and Their Valleys

*Judy L. Meyer*

**River Basin Center, Odum School of Ecology, University of Georgia, Athens**

A Canadian limnologist, H.B.N. Hynes, delivered a lecture entitled "The Stream and Its Valley" (Hynes 1975) at the first scientific meeting I attended as a graduate student. Using research from the Hubbard Brook Experimental Forest (Fisher and Likens 1973) and elsewhere, Hynes argued in this classic paper that the organisms and ecological processes in a stream reflect the conditions in its catchment: "We may conclude then that in every way the valley rules the stream" (Hynes 1975). I was just beginning my doctoral research on phosphorus dynamics in one of the tributaries of Hubbard Brook (Meyer and Likens 1979), so the talk was relevant to my work, and I listened intently. What I did not realize at the time was that the concepts in that lecture would guide stream ecosystem and my own research for the next three decades. If the concepts had been used to guide management of our water resources, they would be in a better condition today.

> ... within the last few years, there has emerged a growing band of workers who are endeavouring to look at watercourses in a holistic way, rather than as conglomerations of processes, phenomena and taxa. *(Hynes 1975)*

I came to the field of stream ecology from oceanography. The change was inspired not only by my aversion to seasickness, but also because studying streams didn't require large research vessels. My work in oceanography had been on nutrient-limited growth of phytoplankton (e.g., Caperon and Meyer 1972), and oceanography students are required to take classes covering physical, chemical, and biological processes in oceans, so thinking about nutrient dynamics in a stream ecosystem from a more holistic perspective seemed natural. That perspective made me somewhat different from many stream ecologists, who chose to study streams because they enjoy fishing and are fascinated by the organisms found in flowing waters.

Much of the research in freshwater science at that time was concerned with cultural eutrophication, the excess enrichment of water bodies by anthropogenic inputs (e.g., from wastewater treatment plants and agricultural fields). Scientists and engineers studying lake eutrophication tended to view streams as sources of water and nutrients, as "pipes" on the landscape delivering materials to lakes. Using the mass balance approach that had proven so powerful in understanding forested ecosystems (e.g., Likens and Bormann 1995), stream ecologists showed that stream ecosystems could not be treated as pipes; biogeochemical processes in streams (Figure 16.1) transform the nutrients and organic matter entering them, thereby altering the quantity, form, and timing of exports to downstream ecosystems (e.g., Fisher and Likens 1973; Meyer and Likens 1979; Triska et al. 1984).

Despite a general recognition that streams are ecosystems, input—output budgets for watersheds are often interpreted as indicating only the impact of terrestrial ecological processes on nutrient exports. Changes in nutrient export have been evaluated with respect to changes in the terrestrial ecosystem, ignoring the nutrient transformations that occur in the stream (e.g., Vitousek and Reiners 1975; Aber et al. 1998). Yet stream researchers have demonstrated significant removal and transformation of nutrients in streams (e.g., Meyer and Likens 1979; Peterson et al. 2001); failing to recognize those stream processes makes it impossible to accurately identify the mechanisms causing observed patterns in nutrient export.

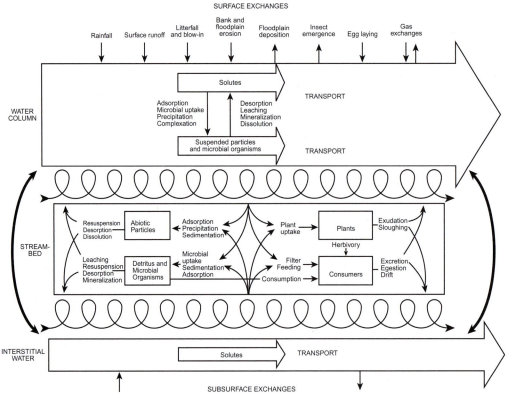

FIGURE 16.1    Conceptual diagram illustrating hydrological and biogeochemical processes that transport and cycle nutrients and organic matter in stream ecosystems. *(From Stream Solute Workshop 1990.)*

V.  CASE STUDIES

The long-term decline in nitrate concentration and export in New England streams illustrates the need to consider both terrestrial and aquatic ecosystems when seeking a mechanistic understanding of observed patterns (Bernhardt et al. 2005). Current models of terrestrial ecosystems (e.g., Aber et al. 2002) cannot explain the marked decline in nitrate concentration and export that has been observed in many New England watersheds (Bernhardt et al. 2005). An analysis of the 40-year record of observations and experiments on nutrient dynamics in streams at the Hubbard Brook Experimental Forest provides a plausible mechanism: Changes in the stream ecosystems have resulted in increased rates of nitrate uptake, benthic storage, and denitrification; and these changes can explain at least 30% of the long-term decline (Bernhardt et al. 2005). Clearly, an ecosystem perspective that extends beyond the boundaries of a single ecosystem is needed to understand the mechanisms leading to declining nitrate export. Although "the valley rules the stream" (Hynes 1975), the stream alters the linkage between the valley and downstream lakes or estuaries.

The publication of the River Continuum Concept (RCC; Vannote et al. 1980) revolutionized stream ecosystem research because it emphasized those up- and downstream linkages (Box 16.1). The RCC manuscript was one of the first I reviewed as a young professor. When I read it, I knew it would change the perspective of stream ecologists, who at the time tended to work at the scale of a single stream reach. The RCC stimulated stream

---

## BOX 16.1

### THREE CONCEPTS THAT ENHANCE UNDERSTANDING OF STREAM ECOSYSTEMS

Try this exercise, which I learned from Stuart Fisher: Take a minute and sketch your concept of a stream ecosystem; do it before reading any further!

When I have used this exercise in classes, students have often drawn a diagram of a reach of a stream, showing inputs and exports and some of the organisms and processes in the ecosystem (much like Figure 16.1). That is what we see when standing on a stream bank. What is missing from this diagram is the recognition that each stream reach is part of a larger network—the many tributaries and channels that comprise a river network. The concept of stream order is used to describe the position of a stream reach in that larger network. A first-order stream is the first channel formed when water comes out of the ground

(identified as solid blue lines on 1:24,000 topographic maps); when two first-order streams converge, a second-order stream is formed. Stream order increases only when two streams of equal order converge.

Stream order influences the physical, chemical, and biological forms and processes occurring in a stream ecosystem, a fundamental idea in the RCC (Vannote et al. 1980; Figure 16.2). Headwater streams (orders 1–3) in forested landscapes are dependent on inputs from the surrounding forest (e.g., leaf litter) and have invertebrate assemblages dominated by benthic species that feed on those inputs and export fine detrital particles downstream. As streams get larger ($\sim$orders 4–6), more light is available to support autochthonous production and the benthic consumers that feed on

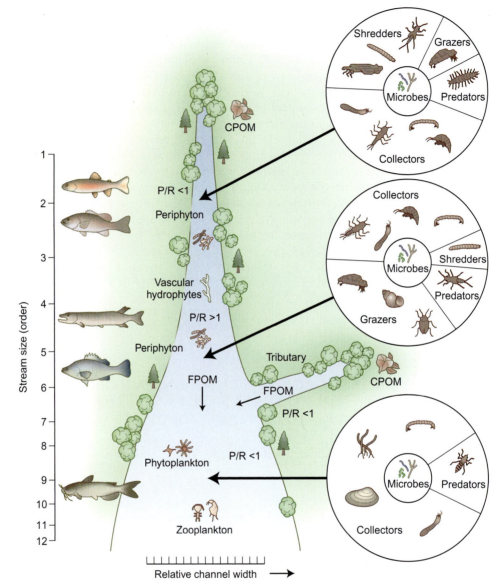

**FIGURE 16.2** Longitudinal changes in organic matter inputs and consumer assemblages postulated in the River Continuum Concept. *(From Allan and Castillo 2007.)*

it as well as filter-feeders that consume the fine particles exported from upstream. Larger and deeper rivers (orders > 7) have less benthic and more water column algal productivity with filter-feeding invertebrate assemblages. The ratio of primary productivity to community respiration ($P/R$) is hypothesized to peak in orders 4 to 6, but nutrients and organic matter transported from upstream are a significant component of the ecosystem in all downstream reaches.

Downstream transport is a characteristic of flowing waters that sets them apart from other ecosystems. The concept of nutrient spiraling incorporates downstream transport into more traditional concepts of nutrient cycling (Newbold et al. 1981). Following a path of an atom of nitrogen serves to illustrate the nutrient spiraling concept: Let's say the nitrogen atom enters the stream as nitrate in ground water and is transported downstream a distance before being taken up by a diatom, which is consumed by a mayfly, which excretes the atom of nitrogen as dissolved organic nitrogen, which is once again transported downstream before being taken up by bacteria on a decomposing leaf. The path just described is a spiral (a cycle plus downstream transport) from water column to benthos back to water column again (as depicted in Figure 16.1). The spiraling length can be measured using tracers (e.g., Newbold et al. 1981) as the average downstream distance traveled by an atom during one spiral from being dissolved in the water, to uptake into an organism in the streambed, to release back into the water. Spiraling length is a measure of the efficiency with which nutrients are utilized in a stream; it is shorter when nutrients are more intensely used.

ecologists to assess not only the influence of the valley on the stream but also the effect of location in the stream network on the structure and function of the ecosystem. That perspective provided direction for a study of a blackwater river that I was developing with my colleagues in Georgia.

The waters of the Ogeechee River are stained with humic acids leached from the floodplain forests that line its meandering path through the Coastal Plain. The tea-colored water reduces light penetration, and primary productivity is relatively low (Meyer and Edwards 1990); yet secondary productivity is very high (e.g., Hauer and Benke 1991). The food web of the Ogeechee River (Figure 16.3) is supported by inputs of bacteria and other organic matter from its floodplain (Meyer 1990; Wainright et al. 1992). Not only are the up- and downstream linkages important, as emphasized in the RCC, but also lateral inputs from floodplains are significant, particularly in larger rivers that have not been isolated from their floodplains by levees or other human actions. Once again, to more fully understand the structure and function of an ecosystem, its context and interactions with surrounding ecosystems must be considered (see chapter 10).

... changes in the valley wrought by man may have large effects. *(Hynes 1975)*

The impacts of forestry practices (e.g., clear-cutting) on stream ecosystems provided an early illustration of the tight linkage between human activities on the land and the structure and function of stream ecosystems (e.g., Likens et al. 1970). Cutting trees increases the amount of water that runs off a watershed, as well as water temperature

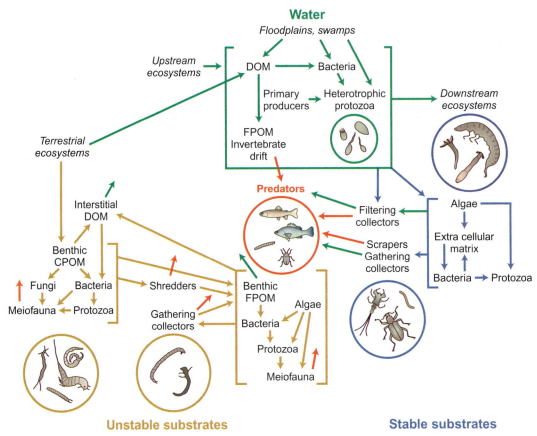

**FIGURE 16.3** Diagram of the food web in the Ogeechee River, a southeastern blackwater river. The food web is a mosaic of webs, each characteristic of a particular habitat type and linked by flowing water. Each habitat is denoted by a different color: water column (green), unstable substrates (mustard yellow), and stable substrates (blue). Brick-colored arrows denote consumption by predators, green arrows indicate movement into the water. *(From Meyer 1990.)*

and inputs of light and nutrients, which alter productivity and food web structure in streams (e.g., Webster et al. 1992). Human actions on the land influence stream ecosystems via many pathways: altered hydrologic and temperature regimes, increased sedimentation, increased nutrient and contaminant inputs, less woody debris, and changes in organic matter inputs (Allan 2004). Understanding the mechanisms by which landscape alteration impacts streams is a difficult task because a change in land use alters many pathways at the same time (e.g., converting a forest to a housing development reduces leaf litter inputs to streams while also increasing sedimentation, nutrient inputs, and light).

To better understand just one of these pathways (reduced inputs of leaf litter), my colleagues and I used an experimental approach in a small headwater stream. We prevented leaf litter from entering the stream by putting a net over it (Fig. 3.6), and observed marked changes in dissolved organic carbon (DOC) exports (Meyer et al. 1998), secondary production of aquatic insects (Wallace et al. 1997), and nutrient dynamics (Webster et al. 2001). Changing just one of those pathways of interaction with the terrestrial ecosystem (leaf litter inputs) had profound impacts on the stream ecosystem. Modern humans are changing many pathways.

Streams in human-dominated landscapes commonly have high concentrations of nutrients, and nutrient export can be directly related to the fraction of the catchment no longer in native vegetation (Allan 2004). Increased input of nutrients (e.g., fertilizers and sewage) is generally considered the primary cause. Yet landscape alteration affects not only nutrient delivery to streams, but also the biogeochemical processes that remove and transform nutrients in streams.

Our understanding of biogeochemical processes in streams has grown considerably over the decades since my doctoral research on phosphorus dynamics. The concept of nutrient spiraling (Box 16.1) represented a considerable advance over the budget approach I used in my earlier research, because spiraling deals explicitly with transport and uptake and eliminates the problem of budget sensitivity to the ecosystem boundaries selected (Fisher et al. 2004). Nutrient spiraling length is the downstream distance traveled by a nutrient molecule (transport) before its removal from the water column (uptake) by biotic uptake or physical sorption; some of the nutrient taken up is later released and transported downstream, resulting in a nutrient spiral rather than the more conventional nutrient cycle (See Box 5.2).

The increased availability of analytical and chemical tools for analysis, such as mass spectrometers and stable isotopes of nitrogen, has enabled stream researchers to explore the impacts of human land use on nutrient spiraling in streams in the Lotic Intersite Nitrogen eXperiment (LINX). I have been fortunate to be a part of this team of several dozen colleagues and students, who have explored nitrogen dynamics in streams in eight biomes, each with catchments in three different land covers: natural vegetation, agriculture, or urban. After demonstrating the effectiveness of small streams in removing ammonium from the water column (Peterson et al. 2001), we showed that nitrate uptake and denitrification rates increased but efficiency of uptake and denitrification decreased with the increasing nitrate concentration associated with agricultural and urban land uses (Mulholland et al. 2008). As excess nitrate enters the stream from human activities, the fraction of nitrate exported downstream increases (Mulholland et al. 2008). Human activities in the valley change both inputs to and biogeochemical pathways in flowing waters.

> We must, in fact, not divorce the stream from its valley in our thoughts at any time. If we do, we lose touch with reality. The real lake is not a basin with two vertical sides as in the textbook. One that is like that, Loch Ness, is so out of line that it harbours monsters. Somewhere, in Australia, there must be a stream with a channel like a gutter, fed by runoff from a landscape paved like a parking lot. There, I predict, will be found the legendary river creature of the aboriginals—the Bunyip. *(Hynes 1975)*

We do not need to go to Australia to find streams like gutters fed by a parking lot. Most college campuses have streams like that (does yours?), although few stream ecologists study them. Engagement with a local watershed group and a personal resolve to study urban streams (Figure 16.4) have added to my conviction that an ecosystem perspective is essential to understand and reduce human impacts on stream ecosystems.

V. CASE STUDIES

Having spent much of my career studying streams in predominantly forested land-scapes where forestry practices were the main human disturbance, I had a great deal to learn about the threats facing streams in more urbanized catchments. Volunteering with a river advocacy group in Atlanta, Georgia (Upper Chattahoochee Riverkeeper) opened my eyes to the ecological conditions in urban streams, the limited scientific understanding of these ecosystems, and shortcomings in current environmental policy and its implementation. Led by several of my graduate students, I began studying conditions in urban streams around Atlanta. A review of urban stream ecosystems (Paul and Meyer 2001) identified the many ways in which humans have altered these ecosystems (Figure 16.5) and the gaping holes in our scientific understanding of them. Many of those holes still

**FIGURE 16.4**  Tanyard Branch, an urban stream on the campus of the University of Georgia, which exhibits many symptoms of the "urban stream syndrome." Its riparian zone has little vegetation, it is choked with fine sediments, it receives storm-water runoff via pipes from the adjacent parking lot, and parts of it are buried in culverts underground. In fact, just downstream of this site, the stream flows through a pipe under the football stadium. Is there a stream under the football stadium on your campus? I've found that to be a fairly common phenomenon on college campuses! *(Photo by J.L. Meyer.)*

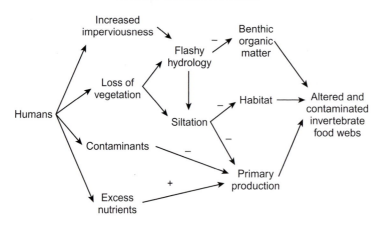

**URBAN STREAM SYNDROME**

**FIGURE 16.5**  A simplified diagram illustrating ways in which the structure and function of urban streams have been impacted by human actions.

remain, although considerably more scientific attention has been paid to urban streams in recent years (e.g., Meyer et al. 2005; Walsh et al. 2005).

Working in urban streams has made me realize the extent to which scientific understanding of stream ecosystems has not been adequately incorporated into environmental policy and enforcement. Nowhere is this more apparent than in society's current treatment of headwater streams. Despite their importance in river networks, these small first- and second-order streams (Box 16.1) are not appreciated, catalogued, or adequately protected.

Although individually small in size, headwater (first- and second-order, Box 16.1) streams comprise over 70% of stream length in U.S. river systems. Their total length is not known precisely because mapping has been done at a scale that does not recognize small streams, particularly those that flow intermittently (Meyer and Wallace 2001). Yet small streams are hotspots of intense biogeochemical activity on the landscape because of tight connections to terrestrial ecosystems and the frequent exchange between flowing water and sediments (Meyer et al. 2003). Small streams are also hotspots of high species richness (e.g., Meyer et al. 2007). Their productivity supplies food resources to riparian communities of insects, birds, and bats as well as downstream ecosystems (Figure 16.6). Ecosystem services provided by small streams include maintenance of discharge regimes, regulation of sediment export, processing and retention of nutrients and organic matter, and providing habitat and refuge for many highly valued species (e.g., salmon; Lowe and Likens

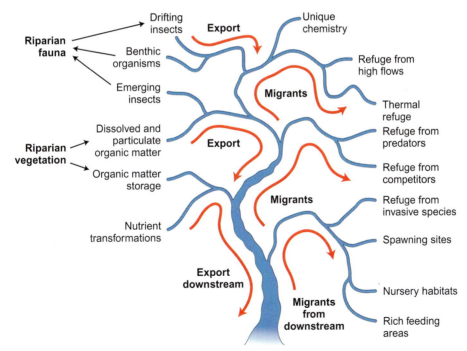

FIGURE 16.6   The role of headwater streams in river networks. Factors on the right result in habitats that support both unique headwater species and migrants from downstream; the contributions of headwater streams to riparian and downstream ecosystems are indicated on the left. *(From Meyer et al. 2007.)*

2005). Small streams also offer recreational opportunities and a point of human contact with nature, particularly in urban settings. I often ask lecture audiences for a show of hands from people who played in streams as children, and I am met with a sea of hands. (See what happens when you ask this question in your ecology class.) Small streams are in backyards and neighborhoods, and are often a child's first contact with "wild" nature.

Despite their ecological importance, small streams are ignored and poorly protected. Rarely are they named. Current environmental regulations allow burying and piping up to 150 m of a stream without an individual permit (Meyer and Wallace 2001). As a result, many streams in metropolitan areas have simply disappeared; for example, the total length of the stream channel was reduced by 58% over 50 years of development in Rock Creek, Maryland (Leopold 1994). Mountaintop-removal-valley-fill coal mining practices bury miles of headwater streams under rock and debris, which has resulted in the loss of over 1400 km of streams in Appalachia (Meyer and Wallace 2001). Recent Supreme Court decisions have called into question whether small streams are even covered under the Clean Water Act, the stated purpose of which is to "restore and maintain the physical, chemical, and biological integrity of our nation's waters."

Although that sounds like an ecosystem approach to environmental regulation, current interpretation of the Act does not adequately recognize the significant role of headwaters in maintaining water quality and biological diversity of downstream rivers, and the cumulative effect of destruction of individual stream reaches. That is, current policy fails to recognize either the uphill or downstream connections to headwater streams (Figure 16.6). Small streams suffer from "the tyranny of small decisions" (Odum 1982): Individual landowners and developers assume their destruction of a tiny stream is of little significance, but the cumulative effects of those many small decisions have been profound changes in river ecosystems.

> ... one could say that some of our most important recent discoveries have been of the existence of hydrologists, foresters and soil scientists. *(Hynes 1975)*

One of the exciting aspects of stream ecosystem research is that most projects are collaborations among people with different expertise. The opportunity to learn from researchers in fields such as hydrology, geomorphology, forestry, and soil science drew me to the field and has kept me there. Doing research as part of a group is both scientifically rewarding and more fun! But to understand stream ecosystems in human-dominated landscapes requires stream researchers to reach out to even more disciplines such as economics, anthropology, and sociology; and incorporating scientific understanding into environmental policy requires even further expansion of collaborations to lawyers and policy analysts.

Although "the valley rules the stream" (Hynes 1975), the valley is controlled by both natural forces (e.g., climate and geology) and human institutions (Meyer 1997). Hence, a holistic ecosystem approach that enhances scientific understanding and influences the interactions between streams and their valleys must incorporate not only the traditional physical, chemical, and biological components of the ecosystem, but also the actions and institutions of humans.

# References

Aber, J.D., McDowell, W.H., Nadelhoffer, K.J., Magill, A.H., Berntson, G.M., Kamakea, M., et al., 1998. Nitrogen saturation in temperate forest ecosystems: Hypotheses revisited. BioScience 48, 921–934.

Aber, J.D., Ollinger, S.V., Driscoll, C.T., Likens, G.E., Holmes, R.T., Freuder, R.J., et al., 2002. Inorganic nitrogen losses from a forested ecosystem in response to physical, chemical, biotic, and climatic perturbations. Ecosystems 5, 648–658.

Allan, J.D., 2004. Landscapes and riverscapes: The influence of land use on stream ecosystems. Annu. Rev. Ecol. Evol. Systemat. 35, 257–284.

Allan, J.D., Castillo, M.M., 2007. Stream ecology. Springer Verlag, Dordrecht.

Bernhardt, E.S., Likens, G.E., Hall Jr., R.O., Buso, D.C., Fisher, S.G., Burton, T.M., et al., 2005. Can't see the forest for the stream? The capacity of in-stream processing to modify terrestrial nitrogen exports. BioScience 55, 219–230.

Caperon, J., Meyer, J.L., 1972. Nitrogen-limited growth of marine phytoplankton. Part I: Changes in population characteristics with steady-state growth rate. Deep Sea Res. 19, 601–618.

Fisher, S.G., Likens, G.E., 1973. Energy flow in Bear Brook, New Hampshire: An integrative approach to stream ecosystem metabolism. Ecol. Monogr. 43, 421–439.

Fisher, S.G., Sponseller, R.A., Heffernan, J.B., 2004. Horizons in stream biogeochemistry: Flowpaths to progress. Ecology 85, 2369–2379.

Hauer, F.R., Benke, A.C., 1991. Rapid growth of snag-dwelling chironomids in a blackwater river: The influence of temperature and discharge. J. N. Am. Benthol. Soc. 10, 154–164.

Hynes, H.B.N., 1975. The stream and its valley. Verh. Int. Verein. Limnol 19, 1–16.

Leopold, L.B., 1994. A view of the river. Harvard University Press, Cambridge, MA.

Likens, G.E., Bormann, F.H., 1995. Biogeochemistry of a forested ecosystem. second ed. Springer-Verlag, New York.

Likens, G.E., Bormann, F.H., Johnson, N.M., Fisher, D.W., Pierce, R.S., 1970. Effects of forest cutting and herbicide treatment on nutrient budgets in Hubbard Brook watershed-ecosystem. Ecol. Monogr. 40, 23–47.

Lowe, W.H., Likens, G.E., 2005. Moving headwater streams to the head of the class. BioScience 55, 196–197.

Meyer, J.L., Likens, G.E., 1979. Transport and transformation of phosphorus in a stream ecosystem. Ecology 60, 1255–1269.

Meyer, J.L., 1990. A blackwater perspective on riverine ecosystems. BioScience 40, 643–651.

Meyer, J.L., Edwards, R.T., 1990. Community metabolism along a black water river continuum. Ecology 71, 668–677.

Meyer, J.L., 1997. Stream health: Incorporating the human dimension to advance stream ecology. J. N. Am. Benthol. Soc. 16, 439–447.

Meyer, J.L., Wallace, J.B., Eggert, S.L., 1998. Leaf litter as a source of dissolved organic carbon in streams. Ecosystems 1, 240–249.

Meyer, J.L., Wallace, J.B., 2001. Lost linkages and lotic ecology: Rediscovering small streams. In: Press, M.C., Huntly, N., Levin, S. (Eds.), Ecology: Achievement and challenge. Blackwell Science, Malden, MA, pp. 295–317.

Meyer, J.L., Kaplan, L.A., Newbold, D., Woltemade, C.J., Zedler, J.B., Beilfuss, R., et al., 2003. Where rivers are born: The scientific imperative for defending small streams and wetlands. American Rivers and Sierra Club, www.americanrivers.org/site/DocServer/WhereRiversAreBorn1.pdf?docID=182.

Meyer, J.L., Paul, M.J., Taulbee, W.K., 2005. Stream ecosystem function in urbanizing landscapes. J. N. Am. Benthol. Soc. 24, 602–612.

Meyer, J.L., Strayer, D.L., Wallace, J.B., Eggert, S.L., Helfman, G.S., Leonard, N.L., 2007. The contribution of headwater streams to biodiversity in river networks. J. Am. Water Resour. Assoc. 43, 86–103.

Mulholland, P.J., Helton, A.M., Poole, G.C., Hall, R.O., Hamilton, S.K., Peterson, B.J., et al., 2008. Stream denitrification across biomes and its response to anthropogenic nitrogen loading. Nature 452, 202–205.

Newbold, J.D., Elwood, J.W., O'Neill, R.V., VanWinkle, W., 1981. Measuring nutrient spiraling in streams. Can. J. Fish. Aquat. Sci. 38, 860–863.

Odum, W.E., 1982. Environmental degradation and the tyranny of small decisions. BioScience 32, 728–729.

Paul, M.J., Meyer, J.L., 2001. Streams in the urban landscape. Annu. Rev. Ecol. Systemat. 32, 333–366.

Peterson, B.J., Wollheim, W.M., Mulholland, P.J., Webster, J.R., Meyer, J.L., Tank, J.L., et al., 2001. Control of nitrogen export from watersheds by headwater streams. Science 292, 86–90.

Stream Solute Workshop, 1990. Concepts and methods for assessing solute dynamics in stream ecosystems. J. N. Am. Bentholog. Soc. 9, 95–119.

Triska, F.J., Sedell, J.R., Cromack, K., Gregory, S.V., McCorison, F.M., 1984. Nitrogen budget for a small coniferous forest stream. Ecol. Monogr. 54, 119–140.

Vannote, R.L., Minshall, G.W., Cummins, K.W., Sedell, J.R., Cushing, C.E., 1980. The river continuum concept. Can. J. Fish. Aquat. Sci. 37, 130–137.

Vitousek, P.M., Reiners, W.A., 1975. Ecosystem succession and nutrient retention: A hypothesis. BioScience 25, 376–381.

Wainright, S.C., Couch, C.A., Meyer, J.L., 1992. Fluxes of bacteria and organic matter into a blackwater river from river sediments and floodplain soils. Freshwat. Biol. 28, 37–48.

Wallace, J.B., Eggert, S.L., Meyer, J.L., Webster, J.R., 1997. Multiple trophic levels of a stream linked to terrestrial litter inputs. Science 277, 102–104.

Walsh, C.J., Roy, A.H., Feminella, J., Cottingham, P.D., Groffman, P.M., Morgan, R.P., 2005. The urban stream syndrome: Current knowledge and the search for a cure. J. N. Am. Bentholog. Soc. 24, 706–723.

Webster, J.R., Golladay, S.W., Benfield, E.F., Meyer, J.L., Swank, W.T., Wallace, J.B., 1992. Catchment disturbance and stream response: An overview of stream research at Coweeta Hydrologic Laboratory. In: Boon, P.J., Calow, P., Petts, G.E. (Eds.), The conservation and management of rivers. John Wiley and Sons, New York, pp. 231–253.

Webster, J.R., Tank, J.L., Wallace, J.B., Meyer, J.L., Eggert, S.L., Ehrman, T.P, et al., 2001. Effects of litter exclusion and wood removal on phosphorus and nitrogen retention in a forest stream. Verh. Int. Verein. Limnol. 27, 1337–1340.

# FRONTIERS

# Frontiers in Ecosystem Science

*Heather A. Bechtold, Jorge Durán, David L. Strayer,*
*Kathleen C. Weathers, Angelica P. Alvarado,*
*Neil D. Bettez, Michelle A. Hersh,*
*Robert C. Johnson, Eric G. Keeling,*
*Jennifer L. Morse, Andrea M. Previtali, and Alexandra Rodríguez*
**Cary Institute of Ecosystem Studies. Millbrook, New York**

## INTRODUCTION

It is easy when reading a textbook such as this one to think of the contents of an intellectual field as fixed and finished—that ecosystem science contains 36 key concepts and facts and will always contain just these 36 facts. However, ecosystem science is a rapidly developing field of which the ultimate shape and contributions are not yet clear. A textbook on ecosystem science written 10 or 50 years from now will certainly not contain the same content as the book in your hands. It is not even possible for today's ecosystem scientists to provide a definitive list of the key unsolved questions in the field, nor to fully anticipate the contents of those future textbooks.

In part, change will come through advances in the subjects contained in this book. Scientists will make more and better measurements of primary production, nitrogen cycling, and so on, and existing theories will be tested and refined or rejected. More exciting and less predictable, though, entire areas of ecosystem science will appear, flourish, and/or disappear. We offer a few examples of areas that seem poised for rapid progress and that hopefully show the vitality of the field. We organize these examples into four broad categories according to the factors (or drivers) that may lead to progress: the pressure of new environmental problems, conceptual advances, technological innovation, and the changing culture of science.

# PRESSURES AND PACE OF ENVIRONMENTAL CHANGE

Many advances in ecosystem science have been driven by the need to meet the demands of a society wanting to understand and solve pressing environmental problems. In the past, issues such as acid rain, the ozone hole, declining fisheries yields, and eutrophication have motivated considerable ecosystem research, and society has benefited from discoveries of that science. Currently, Earth's system is experiencing an increasing number of planetary-scale changes due to the consequences of human population and economic growth. The conditions of the earth, and how ecosystems function, are being modified at unprecedented rates (Schlesinger 1997). The potential severity of these global changes is challenging to predict, and will motivate scientists worldwide to understand and mitigate their socio-ecological consequences. In this section, we describe a number of components of change that, due to their global significance, will draw the attention of ecosystem scientists in the coming years.

## Urbanization

In 2008, for the first time in history, half of the world's population lived in urban areas; by 2050 it is expected that the urban population will double and more than 70% of the world's population will live in urban regions. Although these areas occupy less than 0.5% of Earth's total land area, urbanization and its associated changes in land use are predicted to alter the properties of ecosystems at local, regional, and continental scales (Grimm et al. 2008). As these changes occur, politicians and managers will be faced with decisions about regional planning, conservation, and sustainability.

Over the last decade, scientists have overturned many of our assumptions about urban areas such as the idea that concern about environmental quality is higher among the wealthy, biodiversity is lower in urban areas, lawns are bad, or that urbanization decreases water quality. Indeed, recent work has demonstrated that concern about air quality is independent of socio-economic status, cities are not biological deserts, lawns have some ecological value, and water quality is not always worse in urban areas (Pickett et al. 2008). Ecosystem scientists are now studying urban systems as they have studied "natural" ecosystems. As examples, two urban ecosystem research sites (Baltimore and Central Arizona–Phoenix) are part of the 26-site U.S. Long-Term Ecological Research Network (http://www.lternet.edu/), Miami and New Orleans are part of more than 16 U.S. cities participating in the Urban Long-Term Research Area Exploratory program (ULTRA-Ex), and universities throughout the United States now offer courses in urban ecology. Thus, ecosystem scientists now are using cities as model systems to understand how ecosystems respond to perturbations such as warmer temperatures, increased $CO_2$, higher nitrogen deposition, or invasive species. They have also begun to realize how urban ecosystems function differently from their better-studied nonurban counterparts and that many of the traditional models and monitoring networks that were developed for either "natural" or agricultural systems do not work well in urban systems because human effects on primary drivers of biogeochemical cycles such as hydrology, atmospheric chemistry, nutrients, and land use are fundamentally altered in urban areas. An example of this is what has been called "urban stream syndrome," which in part describes the consistently observed down-cutting of streams draining urban lands. Increased volume and velocity of runoff from impervious surfaces results in stream downcutting and disconnects riparian areas, scours streambed surfaces, and reduces invertebrate and fish habitat (Walsh et al. 2005).

Urban ecology will drive ecosystem scientists to ask new kinds of questions, analyze new kinds of data, and include humans in their conceptual frameworks (Figure 17.2). In addition to asking questions about the distribution of organisms in and around cities and biogeo-chemical budgets of urban watersheds, urban ecosystem science will increasingly combine ecological data with land-use/land-cover data, economic and census data, and social surveys to understand not only how urban ecosystems function ecologically, but their socio-ecological interactions as well. Integrating humans into ecological theory will allow us to ask questions such as how landscaping choices affect the types of bird species in urban areas, how household and authority decisions influence the fluxes of nitrogen and carbon, how to control the proliferation of invasive species in urban areas, and the consequences of new contaminants associated with dense populations.

## Contaminants of Emerging Concern and New Technologies

Safeguarding and maintaining high-quality water, air, and soil represent some of the largest challenges facing humankind. Although advances in technology have allowed the developed world to keep pace with agricultural and health demands, they have also introduced new sources and types of pollution (e.g., insecticides, fungicides, pharmaceuticals, and personal care products). Toxins associated with manufacturing, energy extraction, pest control, and wastewater are discharged into aquatic systems, released into the air, and sprayed onto landscapes. The ecosystem effects of some of these compounds are well known, but the effects of others are just now being investi-gated or have not been studied at all. Thus, assessing and minimizing the environ-mental impact of these compounds will occupy much of ecosystem science in coming decades.

Understanding the influence of anthropogenically derived compounds on the environ-ment is a continuing challenge for future research. Great strides have been made to understand the effects of global contaminants such as DDT, PCBs, mercury, and ozone-depleting CFCs, but the influence of other common human-derived compounds on ecosystems remains unknown. New investigations of pharmaceuticals discharged into aquatic systems have found that they can affect the function of organisms (e.g., fish, amphibians, and invertebrates) by suppressing growth, altering gender, and changing behavior and physiology. However, the effects of pharmaceutical compounds on ecosystem processes, such as alteration of gross primary production or decomposition rates, remain largely unknown (Rosi-Marshall and Royer 2012). Also, new emerging micropollutants may present risks and management challenges. For example, nanotech-nology, the art of manipulating matter at the atomic or molecular scale, is expected to have wide-reaching consequences for society and for ecosystems. Though nanoparti-cles (silver, titanium, gold, and zinc, but also carbon and silicon) have been developed to improve properties of a wide variety of products and services (e.g., cosmetics, microelectronics, water filtration, food production, clothing, and food packaging), studies have shown that nanomaterials may have a greater reactivity and toxicity than larger particles, and may accumulate in tissues, affecting human and organism health, likely having undesirable and environmentally harmful interactions with biological systems (Nel et al. 2006; Arora et al. 2012).

New environmental contaminants and their anticipated widespread production, use, and disposal will likely cause novel environmental hazards with unknown consequences on human health, organisms, and ecosystem structure and function. Accounting for unanticipated environmental effects caused by newly created substances and compounds will continue in the foreseeable future. Thus, balancing the concern of the impact of new technology on ecosystems without hindering innovation or development will certainly prove to be a challenge.

## Challenges Associated with Global Change

Global change (planetary-scale changes in Earth's system, such as climate change, urbanization, land-use change, loss of diversity, etc.) is already affecting ecosystems, and these effects are predicted to increase in the coming decades. Uncertainties related to global change will surely be an important driver of ecosystem science in the twenty-first century. However, it is not easy to comprehend the mechanisms underlying rapid global change, and a substantial amount of research is still needed to understand processes affected by changing environmental conditions at different spatial and temporal scales.

One of the fundamental questions for the coming years will be to understand whether ecosystems will be resilient to pressures of anthropogenic global change, and which characteristics of ecosystems will promote resilience. Ecosystem responses to multiple aspects of anthropogenic change will not be uniform within communities or across landscapes, and may be surprising when effects are not additive or synergistic (Folke et al. 2004). Topics ripe for investigation as potential stabilizing processes include plant phenotypic plasticity, reduced mortality due to release from competition, and enhanced mutualistic relationships under postdisturbance conditions. Ecosystem scientists will need to consider connectivity between protected areas and landscapes that are increasingly modified by human activities, including urban areas (Pickett et al. 2004). Elucidating and managing for ecosystem resilience in the face of global change across spatial and temporal scales will be a true test of ecosystem science.

Another intriguing unknown is the role of biotic feedbacks in global change. For example, under global warming, marine biota could increase the release of dimethylsulfide, resulting in long-lasting clouds, which may mitigate the effects of climate change by increasing the global albedo (Halloran et al. 2010). However, other studies suggest that higher temperatures will stratify the ocean, decreasing the supply of nutrients to phytoplankton, and therefore decrease dimethylsulfide production (Cox et al. 2000). Similarly, higher atmospheric $CO_2$ concentrations can enhance carbon sequestration by forests, slowing down the accumulation of $CO_2$ in the atmosphere; but higher atmospheric $CO_2$ concentrations may also increase the release of $CH_4$ and $N_2O$ (gases with strong greenhouse effects) from terrestrial ecosystems to the atmosphere (van Groenigen et al. 2011). Examples such as these highlight that although it is clear that global change will alter how the biosphere influences climate, and vice versa, it is still unclear if these complex biota-climate interactions, overall, will dampen or amplify anthropogenic global change. Further interdisciplinary research will be necessary to reduce these uncertainties and better identify and understand the role of the biotic feedbacks on global change (Bonan 2008).

Finally, environmental issues related to global change will be difficult to understand because they involve large scales of time and/or space (e.g., climate change, nitrogen deposition, and changes in land use). To complicate matters, these environmental changes can interact, which may generate nonadditive or synergistic effects that cannot easily be predicted from single-factor studies. Experimental ecosystem science is already moving toward new experimental approaches, such as research across larger geographic and temporal expanses, which will allow scientists to improve their understanding of mechanisms of different processes at multiple temporal and spatial scales. Ecosystem scientists will also have to work together to develop research that takes advantage of new and existing facilities and technologies. Use of the sensor and human networks that underpin initiatives such as the National Ecological Observatory Network (NEON; http://www.neoninc.org/), the Global Lake Ecological Observatory Network (GLEON; http://www.gleon.org/), and the Ocean Observatories Initiative (OOI; http://www.oceanobservatories.org/) will become increasingly necessary to accomplish that crucial goal.

## Restoration Ecology

Humans have long sought measures to mitigate or reverse ecosystem degradation. Ecological restoration is the practice of applying management techniques often with the goal of restoring the structure and function of a predisturbance ecosystem (National Research Council 1992), but the term has come to encompass a broader array of management interventions to improve ecosystem function, especially when predisturbance conditions are unattainable (Hobbs et al. 2011). One of the earliest ecological restoration projects that incorporated research was conducted by scientists at the University of Wisconsin Arboretum beginning in 1933 (Blewett and Cottam 1984). The aim was to conduct ecological experiments to compare techniques for restoring native prairie ecosystems. The resulting Curtis Prairie has become well known as a foundational study site in restoration ecology (Jordan 2010).

Restoration ecology provides exciting and important opportunities to use ecosystem restoration projects to test and revise ecological theory and engage with practitioners and decision-makers. Ecosystem scientists have contributed to the practice of ecological restoration by evaluating contrasting methods of restoration and their effect on system function. By monitoring the trajectories of restoration projects, ecosystem scientists have also assessed time frames for structural and functional recovery of ecosystem properties (Figure 17.1; Moreno-Mateos et al. 2012), which could be used by practitioners and regulators to set reasonable goals for these projects. Engineers and policy experts are increasingly interested in restoration as a means to repair ecologically degraded systems, both for their intrinsic value and for the services that restored ecosystems may provide, such as the retention and overall reduction of nitrogen to downstream areas. Restored ecosystems are likely to be subject to ongoing human influence, through management in support of restoration practices or through exposure to continued environmental pressures. Opportunities for interdisciplinary socio-ecological research and for feedback of research into adaptive management (Norton 2005) are therefore plentiful. By partnering with these expert groups, ecosystem scientists can provide and receive valuable information and contribute to designing, monitoring, and evaluating restoration practices.

## CONCEPTUAL ADVANCES

In 1661, Robert Boyle published *The Sceptical Chymist*, in which he introduced a bright idea: matter was composed of many different corpuscles (atoms), rather than the classic elements (air, earth, fire, and water). This original idea, the precursor of modern atomic theory, has inspired scientists since its appearance, and was the seed of countless advances in our ability to understand the world. Similarly, in the nineteenth century, Charles Darwin's theory of evolution marked a critical break from the concept of fixed species in biology. This conceptual shift in the way we understand the species opened new avenues that scientists have used to explore and better understand the world of living organisms, at scales from genes to species. Conceptual advances change the way we think and see the world, and in doing so, catalyze new discoveries. Here we discuss changing views on two long-standing concepts that have the potential to advance ecosystem science: the role of humans in ecosystems and the question and treatment of scale.

### Integration of Humans into Ecosystems

Tansley's (1935) original conception of ecosystems is still widely used, and although its applicability has been contested on occasion (see Chapter 1), it has been adapted to support a broad variety of uses. One adaptation is the gradual assimilation of humans as an integral part of ecosystems. During the Age of Enlightenment, humans were considered separate from nature and this perception prevailed in the Western thought for some time. However, the separation between nature and society was questioned in many different disciplines during the twentieth century. Ecosystem science originally focused its attention on "pristine" systems and models correspondingly excluded humans (Figure 17.2a,b). The incorporation of humans went through a stage in which social and ecological systems were viewed as linked, but separate domains. That is, humans were typically represented as forces influencing ecosystems from the outside, mainly as stressors pushing the system out of equilibrium (Figure 17.2c). More recently, the concept of human-in-ecosystems (Berkes et al. 2003) or the "dwelling perspective" (Ingold 2000) represents a movement toward consideration of the mutual influences of ecological and social processes. This perspective recognizes that ecosystems truly devoid of human influence or manipulation are

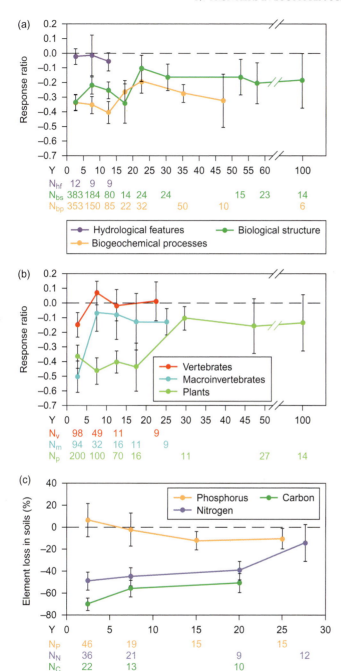

FIGURE 17.1 Recovery trajectories in created and restored wetlands. Chronosequences of the mean response of restored or created wetland ecosystems back to reference conditions (dashed zero line). Restored or created wetlands converge to values similar to what is found in the reference wetland (dashed line), and recovery of function is generally enhanced over time (Y, years after restoration). Response ratio values are calculated by dividing the measured variable in the restored or created wetland by the same variable in the reference wetland. N-values below the x-axis of each panel show the number of sites of each age-class included in the study. bp, biogeochemical processes; bs, biological structure; C, carbon; hf, hydrological features; m, macroinvertebrates; N, nitrogen; p, plants; P, phosphorus; v, vertebrates. (From Moreno-Mateos et al. 2012.)

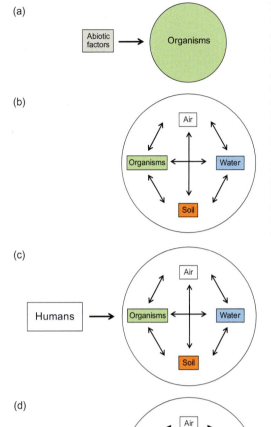

**FIGURE 17.2**  Development of the ecosystem concept. (a) Until the early twentieth century, the world was conceptually viewed as a group of organisms being influenced (note arrow direction) by the environment. (b) In the mid-1900s scientists introduced the term *ecosystem*, and suggested the importance of feedbacks (bidirectional effects, see arrows) between different components of the system. This new model recognized flows of energy and matter through ecological communities, and among the different abiotic and biotic components but did not have a human component. (c) In 1950–2000, many models incorporated the effects of humans as forces influencing ecosystems from the outside. (d) Currently, ecosystem models have begun to include humans (including society and human institutions) as parts of the ecosystem, and acknowledge the mutual influences that occur among all components in the model.

nonexistent. The human-in-ecosystems concept is fundamental to many growing interdisciplinary fields that are related to ecosystem science, such as sustainability science, urban ecology, and adaptive resource management.

These new human-in-ecosystems models will have to account for social and built components of ecosystems and their interactions with the biotic and physical components of ecosystems (Figure 17.2d). In addition, models that integrate humans into ecosystems should incorporate information in addition to matter and energy flows. The wide variety of information relevant for modeling humans as part of complex systems will have to be obtained from interaction with a host of other disciplines such as traditional ecological knowledge, political science, and anthropology (see the following section on the changing culture of science). In the midst of this conceptual revolution, frontiers include exploring alternative ways to consider and interpret the role of humans in ecosystems. These new modeling efforts will offer new frameworks and tools necessary to achieve more comprehensive views of environmental problems and help identify solutions.

## Establishing New Links between Scales in Ecological Research

Scale and scaling issues have become a central issue in ecosystem science, and in many ways, a unifying theme (Levin 1992; Lovett et al. 2005). Although the word "scale" has many definitions, in ecosystem science it most commonly refers to spatial or temporal *grain size* (the finest resolution possible in the data set), *extent* (size of the entire study area or length of the study), or *levels of organization* (e.g., atoms → biological molecules → organelles → cells → tissues → organs → organisms → populations → communities → ecosystems → landscapes → biomes → ecosphere; Schneider 2001). In the future, scientists will increasingly find themselves attempting to connect ecological phenomena across multiple scales, but substantial advances in theory are still needed to establish and refine scaling frameworks in ecosystem science.

The concept of ecosystem heterogeneity is discussed in Chapter 10. Here, we focus on some of the issues and challenges that are at the forefront of ecosystem science research regarding scaling in space and time. First, ecosystem scientists are increasingly using the knowledge gained from fine-scale studies to estimate or model processes at much broader—even global—spatial scales. This aggregation of fine-scale data to estimate ecosystem attributes at much broader spatial scales, while important to our understanding of broad-scale or global processes, is fraught with error and uncertainties (Rastetter et al. 1992; Currie 2011). Recent and future technological advances in areas such as geographic information systems and remote sensing (see the following section on sensors) will greatly aid in estimating ecosystem attributes over large geographical areas (e.g., Running et al. 2004). Temporally, ecosystem scientists are also faced with integrating short-term data on the structure and function of ecosystems with longer-term processes and trends. In global climate change research, for example, knowledge gained from current short-term analyses of climate-change drivers must be integrated with long-term climatic records and trends to understand how the global climate has changed and will potentially change in the future.

Many ecological processes operate at multiple levels of organization. For example, primary production by photoautotrophs can be estimated at the ecosystem level. However, ecosystem-level primary production is the sum of primary production for all individual photo-autotrophic organisms within the ecosystem. This is a result of photosynthesis in the chloroplasts of individual organisms that ultimately determine the potential for primary production in that ecosystem (Allen et al. 2005). Therefore, primary production can be studied from subcellular scales of biological organization to the entire ecosphere or Earth (Field et al. 1995). While ecosystem scientists recognize that ecosystem processes operate at multiple levels of organization, they lack a comprehensive framework that links processes at the level of organization where they occur. Recently, the metabolic theory of ecology (Brown et al. 2004), ecological stoichiometry (Sterner and Elser 2002), or some combination of these two frameworks has been proposed as a basis for assessing ecological processes

(Allen and Gillooly 2009) and interactions at multiple scales of biological and ecological organization. These theories are appealing for this purpose, because each expresses ecological functions and interactions using primary currencies of ecosystem science: energy (metabolic theory of ecology) and matter (ecological stoichiometry; see Chapter 5). Despite these recent advances, considerable research is still necessary to develop and incorporate a comprehensive theoretical framework capable of transcending levels of biological and ecological organization. Such a framework can certainly be used by ecosystem science to determine changes in ecosystems associated with anthropogenic pressures or global change.

# TECHNOLOGICAL ADVANCES

The invention and adoption of new technology allows ecosystem scientists to make new measurements and inspires new directions of research. Examples include the use of molecular genetic markers to describe new communities and functions of organisms, stable isotopes to describe how nutrients and energy flow through food webs, and remotely deployed cameras, sensors, and robot aircrafts to collect images and samples in hard-to-reach or extreme environments. In this section, we show a few examples of promising technologies that may change the direction of ecosystem science in the future.

## Sensors

The rapid development of new technology such as environmental sensors has provided scientists with ways to examine environmental processes and explore data at new temporal and spatial scales. The rich output provided by sensors has become increasingly important in detecting subtle changes that could not be previously observed and has aided in new discoveries. For example, sensors made it possible to identify the reduction of ozone in the stratosphere and its causes, and have helped to discover life in extreme environments by recording output of gases from hot pools, deep sea thermal vents, and under glaciers. Local and global budgets of the production and consumption of atmospheric gases like $CO_2$ and $NO_x$ have been monitored for years with a growing worldwide network of atmospheric flux measurement towers and oxygen sensors in freshwater and the ocean. The analysis of these data will play an important role in understanding climate and weather patterns, and the biological response to changes in these gases. New low-cost sensors capable of detecting micropollutants in real time and at high resolution will greatly enhance our ability to understand short- and long-term processes as well as their drivers, and eventually to protect environmental integrity and human health. For example, the ability to simultaneously detect new emerging compounds of concern such as pesticides, toxins, and endocrine disruptors in water at the resolution of seconds to minutes may uncover unknown sources and promote smart environmental decisions such as improving the design of water treatment facilities.

Remote sensing is a specific example of sensor development that will likely lead to new discoveries in ecosystem science. This term refers to the acquisition and interpretation of

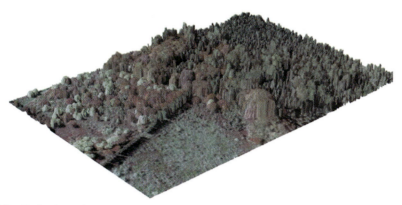

**FIGURE 17.3** Technological advances in data measurement. Remote sensing offers new techniques to collect data at high spatial resolution over large landscape scales. This image was taken over an area of lowland rain forest and cleared lands on the island of Hawaii. Different colors highlight the distinct chemical signatures of trees and other vegetation, canopy heights, and crown sizes, which allow the estimation of relative size and amount of above ground biomass of different plant species. *(Map from Townsend et al. 2008.)*

information about objects or phenomena without being in physical contact with the object or system under investigation, and includes a suite of techniques and tools that have been successfully used for decades in areas as diverse as traffic control, meteorology, the military, and astronomy. Recently, the development of new and more refined airborne platforms and technologies, better spatial and spectral resolution, and the gradual reduction of costs have resulted in remote sensing rapidly becoming one of the most promising tools for the study of ecosystems. By using satellites, aircrafts, ships, or helicopters, it is now possible to collect data in inaccessible areas and at spatial scales and speeds once unthinkable. Technologies such as high-fidelity imagining spectroscopy (HFIS) or light detection and ranging (LIDAR) allow collection of data about plant canopy structure and characteristics (e.g., water content, nitrogen, or pigment concentrations), estimates of species richness, and surveys of coastal dynamics and sediment transport from streams to oceans (Figure 17.3). It is also possible to estimate primary productivity (see Chapter 2) and biogeochemical processes at multiple scales, from the local to the global, and even monitor in almost real-time dynamic processes such as atmospheric concentration of chemicals, deforestation, glacial retreat, or desertification (Campbell and Wynne 2011). Frontiers for ecosystem science are likely to include developing algorithms to link sensor output to ecosystem processes of interest (e.g., spectral output and nutrient content in forests), and the ability to remotely sense soil properties, such as nutrient content, moisture, or organic matter content. The resulting data will offer new opportunities to develop and test ecosystem models and theory across broad spatial and temporal scales. For example, key questions such as how species invasion rates and patterns will vary in response to global change, how albedo and foliar nitrogen can be used as proxies for temporal and spatial controls on the variation in global carbon fluxes and productivity, or how thermokarst lakes (formed by permafrost thaw) change in relation to climate variability will be more achievable for ecosystem science thanks to these new technological advances (Kampe et al. 2010).

## Genetic and Molecular Data

New developments in methods and technologies such as environmental genomics/ metagenomics, transcriptomics, and proteomics will allow the gathering of much larger amounts of molecular data than was previously possible. Using environmental genomics/ metagenomics methods, DNA sequences from environmental samples of microbial communities can be collected and analyzed over large spatial and temporal scales. Environmental genomics studies can include focused surveys of single genes from environmental communities, or shotgun sequencing of all genes in an environmental sample. In transcriptomics, RNA from individual organisms or microbial communities is converted into complementary DNA libraries and sequenced, so that researchers can determine patterns of gene expression. Similarly, microarrays can also test for expression of multiple targeted genes simultaneously. These technologies focusing on gene expression are particularly useful in linking expression of functional genes to microbially driven processes such as nitrogen mineralization. Finally, in proteomics, the complete set of proteins expressed by a microbial community is analyzed, but this new method can be limited by extraction quality and other technological challenges (Vandenkoornhuyse et al. 2010).

Improved technologies for high-throughput sequencing (the production of a large number of sequences at once), such as pyrosequencing and other next-generation tools, have increased our capacity to collect molecular data on microbial communities. This allows us to assess the composition of microbial communities in depth, and evaluate changes in community structure over time or space, or in conjunction with ecosystem processes such as the processing of nitrogen or carbon. Key challenges in using all of these technologies in an ecological context include the development of computational and statistical tools to store, quality check, annotate, and analyze these large data sets, and the improvement of our understanding of previously undiscovered organisms, genes, and proteins of unknown identity or function (DeLong 2009; Vandenkoornhuyse et al. 2010).

These technologies are, and will be, particularly useful in elucidating the structure and function of microbial communities (including bacteria, fungi, archaea, microscopic eukaryotes, and viruses) that carry out so many ecosystem processes of interest. Therefore, they could help ecosystem scientists open the proverbial "black box" of microbially driven processes, linking biogeochemical transformations to cellular mechanisms, microbial communities, and ecosystem function.

## Manipulating and Analyzing Large Data Sets

Although sensor networks, remote sensing, and molecular advances have aided in our understanding of ecosystems, the massive flow of data resulting from this intensive sampling represents new challenges for data quality control and assurance, management, and importantly, how science is conducted through data and idea sharing (Fischer and Zigmond 2010; Porter et al. 2012). Developing national and international observatory networks (e.g., NEON, GLEON, OOI; see earlier section on challenges associated with global change) adds new opportunities for large-scale, cross-system analyses along with new data management and processing challenges, and researchers will have to convert the "deluge of data" (Baraniuk 2011) into scientific understanding.

Management and analysis of larger data sets requires more powerful computational resources and creative analytical tools. Standardization of data formatting across analytical platforms, development of sufficient descriptive documentation to accompany shared databases, and policies for data access, security, and sharing are all important considerations for projects involving large data streams (Michener and Jones 2012). Along with these techniques, we must also supply appropriate ways to verify that final extracted values can be trusted with or without raw information to examine. The developing field of ecological informatics or ecoinformatics attempts to integrate environmental and information sciences by providing tools to analyze and access the large amounts of collected data. One example of ecoinformatics is the creation of "middleware" such as DataTurbine, which can ingest data of all types, reorganize them, and produce transformed structures suitable for archival storage in databases or file systems, and is compatible with statistical software programs (Benson et al. 2009). The ability to analyze and store large data sets using high-performance computing environments, such as cluster-based computing, cloud computing, and heterogeneous computational environments, all offer potential solutions to these challenges (Schadt et al. 2010).

A less obvious problem associated with the increased ease and decreased cost of collecting data is the issue of data storage. The amount of data generated worldwide has been increasing by 58% every year. For example, in 2010 the world generated 1250 billion gigabytes of data, and in 2011, the amount of data collected was twice as large as the world's storage capacity (Baraniuk 2011). The gap between production of data and the ability to store it means that data will be unavailable for further analysis, lost, overwritten, or deleted. Terabytes or even petabytes of data will require inventive ways to be processed and stored, whether by new mathematical algorithms, compression techniques, or other strategies.

Finally, data analysis and modeling approaches that effectively use these newly available data streams are also being developed (Schmidt and Lipson 2009). For example, data assimilation methods that generate weather forecasts can be used to create tools for ecological forecasting (Luo et al. 2011). Although dealing with the increasing amount of information and data is challenging, it will provide unprecedented opportunities to improve our understanding of ecosystems, and aid in developing novel scientific questions.

## THE CHANGING CULTURE OF SCIENCE

The way that we do science affects the kind of science that we do. Although perhaps a less obvious driver of scientific change than technological or conceptual advances, changes in scientific culture will affect ecosystem science in coming decades. Here are a few examples.

The increasing scale, complexity, and urgency of many problems in ecosystem science is pushing ecologists to work in larger, more intellectually diverse teams (Greene 2007).

This trend is likely to continue and accelerate, so ecosystem scientists will need to become even more adept at collaborating with researchers from other disciplines, and may need to develop new reward systems to encourage such collaboration. In turn, working in large, diverse teams will change the questions we ask, the approaches we use, and the technology we import from our collaborators.

In addition, if we expect ecosystem science to be brought to bear effectively on environmental problems, it has become increasingly clear that we must engage productively with policy-makers (Driscoll et al. 2011) and the general public (Groffman et al. 2010; Pouyat et al. 2010). This means that at least some ecosystem scientists must become adept communicators (Hayes and Grossman 2006; Olson 2009) or work with professional communicators or bridge organizations such as intermediary or boundary-spanning groups (Osmond et al. 2010). Ecosystem scientists will need to engage with an

---

## BOX 17.1

## THE ROLE OF SCIENCE AND EDUCATION
### *The Role of Science in Education: What Can You Do?*

Ecosystem scientists are increasingly urged to actively participate in education in the midst of the changing culture of science. Collaboration with teachers, engagement in the community, and citizen science projects can all foster inquiry-based learning by gathering and making sense of evidence. This knowledge will lead to a more informed public, resulting in the necessary critical evaluation of information before making decisions about environmental problems or issues (Resnik and Zurawsky, 2007). Following are examples of ways or opportunities that scientists can engage in education.

- Ecosystem scientists can partner with local schools through collaboration with teacher education and professional development programs. This can be done by serving as experts in courses and workshops for teachers, and aiding in development of education curricula, standards, or assessment (NRC 2012).

- Ecosystem scientists can promote a culture that celebrates science by engaging an increasingly large, diverse, and educated public. Engagement can be done through public lectures, dialogues, panel discussions, debates, hands-on demonstrations, shows, exhibitions, workshops, or science fairs. This can help build relationships and facilitate dialogue between citizens and academics (Durant and Ibrahim 2011).

- Ecosystem scientists can use research-based topics to implement local citizen science projects. These projects typically involve the public or school systems in observation and data collection. For example, middle and high school students have monitored the effects of ground-level ozone by collecting data on observable leaf injury in local plants (Bricker et al. 2010); others have successfully used leaf decay experiments in streams as indicators of stream health.

increasingly large, diverse, and educated public (Durant and Ibrahim 2011) by actively participating in education of citizens and in the communication of their scientific research (Box 17.1). It seems likely that closer engagement with policy-makers and the public will change the research priorities of ecosystem scientists, as well as the approaches that we use (e.g., using networks of citizen scientists to help answer—and ask—research questions).

Historically, science was dominated by relatively few people, primarily from Western countries; however, this trend has been changing over the past few decades, through concerted efforts as well as the rapid development of connectivity tools (e.g., the Internet, see the following). For example, funding competitions often now encourage international

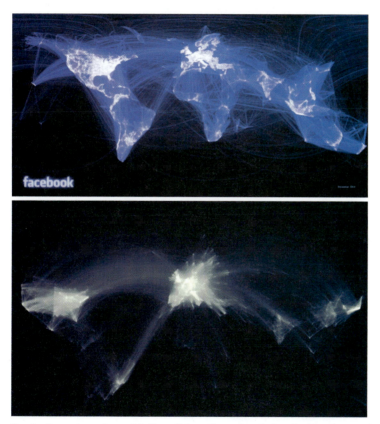

**FIGURE 17.4**  Conducting science in a globally collaborative network. Inspired by the creation of a Facebook friendship map (upper map), the lower map illustrates global scientific collaborations. Each arc represents partnerships between scientists in different cities collected from studies, books, and trade journals found in Elsevier from 2005–2009. The Facebook map depicts how networking technology has created new and widespread opportunities for communication. Similar communication technologies are likely to be used by ecosystem scientists to expand and diversify worldwide collaborations, and to brighten dark areas of the lower map. Currently, most collaboration is centered in the Americas, Europe, and Japan. A zoomable very high-resolution map can be consulted at http://collabo.olihb.com/. *(Lower map created by Olivier H. Beauchesne.)*

teams and collaborations with scientists from developing countries; programs are being developed to increase retention and success of women and minorities in science; and several translation tools are becoming important in broadening the impact of research findings and accommodate cultural and language barriers. Because who does science affects the kind of science that is done, it is likely that broadening the population of ecosystem scientists will change the shape of our science (Uriarte et al. 2007).

Ecosystem science is also being changed by advances in communication and social networking. In 2011, more than 2.2 billion people, nearly one-third of Earth's population, used the Internet. Communication technology has created networks of networks that provide high-speed access to creative and unlimited applications that can be accessed by handheld mobile devices, tablets, and computers at almost any place and time. They also provide important avenues of communication for people. Thanks to the vastly increasing ability to obtain information resources and services using the Internet, and the move toward more web-based social networks and tools, ecosystem scientists will find it increasingly easy to communicate with other scientists around the world (Figure 17.4). These changes are likely to change attitudes about sharing data (from viewing most data as the exclusive property of an individual scientist to viewing at least some data as shared, in fact as community property), expand the range of questions that can be answered, and accelerate the pace of scientific progress.

# CONCLUSION

Even though it may not be possible to lay out the exact shape of the ecosystem science of the future, it should be clear even from this brief overview that ecosystem science is evolving rapidly, in terms of the kinds of questions that are asked, the kinds of questions that can be answered, the research approaches and technological tools that are used, the kinds of people who do ecosystem science and with whom ecosystem scientists collaborate, the applications of ecosystem science to environmental management and policy, and nearly every other aspect of the science. The challenge to address important environmental problems has never been greater, but neither has been our capacity to respond to these challenges.

## References

Allen, A.P., Gillooly, J.F., 2009. Towards an integration of ecological stoichiometry and the metabolic theory of ecology to better understand nutrient cycling. Ecol. Lett. 12, 369–384.

Allen, A.P., Gillooly, J.F., Brown, J.H., 2005. Linking the global carbon cycle to individual metabolism. Funct. Ecol. 19, 202–213.

Arora, S., Rajwade, J.M., Paknikar, K.M., 2012. Nanotoxicology and in vitro studies: The need of the hour. Toxicol. Appl. Pharm. 258, 151–165.

Baraniuk, R.G., 2011. More is less: Signal process and the data deluge. Science 331, 717–719.

Benson, B., Bond, B.J., Hamilton, M.P., Monson, R.K., Han, R., 2009. Perspectives on next-generation technology for environmental sensor networks. Front. Ecol. Environ. 8, 193–200.

Berkes, F., Colding, J., Folke, C. (Eds.), 2003. Navigating social-ecological systems: Building resilience for complexity and change. Cambridge University Press, Cambridge, UK.

Blewett, T.J., Cottam, G., 1984. History of the University of Wisconsin Arboretum prairies. Trans. Wisc. Acad. Sci. Arts Lett. 72, 130–144.

Bonan, G., 2008. Forests and climate change: Forcings, feedbacks, and the climate benefits of forests. Science 320, 1444–1449.

Boyle, R. 1661. The sceptical chymist: Or chymico-physical doubts and paradoxes, touching the spagyrist's principles commonly call'd hypostatical, as they are wont to be propos'd and defended by the generality of alchymists. Whereunto is praemis'd part of another discourse. London: Printed by J. Cadwell for J. Crooke, 1661. In Smith–Boyle Collection. Boyle 33.

Bricker, P.L., Sachs, S., Binkley, R., 2010. Using citizen scientists to measure the effects of ozone damage on native wildflowers. Science Scope, 12–19.

Brown, J.H., Gillooly, J.F., Allen, A.P., Savage, V.M., West, G.B., 2004. Toward a metabolic theory of ecology. Ecology 85, 1771–1789.

Campbell, J.B., Wynne, R.H., 2011. Introduction to remote sensing, fifth ed. The Guilford Press, New York.

Cox, P.M., Betts, R.A., Jones, C.D., Spall, S.A., Totterdell, I.J., 2000. Acceleration of global warming due to carbon-cycle feedbacks in a coupled climate model. Nature 408, 184–187.

Currie, W.S., 2011. Units of nature or processes across scales? The ecosystem concept at age 75. New Phytol. 190, 21–34.

DeLong, E.F., 2009. The microbial ocean from genomes to biomes. Nature 459, 200–206.

Driscoll, C.T., Lambert, K.F., Weathers, K.C., 2011. Integrating science and policy: A case study of the Hubbard Brook Research Foundation Science Links Program. BioScience 61, 791–801.

Durant, J., Ibrahim, A., 2011. Celebrating the culture of science. Science 331, 1242.

Field, C.B., Randerson, J.T., Malmström, C.M., 1995. Global net primary production: Combining ecology and remote sensing. Remote Sensing of the Environment 51, 74–88.

Fischer, B.A., Zigmond, M.J., 2010. The essential nature of sharing in science. Sci. Eng. Ethics. 16, 783–799.

Folke, C., Carpenter, S., Walker, B., Scheffer, M., Elmqvist, T., Gunderson, L., et al., 2004. Regime shifts, resilience, and biodiversity in ecosystem management. Annu. Rev. Ecol. Evol. Syst. 35, 557–581.

Greene, M., 2007. The demise of the lone author. Nature 450, 116.

Grimm, N.B., Foster, D., Groffman, P., Grove, J.M., Hopkinson, C.S., Nadelhoffer, K.J., et al., 2008. The changing landscape: Ecosystem responses to urbanization and pollution across climatic and societal gradients. Front. Ecol. Environ. 6, 264–272.

Groffman, P.M., Stylinski, C., Nisbet, M.C., Duarte, C.M., Jordan, R., Burgin, A.J., et al., 2010. Restarting the conversation: Challenges at the interface between ecology and society. Front. Ecol. Environ. 8, 284–291.

Halloran, P.R., Bell, T.G., Totterdell, I.J., 2010. Can we trust empirical marine DMS parameterisations within projections of future climate? Biogeosciences 7, 1645–1656.

Hayes, R., Grossman, D., 2006. A scientist's guide to talking with the media: Practical advice from the Union of Concerned Scientists. Rutgers University Press,, New Brunswick, NJ.

Hobbs, R.J., Hallett, L.M., Ehrlich, P.R., Mooney, H.A., 2011. Intervention ecology: Applying ecological science in the twenty-first century. BioScience 61, 442–450.

Ingold, T. 2000. The perception of the environment: Essays on livelihood, dwelling and skill. Routledge Press, London.

Jordan, W.R., 2010. Some reflections on Curtis Prairie and the genesis of ecological restoration. Ecol. Manag. Restor. 11, 99–107.

Kampe., T.U., Johnson, B.R., Kuester, M., Keller, M., 2010. NEON: The first continental-scale ecological observatory with airborne remote sensing of vegetation canopy biochemistry and structure. J. Appl. Remote Sens. 4, 043510.

Levin, S.A., 1992. The problem of pattern and scale in ecology. Ecology 73, 1943–1967.

Lovett, G.M., Jones, C.G., Turner, M.G., Weathers, K.C. (Eds.), 2005. Ecosystem function in heterogeneous landscapes. Springer-Verlag, New York.

Luo, Y, Ogle, K., Tucker, C., Fei, S., Gao, C., Ladeau, S, et al., 2011. Ecological forecasting and data assimilation in a data-rich era. Ecol. Appl. 21, 1429–1442.

Michener, W.K., Jones, M.B., 2012. Ecoinformatics: Supporting ecology as a data-intensive science. Trends Ecol. Evol. 27, 85–93.

Moreno-Mateos, D., Power, M.E., Comin, F.A., Yockteng, R., 2012. Structural and functional loss in restored wetland ecosystems. PLOS Biology 10. doi: 10.1371/journal.pbio.1001247.

National Research Council, 2012. A Framework for K-12 Science Education: Practices, Crosscutting Concepts, and Core Ideas. Committee on a Conceptual Framework for New K-12 Science Education Standards. Board on Science Education. Division of Behavioral and Social Sciences and Education. The National Academies Press, Washington, DC.

National Research Council, 1992. Restoration of Aquatic Ecosystems: Science, Technology, and Public Policy. Committee on Restoration of Aquatic Ecosystems-Science, Technology, and Public Policy. National Academy Press, Washington, DC.

Nel, A., Xia, T., Li, N., 2006. Toxic potential of materials at the nanolevel. Science 311, 622−627.

Norton, B.G., 2005. Sustainability. A philosophy of adaptive ecosystem management. University of Chicago Press, Chicago, IL.

Olson, R., 2009. Don't be such a scientist. Island Press, Washington, DC.

Osmond, D., Nadkarni, N., Driscoll, C.T., Andrews, E., Gold, A.J., Allred, S.R.B., et al., 2010. The role of interface organizations in science communication and understanding. Front. Ecol. Environ. 8, 306−313.

Pickett, S.T.A., Cadenasso, M.L., Grove, J.M., 2004. Resilient cities: Meaning, models, and metaphor for integrating the ecological, socio-economic, and planning realms. Landsc. Urban. Plan. 69, 369−384.

Pickett, S.T.A., Cadenasso, M.L., Grove, J.M., Groffman, P.M., Band, L.E., Boone, C.G., et al., 2008. Beyond urban legends: An emerging framework of urban ecology, as illustrated by the Baltimore Ecosystem Study. BioScience 58, 139−150.

Porter, J.H., Hanson, P.C, Lin, C., 2012. Staying afloat in the sensor data deluge. Trends Ecol. Evol. 27, 121−129.

Pouyat, R.V., Weathers, K.C., Haueber, R., Lovett, G., Bartuska, A., Christenson, L., et al., 2010. The role and challenge of federal agencies in the application of scientific knowledge: Acid deposition policy and forest management as examples. Front.Ecol. Environ. 8, 322−328.

Rastetter, E.B., King, A.W., Cosby, B.J., Hornberger, G.M., O'Neill, R.V., Hobbie, J.E., 1992. Aggregating fine-scale ecological knowledge to model coarser-scale attributes of ecosystems. Ecol. Appl. 2, 55−70.

Resnik, L.B., Zurawsky, C. (Eds.), 2007. Science education that makes sense. Research Points vol. 5 (1).

Rosi-Marshall, E.J., Royer, T.V., 2012. Pharmaceutical compounds and ecosystem function: An emerging research challenge for aquatic ecologists. Ecosystems (In press).

Running, S.W., Nemani, R.R., Heinsch, F.A., Zhao, M., Reeves, M., Hashimoto, H., 2004. A continuous satellite-derived measure of global terrestrial primary production. BioScience 54, 547−560.

Schadt, E.E., Linderman, M.D., Sorenson, J., Lee, G.P., Nolan, G.P., 2010. Computational solutions to large-scale data management and analysis. Nat. Rev. Genet. 11, 647−657.

Schlesinger, W.H., 1997. Biogeochemistry: An analysis of global change, second ed. Academic Press, San Diego.

Schmidt, M., Lipson, H., 2009. Distilling form-free natural laws from experimental data. Science 324, 81−85.

Schneider, D.C., 2001. The rise of the concept of scale in ecology. BioScience 51, 545−553.

Sterner, R.W., Elser, J.J, 2002. Ecological stoichiometry: The biology of elements from molecules to the biosphere. Princeton University Press, Princeton, NJ.

Tansley, A.G., 1935. The use and abuse of vegetational terms and concepts. Ecology 16, 284−307.

Townsend, A.R., Asner, G.P., Cleveland, C.C., 2008. The biogeochemical heterogeneity of tropical forests. Trends in Ecology and Evolution 23, 424−431.

Uriarte, M., Ewing, H.A., Eviner, V.T., Weathers, K.C., 2007. Constructing a broader and more inclusive values system in science. BioScience 57, 71−78.

Vandenkoornhuyse, P., Dufresne, A., Quaiser, A., Gouesbet, G., Binet, F., Francez, A.-J., et al., 2010. Integration of molecular functions at the ecosystemic level: Breakthroughs and future goals of environmental genomics and post-genomics. Ecol. Lett. 13, 776−791.

van Groenigen, K.J., Osenberg, C.W., Hungate, B.A., 2011. Increased soil emissions of potent greenhouse gases under increased atmospheric $CO_2$. Nature 475, 214−216.

Walsh, C.J., Roy, A.H., Feminella, J.W., Cottingham, P.D., Groffman, P.M., Morgan, R.P., 2005. The urban stream syndrome: Current knowledge and the search for a cure. J. N. Am. Benthol. Soc. 24, 706−723.

# Appendix: A Primer on Biologically Mediated Redox Reactions in Ecosystems

*Stuart E.G. Findlay and David L. Strayer*

**Cary Institute of Ecosystem Studies, Millbrook, NY**

Most of you know that plants capture energy by oxygenic photosynthesis and release energy contained in organic matter through aerobic respiration according to the following reactions:

$$CO_2 + H_2O + light \longrightarrow CH_2O + O_2 \text{ (oxygenic photosynthesis)}$$
$$CH_2O + O_2 \longrightarrow CO_2 + H_2O + energy \text{ (aerobic respiration)}$$

These familiar equations are examples of *redox reactions*, which involve a transfer of electrons. Many organisms (especially prokaryotic microbes) use less familiar redox reactions to obtain the energy they need for life. These reactions are key parts of both energy flow and biogeochemical cycling in ecosystems; an understanding of ecosystems requires familiarity with these reactions. Because some of you may be unfamiliar with these reactions and their occurrence in ecosystems, we offer a brief primer to biologically mediated redox reactions in ecosystems. Additional information on these reactions is available in books by Stumm and Morgan (1995), Fenchel et al. (1998), Maier et al. (2000), Wetzel (2001), and Reddy and DeLaune (2008), as well as in Chapter 3 on energetics and Chapters 5–7 on biogeochemical cycles.

Redox reactions involve the movement of electrons from one element or compound (the electron donor) to another (the electron acceptor). Such reactions will either yield energy that may be used by organisms or require some energy input to proceed. An easy way to think about these reactions is to use a physical analogy for the chemical potential energy that may be released and used by organisms (Figure A.1). For an element capable of releasing an electron and yielding energy in the process we can think of that electron as an object at the top of the hill capable of doing work as it rolls downhill. There must be an electron acceptor capable of "catching" the electron to complete the process. If the combined process of donating and receiving the electron yields energy, then this energy can potentially be captured and used by organisms. This energy is the Gibbs free energy (represented as $\Delta G$), and if this term is negative, the reaction yields energy.

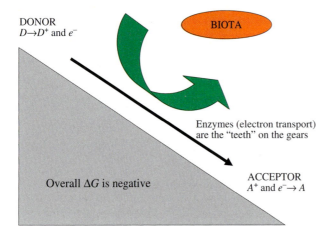

DONOR
$D \rightarrow D^+$ and $e^-$

BIOTA

Enzymes (electron transport)
are the "teeth" on the gears

Overall $\Delta G$ is negative

ACCEPTOR
$A^+$ and $e^- \rightarrow A$

**FIGURE A.1** Representation of the conversion of chemical potential energy into energy useable by organisms. The "stored" energy in the electron donor ($D$) is released as the electrons are transferred to the electron acceptor ($A^+$). Enzymes involved in electron transport capture energy for use in biosynthesis.

More formally, redox reactions can be broken down into two *half-reactions*, one involving the loss of an electron and the other the gain of an electron. The half-reactions of ordinary respiration are:

$$C^0 H_2 O \longrightarrow C^{+4} + 4e^- \quad [\Delta G = -181 \text{ kJ}/4 \text{ electron transfer}]$$

$$O_2^0 + 4e^- \longrightarrow 2O^{-2} \quad [\Delta G = -313 \text{ kJ}/4 \text{ electron transfer}]$$

where the superscripts indicate the oxidation state of the element and $e^-$ indicates an electron. Note that only the elements changing in oxidation state are shown for simplicity and the reactions are not necessarily balanced. Summed, these two half-reactions give the full equation given in the first paragraph of this primer. The terminology for describing redox reactions can be confusing and the easiest thing to remember is that if the oxidation state goes down the element/compound is being reduced, and conversely, if the oxidation state goes up it is being oxidized. In the previous example the carbon in the carbohydrate ($CH_2O$) is clearly being oxidized and the oxygen is being reduced.

The total energy yield of this reaction is the sum of the energy yielded by the two half-reactions, and for this example, both $\Delta G$ values are negative and the overall $\Delta G$ is $-494$ kJ per mole $CH_2O$ oxidized. If one of the half-reactions yields energy but the other requires energy, the summed reaction can still proceed if the yield is greater than the requirement. This allows for a wide combination of electron donors and electron acceptors to be used in energy-yielding reactions by organisms. In the familiar reaction for aerobic respiration, organisms use C as the electron donor and $O_2$ as the electron acceptor, but the principles are just the same if a bacterium uses $SO_4$ as the electron acceptor for an electron derived from the C in organic matter.

$$2C^0 H_2 O \longrightarrow 2C^{+4} + 8e^- \quad [\Delta G = -86.4 \text{ kJ}/8 \text{ electron transfer}]$$

$$S^{+6} O_4^{-2} + 8e^- \longrightarrow S^{-2} \quad [\Delta G = 40.4 \text{ kJ}/8 \text{ electron transfer}]$$

Note that the sum of these two half-reactions yields much less energy (net $\Delta G$ is $-46$ kJ) than the oxidation of a carbohydrate with oxygen as an electron acceptor. Therefore, sulfate reduction occurs only after the more energetically favorable electron acceptors have been depleted.

Similarly, organisms can use electron donors other than C, and when a suitable electron acceptor is present the summed reaction can yield energy, as in the following example of nitrification:

$$NH_4^+ + 2O_2 \longrightarrow NO_3^- + H_2O + 2H^+ \quad [\Delta G = -347 \text{ kJ/mole } NH_4 \text{ oxidized}]$$

Microorganisms use a large number of electron donors and acceptors to capture energy to support life-processes (Table A.1). These different reactions yield different amounts of energy, and the reaction that yields the most energy possible under the ambient environmental conditions tends to prevail. As a result, these microbially mediated redox reactions tend to occur in a predictable sequence (Figure A.2). Thus, organic carbon is usually broken down chiefly by aerobic respiration (the reaction with the highest energy yield) until oxygen is exhausted, then by denitrification, manganese reduction, iron reduction, sulfate reduction, and finally methanogenesis, as successively less profitable (in terms of energy yield) electron acceptors are used and then depleted. This sequence of reactions is often

**TABLE A.1**  Examples of some ecologically important biologically mediated redox reactions (many other examples exist and are important in some ecosystems). Most of these reactions (other than aerobic photosynthesis and oxygenic photosynthesis) are performed Primarily or exclusively by bacteria.

| Process | Chemical Reaction | Location or Conditions |
|---|---|---|
| **A. Oxidation of organic matter (organic carbon is the electron donor)** | | |
| Aerobic respiration | $CH_2O + O_2 \longrightarrow CO_2 + H_2O$ | Where oxygen and OM are present; widespread |
| Denitrification | $5CH_2O + 4NO_3^- + 4H^+ \longrightarrow 5CO_2 + 7H_2O + 2N_2$ | Usually where $O_2$ is low or absent and $NO_3$ and OM are present (aquatic sediments, wet soils, wetlands) |
| Manganese reduction | $CH_2O + 2MnO_2 + 4H^+ \longrightarrow CO_2 + 3H_2O + 2Mn^{+2}$ | Where $O_2$ is absent and OM and Mn are abundant (marine sediments, ground waters) |
| Iron reduction | $CH_2O + 4Fe(OH)_3 + 8H^+ \longrightarrow CO_2 + 11H_2O + 4Fe^{+2}$ | Where $O_2$ is absent and iron is abundant (wetlands, ground waters, wet soils) |

*(Continued)*

TABLE A.1   (*Continued*)

| Process | Chemical Reaction | Location or Conditions |
|---|---|---|
| Fermentation | $2CH_2O + H_2O \longrightarrow HCOO^- + CH_3OH + H^+$ | Where $O_2$ is absent and OM is abundant (wetlands, aquatic sediments, wet soils) |
| Sulfate reduction | $2CH_2O + SO_4^{-2} + H^+ \longrightarrow 2CO_2 + 2H_2O + HS^-$ | Where $O_2$ is absent and OM and sulfate are abundant (salt marshes, marine sediments, wet soils, freshwater wetlands and sediments) |
| Methano- genesis | $2CH_2O \longrightarrow CO_2 + CH_4$ | Where $O_2$ and other electron acceptors are absent and OM is abundant (freshwater sediments) |
| Methane oxidation | $CH_4 + 2O_2 \longrightarrow CO_2 + 2H_2O$ | Interfaces of organic-rich anaerobic sites and oxygenated waters or soils (wetlands, wet soils) |

**B. Oxidation of reduced inorganic species (may provide energy for chemosynthesis; materials other than organic carbon are the electron donor)**

| | | |
|---|---|---|
| Sulfide oxidation | $H_2S + 2O_2 \longrightarrow H_2SO_4$ | These reactions typically take place near interfaces of organic-rich anaerobic sites and oxygenated waters or soils (wetlands, wet soils, thermoclines of eutrophic lakes) |
| Ferrous oxidation | $4Fe(HCO_3)_2 + O_2 + 6H_2O \longrightarrow 4Fe(OH)_3 + 4H_2CO_3 + 4CO_2$ | |
| Nitrification | $NH_4^+ + 2O_2 \longrightarrow NO_3^- + 2H^+ + H_2O$ | |
| Manganous oxidation | $4MnCO_3 + O_2 \longrightarrow 2Mn_2O_3 + 4CO_2$ | |

**C. Photosynthesis**

| | | |
|---|---|---|
| Oxygenic photosynthesis | $CO_2 + H_2O + light \longrightarrow CH_2O + O_2$ | Where there is light |
| Photosynthesis by sulfur bacteria | $2CO_2 + 2H_2O + H_2S + light \longrightarrow 2(CH_2O) + H_2SO_4$ | Sites that are lighted and anoxic or nearly so |

**D. Nitrogen fixation**

| | | |
|---|---|---|
| | $N_2 + 8H^+ + 8e^- + energy \longrightarrow 2NH_3 + H_2$ | Intracellular |

*Note:* OM = organic matter.
*Modified from Stumm and Morgan (1995) and Wetzel (2001).*

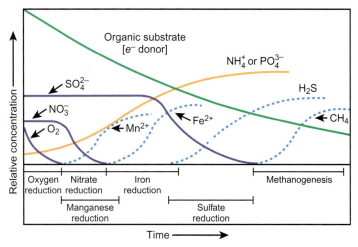

**FIGURE A.2**   Typical sequence of changes in biologically mediated redox reactions and concentrations of redox-active materials that occur after a wetland soil is flooded and the organic material (long green line) degrades. Solid lines show typical electron acceptors that are depleted as organic matter oxidation proceeds. (*Modified from Mitsch and Gosslink 1993, after Reddy 2008.*)

observed either at a single point as electron acceptors are depleted over time, or moving through space away from well-oxygenated habitats, as in aquatic sediments or along groundwater flow paths.

# References

Fenchel, T., King, G.M., Blackburn, T.H., 1998. Bacterial biogeochemistry: The ecophysiology of mineral cycling, second ed. Academic Press, San Diego, CA.

Maier, R.M., Pepper, I.L., Gerba, C.P., 2000. Environmental microbiology. Academic Press, San Diego, CA.

Mitsch, W.J., Gosselink, J.G., 1993. Wetlands, second ed. Van Nostrand Reinhold, New York, NY.

Reddy, K.R., DeLaune, R.D., 2008. Biogeochemistry of wetlands-science and applications. CRC Press, Boca Raton, FL.

Stumm, W., Morgan, J.J., 1995. Aquatic chemistry: Chemical equilibria and rates in natural waters, third ed. Wiley, New York, NY.

Wetzel, R.G., 2001. Limnology: Lake and river ecosystems, third ed. Academic Press, San Diego, CA.

# Glossary

**Allochthonous** Originating from outside the boundaries of the system, as opposed to **autochthonous**.

**Anion** A negatively charged ion, such as bicarbonate, sulfate, or nitrate. A positively charged ion is called a **cation**.

**Anthropocene** The geological epoch in which human influences have become globally important, conventionally set to begin at the Industrial Revolution (late eighteenth century).

**Anthropogenic** Arising from human actions.

**Assimilation** Used in a general sense to mean uptake, but also in a more specific sense in energetics to refer to the amount of energy that is taken up by an organism. For autotrophs, assimilation is equal to gross primary production; for heterotrophs, assimilation is equal to ingestion minus egestion.

**Autochthonous** Originating from within the boundaries of the system, as opposed to **allochthonous**.

**Autotrophic** Used to describe both organisms and ecosystems. Autotrophic organisms are those that synthesize organic matter de novo from inorganic materials, via either photosynthesis or chemosynthesis. Net autotrophic ecosystems are those where total gross primary production exceeds total respiration. The opposite of autotrophic is **heterotrophic**.

**Biogeochemistry** The study of the physical, chemical, geological, and biological processes that determine the chemical composition of the environment.

**Biomass** The mass of living tissues.

**Catabolism** The breakdown of complex molecules by living organisms to form simpler ones and release energy.

**Cation** A positively charged ion, such as calcium, ammonium, or sodium ions. A negatively charged ion is called an **anion**.

**Chelation** The coordinate bonding of a metal with a molecule, usually of organic matter.

**Chemoautotrophy** Primary production in which chemical energy provides the energy needed to fix inorganic carbon into organic matter (contrasted with photosynthesis, in which light provides the necessary energy). Examples of chemoautotrophic reactions include nitrification and sulfide oxidation.

**Chemosynthesis** Fixation of inorganic carbon into organic matter using oxidation of inorganic chemical compounds as a source of energy (contrasted with photosynthesis, in which light provides the necessary energy).

**Chronosequence** A sequence of study sites differing in age (e.g., since disturbance, emergence from the sea, etc.), but as similar as possible with respect to other factors. Used to study long-term dynamics of ecosystems.

**Denitrification** A form of anaerobic respiration in which nitrate is converted into dinitrogen gas ($N_2$) by bacteria. Denitrification represents a loss of reactive (i.e., useful) nitrogen from ecosystems.

**Detritus** Dead organic matter, usually restricted to particulate organic matter.

**Disturbance** Alteration of the three-dimensional structure of an ecological system or part of the system.

**Electron donor/acceptor** The chemical compounds participating in an oxidation-reduction (redox) reaction that contribute or accept an electron, respectively, in the reaction (see the Appendix).

**Energetics** The study of energy flow through populations, communities, and ecosystems.

**Engineering (ecological engineering)** The direct or indirect modulation of resource availability by organisms.

**Epilimnion** The mixed zone that forms the upper part of a stratified lake. The metalimnion (or thermocline) and **hypolimnion** lie beneath the epilimnion.

**Eutrophic** Having high primary production, usually as a result of high nutrient inputs. **Eutrophication** is the process by which productivity is increased, often to undesirable levels, through increased nutrient inputs.

**Feedback** The process by which a component part of a system is controlled in part by the products of its own activities. Feedbacks may be either negative (counteracting the initial activity of the component) or positive (reinforcing the initial activity of the component).

**Fermentation** A microbially mediated, energy-yielding redox reaction in which an organic molecule is split such that one part of the molecule is oxidized and another part is reduced.

**Heterogeneity** Differentiation in structure or process over space or time in any system.

**Heterotrophic** Used to describe both organisms and ecosystems. Heterotrophic organisms are those that obtain their carbon (and energy) from ingestion of organic matter. Net heterotrophic ecosystems are those where total respiration exceeds gross primary production. The opposite of heterotrophic is **autotrophic**.

**Homeotherm** An animal that maintains a nearly constant body temperature, usually above that of the environment. Sometimes also called an endotherm or warm-blooded animal. The opposite of a homeotherm is a **poikilotherm**.

**Humus** Partly decomposed organic matter in the soil.

**Hypereutrophic** Having extremely high primary production, usually associated with high nutrient inputs.

**Hypolimnion** The lower part of a stratified lake. The **epilimnion** and metalimnion (or thermocline) lie above the hypolimnion.

**Hysteresis** The dependence of a variable on the history as well as the present state of independent variables.

**Immobilization** Uptake of dissolved nutrients that are incorporated into organic matter by organisms; usually refers to uptake of dissolved nitrogen or phosphorus by bacteria or fungi.

**Isotope** Any of multiple forms of an element that have different numbers of neutrons, but the same number of protons and electrons, and similar chemical properties. Isotopes may be either stable or radioactive (see Box 1.3 in Chapter 1).

**Leaching** The removal of soluble substances from rocks or soils by percolating waters.

**Lignin** A highly complex, uncharacterized macromolecule present in plants (especially woody species) made up of diverse subunits containing phenolic rings (see Figure 4.7 in Chapter 4) and resistant to decomposition.

**Lithosphere** The crust and upper mantle of Earth.

**Lysimeter** A device for sampling soil water.

**Macronutrients** Elements needed in large amounts by living organisms (carbon, nitrogen, hydrogen, oxygen, phosphorus, sulfur, potassium, magnesium, sodium, and calcium, plus silicon for diatoms and some land plants). Elements needed only in small amounts are called **micronutrients**.

**Mass balance** The application of the law of the conservation of matter to ecosystems. If a substance is subject to mass balance, the sum of all inputs, outputs, and changes in storage must equal zero.

**Mesotrophic** Having moderate primary productivity (less than a **eutrophic** system, but more than an **oligotrophic** system).

**Micronutrients** Elements needed in small amounts by living organisms (iron, manganese, zinc, copper, boron, molybdenum, chlorine, vanadium, and cobalt). Elements needed in large amounts are called **macronutrients**.

**Mineralization** The breakdown of organic matter into its inorganic constituents.

**Net ecosystem production** The difference between gross primary production and the summed respiration of autotrophs and heterotrophs. Net ecosystem production can be either positive or negative.

**$NO_x$, $NO_y$** $NO_x$ includes nitrogen oxides (NO and $NO_2$); $NO_y$ is $NO_x$ plus its oxidation products such as nitric acid ($HNO_3$). $NO_x$ and $NO_y$ are important in the atmospheric cycling of nitrogen.

**Oligotrophic** Having low primary production (and usually low nutrient concentrations as well).

**Oxidation** A chemical reaction in which a substance gains electrons. The opposite reaction is **reduction**.

**Oxidation state** A measure of the degree of oxidation of an atom, ion, or molecule. Many elements of ecological interest can exist in multiple oxidation states.

**Paleoecology** The ecology of ecosystems from the past, often studied by tools such as the analysis of deposited lake sediments.

**Photic zone** The surface zone of an aquatic ecosystem in which sufficient light exists to support photosynthesis.

**Photooxidation** The oxidation of organic matter by light.

**Photosynthesis** The use of light energy to fix carbon dioxide and water into organic matter.

**Poikilotherm** An animal whose body temperature varies along with environmental temperatures, as contrasted with **homeotherms**. Also called ectotherms or cold-blooded animals.

**Primary production** The storage of energy through the formation of organic matter from inorganic carbon compounds. Primary production includes both **photosynthesis** and **chemosynthesis**, and can be expressed as *gross primary production* (GPP; all energy captured by the primary producer) or *net primary production* (NPP; the energy captured by the primary producer less energy expended in its own respiration).

**Radioactive isotope** An isotope that decays into another element or isotope (*see also* **isotope**).

**Recalcitrant** Resistant to decay.

**Reduction** A chemical reaction in which a substance gains electrons. The opposite reaction is **oxidation**.

**Residence time** The average amount of time that a substance spends in an ecosystem before being lost, calculated as the ratio of standing stock inside the ecosystem to the rate of input.

**Resilience** The ability of an ecosystem to recover after a perturbation to its original state.

**Respiration** The oxidation of organic matter by organisms to release energy and carbon dioxide. Respiration may be aerobic or anaerobic.

**Scale** In ecosystem science, scale most commonly refers to spatial or temporal *grain size* (the finest resolution possible in the data set), *extent* (size of the entire study area or length of the study), or *levels of organization* (organisms, populations, communities, ecosystems, landscapes) in a study.

**Secondary production** Production of all heterotrophs, as contrasted with **primary production**.

**Sequestration** Storage, often used in reference to carbon.

**Sink** An ecosystem is a sink for a material if inputs of that material exceed outputs (*see* **source**).

**Source** An ecosystem is a source for a material if outputs of that material exceed inputs (*see* **sink**).

**Spiraling** The combination of material cycling and transport, usually in a stream (see Box 5.2 in Chapter 5).

**Stable isotope** An isotope that is not subject to radioactive decay (*see also* **isotope**).

**Stoichiometry** The ratio of different elements in chemical reactions, organisms, or ecological processes. The simultaneous mass balance of multiple elements in ecosystems.

**Substrate** The organic matter used by a microorganism as its food.

**Trophic cascade** A mechanism by which top predators can control lower trophic levels and abiotic properties of ecosystems through interactions propagated through the food web (see Figure 11.1 in Chapter 11).

**Valence** An integer that shows the number of electrons that an atom or radical will gain, lose, or share when it reacts with other atoms.

**Weathering** The chemical and physical changes that result when rocks are exposed to air and water.

**Zoonosis** An infectious disease that is carried by both humans and some other animal species.

# Index

Note: Page numbers followed by "f" and "t" refer to figures and tables respectively.